How to Fix Absolutely Anything

How to Fix Absolutely Anything

A Homeowner's Guide

Instructables.com, Edited by Nicole Smith

Skyhorse Publishing

Skyhorse Publishing books may be purchased in bulk at special discounts for sales promotion, corporate gifts, fundraising, or educational purposes. Special editions can also be created to specifications. For details, contact the Special Sales Department, Skyhorse Publishing, 307 West 36th Street, 11th Floor, New York, NY 10018 or info@skyhorsepublishing.com.

Skyhorse® and Skyhorse Publishing® are registered trademarks of Skyhorse Publishing, Inc.®, a Delaware corporation.

www.skyhorsepublishing.com

10 9 8 7 6 5 4 3

Library of Congress Cataloging-in-Publication Data is available on file.

ISBN: 978-1-62914-186-2

Printed in China

Disclaimer:
This book is intended to offer general guidance. It is sold with the understanding that every effort was made to provide the most current and accurate information. However, errors and omissions are still possible. Any use or misuse of the information contained herein is solely the responsibility of the user, and the author and publisher make no warrantees or claims as to the truth or validity of the information. The author and publisher shall have neither liability nor responsibility to any person or entity with respect to any loss or damage caused, or alleged to have been caused, directly or indirectly, by the information contained in this book. Furthermore, this book is not intended to give professional dietary, technical, or medical advice. Please refer to and follow any local laws when using any of the information contained herein, and act responsibly and safely at all times.

TABLE OF CONTENTS

KITCHEN

GARAGE

FASHION

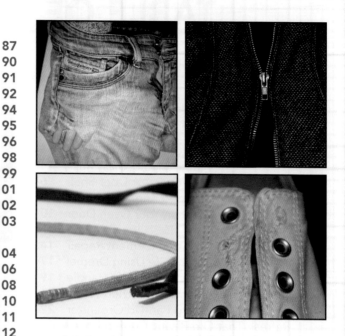

BEDROOM

BATHROOM

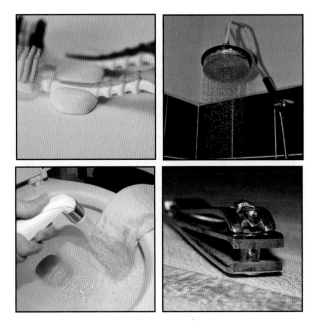

LIVING ROOM

KIDS ROOM

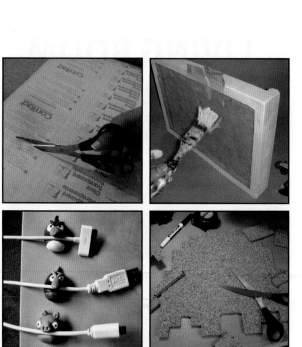

OFFICE

YARD

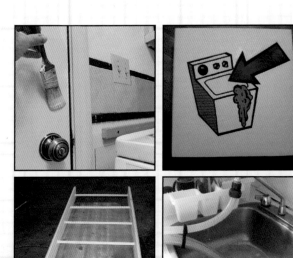

LAUNDRY ROOM

DINING ROOM

Introduction

When something breaks, some people throw it away, but DIYers know the right thing to do . . . fix it! *How to Fix Absolutely Anything* will show you how to fix the things that will break in everyday life, and also show you how to take one thing and make it into something completely different, saving you from having to make other unnecessary purchases. Don't have the room? We can fix that! Don't know how to make it yourself? We can fix that too!

Instead of calling in a professional that could cost you more than the down payment on your home, take a look at these projects to get you started. You won't just find the easy stuff here. The authors on Instructables have gone above and beyond to show you more than just how to fix your shoelace (though you'll find that as well). Take a look and learn how to build your own wood sidewalk to replace that boring old cement one that just cracks every winter. Then learn how you can fix your car from the ground up after getting in a bad accident.

Not everyone is going to be interested in doing body work on their car, but we're prepared for that. We've got plenty of the "why didn't I think of that" fixes. The simple everyone-can-do fixes that make life a little easier. Like how to fix carpet snags and how to keep knobs and hinges in working order. Learn from our community of DIYers who have found fixes for these everyday problems, and are sharing them with you.

Get your tools, get organized, and get ready to learn *How to Fix Absolutely Anything*!

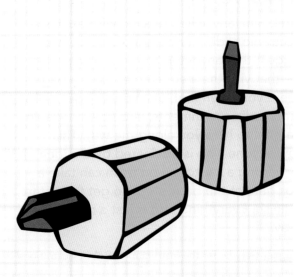

Editor's Note

The wonderful thing about Instructables is that they come in all shapes and sizes. Some users include hundreds of high-quality pictures and detailed instructions with their projects; others take the minimalist approach and aim to inspire similar ideas than to facilitate carbon copies.

One of the biggest questions we faced when putting this book together was: How do we convey the sheer volume of ideas in the finite space of a book?

As a result, if you're already familiar with some of the projects in this book, you'll notice that selected photos made the jump from the computer screen to the printed page. Similarly, when dealing with extensive electronic coding or complex science, we suggest that anyone ready to start a project like that visit the Instructables' online page, where you often find lots more images, links, multimedia attachments, and downloadable material to help you along the way. This way, anyone who is fascinated by the idea of converting a car to run on trash can take a look here at the basic steps to get from start to finish. Everything else is just a mouse click away.

*Special thanks to Instructables Interactive Designer Gary Lu for the Instructables Robot illustrations!

Kitchen

There are always things needin' fixin' in the kitchen. It's a room used daily, sometimes three times daily! If it isn't the stove causing you problems, it could be a dull knife or a broken glass.

Everything in your kitchen needs to be in working order to keep the household running. Don't let your cast-iron cookware rust and your cutting boards get torn to shreds. Learn how to fix these problems and keep everything in tiptop shape so you can keep your family fed!

I currently live in a home that was built in 1957 (the same year I was born) and, like me, some things are just getting old and having issues. We have a very functional kitchen with lots of cabinets, but occasionally a hinge here or there will become loose due to a stripped screw hole. I am going to show you how to do a quick, easy, and inexpensive fix for this problem.

Step 1: The Tools and Supplies
Tools needed:
- Screwdriver
- Utility knife
- Hammer

Supplies needed:
- Toothpicks (round or flat) or bamboo skewers
- Glue (wood glue or white glue)

The screwdriver head should match the type of screw you have (normally a flat or slotted head or a Philips head).

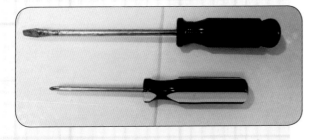

Step 2: First Step
Remove the original screws and hold on to them; you will be reinstalling them at the end.

Step 3: Apply Glue and Wood
You want to apply glue to the end of the toothpick or skewer that you are going to insert into the existing screw hole in the cabinet. I like to use wood glue, but white glue will also work. Push the glued end into the screw hole. Take the hammer and tap the toothpick/skewer into the hole. Run the utility-knife blade around the protruding toothpick/skewer and snap off the excess. Tap the cut area with the hammer to make sure it is flush with the cabinet front.

Step 4: Reinstall the Screws and Pat Yourself on the Back
Align the door and reinstall the screws (the screws you removed and kept) into the cabinet face, and your project is complete. I do not wait for the glue to dry before reassembly because I feel that the new wood and the glue will both help keep the screw secure.

Remember, just because something is broken doesn't mean it needs to be thrown away or trashed. Fix it and reuse it.

In an ever-expanding quest to transmogrify, modify, customize, or hack everything in my daily life, I decided that my tiny apartment required a bar built into a bookshelf. I chose to fabricate the racks from scratch because they would be:

1) Be cheaper (free)
2) Have the correct dimensions (10 ½" deep for an 11" deep shelf)
3) And have that obvious Instructable feel

Step 1: Materials

You will need:

- One wire coat hanger (per rack; I used dry cleaner's hangers)
- Two pairs of pliers
- Drill
- ¼" drill bit
- About two hours

Step 2: Wire Contortionist

Most of this is self-explanatory and varies based on your desired dimensions, style, etc. All bends are 90 degrees unless otherwise provided.

Main Rack:

1. Straighten the hanger, leaving the hook at the end.
2. Bend 3" from non-hook end.
3. Bend 2" from last bend along the same plane.
4. Bend ½" from last bend along the *perpendicular* plane.
5. 10 ½" from last bend, bend 1", ½", 1" to make the square tail.
6. Repeat steps 1 to 4 in reverse order to make the rack symmetrical.
7. Bend the excess with the hook until it breaks off.

4

Support Piece:

1. Take the remainder with hook.
2. Curl the end into a tight circle.

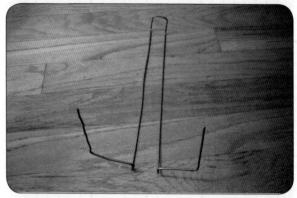

Step 3: Joining Main Rack and Support

1) Slide the support wire's loop onto the main rack.
2) Slide the support wire to the rear notch.
3) Tighten.
4) Remove excess hook.

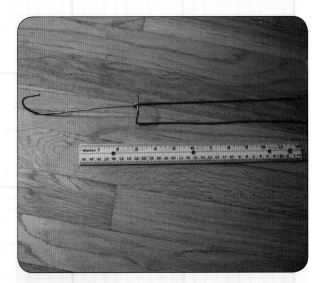

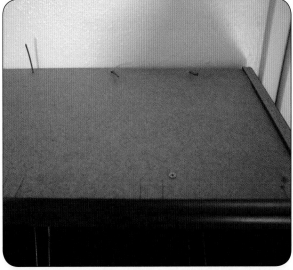

Step 4: Mounting Rack

This step is highly dependent on your mounting location. In the event of a top shelf, it's easy; in other, more unique mounting locations, you may need to mount the racks onto a thin board and then, in turn, fasten the board to your mounting location.

1. Measure the spacing and location of your hangers.
2. Mark drill spots.
3. Drill holes.
4. Insert rear support rod and bend to secure.
5. Repeat for all rear rods and then all forward rods. Now you have hanging glass racks.

This is how I repaired the shelf on my refrigerator door. The hook on the right side busted off and spilled my soy sauce! No need to buy a new part when this is easily fixed.

Step 1: Materials and Tools
- Broken shelf
- Plexiglas or other plastic
- Sandpaper
- Two-part epoxy
- Slamps
- Saw

Step 2: Fix It
1. Clean and rough up (with sand paper) the broken shelf piece.
2. Cut out a piece of plexi or plastic to fit in the broken area.
3. Rough up the plexi with sandpaper.
4. Mix epoxy and apply to the area the needs to be fixed.
5. Add clamps and let it cure.

That's it! It's a very simple fix. With the epoxy and Plexiglas you can't even tell it was broken, and it is now much stronger than before. Plus there was no money wasted in buying a replacement part!

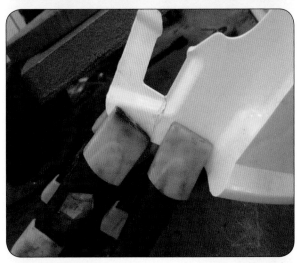

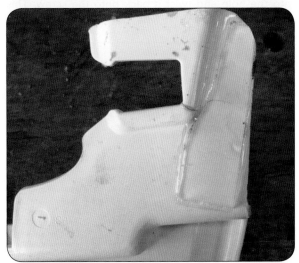

Stripped Knobs and Pulls

By Phil B

http://www.instructables.com/id/Stripped-Knobs-And-Pulls/

It is not fun to deal with knobs and pulls with stripped threads so that the knob or pull come off of the drawer or door when grasped, yet it happens frequently.

Many at Instructables have dealt with this often in their time. This is for the person who has the problem, but does not know what to do about it.

Step 1: The Problem and One Solution

The threads strip out in the first ⅛ inch or so of the threaded post on the backside of the knob or pull. Many simply insert part of a paper matchstick into the hole and twist it back onto the screw. This may last for a very short time, but eventually fails.

Step 2: The Real Solution

The entire length of the post on drawer hardware is threaded. Push a toothpick into the hole and pinch it with your fingernail to indicate the length of the threaded portion inside the post. The distance from where your fingernail pinches the toothpick to the end of the toothpick is the ideal amount of threads to extend beyond the finished surface of the cabinet wood. You really want to shorten this distance by about a millimeter or two in order to allow a little free space for tightening the knob on the screw. Add to the amount of thread extending beyond the finished wood surface the thickness of the cabinet door or the drawer front. You may also need to add the thickness of a washer. See the next step.

Step 3: Small Head?

The screwhead on the left is the screw removed from the knob or pull. The screw on the right is a standard screw from the hardware store. Notice that its head is smaller than the original screw. Adding a washer gives it better support against the wood on the back side of the door or drawer front and is a good idea, but it also adds a little thickness that needs to be considered in preparing a screw for your knob or pull.

Step 4: A Handy Tool Worth Having

The photo shows a wire stripper tool for household electrical work. These are available in many tool departments, particularly in the electrical tools at a big box store. They are not expensive to buy.

Although useful for stripping wire sizes commonly used in homes and for pinching crimp connectors, this one also has five holes on each side of the tool for cutting screws of different common sizes without damaging their threads. The screws for cabinet hardware are 8-32 in thread size (#8 diameter screw, 32 threads per inch).

Step 5: Insert the Screw from the Proper Side

You will not likely be able to buy a screw the exact length you need. Buy a screw that is a bit longer than you need and plan to cut it. Twist the screw into the proper hole on the threaded side of the tool. That would be the side with the threads, not the side that has smooth holes. Notice that there is even an instruction to the user that says, "Insert screw here."

If you were to insert the screw from the other side, the threads would be damaged in cutting the screw to length.

Step 6: Cutting the New Screw to Length

Twist the screw into the tool so the screw will be cut at the proper length. This is indicated by the yellow arrow. Try to be as accurate with this as possible. If anything goes wrong, you can always buy another screw and try again, though. When you are ready, firmly squeeze the handles on the tool and the screw will be pinched off. Turning the screw back out of the tool will make the threads at the end of the freshly cut screw as factory new as possible.

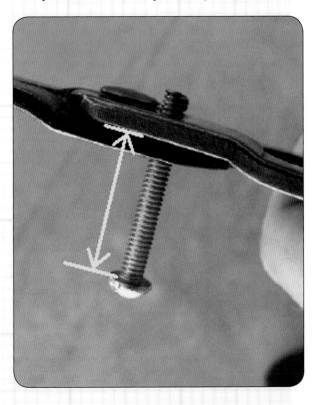

Step 7: The Results

On the left you see an original cabinet hardware screw. On the right you see a freshly cut replacement screw. It is just enough longer to catch fresh threads in the stripped cabinet knob or pull. See also the second photo, which shows the original screw in the cabinet door; and the third photo, which shows the new freshly cut replacement screw. Some of the old stripped threads are only partially stripped and will add some additional gripping power.

You will have saved your knob or pull, which may no longer be available new in the pattern you have on the rest of your cabinets. Cutting a new, longer screw can get you out of a difficult situation.

If your knob is still too loose after cutting to length, you could add extra washers to the head to take up the extra and make it tight. If the screw does not grab enough threads after cutting, you could drill out the back of the door or the drawer front using about a ½ inch bit to gain some length. But, both of these are "desperate measures" for getting out of a special, very difficult problem.

Step 1: What You'll Need
- Silcone sealant — has to be high temperature and costs lots more than normal sealant. You can get it online but I've yet to find a store that sells this over the counter. I've seen special kits, but they claim to be glue and you need the actual silicone sealant.
- Sealant gun
- Clamps or a brick, depending on whether you can remove your whole oven door. If you can, you'll only need a brick!
- Screwdrivers — to remove screws
- General cleaning stuff like washing-up liquid, scrubbing sponges, cloths, etc.
- Glass scraper for removing baked-on grease (optional)

Step 2: Locate All Screws
To locate the screws I had to remove the bottom oven tray drawer. Did that make sense? Good. Ovens are designed by evil men. Once removed, you need to get down on your knees and get out that screwdriver. I removed two screws under the door by the hinges and the second set down the sides of the oven. Unexpectedly, the front of the oven door fell off, which was glass. The inner bit was also glass and as this had also fallen through, I was juggling for a few minutes. Fortunately I caught both, but be aware. Generally it's a good idea to remove the screws on the hinges so you can remove the whole door, but one of the screws on my oven is threaded. Bless those oven designers, so I had to do my oven fix in situ (hence the need for clamps).

Step 3: Remove the Sealant
The old silicone sealant has to be removed completely before you can reapply it. I first used an old flat-head screwdriver to peel the sealant off. Be very careful when you do this; it takes a little pressure to get the screwdriver under the old sealant, and if you slip you'll have a screwdriver in your hand. You could also use a craft knife or similar, but whatever you use try not to hurt yourself. You can pretty much take the stuff off in one go. Once you're done you can carry on using the screwdriver to remove the last bits—any scratches at this point will only give the new sealant extra places to fix into so don't worry too much if you take off any paint. I also used an old, many times reused sponge to remove the last of the rubbish and clean round the oven.

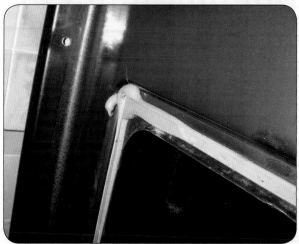

10

Step 4: Cleaning the Glass

You'll also need to clean the glass. If you've got old sealant or old burnt-on oil and stains, you probably want to give it a good clean. I have a window scraper—not an ice scraper—that's basically a razor blade on a plastic stick. It takes off all sorts of stuff off windows such as burnt-on oil, superglue, and sealant. It's rather handy really. Best to do this over a sink. Put a cloth at the bottom of the sink to rest the glass on so you don't chip or scratch the glass or sink. The picture looks really disgusting. Sorry.

Step 5: Applying the New Sealant

You need to slice off the end of the sealant tube with a sharp knife. I used a kitchen knife because I was too lazy to bother to go find a proper work knife. My particular sealant came with a warning to wear gloves as the sealant can cause allergic reactions. I read this after I was scrubbing the black goo off my hands. I'm not dead yet, so I assume I'm not sensitive to it. Probably a good idea to wear gloves.

Load the tube into the gun. To do this, press the metal safety catch at the back, and the long bit of metal slides easily out. Put the tube in, with the beading nozzle on, into the gun, then press the catch again and slide the metal into the base of the tube. You're loaded and ready to go.

Practice first to make sure you know how much pressure you're going to use, ideally with a bit of old card or similar. It's difficult to take a shot at doing beading, but as you practice you need to run right round the oven with the sealant so that it is thick enough to form a seal around the glass and the oven. Since I had extra and I never wanted to use the stuff again (plus it dries out), I went round it a second time once the glass was clamped in place to make a full seal.

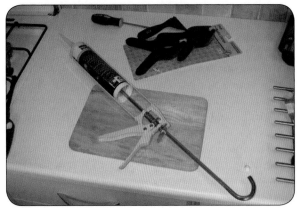

Step 6: Put the Cleaned Glass Back in Place

There's no need to rush about putting the glass back in place—sealant takes a while to set.

Get it roughly lined up and put it back in place. If you're doing this on a flat surface, something simple like a house brick put gently on the glass will probably do just a good a job for putting pressure on, but I had to use clamps.

As you can see, the glass cleaned up nicely. Once in place I ran a second line of beading round the glass to make sure the seal was complete.

The sealant needs to set for 24 hours! Then you can reassemble your oven and you're done!

Rescuing Cast Iron
By Mark Zielinski (theabion)
http://www.instructables.com/id/Rescuing-Cast-Iron/

Cast iron is an amazing cooking surface. Heavy and thick, it acts as an amazing heat reservoir and is excellent for searing steaks and other fine meats at your disposal.

Many a time, an unskilled, forgetful, or uninformed aspiring chef will let the pan soak, leave it in a moist place, or even accidentally run it through the dishwasher. Lo! Ruin and shame! Avert thine eyes!

But no longer!

Bring out the maimed and sad pans from deep within your cabinets! Cast (iron) away your shame! We can fix this. It'll take some elbow grease and time, but you'll be back on the cast-iron horse in no time.

This particular pan met its rusty fate when a wet mixing bowl was left on top of it and ignored for a week or so. View my shame, and learn from my mistake!

Step 1: What You'll Need
You'll need a solution to loosen the dirt/debris, something to buff away the portions where rust has eaten away at the metal, and something to restore the cast-iron seasoning.
- Vinegar
- Lard or shortening
- Scouring pad
- Cast-iron pan in need of restoration
- Elbow grease (now with 100 percent more elbow!)

Step 2: Soak
If you have a self-cleaning oven and a pan with some serious gunk or buildup, run your pan through the self-clean cycle. Any debris will be annihilated,

and you can continue on with the following steps to restore your pan to its former glory.

Depending on the extent of rust damage to your pan, you'll want to soak just the inside, or the whole pan, in a vinegar solution. Anything from an hour to about six hours or so will work wonders to release any caked-on muck and loosen the surface rust/damage. Leaving your pan in an acid soak for any longer than that may start to eat away at your pan, so be careful. I used a 50/50 vinegar to water solution, but I've seen solutions that go with a lower vinegar solution and a longer soak. I don't mind the smell, personally, so I went with the 50/50 solution.

Step 3: Scrub
Let your pan dry before getting to this bit, or you can try scrubbing in the solution as well to pick up any debris. The main idea of this step is to get rid of all the rust that has eaten away at your pan. Scrub like mad until you can't make out the region of damage on your pan. I used a copper scrubber, but depending on the severity of damage, you can use anything from rock salt for spot touches to a drill-mounted metal scour for those heavy-duty jobs. Try to be as thorough as possible—you've already lost the seasoning in those patches, so scrub to your heart's content.

Step 4: Grease

Time to fatten your baby up. Get a nice thick and even coating of your fat of choice all over your pan. Since my pan only had damage on the inside, I didn't coat the bottom of my pan, but if it's necessary for your job, do one surface (inner/ outer) at a time. Pay attention to the smoking point of lard or the shortening you're using! Lard can stomach from 370 to 400 degrees Fahrenheit, while many vegetable-based shortenings will only tolerate a lower range, say 350 to 370 degrees Fahrenheit. Use a higher smoking-point fat if you can.

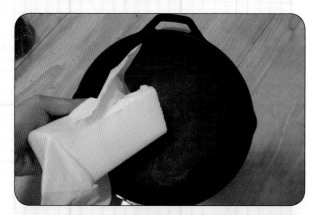

Step 5: Bake

Pre-heat your oven until about 275 degrees Fahrenheit and place your pan in. Use a baking sheet to catch any drippings—you may find that flipping your pan upside-down and putting the cast iron directly on your oven rack (dripping pan underneath) will work better, depending on the extent of lard-ification you sent your pan through.

After letting your pan warm up for 10 to 15 minutes or so, crank up the heat to near the smoking point of your fat. This gradual heating allows for the iron to slowly expand, preventing any cracks or fractures. Let your pan bake at full temperature for 45 minutes, and then let cool.

Step 6: Repeat?

Depending on the appearance of your pan after this baking cycle, you may want to repeat the scrubbing process once again. Repeat the greasing and baking as needed. Ideally you'd repeat the reseasoning step at least four times to let the seasoning take hold, but if you're feeling good about its appearance, it should be ready to go after one cycle. If food proceeds to stick to the bottom during use, you'll definitely know that the seasoning layer did not properly form, and you'll have to repeat this process.

Restoring cast iron is a pain, but maintaining it is quite simple—remember to scrape any food debris away, dry, and coat with a layer of fat while still warm. Stay away from detergents, metal scrubbers, long soaks, and dishwashers and you'll have a great, heavy-duty pan for all of your frying or baking needs. Have fun!

Oven Element Repair

By Josehf Murchison

http://www.instructables.com/id/Oven-Element-Repair/

My wife was making potato wedges when, in the middle of cooking, the bottom oven element caught fire and started to sparkle like a party sparkler. I ran for my camera and when I got back to the kitchen it was over. My wife turned off the stove and when I turned the stove back on nothing happened.

This repair usually takes about twenty minutes if you have the parts.

A point of note: know your stove. I can't count the number of times I went out on a service call for my father on a long weekend just to turn on the oven so a customer could cook their turkey. They only used their oven once or twice a year and the timer had the oven turned off. Minimum charge: one hour for emergency calls and with the holiday double fee it was $250 an hour just to turn their stove on.

Now most repairpersons would come into your kitchen, open the stove, look at it, and say, yep it's broke. Then they would take out the two screws holding the burner in place, pull out the burner, disconnect the wires, and go out to their truck to retrieve a replacement burner. They come back, connect the wires to the replacement burner, screw it in place, close the oven door, turn the oven on, and start to fill out the bill as they wait for the oven to heat up to confirm it is working. A lot of work for two to three hundred dollars, isn't it?

I'm not most repairpersons; I have all kinds of salvaged spare parts, so I just have to find out if I have the right oven element.

Step 1: Safety First

I cannot express this enough: safety first. This stove runs on 240 volts at 30 amps, which is 7500 times what is needed to kill you, so turn off the power before you do anything inside the stove. If your stove is hardwired, turn off the breaker or remove the fuses. Don't just loosen the fuses, take them out. It may be a pain to go back and forth from the breaker box every time you want to test something, but it is not as painful as being fried at 240 volts and 30 amps.

I am lucky my stove plugs in, so all I have to do is unplug the stove when I want to do a repair. First I pull the stove out and unplug the stove; if you don't get back there often this is a good time to clean behind the stove and retrieve your pet's toys.

Step 2: Remove All Damaged Parts

Before testing, remove all visibly damaged parts and render all lines safe; they are a hazard that can be rendered safe, and safety first!

Elements are connected by crimp-on connectors that ether push on or are screwed on; either way, disconnecting the wires is easier from the back.

Remove the back cover of the stove and inspect all the wires, remove all damaged or burnt wires, and cap or wrap in electrical tape. In my case, this part was easy. Nothing was damaged in the back of the stove so I disconnected the leads from the bottom element and covered the crimp-on connectors with shrink tube.

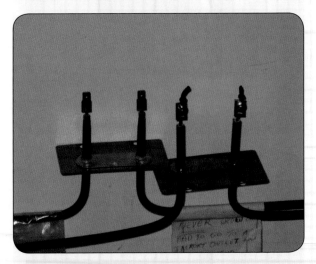

Step 3: Removing the Element

Now that the wires are disconnected from the bottom element it is time to remove the bottom element inside the oven. On this stove the bottom element is held in place with two screws. I take out the two screws, remove the element, and put the screws back in so I don't lose them, as they will be needed to install the new element.

Once I have all the damaged parts removed I sweep away all debris before testing.

Step 4: Testing

Now that you have all the damaged parts removed, test what you have left. Start by connecting your meter to the element leads; safety first, so do this before you plug the stove back in or turn on the power. Set your meter to the highest setting and only lower the setting if you need to. My meter only has two settings for AC, 750 volts and 200 volts, so I set the meter for 750 volts.

Then plug in the stove and test all the oven functions. When on bake, the bottom element leads should register source voltage, in my case 240 volts—much higher than the 200-volt setting on my meter.

When on broil the bottom element should show 0 volts and the upper element in the oven should get hot. Close the oven door and wait for the oven to reach temperature and for the broil element to turn off, this tells you the thermostat works.

Once you have confirmed everything works, unplug the stove and disconnect the meter from the bottom element leads.

Step 5: The Oven Element

The oven's element is a steel tube filled with white powder and a filament like the one in a light bulb running through the center. This one got so hot it was throwing sparks like molten steel, electrical arcs, and flames. The bubbling on the element you see is the melted outer tubing of the element.

An element should be black and smooth with no marks; on some blown elements it may be as subtle as a small crack or swelling in the element.

So I went through my spare parts and found three oven elements, of which only one was close to the one I needed to replace. I could have used this element but I wanted one closer to the original, and it gives my wife a chance to clean the oven without the element in the way.

I decided to put the stove back together so my wife could use the stovetop to cook, and when my local appliance store opens on Monday get a better matching element.

A good repairperson will tell you when he is substituting a part for one that should work.

Step 6: Monday's Here

Well Monday came and the appliance and music store is open. The good thing is they have the exact element I need, $35.00 with taxes.

You can see how the new element is smooth and uniform compared to the damaged one.

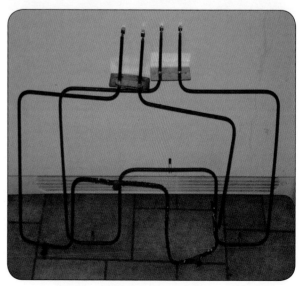

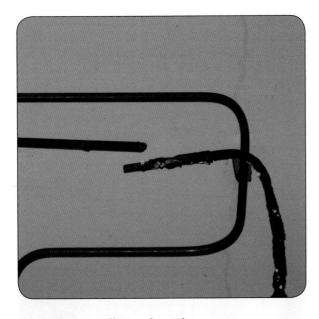

Step 7: Installing the Element

Now that the oven has been cleaned, I unplug the stove and remove the backing as well as the two screws that hold the element in place. I put the new element in place and screw it to the back of the oven, then I remove the shrink tube and attach the wires. I next put the backing on the stove. Once I have the stove assembled, I plug the stove in and push it back in place before testing the oven one last time.

Step 8: Final Test

You can just turn on the oven and see if the element gets hot; however, I like to check the thermostat one last time. You do this by placing an oven thermometer in the oven and watching it go through a couple of cycles while checking the temperature to see if it is the same as the setting on the oven control.

Step 9: The Repairperson

Whether the repairperson is a half-blind, grey-haired, fat S.O.B. like me or not, don't expect them to clean the stove, and at $100+ an hour, that is an expensive maid.

I spend a little more time testing and checking the stove, and the oven element costs $35.00; total cost to me: time, parts, and taxes 30 minutes and $35.

I've had an old and lonely chef's knife hanging out in my knife kit for a while now. I retired it and bought a new one shortly after a coworker used it to and cracked the tip off. Well, I was looking at this knife the other day and thinking about how perfectly usable it is, except for the fact that it has no tip . . . an essential item for speed and/or precision knife cuts. So I thought . . . why not? No job Dremel can't handle!

Step 1: Gather Materials

To put a new tip on your knife you'll need the following:

• Broken knife
• Marking device such as a pen or marker
• Dremel
• Dremel attachments (metal cutting blade, grinding bit, sanding bit, wire polishing brush, synthetic polishing brush, and felt polishing tip with polishing compound applied)

• A clamp for supporting the knife
• A sharpening stone or other sharpening device
• A honing steel

Step 2: Mark the New Tip

Using a Sharpie or other marking device, draw on a new tip. Shade in the section you want to remove. If you want to see the end result, hold the knife up to a cloth of the same color as the pen (e.g., I used a black Sharpie, so I held the knife up to a black cloth). In this way, you will be able to see the shape of your new knife. I wanted to preserve the length of this knife and also avoid having to put a new cutting edge on it, so I opted to shave just a little off the top.

Note: Using this method will slightly change the shape of your knife. To preserve the shape, take some off the top and bottom, then put a new cutting edge on it yourself or have a professional do it for you.

1. Grinding bit
2. Sanding drum
3. Wire polishing brush
4. Synthetic polishing brush
5. Felt polishing tip with a small amount of polishing compound applied to it

Note: I ran my Dremel 3000 at a speed of 4 when doing this and ended up with an identical shine.

Step 3: Clamp the Knife to a Work Surface

Clamp the knife firmly onto your work surface. I do not recommend holding the knife in your hand while trying to do this for two reasons:

1. It is extremely dangerous!
2. You may end up with a jagged or uneven edge.

Step 4: Removing the Excess

Use a Dremel with a metal cutting blade attached to it to cut off the dark-shaded area. Run the Dremel full speed; however, slow and steady motions with very light pressure will produce a nice, rounded cut.

Step 5: Grind, Sand, and Polish

The hard part is over. Now use the Dremel with the following attachments (in numerical order) to clean up the cut.

Step 6: Sharpen the Cutting Edge

Now run your blade along a double-sided sharpening stone a few times to bring back the tip's edge. I used an aluminum oxide, two-sided sharpening stone followed by a diamond-impregnated honing steel to get it nice and sharp.

I have had this bread knife for about 20 years, and it still has a sharp blade. The wooden handle started to rot a while ago (from being left in the kitchen sink too many times), so it was time to make a new handle.

I used a leftover piece of laminated pine board about 1.5 cm (7/16") thick for the handle.

Pretty much any wood that is not too soft or porous could be used.

Step 1: Materials and Tools

Materials:
- One piece of 4 × 10 × 1.5 cm laminated pine
- Approximately 3 mm thick copper wire (possibly 9 gauge, not certain)

Tools:
- Hammer (with a rounded head; ball peen is best)
- Small anvil (or a solid metal surface)
- Handsaw (for wood)
- Hacksaw (for metal rivets)
- Files
- Sandpaper
- Electric hand drill
- Countersink bit

Before

After

Step 2: Remove the Old Handle and Rivets

The old handle on my bread knife had partially rotted off, and I had wrapped it temporarily with packing tape.

I removed the packing tape and the rotten wood. As you can see in the second photo, there are four metal rivets. Two of the rivets are female (hollow), and the other two (male) are inserted into them from the opposite side.

I cut off the rivets with a hacksaw (this can be tricky so be careful). If you're lucky, the rivets may pull apart, so try that first.

Note: Throughout the entire process I handled the knife with the blade taped up to prevent any accidents.

Step 3: Making the Handle

I used a piece of laminated pine from some shelving I made a while ago, so I knew the wood as quite dry (a recently cut tree branch, for example, might split as it dries).

The original handle was slightly tapered toward the center, so I followed the shape of the tang (part of the knife in the handle).

After cutting the wood to the appropriate shape I wanted, I cut a slot down the center for the blade to fit into snugly.

Next, I shaped the wood with files so that it fit the tang of the knife exactly.

Once the shape was just right, I drilled two holes matching the location of the holes left by the rivets.

I also countersunk the holes slightly to accommodate the copper wire spreading slightly at both ends (see next step).

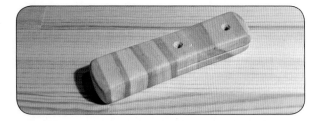

Step 4: Inserting the Pins in the Knife Handle

In this step, I passed two pieces of copper wire through the holes in the wood, with the knife blade inserted.

As I plan to keep the knife dry, I chose to make the handle with only the copper wire pins, but using some epoxy glue in the slot will ensure that it is waterproof (and prevent rotting).

I cut the wire so that about 3 mm protruded on either side, but a bit longer (4 to 5 mm) would have been better.

Using a hammer with a rounded head (ball peen is best), I held the handle on top of the anvil and slowly pounded the copper down so that it spread out. This was done on both sides of the handle, so the ends of the wire filled the countersunk area.

It made a very strong bond; there is absolutely no movement of the blade within the handle.

The last step was to file off the excess copper so the pins were flush with the wood surface.

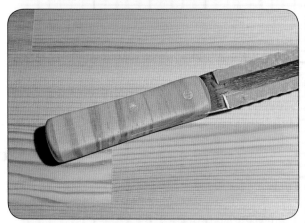

Step 5: The Finished Knife Handle

Once the pins in the handle were complete, I rubbed on a few coats of teak oil (sanding with 400-grit sandpaper between coats) and then a couple of coats of varnish (not varnished in this photo).

I also rubbed down the blade with some polishing compound, which made it look (almost) like new.

With any luck, I'll get another 20 years out of this knife yet!

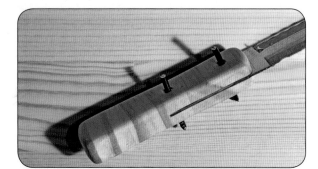

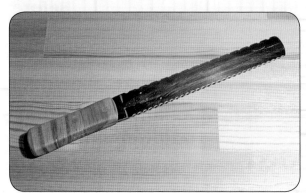

This Instructable shows you how to build a multipurpose holder for displaying everything from fruits and vegetables to your beloved cellphone charger using a simple metallic kitchen whisk.

You'll need a pincer tool, a metallic kitchen whisk (thanks to HBB for this one) and both of your hands.

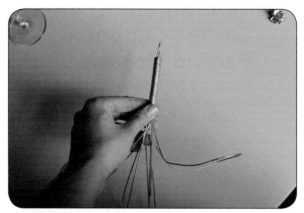

Step 1: Remove Central Metallic Holder

First of all you need to remove that metallic holder piece in the center of the whisk. Use a pincher to cut the metal next to the holes of each "arm" of the whisk. Then you can remove the metallic holder.

Step 3: Fold Rest of Petals Save One

Fold up all "petals" except one : the petal which is in the same plane as the "wall holder" will act as a stabilizer.

Step 4: Tweak Stabilizer

Make sure the stabilizer touches the wall all the way. You can make it more "round" for more stability

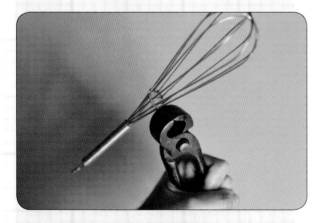

Step 2: Fold First "Petal"

Bend up one of the petal-shaped whisk part so that it is perpendicular to the handle. Make it a little curved up so that it can sustain the weight of a small object. Leave the petal which is planar to the "wall holder" so that it can rest along the wall (see next step).

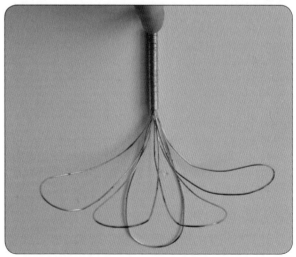

Step 5: Put a Nail on the Wall and Load It Up

Stability can be further enhanced with blue-tack (patafix) or hanging a small load to the stabilizer petal.

Easiest Cupboard Pan-Lid Organizer

By James Williamson (Jayefuu)
http://www.instructables.com/id/Easiest-Cupboard-Pan-Lid-Organiser/

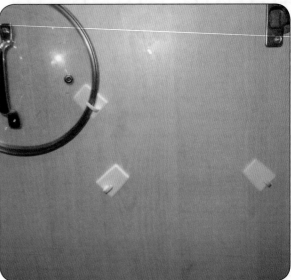

Haters of messy pan cupboards everywhere, rejoice! This quick cupboard-door modification will leave you with more time to enjoy cooking dinner and sipping wine and less time spent searching for that elusive pan lid that's hidden itself inside your deepest stock pot or slipped down behind that slow cooker you've never used.

I first did a similar hack a few years ago whilst a student. Finding pan lids annoyed me as much then as it does now, and so after seeing a very elegant solution on Instructables, I set out to make it even simpler. Here we are: cheap and easily available sticky hooks.

Step 1: Tools and Materials

You will need . . . *drum roll* . . . sticky hooks and a pencil! That is it. I found these sixteen hooks for £1 in a pound store. Be sure to choose ones that aren't too small.

Step 2: Marking

Hold up your selection of pan lids against the cupboard door. Things you may want to consider are whether the bottom one will stick out too far into your cupboard and interfere with objects sitting on the bottom shelf. Position it high enough that it won't do this.

When you think you've got a good layout, hold a pan lid up against the cupboard door and draw a mark in pencil at the 4 o'clock and 8 o'clock positions. If you draw them too close to 3 and 9, the lid will fall out; if you draw them too close to 5 and 7, it might not be so stable.

Step 3: Sticking

Peel the tabs off the stick pad and slap the hooks on the door with the hooks pointing to the approximate center of where the pan will be. No need to be too precise here.

Step 4: Enjoy!

We're done. It's that simple! Enjoy your newly less-hectic pan cupboard.

Refresh That Old Plastic Cutting Board

By djeucalyptus
http://www.instructables.com/id/Refresh-that-old-plastic-cutting-board/

Plastic (polyethylene) cutting boards tend to get worn with use, eventually leading to an unsightly (and often unsanitary) surface. Between cut marks, foods, and cleaners, plastic boards can be left looking pretty ragged.

But not all is lost—a quick attack with some sandpaper can refresh that cutting board, making it as good as new and saving the time and money involved in replacing them! This tried and true food-service-industry trick can help clean up even the worst of boards and prolong the life of your boards while boosting the cleanliness of your kitchen.

Step 1: What You'll Need

Materials in addition to your old cutting boards:
- Dropcloth/newspaper/garbage bag
- Clamps
- Sander
- Sandpaper (ideally 25 grit through 80 grit)
- Metal scrubber or rough steel wool
- Scraper/hand plane/razor blade (not pictured)
- Gloves
- Eye protection
- Dust mask
- Dish soap
- Sponge

For the sander, I'm using a Dremel contour sander. Any sander will do the job, and one with more horsepower will do the job faster. A belt sander or orbital sander would work nicely, I just didn't happen to have one handy at the moment.

Step 2: Clamp the Board

Cover your work surface with a drop cloth, newspaper, etc. to catch the remnants of the sanding.

Using the clamps, securely affix the cutting board to your work surface (I usually clamp the two corners by the handle-edge (if there is a handle cut-out) since those rarely get worn from use. Be sure it's clamped snugly, as scraping and sanding can create a good bit of lateral torque on the board.

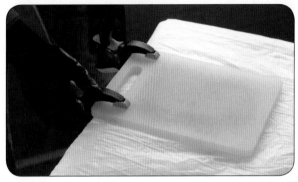

Step 3: Prep the Board for Sanding

Using the metal dish scrubber or extra-coarse steel wool, scrape the surface to remove any loose burrs of plastic and begin to clean the surface. The less excess plastic that is left on top, the less the sandpaper will gum up.

23

Step 4: Sand the Board!

Sand the surface of the board using the coarsest grit of sandpaper. Ideally, I start with 25-grit and progress to finishing with 80-grit sandpaper. If you start too high, the sandpaper won't be successful at removing the top layer of the board.

Be sure to use eye protection and a dust mask, as the sanding will kick up polyethylene dust, which is less than pleasant to get in your system!

And if your cutting boards are anything like mine, this is the stage when you will smell the aroma of everything you've ever cut on the board coming out as the sander gently warms the dust. This can often be a somewhat unpleasant experience!

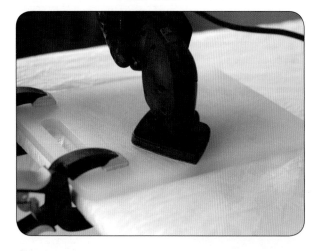

Step 5: If Sanding Isn't Enough. . .

Depending on the depth of cuts, grit of sandpaper, and strength of the sander you're using, sanding alone may not be enough. If you aren't able to sand away enough of the surface to remove cuts, gouges, and slices, it may be necessary to *carefully* scrape the top layer of the board with a razor blade, a knife blade, or, ideally, a hand plane.

Then continue sanding until grooves, scratches, and gouges are removed and the surface is buttery smooth.

Step 6: Clean the Surface While Sanding

To help expedite the process, periodically wipe the surface with the steel wool/scrubber to remove any burrs and the dust that the sander has kicked up. Unlike wood, polyethylene has a tendency to statically adhere to itself, which makes the sanding process more difficult. A frequent wipe will help the process.

Step 7: Clean the Edges

As the sanding process will alter the shape of the board slightly, I take a blade and scrape the edges of the board to get a nice clean bevel after I'm finished sanding.

Step 8: Clean the Board

Cleaning the board should be a three-step process.

First, rinse with water in a sink to remove loose dust and particles.

Second, apply kitchen soap and rub in with your hand—not a sponge—to work more of the dust out. You want to avoid getting your sponge covered in loose polyethylene dust. Then rinse the board.

Third, use a sponge with dish soap to clean the board surface again. Rinse, let dry, and enjoy your like-new cutting board.

Step 9: Enjoy Your Refreshed Cutting Surface!

Not only is the fresh surface more sanitary (deep crevices can collect and breed bacteria), but it will also help prolong the sharpness of the edge of your knives (the worn cutting surfaces can catch and dull knife edges more quickly).

Enjoy!

Magnetic, Under-Shelf Spice Rack

By garrett.tillman

http://www.instructables.com/id/Magnetic-under-shelf-spice-rack/

Spices are an integral part of any kitchen, but, if you're like me and your kitchen is smaller than your closet, they can take up valuable shelf space. Keeping that in mind, here's a way to store your spices in an unobtrusive way that doesn't take up shelf space.

Step 1: Materials
- Spice jars (I got mine from Williams-Sonoma, but you can get cheaper or different ones)
- Magnets (mine are from K&J Magnetics)
- Dremel or drill
- Cardboard
- Pen
- Measuring tape (if you're anal about measurements)
- Epoxy or superglue

Step 2: Preparation
It's important to make sure that your materials are in order before beginning anything. This means laying out your magnets, making sure you have enough, and measuring the space underneath your cabinet.

I laid out my magnets on my spice jars. The tops are metal (steel?), so the magnets stick, but you want to make sure that your magnets are all pointing the same direction.

I also made a quick and dirty template for drilling my holes by tracing the bottles on a piece of cardboard and stabbing it with a knife.

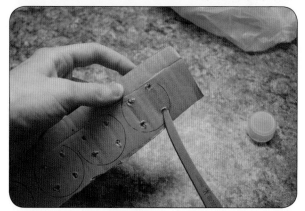

Step 3: Tracing Holes and Drilling
I took the template that I made and used a felt-tip pen to draw my guide holes. These don't need to be perfect, just general guides for where to place your magnets.

I used the burr setting on my Dremel in order to make short, shallow holes wide enough for the magnets and deep enough for the magnets to lay flush once they're glued.

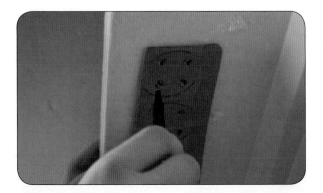

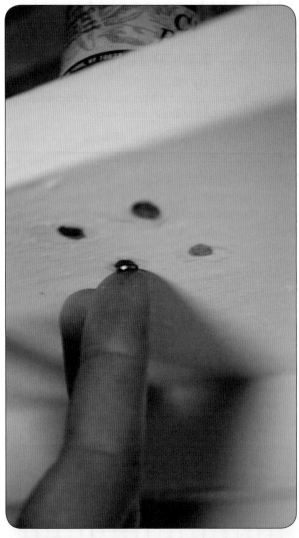

Step 4: Epoxy

Now is the time for you to very safely smear epoxy into the holes. I cannot overstate how important it is for you to wear hand protection. This is why I am wearing my incredible gloves that look almost exactly like my real hands.

It is also important to use epoxy in a well-ventilated space as it will eat your brain tissue and turn you into a zombie.

Smear epoxy into the holes—just enough for there to be a base. Let the epoxy set for about a minute and then push the magnets into the epoxy in order to set them. Make sure to place the magnets into the holes such that they are attracted to the magnets on the lids of the jars; if not, your magnets won't stick (they will repel, in fact!). Then, apply epoxy over the magnets in order to seal them into the holes.

Next, very carefully move the magnets underneath the top of the jar so that they are in the same position as they were previously. You need to make sure they're in the same position so that they magnetically adhere to the magnets you just glued in.

Step 5: Enjoy

Once the epoxy has set for all of the magnets, attach the jars back to the magnets and enjoy your new magnetic under-counter spice rack!

Universal Knife Block

By stroom

http://www.instructables.com/id/Universal-Knife-Block-Design-Martin-Robitsch/

Martin Robitsch designed this knife block, and I immediately loved it.

Because it is quite expensive, but not too hard to make one yourself, I decided to contribute another Instructable.

Materials:
- 4 pieces of 255 mm * 140mm * 9 mm (10" * 5.5"" * ⅜") in nice solid wood (I used Oak), these will be the sides of the box
- 1 piece of 130mm * 130mm * 8 mm (5" * 5" * ⅜"). this will be the bottom, invisible and so it can be some MDF or plywood
- ~2000 bamboo skewers, 25 cm long (9.8")

Other:
- Wood glue
- Wood Oil

Tools:
- Saw: only needed if you need to cut the 5 pieces yourself
- Sander: ideally a Belt sander (I use the Bosch PBS 7 AE) for rough sanding, and a Orbital Sander (I use Bosch GSS 280 AVE) for finishing
- Clamps
- Router (optional, I use Bosch POF 800 ACE)

Effort: takes about half a day

Cost: about 30$ - 25 euro. The Bamboo skewers I bought were 0.85 euro/100 pcs

Remark: You could modify the dimensions if you want to: I just made it to the size of some Oak I had left over, and the final result is about the right size for 3 to 6 knives.

Step 1: Assembling the Box

The hardest part is gluing the box together. I may seem simple, but it is difficult to glue 5 pieces together, keeping right angles everywhere. So I decided to help you with some step by step advice:
1. Put one side on a flat surface
2. Glue the bottom on top of it: Align the bottom, and one corner (in my pictures I aligned the bottom right corner)
3. Glue one extra side at the opposite corner (so I added a side to the left)
4. Apply clamps and some weights (I often use books)
5. Glue the remaining sides, one by one.
6. Finish by applying a bit of glue to all inner joints with your finger.

Remark: Ideally, the side will stick out just a little on all four sides. That's OK (better than being too small). This excess will be removed in the next step.

Remark 2: It is important to take your time, take it one part at a time and let it dry enough. (my glue takes about 30 minutes, but 24h for full hardening out). So patience is your friend here !

Then I finish with the orbital sander, using a grain of 120 or 180.

Important tip : when using the belt-sander, keep the direction of the belt more or less parallel to the grain of the wood. If you you sand it across the grain, you will get visible scratches which are harder to remove. Always keep your belt-sander moving over the piece, never let it rest in one position. If you keep it still, it may leave a groove which is again hard to remove.

Step 2: Trimming the Sides of the Box

On each side, the side panels will stick out a little bit.

This could be removed with sanding it, but I always use a router for this.

You need a straight router bit with a ball-bearing. This will trim the panels to be exactly flush with the adjacent sides.

I understand that not every hobbyist has a router, but this is such a powerful technique, that I want to introduce it here.

You could also do this with a sander, but it will take more time and will not be as precise.

Step 3: Sanding the Box

Now use a sander to finish the box : it should end up nicely square, and all panels need to be clean and smooth.

I usually start with the belt-sander, using a grain of 80.

Step 4: Trimming the Bamboo Skewers

In my case, the Bamboo Skewers were 25 cm, but still they varied a bit in length.

A little variation is no problem, but still I decided to adjust the ones that were sticking out too much. **Here is how I did it:**

Cut a piece of wood that fits in the box.

Then put the skewers in, with the tip pointing down

Because of the extra piece of wood, the sticks will stick out, and the longest ones will stick out the most.

Use the belt-sander to carefully trim them down, so they are more even.

Note: the dust will fall in the box, so be carefull when you remove the sticks, as some saw-dust will fall out.

Remove the temporary piece of wood at the bottom of the box. If it is hard to shake it out, put in a screw so you can pull it out.

Step 6: Adding the Bamboo Skewers

Finally add the bamboo skewers. Make sure they all go in nicely parallel to the length of the box.

Admire your result, and if you are proud, send me a picture of it !

Happy woodworking and happy cooking!

Step 5: Surface Finishing the box

Oil the box, or use any other finishing of your liking.

I like oil, I think if the wood could talk, it would prefer the oil as well :-)

In this case I used Skydd from IKEA. Actually I don't like IKEA's consumerism: cheap, disposable, imported, mass-produced furniture, but I like to use parts of what they sell, and make long-lasting products with them.

After applying the oil, I added 4 felt pads at the bottom, in order to not scratch any surface I later put the Knife-block on.

It is always a good idea to have bulk food supplies available in case of an emergency. There are a couple of challenges to keeping a well-stocked emergency food supply. One challenge is how to minimize the space required to store the food supplies. Another challenge is how to turn over your emergency food supply. Ideally you want to eat the oldest items and replace them with new items. Without a good strategy for turning over your food supply you could (and probably will) end up with a lot of expired food.

Canned goods make good emergency food supplies. The shelf life of most canned goods is in excess of a year, and most canned goods can be eaten cold. There are a couple of issues with storing canned goods. First, most commercially available metal or plastic shelving has a shelf space of 12-18". Even stacking cans two high leaves a lot of unusable space above the cans, and cans stacked two high are unstable without some base material (such as cardboard) between them. Bumping the shelving can cause cans to fall and become damaged, significantly shortening the can's shelf life.

Another issue is turning over your canned food stock. Ideally you would use the oldest cans and replace them with new cans. Minimizing the unusable space above the cans makes it a pain to get at the oldest cans, which typically end up at the back of the shelf when fresh stock is placed in the front.

This is where the gravity fed can FIFO (First In First Out) helps. The can FIFO works by dropping new cans in the top, which then work their way to the bottom (via gravity) as the oldest cans are pulled out the bottom. There are many different commercially available can FIFOs typically made of plastic or plastic-coated wires. I found the commercially available can FIFOs to be very cheap in construction and somewhat expensive, at $1 or more per can stored. Additionally, I did not find any FIFO can storage systems that would allow the area above the cans to be used without imminent collapse of the cheap plastic. Thus, I decided to make my own.

Ultimately, the can FIFO presented here, though not a work of art, is very strong, functional, and can be made with some simple woodworking tools.

Disclaimer: This project requires the use of tools. You can hurt yourself with tools if not used correctly. By attempting this project you are taking sole responsibility for your actions. The author holds no responsibility for any positive or negative consequences of your actions if you attempt this Instructable. Use your head; if something does not seem safe, don't do it!

Step 1: Items Required

Materials:
- One 4'x8' sheet of ⅜" or ¹¹⁄₃₂" finished plywood
- Small ⁹⁄₁₆" nails or staple gun with small brads
- 4d finishing nails
- Wood glue

Tools:
- Pencil
- Tape measure
- Square
- Hammer
- Drill
- ⅛" and ⅜" drill bits
- Reciprocating saw
- Circular saw (optional)
- Polyurethane (spray or brush)

Make sure the plywood surface is sanded and smooth. A rough surface and knot holes may keep cans from rolling smoothly, causing them to jam rather than roll. I purchased a 4'x8' sheet of "Finished" birch plywood for less than $20. It was more than double the cost of the cheapest grade ⅜" plywood, but I think it was worth the extra cost.

Step 2: Cut Out the Plywood Pieces

Use a pencil and square to mark out the pattern on the plywood. Remember the old adage to measure twice and cut once. If you mess up you still have about 22" of plywood left to recover. I used a circular saw to cut the pieces out, but you can use a reciprocating saw if you like. I find that I can get a straighter, more professional-looking edge using a circular saw versus a reciprocating saw. Either way, just be careful not to cut your fingers off. Don't forget to take into account the blade width when marking the plywood. When you are done the pieces should measure close to what is shown on the pattern.

You will also need to cut nine pieces that measure 4 ½" × 2 ½" (not shown in picture) for step 7 of the project.

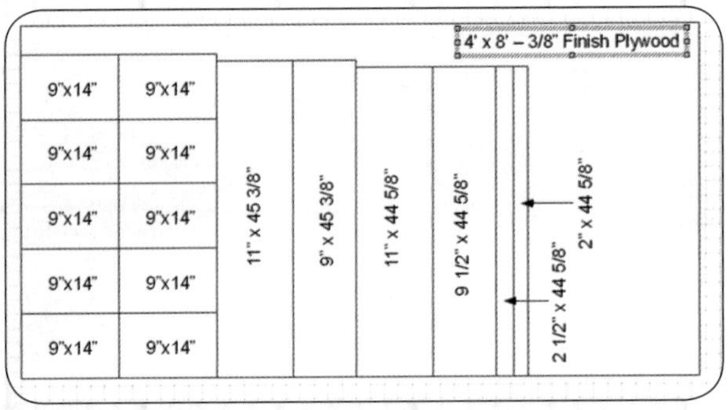

		4' x 8' – 3/8" Finish Plywood
9"x14"	9"x14"	
9"x14"	9"x14"	
9"x14"	9"x14"	
9"x14"	9"x14"	
9"x14"	9"x14"	

(columns: 11" x 45 3/8", 9" x 45 3/8", 11" x 44 5/8", 9 1/2" x 44 5/8", 2 1/2" x 44 5/8", 2" x 44 5/8")

Step 3: Cut Inside Panels

Take one of the 9" × 14" plywood pieces and mark it up as shown in the first photo below. Now drill out both ends of the slots using a ⅜" bit, as shown in the second photo. Finally, use the reciprocating saw to cut out both slots, as shown in the third photo.

When cutting the slots make sure you cut just outside the lines, because they need to accommodate the 9 ½" × 44 ⅝" and 11" × 44 ⅝" pieces shown in the fourth photo. Once you have the slots cut out, test-fit the 9 ½" × 44 ⅝" and 11" × 44 ⅝" pieces as shown. Each board should be able to pass all the way through their respective slots.

Note: The two remaining 9" × 14" plywood pieces will be used for the ends and do not get cut in the next step, so set them aside.

Use the board you just cut out as a pattern and mark up seven of the 9" × 14" plywood pieces, as shown in the final photo. Cut these seven pieces out using the same method you used to cut the first one. Remember to test-fit each piece before moving on.

Step 4: Finish the Wood

Now that everything is cut out you can apply a thin coat of polyurethane to the faces of all 9" × 14" plywood pieces as well as the 9 ½" × 44 ⅝" and

11" × 44 ⅝" pieces. Do not apply polyurethane to the edges of the 9" × 14" pieces, as we will need to apply wood glue on the edges.

Note the knot holes in the surface of the 11" × 44 ⅝" piece shown in the first photo. This side will be used as the bottom, and the cans will roll on the other side. Once the polyurethane is dry, you need to mark the bottom of the 11" × 44 ⅝" piece. Starting from one end, draw lines parallel to the 11" side every 5". After drawing each line, draw an arrow pointing toward the side you started measuring from. The arrow is very important, because this is the side that will align with the inside panels. If you have marked the piece correctly, the last box (opposite side you measured from) will only be 4 ⅝". This is on purpose, because once the inner walls are all placed, each can opening will be 4 ⅝". Mark the 9 ½" × 44 ⅝" piece in the same manner. Don't forget to include the arrows!

Step 5: Assemble Inner Panels and Ramps

Assemble the top and bottom ramps through the holes cut in the eight inner panels. The marked side of the top and bottom ramps should be facing up as indicated in the photo. Align the first inner panel with the mark on the bottom ramp (11" × 44 ⅝" piece) and use a square to keep the inner panel perpendicular once aligned. Now use a drill with a ⅛" drill bit to drill two holes down through the center of the inner panel and through the bottom ramp. The first hole should be about 4" back from the front of the inner panel, and the second should be about 8" from the front. Once the holes are drilled, drive a 4d finish nail into each hole to secure the bottom ramp to the inner panel. Apply this same method to attach the remaining seven inner panels.

Notes: Do not skip drilling the pilot hole, as the plywood is very thin and will crack and bulge if nailing without drilling. This bulge will cause the cans to catch and not roll down the ramp. Also, the top ramp should still be floating in the inner-panel slot once all inner panels are nailed.

not aligned well you risk splitting the ramps, which could cause the cans to get stuck and not roll down the ramp. Since the end is getting glued, you could potentially just use small brads to attach the ends and skip all the drilling, but that is not how I did mine.

Step 6: Attach Ends

The end panels are the remaining two 9" × 14" panels. Place one end panel at the end of the assembled pieces and use the 11" × 45 ⅜" board to align it with the front of the inner panels (see first photo). Now mark the location of the top and bottom ramps on the end panel (second photo). Drill ⅛" holes 2" in from the ends of the top and bottom ramps, as marked on the end panel (you should have four holes). Drive a 4d finish nail into each hole from the side opposite the markings. Only drive the nails in until the point sticks out about ⅛" from the marked side (third photo).

Now place the end panel back on the end as you did to mark the panel and press it into place, letting the nail points mark the top and bottom ramps (fourth photo shows mark). Remove the end panel, and at each marked location on the ramps drill with ⅛" hole about the depth of a 4d nail. Put wood glue on the end panels in the area marked for the ramps (fifth photo). Place the end panel back on the assembly and nail into place. If you were careful the nails should follow the drill holes and not split the plywood ramps. Repeat this process for the other end.

Note: This step is tricky. Be very careful to drill all holes as perpendicularly as possible. If the holes are

Step 7: Attach Back

Position the assembly so the back side of the inner panels is facing up. Run a bead of glue down the back edge of each inner and end panel (see first photo). Place the back panel (11" × 45 ⅜" piece of plywood) over the panels you just glued. Use a couple of small brads to tack the back to be flush with one of the end panels. Now measure from the panel you just tacked to the next panel to make sure the panel-to-panel spacing is 5" exactly. Then tack the panel in place using a couple of small brads (see second photo). Do this for all the inner panels, measuring each time from the end panel you started from, but add 5" each time. Thus, the third panel you tack should be spaced 10" from the end, the fourth 15", and so on.

From the plywood scraps left over, cut nine pieces that measure 4 ½" × 2 ½". Attach these pieces to the inside of the back plywood you just attached. The small 4 ½" × 2 ½" blocks should line up with bottom edge of the back. Use wood glue and small brads to attach them as shown in the last two photos.

I actually added these blocks at the end when I found that the cans could get stuck if they drop and don't roll forward before the next can drops. The small block kicks the can forward so that it cannot get stuck by the next can. The last photo in the series shows the view from above, showing where the cans will fall from the top ramp.

Step 8: Attach Top and Front Rails

Place the top panel (9" × 45 ⅜" piece of plywood) on the top of the assembly flush with the ends and back (see first photo). Mark the front edge of each of the inner and end panels. Remove the top and run a bead of wood glue along the top edge of each panel to the mark. Replace the top and tack it in place at one end using small brads. Measure the spacing from the end panel to the inner panel next to it to make sure the spacing is 5" (see third photo). Now tack the top to the inner panel to hold it in place while the glue dries. The next inner panel should be spaced 10" from the end. Continue adding 5" to the last spacing and tack each panel in place.

Now place the lower rail (2 ½" × 44 ⅝" piece) on the front of the assembly flush with the bottom (see fourth photo). Mark along the top of the rail on each inner panel as you did with the top. Remove the lower rail and put a bead of wood glue along each inner and end panel where you just marked. Then put the lower rail back in place and attach with small brads to each panel.

Now place the upper rail (2" × 44 ⅝" piece) on the front of the assembly flush with the top (see last photo). Mark along the bottom of the rail on each inner panel as you did with the top. Remove the upper rail and put a bead of wood glue along each inner and end panel where you just marked. Then put the upper rail back in place and attach with small brads to each panel.

Wait the requisite amount of time for the glue to dry and you are done! Time to go shopping . . .

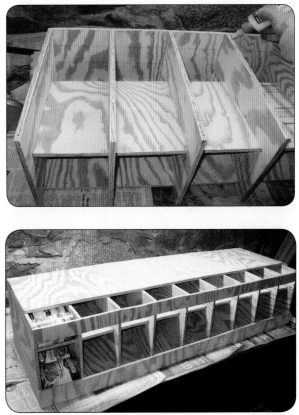

Step 9: Concluding Remarks

To fill the FIFO you simply drop the cans in through the slot on the top. You will notice that the FIFO actually overhangs the end of the shelf it is sitting on by about 2". This turned out to be a blessing as it is easy to remove the cans if you poke them up from below. It is difficult to get a grip on the cans from above to remove them, especially if your hands are really dry. The upside of having the cans be difficult to remove from above is that the cans seem to be well contained, and I have never had an issue with any cans popping out without proper poking and prodding. You will also note from the photo that the top of the FIFO provides a sturdy shelf on which to store more supplies. Just make sure your shelf holding the FIFO is strong enough to support all the weight. Each can weighs about a pound, so there is about 81 pounds of cans alone, and probably another 20 pounds in plywood.

Roll-Out Pantry

By ratmax00

http://www.instructables.com/id/
Empty-Space-
next-to-the-fridge-Make-
a-Roll-Out-P/

With some web-spiration, a 3D-Printer on hand, and some empty space next to the fridge, I decided to make a roll-out pantry.

Step 1: What You Need

Materials:

- (2) 2" × 6" × 8" construction lumber
- (1) ³⁄₁₆" × 4" × 8" plywood
- (1) ¾" × 4" × 4" plywood (scrap used)
- (4) Casters
- (8) Dowel rods (as shelf holders and railings)
- (3) ¼" × 6" quarter-round molding
- (14) #6 ¾" flathead Screws (for dowel railing holders)
- (2) #6 32 × 3 machine screws with nut (for handle)
- (38) 1" wood screws (for casters and scrap pieces to hold backing)
- (6) Scrap pieces of wood (can use leftovers from the 2" × 6" × 8" pieces)
- (48) Finishing nails (guess, not sure how many used)
- (2) Quarts of paint

Tools:

- Drill
- Hand Saw
- Measuring Tape
- Clamps
- Straightedge (square)
- Painters Tape
- Kreg R3 Jr. Kit
- Dowel Rod
- Jig Kit
- Wood Glue
- Hacksaw Blade (off the hacksaw)
- Sandpaper
- Hammer
- Chisel

Optional: 3D-Printer + filament

Step 2: Measure Out Your Space

First you'll need to measure out your space, as everyone's may be a little different. I didn't want my pantry being taller than the fridge and I wanted the pantry to be flush with the fixed wall on the side, so take that into account as well. In my case I had 6 ½" × 29" to play with, so I purchased two pieces of 2" × 6" × 8" construction lumber (as the measured size is 1 ½" × 5 ½") and cut them into two 26" boards and two 66" boards. My fridge is about 5" taller than 5' (66") but that gives me room for my casters.

Step 3: Cut Your Pantry Frame

I measured the distance from my hand-saw blade to the edge of the base assembly. This will be your cut distance. Then I measured my actual size + my cut distance and set up a square and clamped it down for a straight cut.

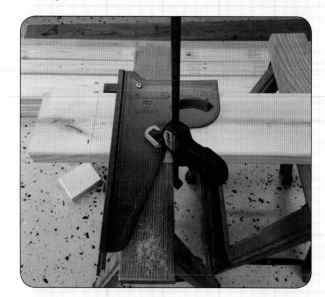

Step 4: We're Starting by Making a Box

Now that we have our boards cut we need to make a box. I used pocket screws for a cleaner look. I used a Kreg R3 Jr. to make the holes, and just guesstimated where they'd be placed. Make sure to get the right size on the Kreg for your lumber thickness and use a clamp to hold it steady. Three holes on the same face of the smaller two 26" pieces will be used so that the outside 66" board will be clean of screws once the box is made. If using regular screws (which I do), use the longest extensions for your drill so that there won't be damage to the wood and the screws get to where they need to be.

Tip: When I don't have a spare set of hands, I use scrap wood clamped on the sides of a vertical piece and then clamp that piece to the wood at a right angle. It's not completely secure but it's enough to get the job done.

Step 5: Pantry Backing

I used some ³⁄₁₆" plywood for my pantry backing. I used some scrap wood to hold it in place and some ¼" quarter-round molding to finish the edges. Using the same principle of hand-saw cutting, I laid out some guides for my plywood and cut away.

Tip: To reduce tearing on the back side of the wood when cutting, I like putting down some painters tape to keep everything together.

As I'm using all the space possible next to the fridge, I inlaid the scrap wood inside the pantry so that the ³⁄₁₆" plywood would be flush with the back. The pantry was then flipped over and the plywood hammered into the scrap wood with finishing nails. I then measured the edges of the pantry for the quarter round, cut the pieces needed, and that was hammered into place as well.

Now's a good time to put your Kreg's pocket-hole covers in, if you haven't done so. A dab of wood glue and they fit right into place.

Step 6: Shelving

Measure out how tall you want your shelves to be (measure some items you'd like to place in your pantry). I came up with a total of about six shelves.

Note: The distance for all shelves + (number of shelves × thickness of your wood) should fit inside your pantry. So six shelves with the following final heights:

- 13" shelf - cereals and bigger boxes
- 9" shelves - smaller items
- 7" shelves - cans

13" + 18" + 21" = 52" + (6 × ¾") = 56 ½" total, which gives me some wiggle room and a small shelf space left as the total inside size of my pantry is 63". Now we'll need to do some cutting. I cut mine out of some scrap ¾" construction plywood I had on hand. Since I kept the 26" boards on the inside of my pantry box, I can easily make shelves this length. I wanted them inset a bit, so I cut them to 5" widths, which comes to a total of six boards at 5" × 26". Once you have the shelves cut, you'll need to cut some grooves out for the ¼" quarter-round molding to fit. The way I did it was to line all the shelves up, mark my wood at ¼" from the edge, and move my saw blade to ¼" deep. I made a few passes with the hand saw, broke the edges, and used a chisel where needed. A quick test fit with all my shelf heights (to make sure I didn't mess anything up) and then some sanding as I didn't want sharp edges.

Step 7: Doweling

I'm sure there are better ways of doing this, as I messed up quite a bit, but here's what I went through. I had a small dowel jig that I had never used, so I thought I would give it a try. I stuck to one side of the pantry and measured out my shelf sizes while working my way up from the bottom. I put in dowels on that one side, then placed a shelf with a level to guide me to where the other side was supposed to be. It worked out well once I got the hang of it. There will be mistakes, but they're easily fixed with some glue, a hacksaw blade, and some sandpaper. I would sand down the end of the dowel a bit to make sure it would take the glue, place the dowel, then use the hacksaw and a wet towel to clean things up. Sand as necessary afterwards and everything should be flush.

Once all the holes are in place you're going need to cut all your dowel rods. I cut my dowels at 1 ½" as the jig I had cut ¾" into the pantry. Now is a good time to put the casters on and make sure everything fits in the space you have.

Note: The way I put my casters on the pantry made sense in my head but wasn't practical as the pantry, once loaded, became top heavy. I went back and widened the casters to fix the problem. I went ahead and used this time to cut seven dowel rods out for the pantry railings at roughly 26" as well.

Step 8: Hardware, or Is It Software?

Now comes the fun (optional) part, as you can probably find items at your local hardware store that can accomplish the same task as below. Using SketchUp I went ahead and designed a handle for the pantry and some dowel rod holders. Once designed in SketchUp I exported the model as an .stl (J. Foltz SketchUp extension), ran it through NetFabb studio (or the online version) to fix the file for printing, and then ported that to my 3D Printer. Print away!

Step 10: Some Assembly Required

Put everything together and make sure you make good use of your new space. The handle was fairly easy as I knew the distance to center for the screws. If you purchase one from a hardware store, just mark those points on your pantry, make sure they're not going to hit a shelf on the inside, and use a drill bit that's about the same size as your screws. The dowel rod holders were put in by measuring up from the level shelves the same distance on both sides of the pantry, which gave me a good level rail to keep things in place. Some of the dowel railings needed some trimming, as they were too long to fit, but after some touch-up paint I put them in place.

Step 9: Paint!

Pick your colors and have at it. At the expert advice of my fiancee, I painted the handle, dowel rod holders, and dowels contrasting colors to the pantry to make things fun.

How to Fix Absolutely Anything

Garage

You've probably noticed Phil B pop up all around this book, but in the garage he really shines! He is the quintessential fixer. A pro at making something work rather than throwing it away or replacing it. Follow along with him as he shows you how to keep your battery fully charged and explains how to switch out a broken ignition switch.

In addition to the great projects from Phil B, you'll learn the basics to keep your car rolling. Everyone needs to change a tire, clean their headlights, or get rid of a nick in their windshield at some point or another. You can take your car in and spend way too much to get these things done, or follow along with these instructions and fix them yourself!

I'm willing to bet, you don't just have a car in your garage. Let's not forget about your tools, motorcycles, and bicycles. Make sure you keep everything in top shape with these tutorials showing you how to fix those minor problems that can hold you back from truly enjoying life . . . in the garage.

Recently I got a crack in my radiator and found out it would be $300 just to buy a new one, and that's If I installed it myself. It would be around $500 to $600 to have someone do it for me. I looked into other ways and here's what I came up with. Total cost: $16, time: 15 minutes.

Step 1: Materials

I went to a local NAPA automotive store and found a kit that is designed to fix cracks and holes in plastic parts on cars and containers. It's a fiberglass repair kit and only cost about $16.

Step 2: Directions

I followed the directions that came with the kit, but there were a few things the directions said to do that didn't work as well as they claimed. I'll talk about what I found that happened or worked better as they come up.

The kit came with a strip of fiberglass cloth, sand paper, a metal tube, a one-time use brush, and a two-part epoxy.

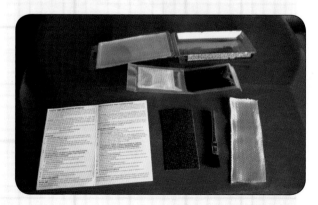

Step 3: Other Tools

- Scissors for cutting the fiberglass cloth to correct shape.
- Some sort of tool to scrape off excess material during the cleaning process. I used a small pick, but a screw driver would work just as well.
- A drill and a drill bit, used to ensure the crack doesn't spread. I'll explain all that in detail.
- Air filter mask (I used a simple painting mask, but any filter mask would be fine.)

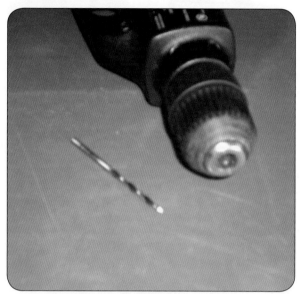

Step 4: Cut the Fiberglass

Cutting the fiberglass is really easy. It is just like cutting normal fabric, so normal scissors work fine.

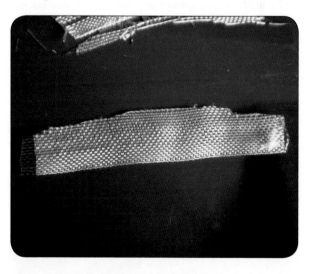

Step 5: Prepping the Area

Make sure you scrape all excess dirt, grease, or any other dirt off and wipe clean with a cloth or a rag. Don't use paper towels because they may leave traces of fibers behind. Then use the sandpaper to sand anything off that is left behind, and to give the fiberglass a surface to stick to.

Step 6: Drilling the Holes

Drill small holes at the end of each crack to ensure the crack doesn't spread any further. I followed the directions that came with the kit for these steps. It was fairly simple. I used a ⅛" drill bit, but depending on the size of the crack you can use whatever size you need; don't go too big as the hole just needs to stop the crack.

After the holes are drilled, make sure you sand the area around the holes again so the fiberglass sticks to the surface.

Step 7: Mixing the Epoxy

The bag of the epoxy tells you to squeeze the black section at the bottom and break the center seal. I found that once the center seal is broken, squeeze both ends to open the entire seal. Once the seal is broken the directions say to mix for 30 seconds, then once you cut the corner you have five minutes to apply. The directions are wrong; once the two mixtures interact you have less than five minutes before it starts to harden.

Once you cut the corner of the packet open, apply some using the supplied brush to the surface of the area on and around the crack. Then spread the fiberglass cloth over the cracked area and cover the cloth with the rest of the epoxy.

After about a minute the epoxy starts to heat up. It got to the point where I could barely hold it as it started feeling like it was going to burn my fingers. Once it gets hot it started coming out of the packet even faster—more like a liquid—and then within 30 seconds started to harden coming out of the pack. So move quick.

Step 8: Done

Once it's done the directions said it would harden within about 20 minutes, but I left it overnight in case it wasn't ready. If you use it too soon and it leaks, it will be almost impossible to scrape off the previous fiberglass and do it over. You can lightly sand the surface if you're worried about the looks. Mine is on my radiator under the hood so I wasn't really worried about making it look good.

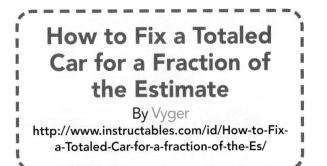

How to Fix a Totaled Car for a Fraction of the Estimate

By Vyger

http://www.instructables.com/id/How-to-Fix-a-Totaled-Car-for-a-fraction-of-the-Es/

A Little History

In 2004 my daughter bought her "dream car," which at the time was a 1998 Dodge Intrepid ES. It was sporty and it was red. It also had a lot of other good things going for it, like a 3.2 liter 24 valve engine, traction control, leather seats, super sound system, auto stick override transaxle, and so on. Overall it was a good car. She took very good care of it, always had the oil changed regularly, had all the maintenance done right.

So when she called me and told me (both angry and crying at the same time) that her car was ruined, it was not a good day for her. Long story short, the airbags did not deploy, but the crash was considered a serious accident and the damage that was done and the age of the car made the insurance company decide to consider the car a total loss. They did not want to spend the money to fix it. Not too long after the accident I went and visited and looked the car over and I thought they were wrong. So I told my daughter to tell the insurance company that we were keeping the car. I paid her the $300.00 salvage that they wanted and I became the owner of the car.

There is a full cost breakdown of the total cost on the last page. It is fraction of the $3,000 that they said it would cost.

I rented a U-Haul car dolly to tow the car to its new home, which cost me about $125.00 in rental fees and gas. I spent another $70.00 to transfer the title and get license plates. Yes, I was confident.

This Instructable will show you how to fix a crashed car for a reasonable cost.

Step 1: Dismantling

First thing to do is to carefully dismantle the damaged areas. Take pictures of where stuff goes so you can use them for reference when it is time to put things back together. Try not to cut any wires, as wires can be difficult to splice back together. Disconnect them when possible, but don't cut them.

Make sure to remove the battery. It should be one of the first things you do. If it still has a charge then any of the wires could have power in them. You can't get a shock from them, but they can short out and burn up an entire wire harness or even set the car on fire. Also, if the battery is still good you need to charge it up right away to keep it from sulfating. If it sits in an uncharged condition for a length of time it will become non-chargeable and no good. If it is below freezing and the does not have a charge then it can freeze, and the ice will warp the plates and cause physical damage and short it out permanently.

A good repair manual will help you a lot in a project like this. It is a reference for how things are supposed to be and can have a lot of tips for dismantling and reassembling.

Resist the temptation to just hammer things off. Remove bolts whenever possible and put all of them in a safe place, like a coffee can with a lid. As you remove parts you will get a better idea of just how deep the damage goes.

Don't throw parts out until it's all finished.

Keep track of the damaged parts, making a list if necessary, because you will need to get replacements. Make a shopping list, and it will be a lot easier when you go looking for parts. Where will you get parts? By far the very best place is an auto salvage yard, more commonly known as a junk yard, and this is why it's important for you to remove your damaged parts. A lot of the time you are going to be getting salvage parts from other cars and you will need to remove the replacement parts unless you want to pay a premium for someone else to do it for you. So make mental notes of what tools you will need and how to get those strange bolts loose and what you will need to do it.

Step 2: Drain the Fluids and Save Them Carefully

If your radiator is intact and holding water, drain out the antifreeze and save as much as you can. Put it in a container that you can seal to keep dirt and also animals out of it. It is poisonous and animals that drink it will die.

If your air conditioner still has coolant in it then you are going to have to vent it. I know that you are supposed to take it to a service place and have them remove and recover the refrigerant but let's be realistic here. The car is not drivable, so you can't take it anywhere. They won't come to you, and if they actually did they would charge you a fortune for it. The value of the refrigerant is not that much. It's about $20 worth. And since this is not Freon it is meant to be environmentally safe. So just accept the fact that some is going to escape. If there is refrigerant in the hoses, it will come out in a big puff and the compressor oil is going to go everywhere. It makes a loud bang. Mine was empty because it had a hole punched in the condenser in the accident. At the junk yard the system in the car I was salvaging was still charged. When I unscrewed the first bolt it all came out. That actually was great because it told me that the condenser I was buying was good. It had been holding pressure for years, so I knew it was good.

Keep your distance when you unscrew these lines. To remove radiator hoses, take the clamps off and slide them back along the hose. Don't try to pull the hose off; instead try to twist it to break its connection, and then twisting and pulling work it off the connector. You can also use a screwdriver but not in the way you might think. If there is room you can put the blade of the screwdriver between the hose end and the radiator and twist the screwdriver. This will push the hose away from the radiator. Use leverage rather than yanking on the hose.

The little hoses are the cooling lines for the transmission. They run through the radiator and also through the little cooling unit in front of the radiator. They will leak transmission fluid when you disconnect them. If you can find a dowel that fits you can plug them temporarily to keep the transmission from leaking fluid everywhere. The transmission fluid in the radiator is going to leak out. Again, try to push the lines off with a screwdriver if possible. Expect them to leak fluid. Keep some rags handy to soak it up.

Then there are those stupid plastic rivets and fasteners. You can just cut them off if you want. I try to salvage them if I can because the stupid things cost almost a buck each for replacements. Push the center pins out with a pair of long-nose pliers and pull the rivets out. Some you can't save and for those a pair of wire cutters works great for snapping the rivets off.

By the way, when you dismantle a car at the junk yard, keep all the bolts and screws and plastic rivets. After all, they are part of the stuff you are buying, and having a few extra can be very handy.

Step 3: Get Ready to Go Shopping

With all the broken and damaged parts removed you now know what you are going to need for replacement parts. Make a trip to an auto wrecking yard, maybe even several of them, and tell them what you are looking for. They will know where the parts cars are and if they have enough parts for what you need. Ask them for an estimate of what it all will cost you. There are no set prices for used parts so feel free

45

to dicker with them if the price seems too high. Let them know you would rather get all the parts from one place for one price but that if you need to look elsewhere you will.

I didn't even take any tools with me the first visit. I was trying to find where I would get the parts from and what was available. They usually will not buy stuff back from you, so find the best parts that you want before you even pick up a wrench.

I needed a hood, an AC condenser, maybe a radiator, the fans, the top metal piece or brace or whatever they call it, two headlights, the plastic pieces that were broken, and the front bumper cover. One junk yard had two different cars that had all the parts I needed between them so we agreed on a price. They charged me $175 for everything, and I removed the parts myself. From a dealer just one headlight is over $300 and a hood is over $400. But these are not in pristine condition. I had to degrease everything and clean it all up.

If you are getting air conditioner parts take some plastic sandwich bags with you and put them over the open hose ends and put rubber bands around them. You don't want to get dirt and water in the lines. Keep track of your tools, as anything you leave behind will belong to the next guy who finds it. If it looks like you will need help with heavy parts have a friend come and help, or you can even hire a high school kid to help. They will love just being there and they are usually interested in learning things like how to salvage parts.

Take all your parts home and clean them up. Lay them in the sun for a few days to dry. You will probably need to clean them several times to get all the grime off.

Step 4: One of the Best Body Repair Tools, the Come-a-Long

When things get pushed in, you need to pull them back out. That is what a come-a-long can do. It is a hand winch with a steel cable. You attach one end to something that will not move, like a utility pole, and the other end goes on what you want to stretch out. Sometimes the hardest part is finding a place for it to grab. I needed to pull the front bumper supports out, and in this case I managed to get a big bolt into them to give me something to grab on to.

Having a collection of things like big old bolts can really be handy. A piece of junk can become a tool in the right circumstances.

Set the parking brake and block the tires of the vehicle so it stays put.

I ran the bolt through the hole, put the nut on, and hooked the cable to it. Take up the slack in the cable and ratchet it until it is tight. When it is tight enough to pluck like a guitar string, stop. This has to be a controlled process. It is possible that just ratcheting the cable will stretch out your dent but probably not. You need to add a little more force, and the best way to do this is to step or sit on the cable and bounce it a little. You will see the dent move forward with each bounce. Be gentle; just do it as much as you need, otherwise you will be pounding things back in the other direction.

Step 5: Hammer Time

Pulling out parts will only work so far. Sometimes you need to get a hammer and pound on things a little.

The sides of the supports got pushed out so, with the cable still tensioned, I hammered on the bowed out parts, and some of them moved back to where they were supposed to be. Don't get carried away with the hammer. Hit it a little and if nothing happens then hit it harder. Do one hit and check your progress. A little bit at a time is the best way to do it.

Some were a little harder because of being crushed in. I used a combination of punches and chisels to push and hammer the metal back to where it should be. Hammering a punch down alongside the front will push the steel out if it's not bent too badly.

You can use any type of steel as a tool for doing stuff like this, but keep in mind that soft steel will likely deform. Punches that are made for hammering on work really good.

After I was satisfied with the results of all the hammering I sprayed everything with a coat of primer. It will help keep the metal from rusting.

One thing I was surprised about in this whole process was how soft the car's metal is. It is very easy to bend. Some things were so thin you could bend it with a pair of pliers.

Step 6: Bumper Bashing

Now that the supports were straight I started putting things back together. That didn't get very far. When I tried to put the bumper on I found that the holes did not match up. They were about an inch off. Well, this actually makes sense, because the bumper is curved and as you can see from the first pictures it was pushed back far enough to crack it in the reverse direction. This means that as it was getting pushed back it was exerting an outward force on the support arms and so bent them outward.

Not a problem.

Take your trusty come-a-long and attach it to each arm and ratchet it together. It worked a little bit but not enough, so now it was time to bring out the big hammer.

Using a sledgehammer and with the come-a-long adding tension, whack the outside of the support arms to force them back into position. Hit them in a place where you won't dent them but can get enough force to make an adjustment. This can take several times. Don't hit it really hard, just a good solid hit, and then check the alignment of the holes. (Also make sure to loosen the bolts of the bottom support so it allows the arms to bend.) When the bolt holes line up you are done. Do not go too far.

Step 7: Straighten the Radiator

When the AC condenser got punched in it bent the radiator behind it. The radiator did not leak, so that meant that it might be possible to salvage it. Why bother? Well, this was a new radiator that was a little more than a year old so it still had a lot of life left in it. Also the radiator I got from the junk yard was not the same. The 3.2 engine has an extra transmission cooler on the other side of the radiator so it is different from the standard. The junk yard did not have any 3.2 engine cars and so no radiators. If I could not fix it I might have to get a new one.

Aluminum is a soft metal and bends easily. The core of this radiator is aluminum. It should be able to be bent back.

First I put it on a flat surface and pushed on the main bulge with my foot. Yes, I stepped on it to make it straight. That got it close.

Next I took a rubber mallet and gently hammered out the high spots using a wooden block in back for an anvil. I checked it with a straightedge to make sure I got it even. It flattened out just fine.

Then I had to repair the little fins that got bent in the accident and that got bent from me hammering it. I used an old linoleum knife and just bent the fins back up. Its tedious but it's part of the job.

Step 8: Assemble the Radiator

Now that the radiator is flat, it's time to put it all together. With this car the radiator is sandwiched in between the AC condenser and the electric fans. It forms a unit when it's all bolted together, and it makes it easy to put it into the car. So put it together and place it on the bottom radiator support. The rubber legs fit right into the holes, so you can't really get it wrong.

Hook up the transmission cooling lines and then the radiator hoses. Plug the fans in and make sure nothing is in the way of them turning. Fill the radiator with the saved antifreeze and check that it's not coming out somewhere as you put it in.

Hook up the AC lines but be careful how you do it. First, don't damage the O-rings in any way. Wipe the connectors with a clean rag so there is no dirt in them. Now, to hook up these lines, do not put the connector in the hole and then try and thread the screw in. This is soft aluminum and the screws can strip the threads out with just a little force. First, hand-thread the screws into the condenser and make sure they are going in correctly. You should be able to turn them with no resistance if they are threaded the right way. Once the screws are started, slip the AC line over the bolt and then push it into the hole. Now tighten down the bolt. It will draw the hose into the right position, and when it is flat with the surface it is seated properly.

Step 9: Put In the Battery, Start It Up

This should be the fun step. With the radiator in place and hooked up you can start the engine, once you put the battery in.

Don't run the engine without the radiator hooked up. Why not? Because there is still a lot of antifreeze in the engine block and with this car the water pump is powered internally, so if you start it up it will spray out all the antifreeze and make a big mess and add the cost of antifreeze to your list. Second, the transmission will pump fluid through those little cooling hoses and you will have that nice red fluid everywhere except in the transmission.

I had to get a new battery for this car because the old one was damaged in the accident. Some of the plates shorted out and it would not keep a charge.

The battery in this car is mounted in what has to be the worst place they could think to put it. You actually have to jack the car up and take the wheel off to get access to where it goes. You also have to take the headlight out in order to service it. It's a half-day project just to put in the battery.

So, I finally got that in place, had power again, and cranked the engine over. It started with no problem.

But it was making a racket. I tracked down the noise, which was coming from a tensioner pulley. But much more serious than that I noticed that the crankshaft pulley was wobbling. It is also called a harmonic balancer. Apparently it was bent from being impacted in the accident. It was about ¼" off. This was a problem. If the balancer wobbles it will tear up the bearing and the seal of the crankshaft. It is also possible for it to actually cause the shaft to break since the shaft is hardened but brittle steel. I would need to replace it. That meant that I was going to have to drain the radiator and disconnect all the hoses and remove the whole assembly so I could pull the pulley off. What a pain.

Step 10: Changing the Harmonic Balancer

Some parts you need to buy new. The harmonic balancer is a key part. It drives all the belts among other things. I did not want to put in a used part here because this is such an important part. So I got a new balancer for $65.00.

To take it off you need to use a puller. I took out the center bolt and then set up the puller to take the pulley off. These things are on really tight; you cannot just pry it off.

What NOT to do: I used a socket extension bar in the shaft hole for the puller to push against. I thought it was a good idea. It fit perfectly. This turned out to be a bad idea. The pulley did come loose and start to move off the shaft the way it is supposed to. Then it reached the socket flare, so I had to change to something else. Only problem was, I found the extension was stuck. I guess it was softer steel than I realized and it somehow jammed itself in the bolt hole. What fun. I could not get anything to get a grip on it, including vise grips. It finally dawned on me that there was a way to grab it, sort of, and that was to put a breaker bar in the socket hole. So, with that I managed to jerk it back and forth and got it loose. With the breaker bar and a nail-puller crowbar I finally got the thing out. What I ended up using there instead to get the pulley the rest of the way off was a large drill bit. I put the bit in the hole and the puller against the butt end and that got the pulley off. I also figured that if the bit got stuck I could attach it to a drill and spin it out, but that wasn't necessary.

Just another little job that ended up taking all day—it's how we learn to do things better: I tried putting the bolt into the hole, just out of paranoia, and sure enough it tore up the bolt threads. So I now needed to get out the tap and die set and clean up the threads on the bolt and the threads in the shaft as they apparently were damaged by my socket extension. The tap cleaned it out with no trouble so it wasn't damaged badly. I shot a squirt of WD-40 into it to wash out the metal bits and then blew it out with compressed air.

It is recommended that the pulley be put on with a special tool. I didn't have one. I really didn't want to buy one. I did a Google search and found a lot of comments about it. If you hammer on the front of the pulley, trying to hammer it onto the shaft, it can flatten the steel and make it impossible to get on all the way. In addition, hammering on the crankshaft can do damage to the bearings inside the engine. Instead use a rubber mallet to hammer it part way until the center bolt can reach the inner threads. The mallet won't do any damage to anything; it will just take a few extra hits to get it on. It worked perfectly. So, bang on it with a rubber hammer like a preschooler until you can get the center bolt to grab. Then just use your ratchet and the bolt will seat it the rest of the way. Ta Da. Put the belts back on and tighten them to the recommended amount. Then quit for the day while you are ahead.

As it turned out the idler pulley for the air conditioner belt was bad also. So I ended up replacing all of them. I would highly recommend that if you are ever in the position that the front of the engine is open that you go ahead and replace the pulleys and maybe even the belts as it is a lot easier to do when it's all open.

Step 11: Some Assembly Required

With practice you get better. Now that the crankcase pulley is done I can go back to putting things together. Put the radiator assembly back in and hook up all the hoses again. Fill it with antifreeze and then start it up again. This time it's very quiet. No noise other than the engine noise, so that was a success. Run the engine until it gets warm and the fans turn on. You need to check to make sure the fans are working so you don't run into trouble later.

Now the top piece can be put in place. This is actually a pretty important part. It ties together the top part of the engine. It keeps the radiator in place, provides a place to secure the plastic bumper and provides a way to mount the headlights. I could have tried to hammer out the bent one but I thought it would be better to get one that was factory correct so I could tell if everything was lining up right. If some of the holes were off then it was due to the parts underneath being out of alignment.

Once again the friendly come-a-long comes into play. If something has been pushed back you can hook on to it and pull it into alignment. Just be careful not to over-pull something and not to bend something that is not supposed to be bent. This part also holds the hood in place, so it's important that it be pretty close to where it's supposed to be.

It's actually beginning to look like it should. After you get all the bolts in go through them again and give them a last turn. Don't over tighten them so they strip, but don't leave them loose either. Always, after you bolt something down, run back over all the bolts again and give them a final crank.

Step 12: Headlights

Now that the front frame is in place, the headlights can be put in place. This is when you can make sure the wiring harness is in the right place and secured.

A word about the headlights: Almost all the lights on older cars are foggy. This happens from weathering and such. Buying used lights you are almost assured that they will be foggy, but this can be fixed. There are kits available for restoring the lights, and they really do work. The best one I have run across so far is made by Turtle Wax and is simply called "headlight lens restorer." It did a fantastic job on the lights. I took one of the broken lights that was really foggy and

cleaned a spot on it. You can really see the difference. This stuff makes them like new. For only $8 you get like-new lights. One of the lights I got was so foggy that I couldn't really see the inside. When I did clean it up I discovered that it had had water inside it and so had tarnished the reflective coating. Oh well, that one is a little duller than the other one. I might get a replacement if it bothers me too much.

The lights are made to be adjusted. After you bolt them in place, check to see that they line up correctly. They will almost for sure need to be adjusted.

If a light unit does not go in easily or seems to fit wrong don't force it. You may still have some frame elements that are off. Make fine adjustments if you need to by pulling out or even pushing in mounting brackets. Remember, this is a traumatized vehicle, it's going to be a little off. Be patient with it and you can get it right.

Step 13: Really Stupid Stuff

In the process of putting in the headlights and connecting up all the various wires I found a couple of bolts missing from where the fender bolts to the body on the driver's side. No problem, I have a can full of extra screws and bolts. I wondered though why someone would have taken them out while removing the torn up plastic bumper since they had no connection to it. Whatever, I screwed them down. Later when I went to open the driver's side door to turn on the lights, the door edge hit the fender and ground against it. This made no sense because this had not happened before. Then I remembered my daughter had complained after getting the car back from the repair shop that the door hit the fender when it was opened. I called her and talked to her, and she said the shop had fixed it after she complained. Yeah, "fixed it" by removing the bolts from the fender so it hung loose. Brilliant. Didn't it occur to them to just adjust the stupid door? The door was in fact too far forward. The gap in the doors on the driver's side was larger than on the other side, and the door had not been sealing correctly since the repair shop visit. This was just stupid.

I removed the fender, as it just bolts on, and tried to see what was going on. It is possible that there was someplace where it had been bent and so did not line up. I could not see anything. I loosened the door hinges and slid the door back an eighth of an inch or so. When I put the fender back on everything was just fine: the door cleared the fender, seated correctly in the frame, and all the bolts were now in the fender. This is really basic body stuff; how did these people get this so wrong?

So I suppose the bottom line here is never trust a repair shop. If they say they fixed something have them show you how they fixed it.

Step 14: Replace the Hood

Hoods are not heavy, but they are large and difficult to change by yourself. You really need an assistant for this step. And keep in mind that it is possible for the hood to slide down and hit the windshield. The pointed edges would probably punch a nice hole in it, so get help for this.

All you have to do is take the bolts out and lift the hood off. Then bring over the replacement and put the bolts back in. You can adjust its position by sliding it around on the supports. The bolt holes are big enough so you have a little room. On this car the hinge hood supports were not bent by the accident, but they easily can be. They are not really heavy duty, as their job is mostly just to hold the hood in the right place. If you do have bent hinges get replacements when you get your hood. It is also possible to bend the hinges to adjust them if they are not mangled too badly. You can put a block of wood under them and close the hood to bend them. Just figure out which way you have to go and use the leverage of the hood. Again, make small adjustments a little at a time.

My hood did not line up straight with the fenders. It did on one side but not the other. Again, it is possible that the car was bent ½", but there is no way for me to fix that. Instead I adjusted the fender to match the hood.

The hood latch is usually adjustable also. Once you get the hood in the right position and the hinges bolted tightly, lower it and see where it hits on the latch. Loosen the adjusting bolts and move the latch to match up with the catch. Tighten those down and then close it tight and check it for fit. There are a number of adjusters and bumpers that will allow you to get the hood to match up with the rest of the car. A car book will have all the details.

I left the headlights unbolted while I was adjusting the hood. I didn't want to take a chance on the hood being too low and hitting them. You might want to do the same thing. Plastic will always break before steel, so watch out for plastic parts.

Step 15: The Last Piece, the Big Plastic "Bumper Cover"

It's called a *bumper cover* and not a *bumper*, I found out. It's basically a big piece of molded plastic, but it hides all the internal stuff and makes the car look good. It does not do much in a collision except break into pieces. There is a chunk, or perhaps chunks, of foam behind it that fill in the gaps between it and the steel bumper support. It is held in place by those stupid plastic rivets and perhaps a few screws. A car dealer will charge you a lot for one, around $400.00. You can buy a new one on ebay for $100.00 that is primed and ready to paint. Or you can get one at a auto salvage yard for next to nothing, but it almost for sure will not be the color that matches your car and probably will have scratches on it and maybe a coating of bugs. I wasn't really worried about the color; I wanted cheap.

These are pretty easy to put on. This one has holes that line up to the holes in the main support for the hood. Slide that on first and just stick bolts through the holes to keep it in place. Then go around to the fenders and lift and slide it into place. With mine there is a support that it slides onto to hold it and then a that screw goes through the bumper, the wheel-well liner (also plastic), and then is secured into the fender. Once that is in all you have to do is stick the plastic rivets into the holes and push them tight. You're done, it's that easy.

Step 16: Charge Up the Air Conditioner

After you test drive the car and are certain that you are not going to have to take the radiator assembly out again, you can charge the air conditioning system.

I have had to have this done several times, and the minimum I paid was $75. It is not the coolant that costs that. So I decided to buy the equipment to do it myself since only two uses would pay for it. I bought a vacuum pump so I could evacuate the lines and a manifold valve thingy that hooks up to the lines and lets you know if things are going the way they are supposed to go. It cost me $150.00. I have now told my friends that I can recharge their air conditioners because I have the equipment, and that it will cost them $40.00 and they buy the coolant. All I need is four cars and I am making a profit.

Hook up the lines and the vacuum pump and let it run for a little while, maybe five or ten minutes. You should read a vacuum on the gauge. Shut the pump off and close the valves and let it sit for half the day (or a whole day). It should still show a vacuum. It might go up a little but if it has lost its vacuum completely then you have a leak somewhere.

If you have no leaks then disconnect the pump (after running it again to get out as much air and moisture as possible) and hook up the lines for the coolant. Start the engine and follow the directions on how to add the coolant. It's pretty simple. It does take a while for it to all get in there. Add as much as they recommend. I bought some special leak-sealing additive and a lubricant also. It is designed for older systems that have some wear. All together I put in one can of that and one can of coolant and it cost me $20.

Step 17: On the Road Again

I am not going to tell you that this was a simple and easy project. Just about each of the steps could be an Instructable by itself. This is really an overview in that there are a lot of little details left out. But the point is that if you want to take the time and tackle a project like this, it is possible to do so and at a considerable savings. Nothing was really hard. It just takes the tools and you. You need to believe in yourself that you can figure out a way to get things done. And you need to be determined and able to devote enough time to it to do it right.

The Cost Breakdown
- I paid $175.00 for parts at the junk yard
- I bought a Harmonic balancer for $65.00 and the replacement pulleys were about $20 each, so that was another $40.00
- I bought about $15 worth of those stupid plastic rivets
- The air conditioner coolant was $20
- I spent about $5 for degreaser
- A new battery cost me $75.00
- That all totals up to $400.00

So, I repaired $3,000 in damage for $400 worth of parts. Now to be fair, it's not painted the right color. I have been thinking about that because I have several vehicles that could use some paint. So right now my thinking is to get a good paint spray gun and do that myself also. Maybe yet another Instructable!

If you add in to the above, the $300 for the salvage cost, the $125 for towing, and the $70 to transfer the title, I have invested about $900 in this vehicle. With a book value of over $2500 that is not a bad investment. And I know the car—there are no surprise issues.

And it drives really great!

So, how ironic is it that the daughter is now driving a conservative, gray, economical car and the dad has the almost all-red sporty car that goes from 0 to 60 in eight seconds.

Fix Stripped Bike Pedal Threads

By joker31698

http://www.instructables.com/id/Bike-Pedal-Fix/

During a recent bike ride, my son went to pedal after walking across a section of grass, and as he did his pedal just dropped out from under his foot. It must have been loose, working its way out, and when he pushed down it ended up stripping out the threads, making it difficult to screw and tighten back in. The following steps are not ideal, but they will work well for a long time. I hope this helps.

Step 1: Materials
- The un-attached pedal
- Correct size wrench (in our case, ⅝ths)
- Small file
- Pick (since I do not have the tools to rethread properly with a tap and die set)

Step 2: Cleaning the Threads Out of the Crank Arm

Using the pick, clean up the inside threads to clear any significant obstructions. This will also help open up any threads that were smashed down. You will want to pull out the threads that were broken out, being careful as there are metal slivers that can hurt you.

Step 3: Pedal Threads Clean-Up

This step may not be necessary, but it can help. Using the good edge of a small file, go in between the threads and make sure they are smooth. Be careful not to take off points as you will want them to bite in.

Step 4: Screw the Pedal Back In

This step may take a little bit, as it takes some wiggling and working to get the threads started. Since some were stripped out of the crank arm, it proved impossible to align it all back up, so we got it started the best we could.

Step 5: Tighten the Pedal

This is pretty self-explanatory, but a good thing to know is that to tighten a left-side pedal you have to disregard the good old saying "Righty tighty, lefty loosey," since on a left pedal the threads are reversed. Because the threads were pretty messed up, we had to really crank the pedal down; at one point we were cutting new threads. We got it tight, and it will hold for a while. Also, if you want, you can use a product like a mild thread locker.

This is my 2012 Hyundai Sonata. I did not drive it for ten days. When I returned home, the battery was dead. I have never had that experience on any car that I have ever driven.

This Instructable applies to my car, but with all of the modern electronics running in the background on today's automobiles, your car may have this problem, too. This Instructable tells about the solution to my problem, but may be helpful with a similar problem on your car, too.

Step 1: Tools
- Multimeter with an ammeter scale capable of reading up to about three amps
- 8 mm socket wrench and ratchet
- Spring clamp for connecting a small alligator clip to the battery post

Step 2: How Much Is the Current Draw?
I disconnected the negative (-) battery cable and connected my multimeter between the cable and the battery post. (Check to be certain it is safe to do this on your car. I was reading the manual for another new vehicle and it seems some things need to be reset if the battery is ever disconnected.) The meter was set to measure DC amperes. Check the terminals on your meter to be certain you have the leads connected properly for the scale on the dial. The leads plug into the meter at different terminals for a current reading than they do for a voltage or a resistance reading.

With everything off, the doors closed for a few minutes so all dome lights have gone off, and the key removed, there is a current draw of 470 milliamps, or nearly half of an amp. At a recent visit to the nearest dealership for routine warranty service I asked about this. I was told that is normal. If I am concerned, I should connect a trickle charger when I will leave the car unattended for more than a week. See the second photo. This is a battery conditioner we bought a few years ago for another purpose. I could mount it in the engine compartment and connect an extension cord to it when we will be gone for more than a week.

My question of the dealership was, "What do I do if I need to leave the car in an airport parking garage for a couple of weeks?" There are no electrical outlets in the parking stalls at any airport garage I know.

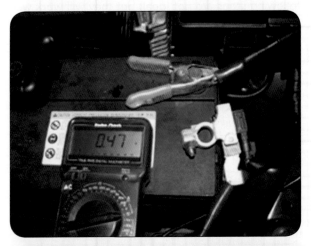

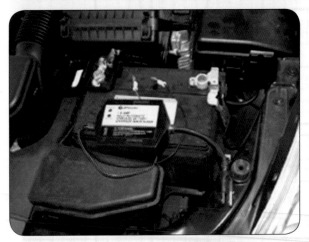

Step 3: What the Dealership Did Not Tell Me
The dealership might have told me there is information in my owner's manual that advises me to pull a special fixture on the fuses to reduce the current draw to a very low level. Yes, I should have read the entire manual after I bought the car, but it is hundreds of pages long.

The graphic is a page from my owner's manual in the section on fuses. It describes a memory fuse that can be pulled when leaving the car unattended for long periods of time in order to avoid a dead battery. Even if I had read this, I am not sure I would have remembered it or that I would have made the connection in my mind. From doing searches on the Internet, particularly on an owner's forum, I suspect this information has escaped others, too.

But the search for a solution to my problem is more complex and confusing than it would seem. Some have had the dead battery problem because of a bad cell in the battery, faulty battery cables, a bad diode in the alternator, or even a problem in the car's radio. A dead battery after a few days has been a problem on several makes of car, not just my 2012 Hyundai Sonata.

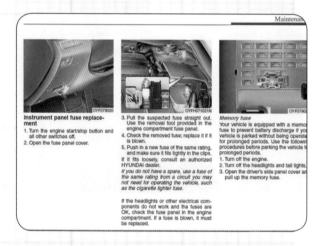

Step 4: Fuse Information, with Photos

The photo shows how to remove the panel covering the memory fuse that needs to be deactivated when the car will be unattended for a longer period of time. Just lift the panel to remove it. It is on the left side of the dashboard between the steering column and the door.

Step 5: Find and Pull the Fuse

Two fuses are grouped together in a yellow plastic holder. You cannot see it while sitting in the driver's seat, but rather you must kneel beside the car with the door open. However, you can locate the fuse holder from the driver's seat by touch without seeing it. Grasp the yellow fuse holder with a thumb and finger. Pull toward yourself. There will be a little click and the dome light will go off. To restore, just press on the yellow fuse holder with your thumb and replace the fuse cover.

There are two fuses in this holder. To remove the holder from the car, squeeze it under the extensions you grasped on each side and pull. This releases two small catches. Each fuse can be removed separately from the yellow holder and replaced as necessary.

Step 6: Big Difference

Here you see the reading on my meter after pulling the memory fuse holder. It is only 40 milliamps. That is not enough to make my battery go dead, even if left unattended for weeks.

Check the owner's manual on your car to see if it has a fuse like the one on my Hyundai Sonata, especially if you have had a dead battery problem after only a few days.

Change an Ignition Switch without Removing the Dashboard

By Phil B

http://www.instructables.com/id/Change-an-Ignition-Switch-without-Removing-the-Das/

This Instructable will show how I replaced the ignition switch in my car without removing the dashboard.

I was having problems with the instrument cluster on my 1999 Oldsmobile Alero. I wondered if my 12-year-old car with 110,000 miles could be suffering from an ignition switch in the early stages of failure. I decided I wanted to remove the ignition switch from my car for examination and possible replacement, but do it without removing the dashboard.

The Oldsmobile Alero has some "cousins," like the Chevrolet Malibu. But the dashboard trim in the Malibu is different from that in the Alero. In the Malibu the bezel around the radio simply pries off, and when it is removed the two bolts that hold the ignition switch in place are fully accessible. The Alero is different, though. The same two bolts are hidden behind the dashboard.

Step 1: Materials and Tools

- A 10mm open-end and box-end combination wrench that I could sacrifice
- A couple of screwdrivers
- A nut driver with a 7mm wrench socket attached
- A torch for heating and bending the wrench as needed (I used a carbon arc torch on an electric welder.)
- A vise (for holding the wrench while heating it for bending)
- A hammer for making the bend in the wrench as sharp as possible
- A Dremel tool with a cylindrical grinding bit and a burr bit
- A mechanic's inspection mirror
- Auxiliary lighting (flashlight or a mechanic's trouble light)
- A Haynes manual for my car
- A multimeter
- A new ignition switch

Step 2: Ignition Switch Bezel

Before beginning it is a good idea to disconnect the negative lead from the battery to keep the air

bags from deploying accidentally. If your car has an anti-theft code set for the radio, deactivate that first.

The ignition switch bezel lifts off when pried around its perimeter with a common screwdriver. I would need to trim away some of the dashboard behind the ignition switch bezel and use the extra space to access the bolts.

Step 3: Working with a Dremel

I used a burr tool on my Dremel to chew away some of the plastic dashboard so that there was a chance I could get a wrench onto the two ignition switch mounting bolts. See the yellow text boxes for the location of the two bolts, each with a 10mm hex head. My plan was to remove dashboard plastic right out to the edge of the ignition switch bezel, but not so far that a gap is visible. This works because the ignition switch bezel fastens to the ignition switch and not to the dashboard.

Step 4: A Suitable Wrench

I decided to buy a 10mm combination box-end and open-end wrench for this project. But, I needed to modify it to work within the spatial confines presented by my dashboard. I decided to use the 12-point box-end portion of the wrench, but it was too thick. So I ground it from both sides to make it thinner. It would not fit between the inner surface of the dashboard and the top of the bolt heads before grinding. It really needs to be no thicker than the bolt head is high. I also heated the wrench to bend it in two places for a large offset. For heating prior to bending I used a carbon arc torch on a 230 volt stick welder. See additional details in the yellow text boxes.

Step 5: Fitting the Wrench onto the Bolt Heads

In these two photos you can see how the wrench fits through the opening, around the ignition switch, and onto the bolt heads. After the bolts were a little bit loose, I was able to reach around through the instrument cluster opening and turn the back end of the upper bolt by hand. I could also get enough of a finger into the area around the ignition switch and push at the bolt heads to speed their removal. This also helped during installation of the new switch. I could twist the bolt between 1/12th and 1/6th of a turn before I had to reset the wrench on the bolt. This was slow, but it worked fine and I was able to get the bolts as tight as I wanted.

Before beginning I had some concerns about either of the bolts falling out of its hole when fully loosened and lodging down low behind the dashboard. I considered stuffing some newspaper behind the dashboard under the ignition switch, but that really was not necessary. Although the bolts tipped precariously, they never fully came out of their holes and they stayed in place quite well.

Step 6: Removing the Instrument Cluster

First, lower the steering column and remove the top half of the steering column cowl. Fingertip pressure is enough to separate and lift the upper cowl. (1st photo)

Remove two screws from the upper part of the instrument cluster bezel. (2nd photo)

Pry the instrument cluster bezel loose on opposite sides of the steering column. (3rd photo)

Disconnect the wiring harness at the switch on the bezel that changes the odometer display between the trip meter and the odometer reading. Remove the instrument cluster bezel and set it aside. Remove the four mounting screws around the perimeter of the instrument cluster. Tip the instrument cluster and pull it from its nesting place. Disconnect the wiring harness. (4th photo)

With the instrument cluster removed, you can see the upper portion of the ignition switch from the lower-right portion of the instrument cluster opening.

Step 7: Access the Switch

The ignition switch can easily be accessed through the opening for the instrument cluster once the cluster and its bezel have been removed. At this point you may want to consult a repair manual for your vehicle. Some things are certain to vary. The harnesses connected to the ignition switch restrict the degree to which the switch can be moved for better access. I found a mechanic's inspection mirror and a flashlight very helpful when something would not release as I thought it should. Also, some things cannot be removed from the ignition switch until the lock cylinder has first been removed. Consult a manual before forcing something with more leverage.

My ignition switch uses an interlock cable to connect the gearshift lever to the ignition switch so the car cannot be started unless the transmission is in park or in neutral. The Haynes manual fails to mention that this cannot be separated from the switch until the lock cylinder has been removed. The lock cylinder is removed by inserting the key into the ignition switch and turning it to its "Run" position. There is also a metal retainer in a rectangle on the side of the ignition switch. Press it inward and the lock cylinder can be pulled from the switch. Also, the Passlock wiring harness (white and yellow wires) cannot be removed until the lock cylinder has been removed.

Step 8: The Switch

The first photo shows the old switch as viewed from the front, but with the lock cylinder removed. Notice the two arms with metal threaded sleeves to receive the mounting screws. The switch is turned counter-clockwise just a little. The lower threaded sleeve would be at 6 o'clock and the upper at 2 o'clock when in place.

See the second photo for a view of the back and underside of the switch. The two wiring harnesses and the interlock cable attach here. Even though I pressed the releases on the wiring harnesses, both were very difficult to remove, especially in the confined space behind the dashboard.

The third photo shows the metal tabs in each of the two harness connectors on the switch. The diagram below is from the Haynes manual. Not all tab positions shown in the manual are filled with a metal tab. The table below tells which sets of tabs should have continuity in the various key positions. I decided I would spend the money and buy a new ignition switch.

The auto parts store I use is part of a chain. I was able to go onto their web page and locate the specific ignition switch my car uses and determine that my local store had one in stock. The price was also listed. These things were good to know before I had removed enough things that the car no longer starts.

Step 9: Finished

This is an actual photo of my dashboard after I replaced the ignition switch without removing the dashboard. Nothing in what you see hints that some of the dashboard has been cut away behind the ignition switch bezel with a Dremel tool. And my car now works as it should. Although a new ignition switch is almost $100, I can avoid buying a new car for a while. I sacrificed a wrench that I may yet use again for another special job in the future, but it was well worth the extra cost of a few dollars.

Fix a Motorcycle Flat Tire

By TimAnderson
http://www.instructables.com/id/Motorcycle-Flat-Tire-Fix/

It's just like fixing a bicycle flat tire, but *much* bigger. For instance, contrast these "tire irons" with the little plastic things you use to pry the tire off a bike rim. Some newer/larger motorcycles don't have innertubes. Fixing one of those is more like fixing a flat in a tubeless automobile tire. Just keep in mind you *can* put an innertube in any tire, even a "tubeless" one.

Step 1: Motorcycle Stand from Milk Crate

We're going to remove the front wheel. I made a hasty motorcycle stand from a milk crate. I put a slab of 2" × 6" on top of that to spread the load. I propped the engine up on that. Fortunately there's a flat spot on the bottom of the skid pan that makes this arrangement very stable. Don't store your bike this way though, as the milk crate plastic will sag and eventually your bike will fall over. A double kickstand would hold the bike up just fine with the front wheel off, but this bike doesn't have one. This is my 1987 Honda TLR200 trials bike. It was stripped for racing, and I'm in the process of putting improvised street-legal signals and lights on it. That's why the lights on this bike look a bit odd.

Step 2: Wheel Removal—Don't Lose the Little Parts

Taking a wheel off is slightly different for every bike. Usually you need to disconnect the brake cable and speedometer cable. Usually there's an axle bolt. Sometimes there are other bolts clamping the axle bolt in place. Sometimes when you remove the axle bolt there are little bushings like this that can fall out of the wheel. Don't lose these parts. They are very important.

Step 3: Tire Irons

You'll need three "tire irons" to pry your tire off the rim. One of mine is an official tire iron on the end of an old lug wrench. The other two are stainless steel bars that came off the broken mast of the free yacht. Make sure the ends don't have sharp corners or edges. You don't want to poke holes in your inner tube while putting it back in.

Step 4: Pry the Tire with the First Iron

Push the tire down away from the rim all the way around. That unseats the tire's "bead." That makes it loose enough to pry it up and over at one end. Take the first tire iron and pry the tire over the rim. If it's hard to do this, push the tire down on the other side to keep it from springing up and reseating on the rim. Make sure you don't pinch the innertube between the tire iron and anything else. That would puncture it.

Step 5: Second And Third Irons

Repeat with your other two tire irons. You might want to put your knee on the first one to keep it from getting levered up and hitting you in the face. If that happens you've got other problems as well. Most likely the tire has reseated itself on the rim and isn't loose enough. Push it down away from the rim all the way around and things should get easier. This tire is pretty badly cracked from SUV pollution in the air. It was stored in the shade but wasn't covered. It cracked badly anyway. I'll need to replace it soon so I'm not being careful with it. If you care about your tire you can lubricate the edges with soap like they do at a tire shop before prying it on or off. If you ask a mechanic at a tire shop for some of that grease-looking rim soap they'll be happy to give you some. They'll be glad that someone knows about it and will interpret that as a sign of respect for their profession.

Step 6: Pull

Now you should be able to pull the bead of the tire over the rest of the rim by hand.

Step 7: Pull Out the Tube

Usually there's a little nut on the metal valve stem. Remove the nut. Push the valve into the rim. Reach in and pull the whole innertube out. Look and feel around inside the tire to find what caused the leak.

Nails and staples are pretty common. Sometimes the head wears off from driving, so it's really hard to spot from the outside. You need to find it and pull it out or you'll get another flat right away.

Step 8: Inflate and Bubble Test

Put some air in the innertube to puff it up. Fill a tub with water. Push the tube underwater and look for bubbles. Once you find the leak, go look and feel around inside the tire until you find the nail/thorn/bullet hole or whatever caused it. Don't forget to fix the cause of the leak so you don't just get another leak. These leaking bubbles are coming from around the valve stem. That's trouble. I don't have any patches with a built-in valve. They exist, but the nearby auto parts store doesn't carry them.

Step 9: Maybe Slime?

Sometimes when I cut an innertube up for lashings a lot of slimy stuff comes gushing out. That's a product called "slime" that's supposed to fix flat tires. Or competing products with equally revealing names. I considered getting some to try to fix this one. Then I realized there was something slimy inside this tube already. Sure enough, it already had slime inside it but it leaked anyway.

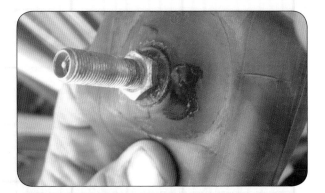

Step 10: List of Other Repair Alternatives

If the leak hadn't been right by the valve, I could have patched it with a regular bicycle tire patch. That process is exactly the same as patching a bicycle innertube.

A replacement 21" motorcycle innertube costs between $8 and $15 online. That would be the best option for this tire. Retail price is probably similar. Unfortunately there's no motorcycle parts store nearby.

A pack of innertube patches with a built-in valve is $10 for four patches on eBay. It might be a good thing to have handy, but by the time I needed it again it probably wouldn't be handy any more.

I considered cutting a patch and valve from a bicycle innertube and gluing that on. But the slime inside this tube would have made it hard to glue that on properly.

Then I remembered my parts bike. It has the same size front wheel, and it even holds air! I deflated the tire and pried the tire off the rim. I pulled the tube out without removing the wheel first. Obviously I'm not thinking clearly. I could have patched the tube without removing the wheel, but I have to remove the wheel to get this tube off the fork.

Step 11: Install the New Tube

I left a little air in the tube so it wouldn't collapse. That helped keep inside the tire so I didn't puncture it with the tire irons. I put the valve through the hole in the rim and installed the little nut on the valve so it didn't pull back into the rim.

Step 12: Pry the Tire Back Onto the Rim

I used a tire iron to pry the tire back onto the rim. Once again I pushed the tire down on the other side so it was loose enough to do this. Watch for the dot! New tires usually have a dot on the sidewall indicating the heavy end of the tire. Put this dot away from the valve stem. That will make the wheel more balanced. This tire also has an arrow indicating the direction it should rotate. We never took this tire all the way off the rim, so the arrow still points the right direction.

Step 13: Testing!

Inflate the tire, let the air out again, and inflate it again. This is a trick I learned from my brother. It makes the tube and tire shift around and get evenly seated around the rim. Then you can let it sit around for a while to see if it holds air. If you're in a hurry to know for sure, put it in the dunk tank. Put the wheel back on the bike and go for a ride!

How to Fix a Bike Chain

By dan

http://www.instructables.com/id/How-To-Fix-a-Bike-Chain/

Fixing a bike chain on the street is no harder than fixing a flat tire if you are prepared. Read on. . .

This article is sponsored by *Momentum* Magazine and MonkeyLectric. An edited version of the article appears in *Momentum* issue 50.

Step 1: What You Need

To fix a broken chain, all you need is a chain tool. These are compact and built into many common multi-tools like the one shown. You may even have one on your multi-tool that you never even knew what it was for!

At home in your garage it's possible to repair a chain with just a hammer and pliers, but a chain tool is easier, and really the only option on the street.

Step 2: How Do Chains Break?

The most common way chains break is by pedaling full force at the same moment that you are shifting your front derailleur. Other breaks I've seen were caused by an assortment of seemingly one-in-a-million occurrences, yet I've seen enough of those cases that I guess if you ride long enough one-in-a-million still happens. Things like a nail getting thrown up by my front wheel and lodging in the chain, then getting cranked across the sprocket. Who'da thunk?

Step 3: How Do Chains Work?

Each link of a chain is held together by a steel pin or peg. With the chain tool (or a hammer) you can push out and push in the pins, allowing you to remove or attach links. Fixing a broken chain amounts to removing the broken link and reattaching the remaining ends. On bikes with derailleurs there's enough extra links that you can remove a couple without a problem. On a single-speed bike you probably won't have enough slack in the chain to remove a link, so you'll need to borrow some links from an old chain or else buy a new one.

Step 4: Your Chain Just Broke, Now What?

Are you wearing nice clothes that you care about? Probably best to lock your bike and take the bus home. Come back later with your old jeans and we'll fix it then. Fixing a chain is the dirtiest job there is on a bike.

Step 5: Take a Look at the Chain

Okay, you're back and ready to go. Flip your bike over so you can get to the chain more easily.

Take a look at the two broken ends. One end (possibly both) is damaged and needs to be removed. What you will do is to remove two segments of the chain at the damaged end. You need to remove two segments instead of 1 because the two types of segments alternate. If you just remove one segment you can't reattach it.

Place the chain into the groove in the chain tool (see photo) at the spot you want to disconnect. If you are replacing a worn but non-broken chain you'll do the same thing here.

Step 6: Separate the Chain

Turn the screw on the chain tool to start pushing the pin out of the chain (see photo). Be careful to keep the pin on the chain tool lined up with the pin on the chain; sometimes they like to slip around a bit.

Don't push the pin all the way out! Only push it just far enough so the chain comes apart (see photo). You need to leave the last bit of the pin in the chain so you can push it back in later.

If you want to do this without a chain tool: drill a hole in a piece of wood and place the pin you want to remove over the hole. find a machine screw about the size of the chain pin and use it as a peg to bang the chain pin out with a hammer. It's tricky because you don't want to bang it out all the way.

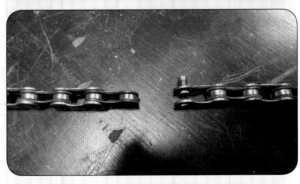

Step 7: Reattach the Links

Okay, now feed the chain back onto your sprockets. It helps a lot if you have a friend who can hold the two ends in position while you reattach them.

Use the chain tool to push the pin back in (see photo). This is the trickiest part—to keep the tool lined up with the pin.

Note: if you are putting on a new chain here, many new chains come with a special link that makes the first-time installation possible without pushing any pins in.

Step 8: Work It Loose

Once the pin is in, the link you just attached will be stiff. Work it back and forth (see photo) until it loosens enough to bend around the gears.

Take a look at your hands and feel proud. You have done something real today.

Step 9: Reuse

If you were just putting on a new chain in the comfort of your home, now you have an old worn chain to reuse! Since you know how to remove links and reattach the segments, you can use part of the old chain as a cable to lock your seat onto your bike. This is very handy in urban areas.

You can also make yourself a bike chain bracelet or an earring. You'll need a fairly big piercing and a tough ear to get that stud through.

Sharp drill bits are fun to use. They work so well. Dull bits are dangerous. They can break. One broke for me once and went through my thumbnail and out the other side of my thumb.

Step 1: A Dull Bit and a Sharp Bit

The bit on the left is a little dull. Notice the glint of light on the cutting edge between the two flutes. Compare that with the crisp edge on the freshly sharpened bit on the right.

Step 2: My Favorite Sharpening Tool

People who know what they are doing can sharpen bits by hand. In theory, hold the bit with the shank angled off to the left at about 59 degrees. As the bit contacts the grinding wheel, simultaneously move the shank farther left and downward while twisting it clockwise. I have tried, but I have never been able to make it work for me. I bought this bit-sharpening tool almost 30 years ago for less than $20. The same tool is still available at Amazon and other places, and it is still less than $20. A Drill Doctor is a very nice tool, but it costs four or five times the cost of this tool. I do not sharpen bits often enough to justify the cost of a Drill Doctor.

Step 3: Set to 59 degrees

This sharpening guide can accept drill bits with several different profiles. My bits have a 59 degree profile on the cutting edge. Set the tool to 59 degrees and tighten the thumbnut.

Step 4: Catch the Edge

The tool has a small tip, and the edges of the bit's flutes rest against it. You may have to raise or lower the tip so it fits against the flute edges properly.

Step 5: How Much Overhang

As a starting point, make the overhang (space between the yellow lines) equal to the radius of the bit (space between the green lines). See the next step for why it matters.

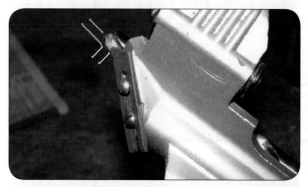

Step 6: Width and Angle of the Cutting Edge

Notice the angle of the red line. If there is too much overhang in the previous step, the red line will approximate the cutting edge at the tip of the bit. If it is too wide the bit profile will be too flat. The bit will skate on a metal surface and the hole will be hard to start. You can reduce the bit's overhang quite a bit, but be careful. If you reduce it too much, the tip you adjusted in step 4 may come into contact with the grinding wheel and you will damage your sharpening guide.

Step 7: Ideal Cutting-Edge Angle

The ideal is to have the shortest cutting edge possible. This would be a cutting edge that runs between the low points in the valleys of the fluting. See the yellow line. This bit is close to ideal and will cut steel very well.

Step 8: Clamp the Bit in the Tool

When you have the overhang set, turn down the screw that clamps the bit in the tool's trough.

Step 9: Set the Tool for Bit Length

Set the sharpening guide for the length of the bit you want to sharpen. Keep the end of the bit in the moveable trough, not hanging in the air. Loosen the metal-colored nut. Adjust the black nut. Tighten the metal-colored nut.

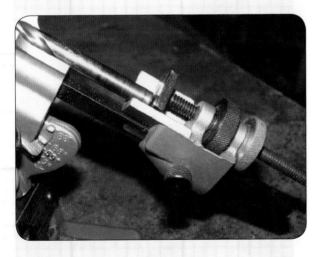

Step 10: Align for Height

The end of the bit should be squarely aligned with the grinding wheel. I use a radial arm saw for my grinding. The tip of the bit should be even with the center of the motor shaft.

Step 11: Clamp the Tool to the Table

You want the bit to kiss the grinding wheel while sharpening it. If the bit is too close to the grinding wheel, sharpening will be difficult, the bit will become too hot, and you will remove a lot more material than necessary. Keep the base of the sharpening guide square to the surface of the grinding stone (green lines), but turn the upper portion of the guide so the tip of the drill bit is just a little to the left of the center (angle between long green line and the yellow line). Slide the guide forward so the bit lightly touches the grinding wheel's surface. Clamp the guide to the table.

Step 12: Get Ready to Grind the Bit

Swing the tip of the bit to the right. Start the motor.

Step 13: Grind

Swing the rear of the sharpening guide to the right (red arrow) so the tip of the bit moves into the wheel. The yellow shower of sparks is added in a photo-editing program, but the actual grinding happens when the bit is in about this position.

Step 14: Rotate the Bit One-Half Turn

Continue swinging the guide until the tip of the bit is beyond the cutting wheel. You need to rotate the bit one-half turn and repeat the process in order to sharpen the other half of the bit. It is safer to turn the motor off and wait for the wheel to stop. Loosen the hold down on the bit and turn the bit one half turn. Make sure the flute rests on the guide's tip. Repeat the process from the last two steps. Shut the motor off. Remove the bit. Check width of the center cutting edge on the bit. Adjust the overhang and repeat the grinding process if it is not satisfactory.

Step 15: The Finished Bit

This is how your bit should appear. Notice there are no longer any worn, rounded cutting edges casting glints of light. Everything is sharp and crisp. The length and angle of the cutting edge at the tip of the drill bit are good, too.

Step 16: Small Sizes

A sharpening guide like this one works well for bits ⅛" and above. It does not work with smaller bits than ⅛". Make a special wooden block to serve as a guide for a handstone when sharpening small bits. The angle of the lines in red is 77 degrees. Make the block about 4" long.

Step 17: Compound Angles

This is the edge of the block. The angle between the red lines is 59 degrees.

Step 18: A Guide Line

Notice the "V" in the top surface of the block. It runs the length of the block and makes a place for the small bits to be cradled. The angle between the red lines is also 59 degrees. This serves as a guide line to align with the leading edge of each half of the bit. A visual alignment is satisfactory.

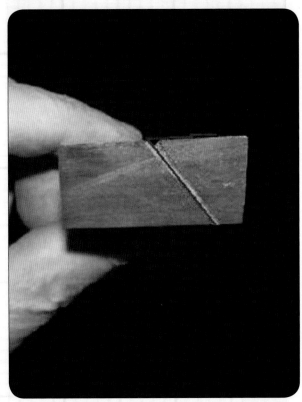

Step 19: Placing the Bit against the Block

Place a bit into the "V" groove on the back face of the block. Place the block into a vise so the end of the bit rests on top of and against the jaws and so that it just barely extends above the angled surface of the block. Turn the bit so the leading edge of the first half follows the guide line. Use a "C" clamp to hold the bit in place. Put some oil on a small handstone, like those used for sharpening fishhooks. Stroke along the angled surface of the block so the bit is being sharpened at the same time. When the stone is no longer cutting on the bit, turn it half of a turn and sharpen the other side. Inspect the bit with a magnifying glass, if necessary.

In many older cars the rubber door seals don't seal the way they should. Often the seals have pulled away from the door frame, leaving gaps, almost always in the corners. This lets in cold or hot air, sometimes water, and almost always excess noise. So, many older cars have a noisy, drafty ride because the seals are not tight.

Many people think that the reason for the seals not staying in the frame is that they have come unglued. They will often try to glue them back in place, but the seals will not stay there. That is because they are not glued in to begin with. The door seals are held in place by simple pressure. When the rubber seals get older, the rubber shrinks—the older the seal, the greater the shrinking.

But there is a simple and very cheap fix for the problem that is permanent. You have to make the door seal bigger. It's a lot easier to do than you might think.

Step 1: Find the Seam Where the Seal Is Joined

The first step is to find the seam were the seal is joined. This will almost always be located under the plastic sill that protects the bottom of the door frame. Pry the sill up and off to get access. If yours is screwed down then remove the screws. Most have plastic connectors that go into holes in the floor, and they are just pressed in place. They should pull up easily.

Once you have that out of the way, you should be able to see the place where the seal is joined. It will probably look like it has been glued or fused together. This is the easiest place to cut the seal.

After you have cut it, you can push the seal back into the door frame corners where it is supposed to be. Sometimes it is easiest to pull a section off and then start at the top, pushing it back in tightly, working your way back to where you cut it. Now you will be able to see how much your seal has shrunk.

Step 2: Add an Extra Piece

Find an extra chunk of door seal—a foot or so will do. You can get this from a junk yard or from another car. You can also buy seals, but they are expensive. I took a piece out of a minivan that is used as a parts car. The best one to get is one that matches your car. If you can't get that then try to get one that is a close match.

After you get your seal material, figure out how much to cut in order to fill the gap. First, make sure the seal is pushed completely into the door frame. Next, mark on your chunk of seal where to cut. Make it *bigger* than the gap by about a half inch. This way, when you put it in place it will push against the rest of the door seal and help to force it to stay in place.

Push the piece you cut into the gap and hammer it down with your hand. You should not have to do it very hard, as it goes in pretty easily. You don't need to use any type of glue, since the pressure and the sill cover will keep it in place.

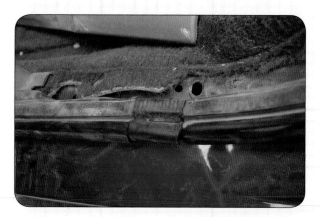

Step 3: Now Do the Rest of the Doors

After you get the filler piece in place, put the plastic sill cover back on. Again, just a hit with your palm should be enough to snap it in place.

Do this same procedure for all the doors of your car. If one has shrunk, then they all have shrunk. Enjoy the quieter ride.

One day, you'll get a puncture. And I guarantee, it will be at the worst time possible. Here's how to install a spare tire.

Note: Some cars have locking wheel bolts. If yours does, check your glove box for a special key. If you don't have this key, and have a lock, you will not be able to remove your wheel.

If you are uncomfortable with changing your tire on the side of the road, call for assistance—do not drive with a spare tire or punctured tire unless you have run-flat tires.

Never raise a vehicle with people inside. It is beneficial to practice this operation in your driveway so you can complete the task quickly and comfortably on the side of the road.

Check the pressure of your spare tire frequently (at least once a month) and before long trips. There's nothing worse than finding all you have to replace your flat tire with is . . . a flat tire.

Avoid products like "Fix-A-Flat" and the like. These make tire repair, if not impossible, much more difficult. Only use these as a last resort.

Step 1: Get to a Safe Location
Once you've determined you have a flat or a puncture, turn on your hazard lights and pull off the road. Ideally, you want to park on a hard, level surface that is visible to other drivers. Once you've come to a stop, make sure that you can safely open your door.

Step 2: Preparation
First, open your hood; leave your hazard lights on. An open hood on the side of the road indicates distress and makes your car more visible. Now, open your trunk (or wherever your spare tire is located).

Step 3: The Road-Side Kit
Here we have a few items—but we only need three.
1. Screwdriver and plastic lug wrench (to unscrew once they have been freed)
2. Jack (this one is known as "The widow maker" among the VW community
3. Lug wrench (if you thought ahead, you might have also included gloves, to keep your hands clean.

Other good things to have:
1. Flashlight (preferably a human-powered one)
2. Road marker
3. Road flare
4. Jumper cables (that's another Instructable)

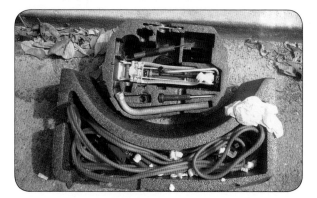

Step 4: Clear Trunk Space and Remove Spare

My trunk was full of stuff, so all if had to come out. Once the trunk space is clear:

1. Lift the trunk floor
2. Remove road-side kit
3. Unscrew spare-tire tie down (this keeps the tire from rattling)
4. Remove spare tire

You'll notice I have a full-sized spare. This mean, I can replace any tire of my car with it. For those with a "donut" spare—you can only replace a wheel that is not driven. That is, if your car is front-wheel drive, AND you have a puncture on your front wheel, you'll need to replace a rear wheel with the spare, and then replace the flat/punctured wheel with your full-sized rear wheel. This is to prevent excessive wear on your transmission (specifically, differential). Additionally, driving with an undersized tire on a driven wheel can be dangerous.

Step 5: Secure Your Vehicle

When you lift a car with an emergency, the wheels need to be able to roll a tiny bit. Otherwise, you'll find out why this VW jack is known as the widow maker. If the wheels are not able to roll, any force applied to the jack will cause it to twist off. Luckily, we can secure either the front or rear without problems.

For flat ground (that is, the car doesn't roll on its own): If you're replacing a front wheel, engage the parking brake OR chock the opposite rear wheel (if possible). Leave your transmission in neutral. If replacing a rear wheel, put your car in first gear (for manual transmission) OR chock the opposite front wheel and leave the parking brake off.

Step 6: Free Wheel Bolts/Lugs

Remove any wheel center caps to reveal your lugs/bolts. Using your lug wrench, loosen each lug to break it free. DO NOT continue removing them at this point. DO NOT raise the vehicle off the ground at this time.

Step 7: Place Jack and Raise

My jack uses my car's unibody to lift the car. There is a bit of metal that comes down vertically that the jack settles into. Not all vehicles are like this. Check your owner's manual for the proper lift points. Place the jack down so its "feet" are even on the ground and level. Begin raising the jack and make sure the jack cup fits into the proper portion of the frame. Once the cup is in place, begin to lift the car slowly. Check that the jack is not twisting and that its base is level on the ground. Should the jack start twisting or go off center, immediately lower the jack and try again. Raise your vehicle so that there is a little space under your wheel. DO NOT place your jack on soft ground such as dirt, soil, or grass.

Step 8: Remove Lugs/Bolts and Wheel

Now, unscrew the lugs and remove them. Place them in a pocket or anywhere that they won't get lost. At this time, you should be able to remove the wheel. Remove the wheel and place it under your car as shown. In the event that your jack fails, your car will not fall on to an unprotected wheel hub. Yes, I've had a jack fail on me while rotating my tires. No, my wheels were not destroyed.

Step 9: Attach Spare

Place your spare onto your wheel hub. You may need to lift your vehicle a little more, as the spare may be larger compared to a flat tire. In my case, the wheel sits on a hub (not the bolts). So I have to place the wheel on the circular ring (pictured) then bolt it on. Screw in all of your bolts/lugs until hand tight (do not use lug wrench to apply a great amount of force).

Step 10: Partially Lower Your Vehicle: Tighten Lugs

Now, remove your flat tire from under your car and lower your car so that some of the vehicle's weight is place on the spare. At this time, use your lug wrench to tighten all lugs in a star-shaped criss-cross pattern. This ensures the wheel tightens evenly. Look at image notes for the proper order. After doing one pass with your lug wrench, do a second and a third. Now Lower your vehicle completely.

Step 11: Finish Tightening and Clean Up

With the car lowered completely, tighten the lugs/bolts as hard as you can with your wrench. Put your flat tire in your trunk (in the spare tire well if applicable) and put away your road-side kit.

This is my trouble light, also known as a work light. It needed a new guard to protect the bulb. I decided to make my own.

Step 1: What You Will Need
Materials:
- Sheet metal from the outer cover of an old washing machine
- 1/8" steel rod (from concrete reinforcement wire stubs)
- Two #8-32 machine screws and nuts
- An old speaker magnet

Tools:
- Flux-core wire-feed welder
- Angle grinder with a cutting wheel
- Dremel tool with cutting wheels and grinding stones
- Vise
- Electric hand drill and bit
- Grinding wheel
- Screwdriver

Step 2: The Old Guard

My trouble light is a cheap plastic unit that still works well, except for the broken guard. The grill was plastic and broke many years ago. I used a piece of coat hanger wire to make a protector for the bulb, but it easily pushes away and is little help. The old guard is also badly cracked. I never liked the swivel hook, either. It has never broken, but a twist in the cord will cause the light to turn away from the direction I want it to shine.

Step 3: First Step

First I cut a strip of sheet metal ⅝" wide by about 7" long and cut this into two equal lengths. These would become straps to fit around the body of the trouble light. I bent them to the contour of the trouble-light body and left a flat tab at each end. Here you can see the front strap attached to the trouble light. The old plastic strap in the foreground was used as a guide. One of these will be welded to the body of the guard. The other will simply attach with screws.

Step 3: Mark to Cut a Circle

A can of wheel-bearing grease had just the right diameter (about 4") to use as a guide for marking a circle to be cut for the bottom and top parts of the guard body. I would like to have found an existing steel can from which I could remove half of the can's side. I could have folded over a lip to protect against sharp edges, but we did not have a can that large in our pantry. Such a can would have saved a lot of work, but the final product on my guard is very sturdy.

Step 4: The Discs

Make two 4" discs. After marking, I tried to cut one with a Dremel tool and cutting wheels. This works very well and is very precise, but it is also very slow and uses quite a few cutting wheels. One of the 4" steel discs needs a center hole cut into it so it can slip over the body of the trouble light. I cut and fitted a hole a little larger than 1 ⅝" in diameter.

Step 5: Weld a Strap to the Bottom Disc

I was able to slip the disc with the hole over the body of the trouble light and position it so it would stay in place. I rested one of the straps on the disc and against the body of the trouble light. I tack welded the strap to the disc at the flat tabs so the heat was away from the plastic trouble-light body. I have had this trouble light more than 30 years and discovered some of the plastic is becoming a little brittle. There was a lip at the top of the trouble-light body I wanted to preserve, but much of it cracked and broke away while I was wrestling with fitting the disc over the body of the trouble light.

I removed the strap and disc from the trouble light and made a series of tack welds along the length of the strap so it is very firmly attached to the disc. If I had a MIG welder, I could have made just the proper setting to make a continuous weld bead, but that is not really possible on my flux-core welder. This is not a cosmetic project, anyway. But, my flux-core welder will dig through old paint and a bit of dirt to make a weld whereas the metal would need to be bright and clean for a MIG welder to work. Drill screw holes in the tabs on the straps. Attach the guard to the trouble light when finished with the all of the welding.

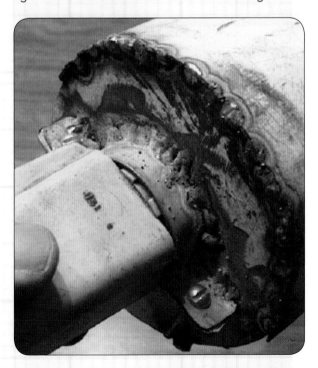

Step 6: The Main Part of the Guard

I measured half of the circumference of the discs and found it to be right at 6". The old guard is about 5" high. I cut a rectangle of sheet metal 5" × 6" and bent it to a half pipe to fit the discs. I did not have a pipe about 4" in diameter and just made a series of crimps in my vise to get as close as I could. Then I began tack welding the main part of the body to the disc at the base of the guard. This allowed me to pull the main part into place so it fit the disc before each weld.

Step 7: Weld the Top Disc in Place

Use the same process to weld the top disc into place.

Step 8: Solving One Irritation

The grill on trouble-light guards is designed to open so it is easy to replace the bulb. The hinge system is usually a weak spot. Any bend to the guard causes the grill not to fit as it originally did. I decided I could weld a permanent grill in place, but plan the spacing of its parts so that I can still change the bulb easily. I positioned the rods for the grill so I can easily screw in a light bulb without removing or opening anything. Yet, the bulb is well protected when the light rolls around on the concrete floor.

Step 9: Solving Another Irritation

As I mentioned earlier, the swivel hook on my light's original guard does not always stay where I want it, and the light twists to one side or the other rather than shining on my work. I wanted a way of turning the hook so it stays in place. I decided to weld a hook I made to the back of an old speaker magnet. I can position the magnet wherever I want it, and it stays in place, even when the cord has a twist in it. This magnet makes my trouble light a little top heavy, but I can easily remove the magnet and hook when I do not need to hang the light from anything.

One additional thing—a trouble light takes some bumps and jarrings. A rough-service bulb costs very little more, but lasts so much longer.

If you have a chip on your windshield, it is necessary that you get it repaired as soon as possible. A small chip on your windshield can turn into a big problem quickly. After the first layer of your windshield is penetrated, it is likely to crack out, causing further damage, plus the need for a costly replacement.

Repairing your windshield when you notice a chip will save you money in the long run. You can call a windshield repair company or do it yourself. They do sell inexpensive windshield repair kits at your local auto parts store, but if you are not comfortable with the process, call a professional.

Step 1: Windshield Repair Tools and Supplies

You can purchase a windshield repair kit from your local auto parts store, which will include all the necessary tools and supplies. I will be using a professional-grade windshield repair kit, but the concept is the same.

You will need:
- A mirror to place on the inside of the windshield
- A bridge and injector
- Windshield repair resin
- Windshield pit filler
- Plastic curing tab
- Razor blades
- A Dremel tool with special glass bit for cracks

Step 2: Beginning the Repair

The first step is to prep the chip and windshield for repair. I recommend using an alcohol pad to clean the area and gently scribing out any loose glass from the impact point.

Next, hook your mirror up on the inside of the windshield, centered on the chip you are going to be repairing. This will allow you to keep an eye on the chip from all angles, which is very helpful with all windshield repairs.

Step 3: Make a Seal over the Chip

You want to center your bridge, or whatever tool you are using, directly on the chip. You basically want to create a seal over the area of the chip that is missing glass.

Step 4: Drop Resin

After you have effectively created a seal around the chip, put three to eight drops of resin into the injector area.

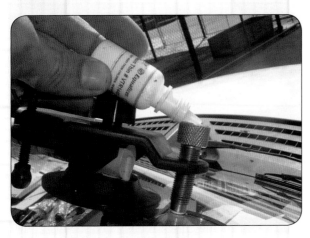

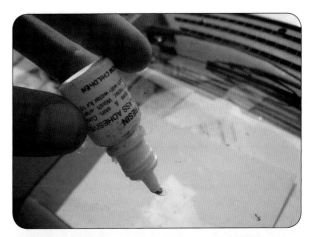

Step 5: Injecting the Chip

Next, use the injector to push the resin into the windshield chip. You should be able to see it start to clear up through your mirror. Keep an eye on it, releasing air and re-injecting the resin when needed. Leave it alone for about five to ten minutes.

Be sure to keep the area covered if you are in direct sunlight, as you do not want the resin to cure prematurely.

After you have let it sit, and it appears as if the chip has cleared up, you can remove the bridge.

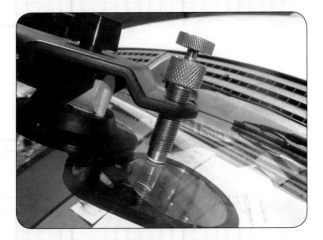

Step 6: Fill in Missing Glass

The repair is just about complete, but we still need to fill in the "pit" of the chip.

The *pit* is the area where little bits of glass are missing.

This step will give the glass a smooth finish once again.

Get your pit filler and drop a tiny bit directly on the impact point. Grab a plastic curing tab and place it over the area. Leave it alone in direct sunlight for a minute or so to let it cure.

Step 7: Scrape Off Excess

Grab a razor blade and hold it securely upright. Scrape off all excess pit filler, leaving only the area where glass was missing filled.

You can even go an extra step and use a light polish on the area to be sure that the area is flush.

Cosmetically, windshield repairs clear up anywhere from 30 percent to 80 percent depending on many variables. Age, moisture, dirt, location, and temperature all play a role in the appearance of a repaired windshield chip.

Structurally, the glass should be back up to 100 percent.

Clean Your Headlights with Toothpaste

By Jessy Ellenberger (jessyratfink)
http://www.instructables.com/id/Clean-your-headlights-with-toothpaste/

So you're driving around super late at night in the middle of Nowhere, NM and you realize you can't see a thing.

You and your significant other talk about cleaning the headlights or getting new bulbs, but the store-bought kits cost way more than you can afford because you just spent all your money on a cross-country move. And then one of the lights goes out and you replace it, and it doesn't make much of a difference.

So what do you do? Google it and then wind up cleaning them with toothpaste.

I have to admit I didn't know if this would work, but I am pleasantly surprised.

Step 1: What You'll Need:

- Regular ol' toothpaste
- Old towels or rags
- Water for rinsing
- A pair of filthy headlights

I'm using old bar-mop towels and Arm & Hammer toothpaste. We bought it to actually clean our mouths, but it is the worst thing I've ever put in my mouth. Hooray for reuse!

Step 2: Scrub!

Squeeze out a bit of toothpaste on the rag and scrub the headlight.

Scrub however you want. Circular motion adds nothing.

Watch how fast the grime comes off!

Step 3: Admire Headlight Dirt

Your rag/towel/cloth of choice will look gross. Good job!

I can't say that yours will look much worse than mine, though . . . our Altima is old and very dirty. I'm pretty sure it got vacuumed for the first time ever in more than twelve years before we moved to Oakland.

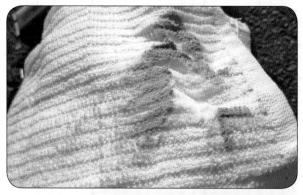

Step 4: Rinse and Be Excited

I rinsed them with a little water and wiped them down again to make sure all of the gunk was gone. Easy! I included some before and after photos to convince you.

So now you know what to do: go buy toothpaste instead of a $30 kit.

How to Fix Rust Spots on a Car

By intoon

http://www.instructables.com/id/How-to-Fix-Rust-Spots-On-a-Car/

I drive a 1985 VW Golf (diesel), and it's in pretty good condition for being 21 years old. There are three spots on the front left fender that have rust on them. These spots are not only an eye sore, but they are sure to spread in the salty Nebraska winters. My goal in fixing these was function and not so much glamour. The car is kind of a beater, so I wasn't too concerned with making it look perfect. As long as the rust was gone, it would look better, and I wouldn't lose a fender.

Step 1: Assess the Situation and Remove Wheel

Having never done this, or any other body work on a car, it took me a little longer to figure out what exactly I was going to do. My original plan was to take the entire fender off, but after inspecting it, that would be too much of a hassle and would require me to disassemble a lot of the front of the car.

Instead, I jacked the car up, then I pulled off the wheel. I unscrewed the plastic thing protecting the wheel well and set it off to the side. That gave me really good access to see up behind the sheet metal on the car. I was originally going to pound out the dent on the upper part of the fender, but space was tight and I couldn't easily do it. Having the wheel well open will help when I'm grinding and painting.

Step 2: Remove Paint

The first thing I did was remove the paint around the rust. I used a 4 ½" grinder with a 120-grit 3M Sandblaster wheel. It worked really well for taking off the thick layers of primer and paint. I carefully worked my way around the rust spots and removed paint until I could see clean metal surrounding the rust. I also used that wheel for removing all of the light rust that hadn't pitted the metal.

Note: Before grinding, cover up anything that you don't want to get dusty. The paint dust is super fine and covers everything. I had my hood open to help access some rust, so I got a tarp to cover up the engine. Having your windows rolled down here would be a bad idea.

Step 3: Grind Some More

After I got all I could with the sanding wheel, I changed over to a metal grinding wheel. When using this, be super careful, because these can do a lot of damage. I worked really slowly so that I could get a nice finish on the metal. It was really good for taking the thick rust off and getting into those pits. After 99.9 percent of the rust was removed, I sanded by hand (with 120-grit 3M Sandblaster sandpaper) to get a nice smooth metal surface. If I wanted, I could have used Bondo to even out some of the dents and fill the space where the paint is gone.

Step 4: Prep for Painting

I went to NAPA auto parts to find some primer and paint. I found some really good primer that is ideal for painting on bare metal: Dupli-Color Self-Etching Primer. Then I found some auto spray that matched the color of my car: Dupli-Color Auto Spray in Sunburst Gold Metallic.

I followed all of the instructions on the back of the primer: I mixed up a little bit of car-wash soap and water and washed the areas that I was going to paint. Then I got a 400-grit wet sandpaper and sanded the areas, then wiped clean. I then masked off the areas with tape and taped newspapers on all the surrounding areas within at least three feet. Paint spray can get everywhere because it gets suspended in the air and blown around and settles. Once everything was masked off, I was ready to prime.

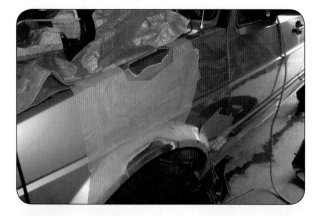

Step 5: Prime and Paint

When applying paint, it is important to spray thin coats and keep it even. The paint that I was using was really nice and went on very smoothly. I ended up spraying three coats of primer, waiting about two minutes between each coat for it to tack up. I let that sit all night and sprayed the paint in the morning.

I had to spray the paint on in even thinner layers, because it really wanted to run and sag. I ended up having five coats of paint on top of the primer. That gave me a nice color and a nice finish. I let it set at least 24 hours before I pulled off the tape. The paint turned out pretty well, and it just looked like little patches over the old rust. The color wasn't quite the same as the old, but it was pretty close. It also had no clear coat on it, so it had a slightly different finish.

I didn't bother buffing the edge of the paint so that it blended with the old paint.

Step 6: Wash and Wax

After the paint had cured a good 48 hours, I washed and waxed the car to bring back the shine. It ended up looking fairly good. It cost me less than $15 and four to six hours of labor. I spent an additional four hours washing and waxing. If I had taken it to a body shop, it could have cost me $200, so I saved a lot of money and got the satisfaction of doing it myself, which is the best part.

On a typical morning I head out the door and bike to work. Well, I try to head for the door. Usually I'll get to about spitting distance before stumbling over a Specialized or a Giant. I'll move those to the side and get about two more steps. Then I'll be in the thick of it. To my left is the formidable fortress of Fujis. To my right, the towering tangle of Trek. Dead ahead, stupendous snarl of Surly. And underfoot—you guessed it—Univega. After about 10 minutes of snagged up pedals, chains, and spokes I've got my ride out. Whew! Then I enjoy a peaceful ride to work.

Of course we tried keeping the bikes in other places—the garage, the backyard in the summer, on the porch—but that was just moving the problem from one department to another. Things were getting ridiculous! If you're like me you've got 11 bikes. And your housemate has six. And your other housemate has three. And that girl couchsurfing is fixing up two.

So I set about to thinking—maybe I can make some kind of storage rack for these things? My engineering instinct kicked in. What's the most compact way to store bikes anyway? Eventually I devised a two-level hanging rack. It's easy to build with a minimum of tools, and it stores almost twice as many bikes in the same space as a standard single-level hanging rack. The bikes are still easy to get in and out, and this rack can work in a garage, foyer, porch, or yard. You just need a wall or some posts.

The rack system shown is very easy and inexpensive to build, and I believe it is the most compact, tangle-free storage possible for four or more bikes. For two to three bikes it's still a good rack but will use about the same space as some other options.

Step 1: What You Need

First, measure the width of the wall you plan to use. You need 1' (300 mm) per bike, plus another 1'. So, four bikes will need 5' (1.5 meters) at the widest point. If you only have road bikes with narrow handlebars you can get away with a little less—maybe 11" (270 mm) per bike. Once you've figured out how long the rack will be, you need two pieces of wood (2" × 4"s) of that length. The big home improvement stores often can cut the wood to length for you, or cut it yourself if you have a saw.

You need:

- Two wood 2" × 4"s as long as your rack will be
- Drill
- Saw if you need to cut the 2 × 4's
- Wood screws between 3 ½" and 4" long (8 to 10 cm)
- Large metal screw-in hooks (available from most home improvement stores; the ones I found were helpfully called "bike hooks")
- Plastic tubing that will fit over the metal hooks (I used ⁷⁄₁₆" tubing with ⁵⁄₁₆" ID [8mm]), or some old innertubes
- Tape measure
- Pencil
- Stud sensor (or you can make one by hanging a magnet from a piece of string)

- Thick plastic or thin plywood sheet the full size of the rack (width and height) if you want to protect the wall from tire marks (optional)

Step 2: Dimensions Are the Key

This whole setup is totally simple. The only trick to the double-level rack is to get the correct spacing of the bikes both horizontally and vertically.

In order to not have the bottom row of bikes flop all around the rear wheel MUST be off the ground.

The bottom row of hooks should be 65" (1.65 m) off the ground.

The top row of hooks should be 14" (350 mm) higher than the bottom row; this keeps the handlebars and cranks of the top row clear of the bottom row.

Spacing between hooks at the same level: 24" (600 mm). This gives you 11" or 12" overall bike spacing.

You can reduce the spacing a little—the more you reduce the more tangling you will have trying to get the bikes in and out. At 24" the handlebars on mountain bikes will be just next to each other. If you only have road-bikes you can do 22" spacing.

Step 3: Just in Case You Are Worried about Your Rims

1. Using a metal hook could scrape up your fancy aluminum rim. As shown in the project, I recommend covering your hooks in vinyl tubing or innertube wrap, which will create a thick and tough rubberized surface to protect the rim.

2. Too much leverage on the hook will deform the rim itself. This is not possible if you use metal hooks that extend at least 4" from the wall, like in all the project photos. The only way you could risk deformation is by using a much smaller metal hook; however, a hook small enough to deform your rim would also make hooking the bike on and off the wall very difficult in the first place.

Here's the math on this just in case you are not convinced:

(2a) How strong is your rim? Very strong! It is designed to handle at least a 200lb. person riding over the edge of a curb or pothole. At very slow riding speed you could estimate that the contact area of a pothole corner is similar to the hook we are using. Fortunately, when your bike is hanging from the rack it is only supporting itself (25lbs.) and not 200 lbs., and your rim can handle that pothole at speed too.

(2b) How much leverage do we have? As shown in the photo, the weight of the bike "X" is pulling down at the hub. This sets up a torque around point A. If I recall my high school physics properly this means:

$$\text{torque} = \text{force} \times \text{distance}$$

Since there is no motion, there must be equal and opposite torques applied around A.

So, the force at the hook $Y = (L1 / L2) * X$

(2c) The hook point B is about 5" from the wall. This sets the distance L2 nearly as long as L1. that means the force at Y is only slightly more than the weight of the bike; no chance of deforming your rim!

(2d) Let's say you used a really small hook that only extended 2" from the wall and hooked at point C. First off, it would be fairly tricky to even get your bike on and off this hook. But you do get a leverage ratio of perhaps 5:1. Even that is not likely to be able to deform the rim from the bike weight alone. Perhaps then your buddy is drinking some beers while you are cleaning up from a long ride, and he stumbles, flails about, and catches his entire drunken weight on the hanging bike! Now you've got 200lbs. at a 5:1 leverage. Based on some unrelated experience trying to hang a large sculpture from my ceiling, if you used the same ¼" steel hooks that I did you still won't bend your rims. Instead the hook is going to unbend until the bike unhooks itself and falls off. If you did happen to use some industrial-grade hooks here, and they don't rip out of the wall, then perhaps your rim is toast.

Step 4: Find Your Studs and Measure Them

In a house or garage your rack needs to have firm support—it needs to be screwed into the "studs" (the vertical frame timbers of the house). You can use a stud sensor or a magnet hanging from a string to find these. Measure up from the floor and mark the spots to whichyou will attach the two pieces of wood for the rack—each end of each piece should be screwed into a stud.

Step 7: Put in the Hooks

Now drill pilot holes for your hooks into the rack. On the bottom row, space the hooks 2' (600 mm) apart. On the top row, offset by 1' (300 mm), and again put the hooks 2' (600 mm) apart.

Step 5: Drill the Wood and Screw It On

Find a drill bit a little less than the diameter of the screws you are using (try to match the screw "body" with the drill bit). We'll use this to make a pilot hole into the wood—the screws go in easier and they won't split the wood. Have a friend hold the first piece of your rack onto the wall in the correct spot. At each stud, drill two pilot holes through the rack and into the wall. Remove the rack and drill the holes in the wall deeper in. Next hold your rack back onto the wall and screw in the wood screws all the way. You need to attach the wood to two different studs so it doesn't tip or rip out.

Step 8: You're Done!

And your mess of bikes is history. Note that your bike tires will leave some marks on the wall; if you want to keep things "nice" I'd recommend putting a thin sheet of plywood across the whole wall before attaching the rack.

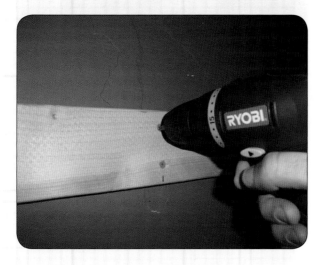

Step 6: Prepare the Hooks

Once you've got both of the wood pieces firmly secured, it's time to add the hooks that hold the bikes. All the home improvement stores around here seem to stock the identical bike hook; it's a large metal hook with a thin rubbery coating. The hook part is fine, but I always find that the rubbery coating gets ripped up after a short time. You don't want a bare metal hook scraping up your rims, so here's an easy way to fix it: you can wrap the hook with an old innertube, or you can get some flexible plastic tubing at your home improvement store. Just remove the crappy coating and slip the plastic tubing over the metal hook.

Repairing a Car Console Armrest

By Winged Fist

http://www.instructables.com/id/Repairing-a-cars-console-armrest/

My wife and I recently purchased a "new" used car, and one of the defects was damaged upholstery on the armrest, which also serves as the lid for the compartment between the two fronts seats. This wasn't a deal breaker, but it was annoying enough that I set out to replace it.

What I quickly found was that it was nearly impossible to replace just this part without replacing the entire console. I found replacement consoles online, and I even found one in a local salvage yard, but both options involved removing and replacing the entire console—way more time and money than I was willing to invest! And why scrap a perfectly good console when all I needed to replace was the armrest/lid upholstery?

So here is how I reupholstered a damaged armrest in under an hour, for less than $5!

(My car is a 2007 PT Cruiser, but I imagine there are plenty of damaged armrests out there on different make/model cars that can be restored in the same way.)

Step 1: Materials and Tools

- A few feet of vinyl
- 3M Spray adhesive
- Packing foam
- Torque bit and screwdriver
- Stapler
- Scissors

Step 2: Remove Armrest

This is pretty easy, as long as you have the correct tool. I believe I used a 10- or 15-torque bit to remove the three screws holding the armrest in place. Yours may be held in place with different screws, but are still likely easy to remove.

Step 3: Disassemble Armrest

My armrest is made up of three layers of plastic parts; the part that screws into the base, the underside of the lid, which also includes plastic tracks that allow the armrest to slide forward, and the top cover (with the damaged vinyl).

First, remove the two screws that attach the base bracket to the underside of the lid, then remove the six screws that hold the remaining pieces together.

(One of the plastic tracks on my armrest was broken, likely from a previous owner who tried to pull the lid open without first pushing the release button. I glued this piece back in place during this process.)

Step 5: Spray Mount Foam

To give the armrest a bit of cushioning, I used a bit of packing foam that came with some electronic component I bought ages ago.

Place the plastic lid on top of the foam and then spray the lid with adhesive. I used 3M 90 HI-Strength spray adhesive, which did the job perfectly.

My foam wasn't quite large enough to cover the lid, so I mounted one piece and then used a second to complete the job.

Once the top surface was covered, I sprayed a bit of adhesive on the underside then folded the foam over the lid.

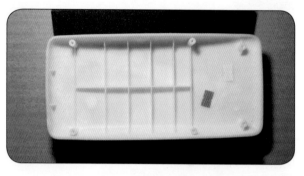

Step 4: Remove Vinyl

The vinyl cover is held in place with way too many staples. Remove these staples with needle-nose pliers or a small screwdriver.

Step 6: Cut Vinyl

I decided to use a piece of vinyl that matched my car's interior, a light grey. But of course any material can be used—scrap leather, denim, or your favorite old sweatshirt. Keep in mind that this piece will get a lot of wear, and vinyl is very easy to clean (and cheap! I paid about $4 for a half yard at a fabric store).

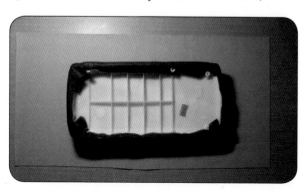

Step 7: Staple Vinyl

This I found to be the trickiest step in this process. The difficult part is getting the vinyl to wrap around the lid as tightly as possible. I chose not to glue it with spray mount, as this would make replacing it in the future more difficult.

The trick I used was to first staple the vinyl on the underside length-wise, then widthwise, then I folded the corners inwards, creating a bit of overlap in the corners. You want to try and make the corners as tight as possible in order to make the final product look close to factory original.

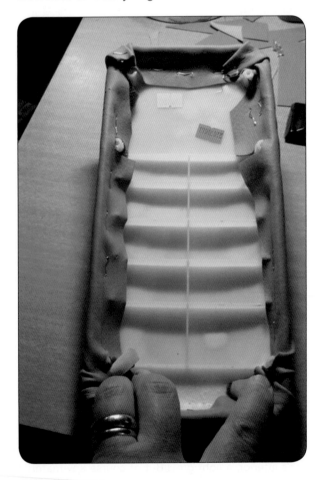

Step 8: Reassemble

Once you're done stapling the vinyl inside the lid, you're ready to reassemble the whole cover, reversing the steps you used to disassemble.

Step 9: Finished

Here are a few photos of the finished product. Had I purchased a replacement console, it would have cost me between $50 and $100, and it would be in the same range to have it professionally installed.

This isn't my most exciting or creative Instructable, but it saved me between $100 and $200 that I now have to spend on more important things, like fuzzy dice!

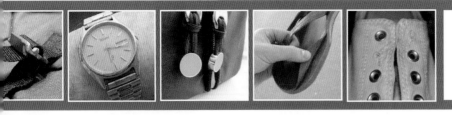

Fashion

We wear through shoes way too fast nowadays and with the price of clothing and accessories we can't always afford to just throw away and buy new. Find out how you can get a couple extra miles from your flip flops and favorite pair of jeans.

Don't expose yourself to unnecessary clothing purchases that will just wear another hole in your pocket. Check out these fixes and save your wardrobe while going easy on your wallet!

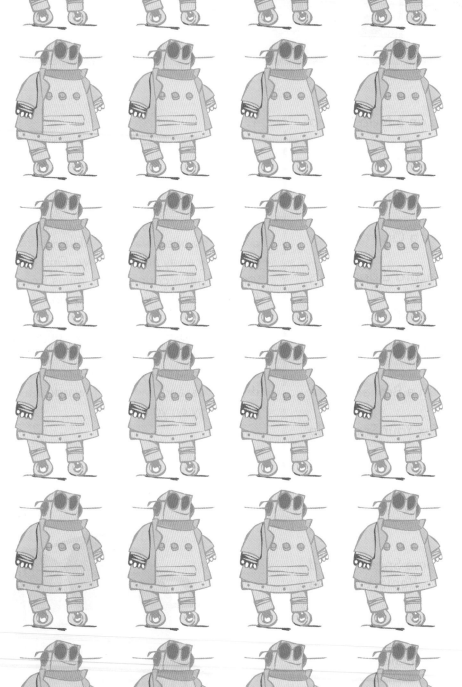

I use a backpack when I commute to meetings on my bicycle. A few days ago I stooped down to pick up something and the extra stress on the backpack straps caused the plastic ladder-lock buckle to snap. The rest of the backpack is in good condition. Backpacks are only one of many items that use nylon straps with adjustable buckles.

This Instructable will provide two solutions to a broken ladder-lock buckle. One is for those who can weld and one for those who cannot. The welded version will show how to make your own ladder-lock buckles. The non-welded version will show you how to use D-rings, either those you purchase or those you fashion yourself.

If you make the D-ring version, you will need D-rings you purchase and a hacksaw or a Dremel tool with a cutting wheel.

If you make the ladder-lock-buckle version, you will need a hacksaw, a grinder, a vise, a hammer, and a wire feed welder.

Step 1: Stitching

I wanted to fix my backpack without cutting the stitching on any of the nylon straps. That means I will make a ladder-lock buckle that begins by feeding part of it through the nylon strap loop sewn to the backpack. Shown is the beginning of the welded version.

The next steps will describe using D-rings for the non-welded version. Then I will explain how to make the welded ladder-lock buckle. The ladder-lock buckle will be easy to release with one finger. The

D-ring, non-welded version will be easier for most people to manufacture at home, even if it is a little more difficult to release.

Step 2: Non-Welded Version

It is possible to buy D-rings about the same size as the width of the nylon strapping. Look for them in fabric stores and in generic hardware stores. Cut about ⅛" from the center of the straight side on each. See the photo. Slip the nylon loop through the opening you make in the straight side. Two D-rings are needed for each nylon loop. While this works very well, the straps may not release as easily or as quickly as they do with a ladder-lock buckle. But this makes a quick and effective solution.

The photo shows two D-rings I made. See the next steps for more details.

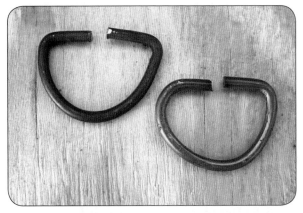

Step 3: Making D-rings

If you wish, you can make your own D-rings from a rod. Bend a half circle in the rod using a piece of pipe. (The diameter of the pipe should be about the width of the nylon strap.) Bend the ends sharply. Leave an opening where they meet. Slip the nylon strap through the opening you made in each ring. Thread the strap under the bottom ring and the upper ring. Loop the strap around the upper ring and under the bottom ring. Pull tight.

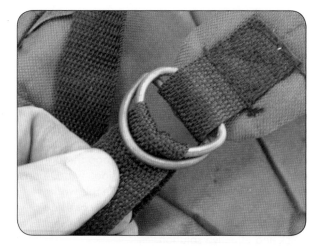

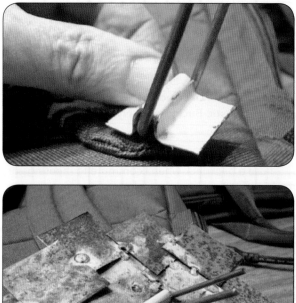

Step 4: Protect the Strap Loop from Heat

In the welded version, some welding will need to be done on the ladder lock while it is on the backpack. The nylon from which the backpack is made will melt with too much heat. The nylon needs to be protected.

Cut strips of paper, fold them over, make a roll, and insert the rolled paper into the nylon strap loop. Use four or more thicknesses of paper. These strips of paper will insulate the nylon strapping from the welding heat in the rod used to make the ladder lock. The paper can remain inside the nylon strap loop forever.

Step 5: Protect the Backpack from Weld Spatter

Weld spatter will burn holes in the nylon backpack. Surgeons cover bodies with sheets that leave a hole where the surgeon wants to operate. I made something like that to fit around the nylon strap loop, using scraps of sheet steel (first and third photos). I also bent a U-shaped piece to cover the nylon strap where it came through the hole in the protective cover (second photo). This U-shaped piece goes into place first, then the cover for the field slips over it (third photo).

Step 6: Bend ⅛" Rod

I used some ⅛" steel rod that had been part of the mesh used to reinforce concrete. A friend built a garage and gave me stubs of wire about five inches long after breaking them off from the finished concrete foundation. Bend a piece of the wire so the space between the two halves is the width of the strap. Insert it into the nylon loop so it is surrounded by the paper from the last step.

Step 7: Buckle Design and Strap Pathway

This shows a profile view of the strap (red line) in its pathway through the ladder-lock buckle. The gray portions show cross sections of the parts. The black area is the ⅛" rod from the previous step. The green areas are welds. The relative positions of the different parts are important for the strap to bind and release well. As much as possible, the orientation of the parts follows those of the original ladder lock buckle.

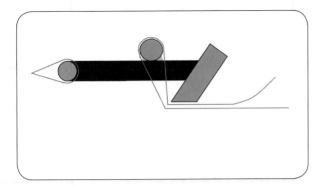

Step 8: Cut Strap Iron

Cut a piece of ½" strap iron so it is as long as the strap is wide. Grind one long edge to 45 degrees.

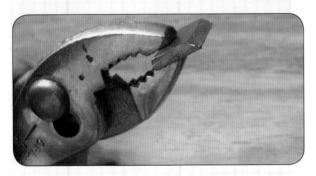

Step 9: Begin Welding

Position the strap iron and tack weld it in place. When welding on the ladder-lock buckles, keep a wet sponge nearby to cool the steel before excess heat can soften the nylon strapping. This is mostly a precaution. The paper strips from step 4 should be adequate to protect it from excess heat.

Step 11: Pull and Release

The first photo shows how to pull the nylon strap to tighten it. The second photo shows how to push upward on the ladder-lock buckle to release the strap. This works well with the backpack. It is easier to put the backpack on and take it off if the straps are loose. But, the backpack fits better, especially while riding a bicycle, if the straps are snug. Fortunately, backpack buckles are located at the front and side of the rib cage on each side, making the strap ends and the buckles easy to reach and manipulate. An advantage to the ladder lock buckles is that they can be operated easily with one hand. D-rings are more likely to require two hands, especially for releasing them.

Step 10: The Rest of the Ladder Lock

Weld a ⅛" rod across the ladder-lock frame. Cut excess from each side. Grind smooth. Be careful about the shower of sparks from a grinding wheel or a cutting wheel on a Dremel. A concentration of sparks can burn a hole in the nylon backpack. Make the spacing approximately the same as that on the original plastic ladder-lock buckle. See the finished ladder-lock buckle in the second photo.

Fix Broken Pin Badges
By Kryptonite
http://www.instructables.com/id/Making-the-pin-for-a-badge/

The other day I found a badge that didn't have a pin for me to pin it on my shirt with, so, getting creative, I thought I'd make one!

There are many other alternatives around, as you may have seen, but done right, this looks much more professional, is cheaper, and can be done without much at hand.

Step 1: Materials Required

Because this is so amazingly simple, there aren't many tools required.

- A paper clip
- Pliers
- Side cutters, but not needed if your pliers have the cutting bit on them
- A pinless badge
- Sandpaper, or a bench grinder

Step 2: Starting Off

Straighten out your paper clip; it doesn't have to be really straight, but mostly so. Eyeball the distance from one side of the badge to the other, minus about 5mm, and with the same distance from the end of the paper clip make a 90 degree bend.

Step 3: Continuing On

From there, make a semi-circle that goes round from there to the very end of the straight bit you made earlier. Make a sharp 85 degree angle (about there) upwards, and then back down again. From there, continue about ¾ the way round and cut it off. Next, with your pliers, grab the lip that went up at an 85 degree angle and bend that inwards towards the middle of the circle. With the straight section that you made first, bend that upwards (to the same side of the circle as where the lip is).

Step 4: Sharpening

Essentially, you are done. But because the "pin" (straight) bit is not pointy it won't go through your clothing very well. Here, grab your sandpaper and hone down the straight end to a nice sharp end. I used a bench grinder, but because it's such a small job I just cranked it by hand.

Step 5: Inserting It in the Badge

Hook your circle under the lip of your badge with the sharpened straight "pin" pointing outwards, along with the "lip" that it will slide under.

Step 6: Done!

You're done! The insert that you made can still slide about inside, but, if you want, a tad of glue won't hurt. I prefer it the way it is so I can turn it without having to take it off, and it stays firm in the meantime. Hope this was helpful!

How to Fix a Drawstring Waistband
By DizzyMissLizzy
http://www.instructables.com/id/How-to-fix-a-drawstring-waistband/

Here's a simple little clothing hack I devised for fixing your drawstring elastic waistband (or hoodie sweatshirt cord) when it comes out of the loop it's supposed to stay in.

Step 1: Materials
- Clothing plus lost band
- Ballpoint pen
- Scotch tape

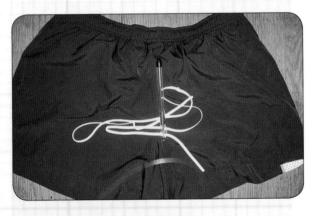

Step 2: Preparing the Pen
The trick was to find a needle-like object that is pointy, skinny, and flexible. After ransacking my apartment, I stumbled upon the center ink thing from my ballpoint pen. I removed it from the pen and fastened it to the elastic with tightly wound Scotch tape.

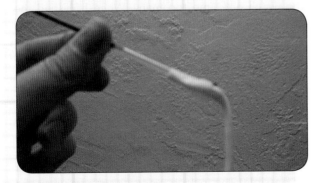

Step 3: Threading It
It's important to move the pen/elastic combo slowly and to know when to push against the fabric and when to ease up. Once you begin to trace the path around the waistband, beware of snags where the fabric leaves only a small space between the stitching for the drawstring, and also of poking through the fabric instead of following the elastic band path.

Step 4: Bunching
I found that a bunching technique works pretty well. With one hand I pushed the fabric over the ballpoint, and I used the other hand to pull it through.

Step 5: And Out the Other Side
Eventually you should come out the other end again. Hooray!

Step 6: Preventative Measures
Be sure to tie those big knots in the end that you were too lazy to do in the first place. Enjoy your old clothes all over again!

This is my Seiko quartz analog watch. It is almost 19 years old. In recent months I have noticed it slowly drifts a couple of minutes from the correct time. I checked prices for cleaning and lubrication through an online watchmaker. By the time all fees are paid, repair costs would be almost equal to the price of a new watch. Repairs could cost more yet if any parts need replacement. Similar watches to mine are available on eBay, and I might be able to find one for less with a movement I could substitute in my watch case, if all dimensions are the same. But, that would be a big risk. Because this watch was given to me by my wife on our 25th wedding anniversary I really want to keep it rather than replace it.

Step 1: A Local Watchmaker

We live a couple of miles from one of the few watchmakers in our very metropolitan area. Because droplets of moisture have sometimes gotten into the watch and condensed on the inside of the crystal, I wanted to talk with him about cleaning and lubricating the watch. The watch also stopped recently, but I got it going again by gently poking with a toothpick at the wheel that drives the second hand. I thought there may be a tiny piece of debris inside the watch, and cleaning would be a very good idea. The watchmaker has a very thick foreign accent and shook his head "No!" when I asked about cleaning. He said, "New battery! One year!" When the watch was new, the first battery lasted 7 years. I have 3 ½ years on the present battery. This watch is still supposed to keep accurate time when the battery is getting low, but the second hand begins to jump in

two-second increments every two seconds as a sign the battery needs to be changed. I have not seen that yet, so I assume the battery still has some life in it... Still, some sites urge replacing the battery every two years, even if no inaccuracy problems are evident. I do not know if it makes a difference, but the watch came with a silver-oxide battery. The present battery is an alkaline battery.

Tools:
- Spanner wrench to remove the back
- Ballpoint pen or jeweler's screwdriver to depress the stem lock

Materials:
- Canned air with a guide tube
- Rubber cement or a properly sized "O" ring

Step 2: A Really Bad Idea That Worked

I decided to attempt blowing a little compressed air through the watch movement in order to remove any loose dirt that might be slowing my watch. Note: It is generally a bad idea to assault fine mechanical devices with air under pressure.

I began by removing the back.

Step 3: Take the Movement Out of the Case

If possible, you may want to avoid removing the movement from the case. I decided to tinker with the watch one time too many. When I finished the stem would not go back into place fully. I probably could have lifted the movement enough to use the compressed air as described in step 4 without removing the stem. Now that I cannot get the stem back into place, I will either need to pay a watchmaker to repair the watch, or put the watch aside in a drawer.

If you do decide to remove the movement, do it as follows. Lift the plastic retainer out of the watch case and depress the lock that holds the stem in the movement. The stem must be pressed inward as far as possible. The locking piece disappears when the stem is pulled outward without releasing the lock. On Seiko watches the stem lock is very often a springy piece of metal near the stem and it has a small hole in it. Look in the photo, near the end of the toothpick. See also the second photo. Push downward on the piece with the hole while pulling the stem out of the watch case. A ballpoint pen works well enough for this, or you may use a jeweler's screwdriver. A toothpick splinters and leaves debris in the watch case.

Step 4: Canned Air

I used short bursts of canned air I bought at an office supply store. This is the kind of canned air that is free of dust and humidity. It is often used to blow dust from inside a computer. I tried to avoid spraying air at the delicate watch hands to keep from pushing them hard if blocked and to avoid bending them, but I focused on aiming air into the open sides of the watch's movement. If this were a mechanical watch with a balance wheel to regulate the movement, I would be very careful with pressurized air near the dainty spring on the balance wheel.

(When assembling the watch in its case, do not force the stem through the case and back into the movement too hard. A little pressure is needed, but too much may mean something is not properly aligned or installed in the proper orientation.)

Step 5: Checking the Results

A watch needs to run 24 hours to determine what effect adjustments have made in the performance and accuracy of the watch. I chose to use the World Clock application on my phone to check my watch's accuracy. I could also have used the clock face that opens in the lower right corner on my Windows PC screen. Choose one clock and do all checking with it. Clocks that are supposedly steered by an atomic clock somewhere can vary from one another by a second or two, and mixing clocks could make you think your watch is less accurate than it actually is. Notice the red second hands in the photo all indicating 55 seconds. I synchronized my watch and its second hand with the display in the World Clock app. So far it appears that my watch is running accurately again, and it cost me almost nothing. Try this on your own watch with caution. It is, as I mentioned, a really bad idea, but one that did work very well for me.

The black clock faces on the app indicate it was dark in those parts of the world when this photo was taken. The clock faces are white during hours of daylight in the respective parts of the world. Still, the second hands on these clocks are easy to see.

Step 6: Gasket

I could probably get a new O-ring gasket for the back of my watch through a jeweler or a watchmaker. My gasket stretched, which is normal wear and tear for a watch, and I discarded it. But, if I need to replace the battery only every several years, I will start putting the back on again, allowing the threads to just barely start catching. Then I will smear some common rubber cement into the gap between the back and the watch case. I will tighten the back the rest of the way. I should get a good seal and I can still open it again easily when I need to access the battery, and no shreds of hardened cement should reach the delicate moving parts in the works. I have actually worn my watch for a few months without a gasket or a seal. Moisture was not collected inside the crystal if I was not perspiring.

O-rings for watches are available from Amazon and from watchmaker's supply houses, like Esslinger. Some are sold in assortments and some individually. Unfortunately, Seiko uses part numbers rather than dimensions on its O rings, and I have not found a key to the numbers so I can order the right gasket for my watch. The Esslinger site also has some tutorial information for the amateur.

The graphic is a depiction of an O-ring, including a cross-sectional view. The diameter of the material and the internal diameter are the key measurements for a watch back.

Sugru Paracord Zipper Pulls

By Brent Garcia (Mrballeng)
http://www.instructables.com/id/Sugru-Paracord-Zipper-Pulls/

I made these zipper pulls for my son's lunch bag using ½" electrical conduit, paracord, and sugru. The sugru was textured using poly netting. It'll make for a good conversation piece during lunch.

Step 1: Machine the conduit

To start I machined and sanded off the zinc coating.

Step 2: File and drill

Next I marked out the rings for the zipper pulls and cut them with a pipe cutter. I filed off any sharp edges. I then marked and drilled 2 holes in each ring. That was followed up with a buffing wheel.

Step 3: Thread and melt

I gutted some paracord and threaded it through the holes. After cutting the ends I melted them so they would no longer slip out.

Step 4: Texture the sugru

To texture the sugru I used the mesh netting on the back of a jogging stroller. First I wet both the sugru and netting. I then pressed it in-between my fingers to set in the pattern. After sitting overnight it was ready to go.

Thanks for reading.

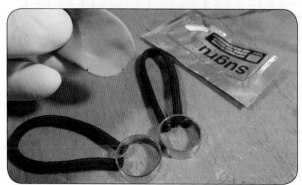

Patch Your Jeans without a Patch

By Sarah James (scoochmaroo)
http://www.instructables.com/id/Patchless-Patch-Fix-Your-Jeans/

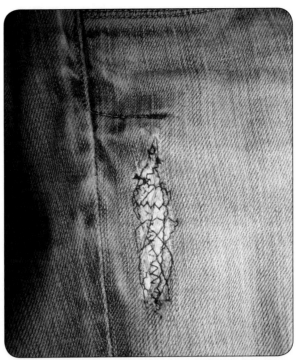

Trendy jeans these days come pre-distressed with holes and gashes galore. Sometimes gashes become holes, and sometimes holes become bigger holes, and sometimes these holes happen right where you wish they wouldn't. Sewing an actual patch of something over these holes would infinitely reduce the jeans' coolness, meanwhile indicating how uncool the wearer is for not appreciating the inherent coolness of the holes. So I came up with a quick tutorial on how to repair a hole in your clothes without using a patch, in a way that can coexist with the intrinsic coolness of the jeans themselves.

Step 1: Materials
- One holey garment
- Thread in at least one cool color
- Sulky (or other) water-soluble stabilizer (that's where the magic lives! I had the "paper" kind around. They make a bunch of different weights of the stuff—pick what you like best. They'll all work for this.)

Step 2: Sew
Tear a piece of stabilizer big enough to cover the hole and pin to the wrong side of the garment (the inside of the jeans), closing the gap the hole makes. Sew crazy! Unpin.

Step 3: Wash
Remove the stabilizer by running it under water

Step 4: Wear
You're done! You may want to dry them before you put them on. Personal preference.

95

This Instructable will show you how to fix a belt in about ten minutes using basic tools. Due to the terrible economy, low quality of most belts made these days, expanding average waistline, and lack of leather tools in the standard household, this is a good skill to have.

Background: A friend of mine has this belt that she really likes, but is actually rather badly made. It broke the other day, and I saw a perfect opportunity to make an Instructable to show how I fix belts (not to mention help a friend who is rather, um, repair-challenged.)

Here we go.

Step 1: Tools

This step can be loosely interpreted.

Basically all you need are two things:

Something to cut and bend wire with: Depending on the type of wire you use, you may also need something to strip the wire with. I used a pair of wire strippers and some needle nosed pliers.

Something to poke holes: I used a drill because it was fast and sitting on my work table already. You could use a knife, nails, an ice pick, a small screwdriver, pretty much anything small and relatively pointy that can be forced through the material.

Most multi-tools will probably have all the bits required for this fix.

Step 2: Materials

What you need:

Broken belt: this one was pretty cheap, made of something that seemed to be halfway between cardboard and leather. It had broken straight across, so fitting the pieces together was simple.

Wire: I used some tough copper wire from a reel I found on the side of the road a while ago. Depending on your wire, you might have to strip off insulation. Any kind of tough solid-core wire will work.

Super Glue: I used Krazy Glue. Any kind of fast-drying super glue should work. In a pinch, you don't even need super glue, but it dramatically increases the life span of the repair.

Step 3: Poke Holes

Use your poking device to poke holes as shown in the photograph. Make sure the wire will fit through the holes, but don't make the holes really big, since that might damage the belt more.

Step 4: Cut wires

Cut wires as shown in picture, two shorter and two long. Make sure the wires are at least an inch longer than the distance between the holes they are meant to go in.

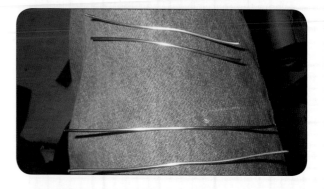

Step 5: Stick in Wires

Push the bits of wire into the holes as shown in the pictures. Crimp the wires flat.

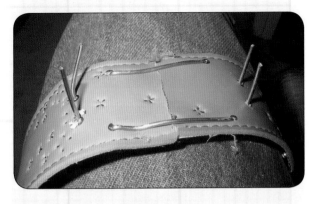

Step 6: Glue

Put super glue in the holes, around the wires, and anywhere else you think might need it. Let it air dry for a few minutes and your belt is fixed.

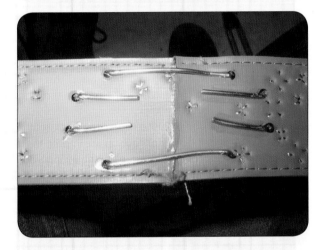

Step 7: Bonus Step: Reinforcing a Lengthwise Tear

The owner of this belt poked an extra hole in it for the buckle tooth to go in. This hole had started to tear lengthwise, so I added a few more bits of wire to reinforce it. You should be able to understand this step from the pictures.

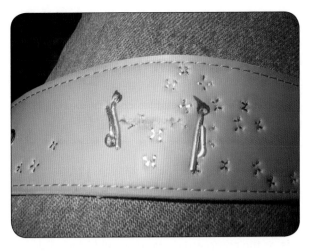

Step 8: Done!

This repair is pretty strong, and I have yet to have it fail on me from normal use and abuse. Don't try to flex the repair that much, as that will surely make it begin to degrade. This repair is designed more to be functional rather than look very good, as you will still have bits of wire visible on the belt, as you can see in the pictures.

This repair could probably be used for other kinds of straps too, like backpack straps, or rifle slings, but I have so far only used it on belts. Use your imagination, and remember that this repair won't hold an elephant.

Have a nice day.

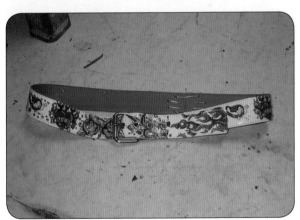

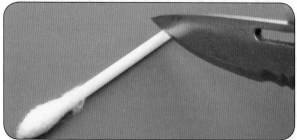

Broken zips can be a right pain in the rear end, in this Instructable I will show you how to effect a repair to a zip (zipper to all you Americans out there) that has one of its teeth missing. Rather than buy a new one as the corporate overlords would have us do, or indeed to fully replace the zip, I will show you how to repair the missing tooth using sewing skills and a piece of a cotton bud (Q-Tip).

Step 3: Sew the U-Piece in Position

In order to retain the U-piece, sew it to the tape. If the U-piece is similar to the one I made, then you can sew though it, although you may need the help of a thimble or some pliers to get the needle through the plastic.

When you have tested the repair to check that it works and the slider does not foul on the repair, then you can make it double permanent by covering your new sewing with cyanoacrylate adhesive (superglue).

Step 1: Reassemble the Zip

If the slider has come away from the teeth of the zip, as it will be prone to do if a tooth is missing, reassemble the zip by pushing the slider back on to the teeth, making sure to get the tape smooth and un-kinked between the groove in the slider. Push the slider as far away as possible from the missing tooth whilst you are working.

Step 2: Fashion a U-Piece

In order to stop the slider coming away from the zip again we must replicate the effect that the tooth had in keeping the slider on the tape. To do this use a small U-section cut from the middle of a cotton bud. A small brass clip would be a superior solution. This U-piece will not help the zip stay together, hopefully there are already enough teeth for this, but it will prevent the slider coming away again.

Desperate-Quick-Fix Your Shoe Sole

By faizzohri

http://www.instructables.com/id/Quick-fix-your-shoe-sole/

Someone wise once said, "New shoes are ugly, my worn out ones are a beauty." Agree. Like real people, I keep wearing this pair all the time because it is wonderful. Here, I have developed a way to quick-fix my favorite soles. It may help your soles too. Duration: 10 minutes or so.

Step 1: What You Need
- A broken sole
- The cheapest bicycle-tire repair kit money can buy

Step 2: Find the Worn-Out Area

Mark the worn-out area with a cheerful-colored crayon. This is to prevent us from missing the area that needs to be repaired. Decide on the tab (from the repair kit that you bought earlier) that fits the worn-out area perfectly. Make the decision.

Step 3: Applying Adhesives

Clean the marked area and apply a thin layer of adhesive to it (the adhesive is from the repair kit too). Let the adhesive become tacky. This may take a few seconds.

Step 4: Fix It

When the adhesive is tacky enough, place the tab over it.

Step 5: Done

Let it dry for a few minutes—and done. Hope that helps!

Fix Your Peeling Flip-Flops or Shoes

By sk8ter20art

http://www.instructables.com/id/Fix-your-Peeling-Flip-flops-or-shoes/

The other day my wife was complaining that her favorite pair of flip-flops had started to peel apart. I decided to fix them for her. This pair of flip flops was starting to peel all around the edges, as can happen to shoes over time. Many times it's parts that are not stitched but glued. Well, luckily it's not that hard to fix!

Step 1: Things You Need
- Shoes or flip-flops that are peeling or separating
- Contact cement
- Q-tips (or cheap small paintbrush)

Step 2: Preparation

The first thing to do is to clean the surface well with a damp rag or paper towel then let dry. Once the surface is clean, use the Q-tip to spread the contact cement on one surface. When you are done spreading the glue, squeeze the two surfaces together to spread the glue evenly. Try not to put on too much glue or it will ooze out. Only hold it together for a few seconds then pull apart and let dry. Or you can spread the glue on each side and let dry. Contact cement requires the glue be dry to adhere properly.

Step 3: Final Step

Once the glue is dry on both sides, carefully push the two sides together. I say "carefully" because you will not be able to pull it apart once the glue touches. Using this glue is easy, and it doesn't ooze out or discolor.

Fix Your Velcro Sandals to Handle Wide Feet

By exabopper
http://www.instructables.com/id/Fix-your-velcro-sandals-to-handle-wide-feet/

I have feet that are wider than average, and like most wide-foot sufferers, I have learned to live with it. When buying footwear, I buy a size or two larger than normal and just ignore the huge gap between the tips of my toes and the tips of the shoes. With sandals, however, having a huge gap like this should not be necessary, since the Velcro straps will allow you to adjust the sandals to fit any size foot, right?

Unfortunately not. I have found an easy way to increase the Velcro strap length on your sandals, though—no sewing, gluing, or anything else required.

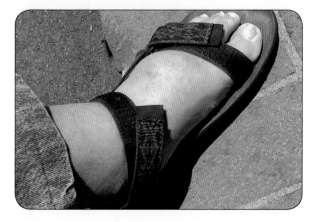

Step 1: You Will Need

Home Depot (and probably Amazon.com and others) carries a product called Velcro Brand One-Wrap. Velcro usually comes in a kit with two strips, one with hooks and one with loops. However, One-Wrap comes as a single strip, with hooks on one side and loops on the other, so that you can wrap this strip around things and the strip will stick to itself.

Because it combines both hooks and loops in one product, you can attach the loops on the One-Wrap to the Velcro hooks on one of the sandal straps and then attach the One-Wrap hooks to the Velcro loops on the other side of the sandal strap, effectively extending the length of the Velcro strap but still keeping its strength.

Step 2: Cut the One-Wrap to Fit

Your mileage will vary depending on how you attach the One-Wrap to fit your sandals. My Tevas needed to have the toe strap and the ankle strap extended, but other sandals I have worn needed a heel strap extension while the toes were okay, and so forth.

For each strap extension you need, adjust the strap to a comfortable fit and then note the length of the Velcro hooks that are not engaged on one end, and the length of the loops that are not engaged on the other end. The One-Wrap strap extension should be just about as long as these two lengths combined, so that all of the Velcro of the sandal is engaged. On mine, however, some of the Velcro was looped through the buckles, so I had to extend the strap after that point.

Step 3: Install the Strap Extensions to the Sandals

Now, undo the sandal straps completely and attach the strips of One-Wrap to the sandal straps so that all (or most) of the Velcro on the straps is engaged. Pinch it nice and tight.

Then, wrap the extended straps back over your feet, engaging the One-Wrap with the Velcro on the other sandal strap. All (or most) of this Velcro should be engaged.

The sandals should now be far less likely to undo themselves.

Step 4: Success!

As the sandals now have a lot more Velcro strength in the straps, they will be a lot more effective for you, so go out and start that triathlon you've been putting off.

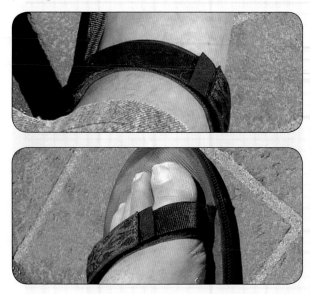

How to Fix Torn Converse Sneakers and Replace Eyelets

By Pavelos

http://www.instructables.com/id/How-to-fix-torn-Converse-and-replace-eyelets/

While riding my bike my shoelace got stuck in the pedal, and I tore my new Converses. I went to the local shoemaker and he told me that this is hard to fix and that it would cost me 35 EUR (45 USD). I decided to fix them myself

Step 1: Essential Tools

I purchased eyelets, fabric glue, and a piece of linen cloth from a local fabric shop; total cost was about 15 USD.

Step 2: Sewing

Now we have to sew the torn parts. I recommend using quilting thread for durability. Take your time and sew carefully.

Step 3: The Patch

Measure width of patch and fold it in half with glue. Let it dry for a couple of minutes.

Step 4: Glue the Patch

Place a thin layer of fabric glue first on the shoe and then on the patch. Use press tool for better result. I left shoes drying for three hours, but I recommend you read the instructions on your fabric glue.

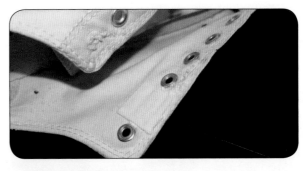

Step 5: Attach Eyelets

There are different tools and ways to attach eyelets, and usually there's instructions on the back of package. Follow them.

Step 6: Sew the Patch

Just to be sure that the patch will stay properly attached in use, I decided to sew the edges. The patch is pretty thick, and you may have to use pliers with your needle.

103

Repairing a Zipper (Cheap)

By J. M. Claassens (theexternaldisk)

http://www.instructables.com/id/repairing-a-zipper-cheap/

In this Instructable I'll try to explain how I fix a zipper. Take a look at the picture below. The zipper isn't attached to the fabric anymore. This happens very often (at least to me). The thread from the zipper wears off after a while, and the zipper detaches.

You might ask why I repair it myself. Well, the answer is simple: it's cheap and fast. It's cheap because you don't need someone else to fix it for you. It's fast because you don't need to wait weeks before your zipper is repaired.

Step 2: Cleaning Up

The first step will be removing the old worn-out thread. If you don't remove the old thread, sewing the zipper back on will become more difficult. Pull the thread away but make sure you don't go any further then needed. You don't want to detach more. At the end remove the thread by cutting it off.

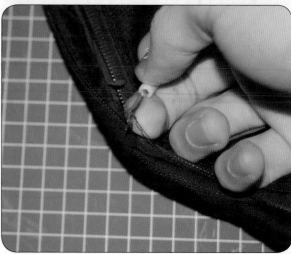

Step 1: What You Will Need

- Needle (it needs to be thin enough to fit through the zipper's teeth)
- Thread (doesn't need to some sort of super-strong thread)
- Small scissors
- A seam ripper

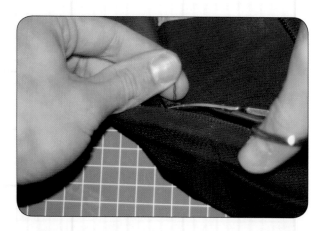

3. When done with B2, start repeating B.
4. Keep repeating B until you are about half a centimeter from where the zipper has come loose.
5. End with A.

When you are sewing, make sure that the zipper is lined up correctly.

Another important thing is to stay in the middle of the zipper's teeth.

Step 3: The Thread

For the length of the thread I multiplied the length of the detached zipper by five. So, my zipper was detached for about 2cm. 2x5=10. I needed 10cm of thread.

When you have your thread measured, try to get it through the needle (this is probably the hardest step of all).

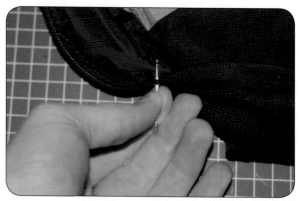

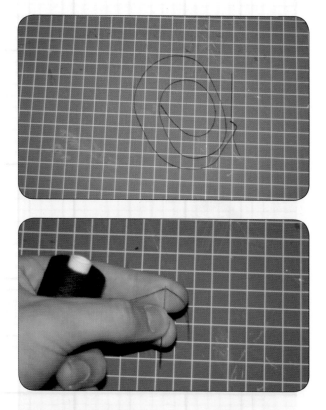

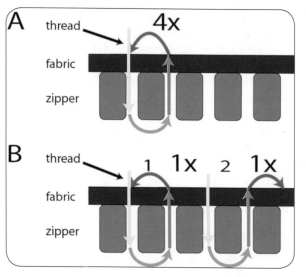

Step 5: You're Done!

You're practically done now. The only thing you have to do now is cut off the thread that's sticking out.

Step 4: Sewing

This step is going to take most of your time. Go to the second picture for the sewing instructions. You have to start sewing about half a centimeter from where the zipper has come loose. Pull the thread almost all the way through and leave about 1cm sticking out.

1. Start with A.
2. When you're done with A go to B2.

Repair Broken Glasses Hinge

By laxap

http://www.instructables.com/id/Repair-Broken-Glasses-Hinge/

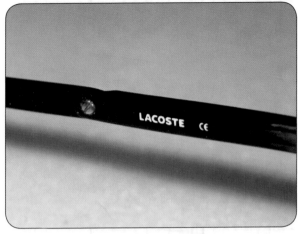

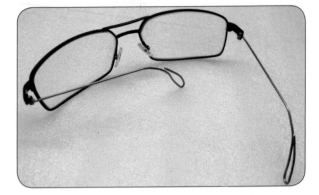

Due to poor mechanical design, the spring hinge of my glasses broke twice. Once it happened while they were still under warranty, and it got exchanged for free, then once again now, but the warranty is over. Being self-darkening prescription glasses, they were not cheap.

I decided to repair them using 1mm thick steel string* to form a hinge and temple in one single piece.

This method may not apply to all glasses. It depends on how the hinge is made.

*used in RC models to transmit the force from servos to controls.

Step 1: Make a New Hinge

With pliers, make a loop with the steel string. You can use a small screwdriver to roll the string around.

The internal diameter must correspond to the original hinge screw.

Cut out the excess string and hammer the loop flat.

Adjust the loop so that it turns smoothly into the hinge, with proper angular limitation. This is the only tricky part.

Assemble using the original hinge screw.

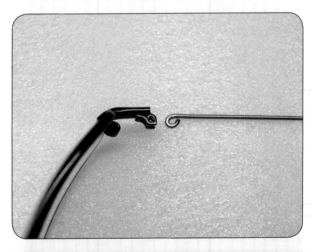

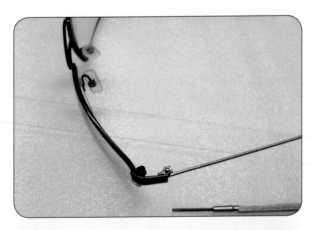

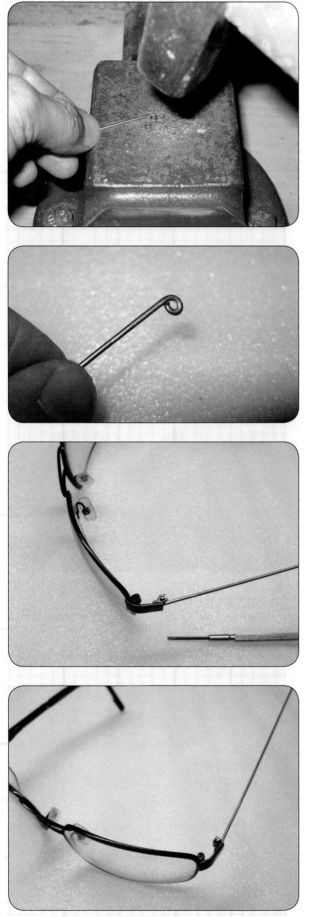

Step 2: Shape the Temple Tip

Determine the proper temple length and bend the string to form the tip. Cut out excess length.

This repair was so much more stable than the original design that I decided to also replace the other, non-broken temple.

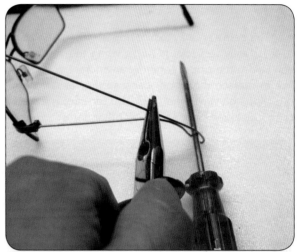

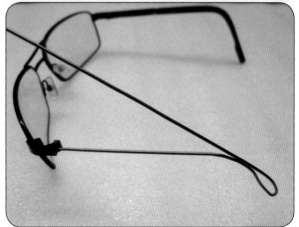

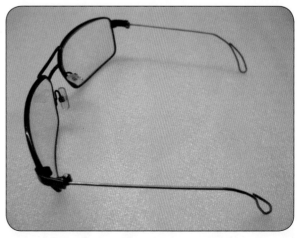

Step 3: Done

Now the glasses can be used again. For more comfort the tips could be coated with Sugru or similar.

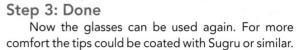

How to Fix a Zipper
By marcellahella
http://www.instructables.com/id/HOW-TO-
FIX-A-ZIPPER-NO-REPLACE/

This is an easy way to fix a zipper without replacing it. It is really fast too. It works when the zipper pull can't close the zipper together anymore. I don't really like to replace the zipper because they always come out a little bit wavy when I do. You can save a jacket, a tent, a sleeping bag, and many other items.

Step 1: What You Need
You need only some pliers. If the zipper pull is really destroyed or is made with plastic, you need a new one of the same size. I found one from an old jacket.

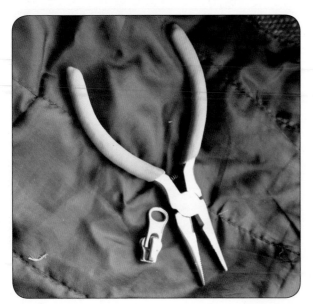

Step 2: Remove Teeth
Remove the little iron teeth of the very top of the zipper (on the same side of the jacket where the zipper puller is).

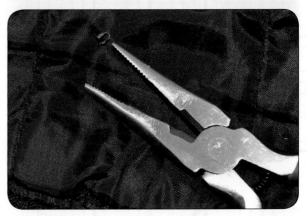

Step 3: Remove Zipper Pull
Remove zipper pull. You can probably see that is all distorted.

Step 4: Adjust The Zipper Pull

(This is only for iron zippers.) With the pliers, close the two sides of the zipper pull, trying to make it look like the original shape again. If your zipper pull is not too worn out you can try to close it directly on the zipper, without removing it.

If it is made out of plastic, if it is too bent, or if it breaks doing this you need to find another one of the same size.

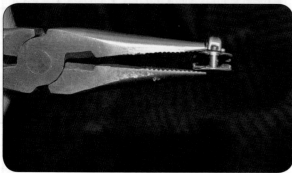

Step 5: Put Back the Zipper Pull

Put back the zipper pull. It may take a little bit of time. . .

Step 6: Put Back the Tooth

Put back the iron tooth with the pliers.

Step 7: Done!

Done! Faster than changing it!

Shoe Sole Repair/ Improvement

By Luke Wardensky (NearSpaceLuke)
http://www.instructables.com/id/Shoe-Sole-RepairImprovement/

This instructable shows a way of repairing or replacing the sole of a shoe with urethane rubber.

Step 1: The Materials

For this project I used:
- Plaster of Paris for the mold of the shoes
- Cake pan for the mold container
- Ease Release 200 mold-release agent
- PMC-790 urethane rubber
- Plastic mixing cup
- Stir stick
- Kitchen scale

Step 2: The Mold

1. Mix up the plaster to about peanut-butter consistency
2. Press the shoes into the plaster to capture the shape of the bottom of the shoe (keep the shoes level front-to-back and side-to-side or you'll have a funny walking feeling on uneven shoes)
3. Add traction or designs to the bottom of the new shoes by drawing lines, shapes, or words into the plaster
4. Let it dry thoroughly
5. Spray the release agent on the mold as recommended by the instructions on the can (the picture is actually of the shoes being cured to the rubber, but you get the idea)

Step 3: The Urethane Rubber

Follow the instructions on mixing the rubber you purchased. PMC-790 is a two-part rubber that can be mixed by weight or volume. There is a big difference between weight and volume. The following method shows how to mix by weight. Mixing for PMC-790:

1. Place the mixing cup on the scale and press "tare" (if your scale doesn't have tare just write the weight down so we can subtract it later)
2. Weigh out an appropriate amount of part A into the mixing cup and write down the amount (if your scale doesn't have the tare function then you need to subtract the weight of the cup from the current weight to get the weight of part A)
3. Press "tare" and add part B until the scale reads ½ the weight of part A (if your scale doesn't have tare, just add ½ the weight of part A to the current weight and that's you're target weight)
4. Follow the mixing instructions on the bottle to make sure you get the two parts mixed well

When you've got the rubber mixed, pour it into the mold all the way to the top. Then lightly press the shoes on top. Again, make sure the shoes are level front-to-back and left-to-right.

Step 4: Trimming the Rubber

When the rubber is firm it's time to remove the shoes. If you let it cure all the way then it will be hard to trim the excess rubber off. For this step, just pull the shoes out of the mold. You can break the plaster if you need to, just get the shoes out. Then use a sharp knife to cut away any excess rubber around the edges and let the shoes cure for the rest of the time recommended on the bottle of rubber.

Aglet/Shoelace Repair

By MrPumpernickel
http://www.instructables.com/id/Aglet--Shoelace-Repair/

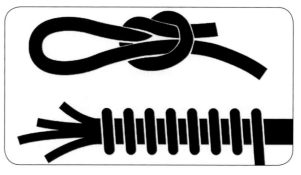

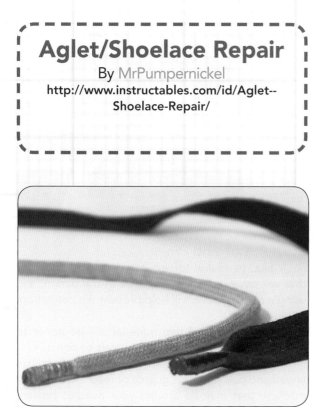

Step 1: Starting Off

First, you should get a hold of some extremely fine plastic line. Fishing line would probably work, as long as you can find one thin enough.

Second thing you're going to need is superglue—the faster it dries the better. It's also easier if you can find superglue with a brush already in the bottle, as it will facilitate steps further down the road.

Third, you need an X-Acto knife for all your cutting needs. Though, a scalpel or a really sharp knife, or even scissors, would work too.

Step 2: Wrapping the Shoelace

Take a length of the plastic line, as long or short as you deem necessary (at least 12"). Since we're going to wrap this line over the shoelace to both crimp it and give it rigidity, it helps if you can attach it first and just concentrate on wrapping. As you can see from the top illustration on the image below, you could make a simple slipknot, thread it over the shoelace, and tighten it. From there it's easy just to wrap, and it gives a rather neat result as well. The bottom illustration shows what we're after: a nice uniform wrap, though not necessarily as spaced out as mine, all across the length of what will be your new aglet.

Doing one lap is a bare minimum, but if you have enough plastic line and enough patience, going over it a second time is definitely recommended. The neater you are the better the end result will be. The aim is to get good coverage and good crimping.

Secure the plastic line with a knot after wrapping and move on to the next step.

Step 3: Glue

What you need to do after wrapping is to glue the plastic line in place. Here's why it helps to have a brush in your superglue bottle: cover all the plastic line with glue uniformly, making sure that you missed no part and making sure you don't cover more than you have to. Set this aside to dry or gently roll it between your thumb and index finger to stimulate drying. A word of caution though, this will cause your fingers to become encrusted.

Step 4: Almost Done

Take out your X-Acto knife (granted your parents or significant other has given you permission to play with sharp objects) and simply cut away the frayed edges of the shoelace. Add a drop of superglue to seal up the edge and then cut away any possible stray parts of the plastic line sticking out.

Once dried, you're done. There you have an aglet that will last you a lifetime, though no guarantees for the rest of the shoelace.

Step 5: Last (Optional) Step

Now this is the last and optional step. Whether you utilize it depends quite a bit on both your shoelaces and your needs. The method I described can be used on nearly any type of shoelace or cord, as long as it's suitably thin. If you use paracord and don't want to burn the edges, this is a good alternative. If you have wider shoelaces, like the black one pictured below, it helps to fold it in half before you start wrapping with the plastic line. It gives a neater result.

Patching Denim

By Audrey Love (audreyobscura)
http://www.instructables.com/id/Patching-Denim/

I very rarely buy new clothes, and instead recycle and repurpose my clothes until they are unwearable.

The most common repair I have to do is fixing the crotch/inner thigh of my pants. I have performed this operation on dozens of pairs of pants, and it is very easily fixed, if you have a little bit of patience.

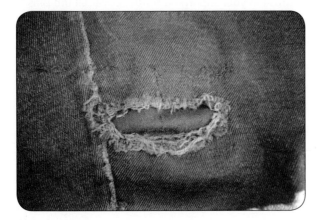

Step 1: Materials and Tools

For this project I used:

- Pair busted pants (the inner thigh ripped out on this pair)
- Scrap material from an old pair of jeggings I cut up into a skirt
- Scissors
- Sewing machine (you can hand stitch, but just try and keep really tight tension)
- Dark thread
- Pins

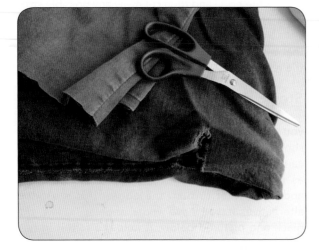

Step 2: Cut and Pin

I like to make square or rectangular patches that will cover the damaged area of the denim, and using a stretch fabric will help prevent the patch from ripping out.

Using a stretchy, thin material will be easier to sew through, versus sewing two layers of denim.

If you are going to machine sew a patch on, go ahead and pull whatever guards or feed trays off your machine that may be around your needle; you are going to want to have access to various grip points on the denim when feeding something like pants into the machine.

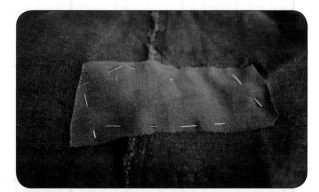

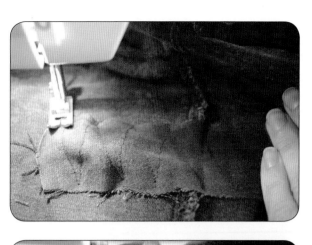

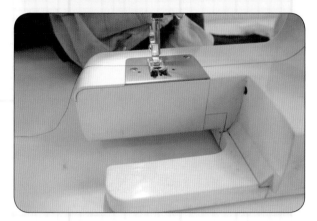

Step 3: Sew It!

To sew the patch on, I make a zig-zag pattern, pulling the material to the right as I go, using really short, tight stitches.

Start by stitching down, then, holding the reversing button/lever (that differs on every sewing machine I have ever used), gently pull the pants to the right.

Repeat this sequence up and down the patch until you get to the left border of your patch.

I then sunk my needle down in to the material and rotated it, sewing a final perimeter box around the patch.

That's it!

Make sure you don't have any pins in it and then wear 'em!

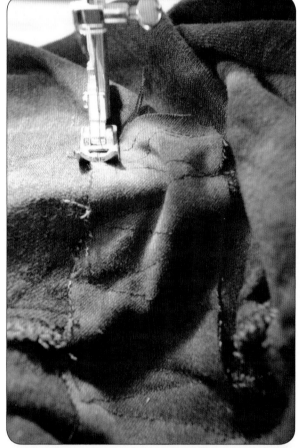

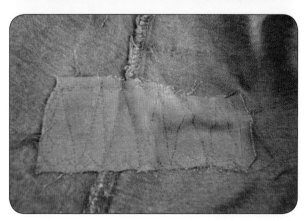

Bedroom

We always seem to run out of space in our bedrooms. We need to tuck, hide, slip, and slide things out of the way to make the whole arrangement work. Learn how to hang your bed or fold it up and away to fix a cluttered floor. Getting too much light in the morning? You can fix that with homemade cardboard blinds!

This section really puts the "room" back in bedroom. Ba-dum-tish!

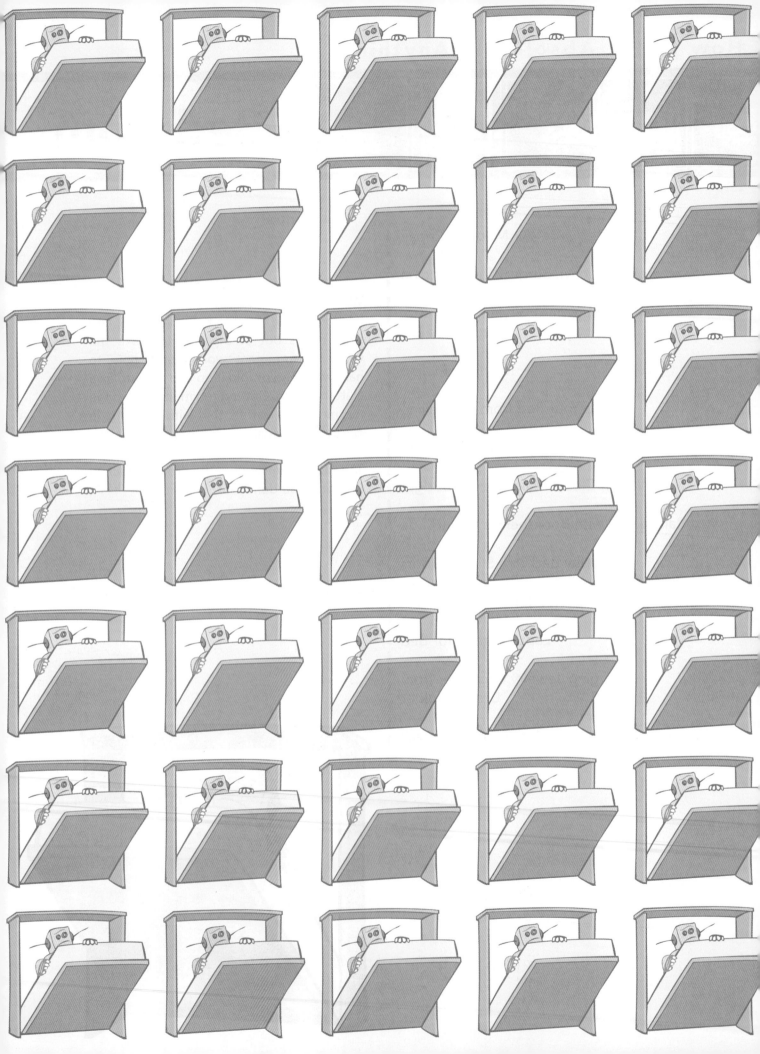

Psssssshhh. . . uh oh. Is that a leak in the air mattress I hear?

Don't worry, you can fix your air mattress with an ordinary bicycle inner tube repair kit and some sandpaper, all in less than 10 minutes!

Step 1: Tools and Materials

Tools:
- Sandpaper (150–200 grit)
- Vacuum

Materials:
- Bicycle inner-tube repair kit
  - Rubber patch
  - Contact cement
  Time: 10 minutes

Step 2: Sand and Score

First, find your leak. There are a variety of methods, such as using soapy water to see where bubbles form or submerging your mattress in water to find where the leak is coming from. In most cases the leak will be obvious enough to find by sight or sound.

Once your leak has been located, deflate your mattress. If the leak is not in a flocked area of your mattress, proceed to the next step.

If your leak is on the flocked upper area of your mattress, start gently sanding away the flocked surface around the leak to reveal the smooth, rubberized surface below. By removing the flocked surface around the leak you are creating a surface that will allow the patch to create a good seal.

Make sure not to sand through mattress or make the leak opening too large from excessive sanding. Then, use a vacuum or damp cloth to clean the area of debris.

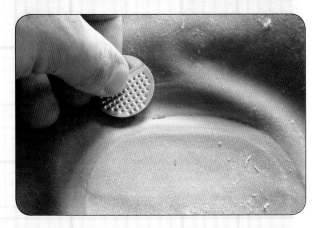

Step 3: Apply Contact Cement

Following the directions on the bicycle repair kit, place a dab of contact cement on the area around the leak. Then, place a dab of glue on the rubber bicycle tire patch. Allow both to dry (about 2–3 minutes).

Contact cement works when you put two sections that have the cement applied together. To bond, the cement needs to be dry.

When the cement has dried, line up the patch over the leak and firmly press the patch into the mattress. Rub the patch in small, circular motions to remove any air bubbles and to ensure a good seal between patch and mattress. If any corners or edges are not adhering right, use small dabs of contact cement, following the same application procedures as before.

For good measure, I usually run a bead of cement around the perimeter of the patch, just in case.

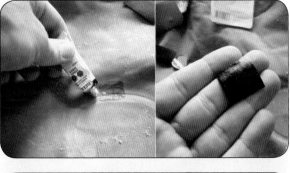

Step 4: Inflate

That's it! Once the patch has been applied you're ready to inflate your air mattress and test to see if your patch holds.

As an added precautionary measure, I usually put a small amount of talc over the patch after it's been applied. The talc acts as a lubricant over the sometimes sticky rubber and cement and reduces the possibility of fabric sheets catching an edge of the patch and tearing it off.

Good luck!

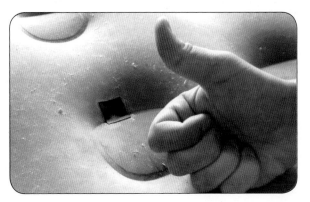

Reconstructive Surgery for a Suitcase

By Phil B

http://www.instructables.com/id/
Reconstructive-Surgery-for-a-Suitcase/

Suitcases with wheels and extendable handles are a boon to travelers. But something heavy resting on your suitcase can bend the telescoping handles during your flight so they no longer extend. That is what happened to this suitcase.

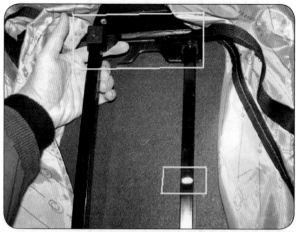

Step 1: Examine the Damage

The telescoping tubing for the extendable handle is below a zippered lining. By opening the zipper, the mechanism is visible. It was not just that the tubing was bent; its mount was shattered, too. In the larger rectangle you can see the plastic is broken, so one set of tubes is now free floating. To the right of my index finger you can see a long crack that breaks the mount into two pieces. Part of the socket for the right tubes is broken away. The smaller rectangle shows a dimple in the tube from a bend caused by something heavy on it. This all happened during only a one-hour flight. Normally, we have no damage to our luggage. The rest of the suitcase is too good to discard just yet.

Once, a humorous flight attendant apologized for the delay in taking off. He said, "The machine that normally rips the tags from your luggage is broken and the crew had to do it by hand." The damage to this suitcase lends credence to his statement.

118

Step 2: First Step in a Repair

The first step is to remove the broken tubing mount. Drill out the peened rivet heads.

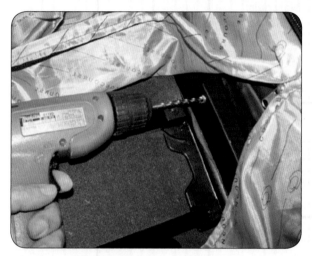

Step 3: Drive Out the Rivets

I used a small punch and a hammer to drive out the rivets. If they do not come out fairly easily, check to see if you need to drill away some more of the peened part.

Step 4: Straighten the Tubing

Check the tubing by eye or with a straightedge. I used a C-clamp, a small wooden block, and a heavier piece of wood to straighten the bent tube set. It is necessary to push the tube set past straight because it will spring back a little. This is also not exactly rocket science, either.

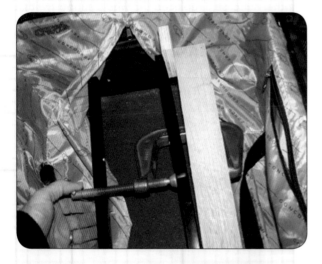

Step 5: A Second Bend in the Tubes

I was surprised to find a second bend in the tubing. This one was not lateral, like the first bend in the previous step, but was from the back of the suitcase inward. I placed the heavier piece of wood from the previous step under the outside of the suitcase. The block visible in this step is directly above the heavier piece of wood. I bore down with the palms of my hands and the weight of my body to straighten the tubes as best I could. Suddenly I was able to extend the handle to about half of its normal full travel.

Step 6: Bends and Bulges

With a little muscle I was able to extend the handle fully. There was a bulge in the side of the more heavily damaged tube when fully extended. I

pressed the bulge back in as close to flat as possible with a C-clamp. I also used the pieces of wood and the C-clamp to straighten this tube. The previous attempts at straightening had a positive effect on the tube inside the suitcase, but this tube inside it was still bent a little.

Step 7: Replacement Mount

I considered using a couple of pieces of wood 1" × 4" and 1" × 3" to anchor the tubes to the bottom of the suitcase on the inside. If I did not have a welder, that is most likely what I would have done. The additional graphic for this step shows how two wood pieces could be used. The 1" × 3" has two square mortises in it to receive the ends of the steel tubes.

But I was able to use a piece of old bedframe and some ⅛" × ¾" strap iron to weld up a replacement for the broken mount. I formed the sockets for the tubes from strap iron bent around a solid piece of square steel bar the same size as the steel tubes. I used a carbon arc torch on my arc welder to make bending easier and more precise.

There is always the risk that adding anything metal to the structure of a suitcase increases the curiosity of TSA (Transportation Security Administration) screeners. But, I figure the increased strength in the suitcase structure is worth it.

Step 8: Install the New Mount

Here you see the new steel mount installed. All that remains is to vacuum shavings from the suitcase and to zip up the lining.

Step 9: The Handle Works!

If you compare the photo in the introduction, you can see how much more the handle extends after straightening the tubes and making a new mount for the tubes. It is not quite as smooth extending the handle as when this suitcase was new, but this suitcase will serve us for quite a long time, yet, at least until the zippers wear out.

Step 10: From the Outside

I used finish washers and bevel-head screws for a nice finished look, as if anyone looks at the bottom of a suitcase, anyway. I used self-locking nuts on the inside. The ends of the screws are flush with the face of the nuts, so nothing can catch or be damaged by the screws extending beyond the nuts.

Step 11: Another Victim of the Airlines

Most wheeled suitcases have plastic extensions to make the suitcase stand up straight. These are easily broken off in flight.

Step 12: Replace with Wood

When half of the extension support broke off of another suitcase, I replaced the whole support with a piece of wood and painted it black. Some of the paint has begun to wear off. I drilled out rivets as described above.

Step 13: What Holds It in Place?

I used a piece of aluminum inside the suitcase and sheet metal screws to hold the extension support in place. So far, no one from the TSA has left a note that he or she looked inside to see what the metal might be. It is a shame to discard a good suitcase just because of some damage to plastic parts or bent handle tubes. I am pleased to extend the useful life of these two suitcases. We do use them often.

Minimalist-Style Dresser with Electronics Bay

By dogtooth

http://www.instructables.com/id/Minimalist-Style-Dresser-with-Electronics-Bay/

This is a design for a minimalist-style bedroom dresser with one of the drawer spaces enhanced to support cable box, stereo, and so on. Now you don't have to choose between a dresser and an entertainment center.

Constructed from plywood using pocket-screw construction, it can be built with a table saw, pocket-screw jig, and a drill. It's about as easy as furniture construction can get.

Step 1: Materials and Tools

Materials:

- 1 + ½ sheets ¾" veneer-face plywood (top, sides, bottom, braces, drawer faces)
- Half sheet ½" plywood (drawer frames)
- One sheet ¼" lauan plywood (drawer bottoms, back)
- 40' edge-banding veneer (optional)
- Fifty (approx.) ¼" pocket screws
- Twelve 4" × ¾" wood screws (for back)
- Forty-eight 1" finish nails or brads
- Six drawer handles
- Five sets 14" drawer slides
- Wood glue

- One pint varnish
- 220-grit sandpaper

Tools:

- Table saw with a good plywood blade
- Pocket-screw jig (with drill bit)
- Drill
- Screwdriver
- Clothes iron (for applying veneer)
- Vibrating sanders
- Two to four bar clamps (optional)

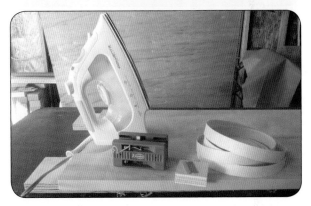

Step 2: Planning

Draw out all the pieces and double check your math!. The dimensions I used were 48" width, 18" depth, and 30" height.

The carcass is a basic box with a top, bottom, two sides, and a center divider. ½" braces provide a facing at the top, bottom, and in between each drawer.

Drawer slides fit flush with the top of each brace. Drawer faces are flush (not inset) with the sides and recessed under the top.

The electronics bay is simply a shelf, flush with the top of the top door brace. It can be converted into a drawer without removing the shelf—just add drawer slides.

It is a good idea to include 4" wide back braces. These can be pocket screwed from the top and base and will add significant strength. A third brace in the middle is not a bad idea either.

Drawer boxes are standard ½" ply with a dado cut to receive the drawer bottom.

Step 3: Cutting

Cut the top and sides out of the ¾″ ply. Cut a relief along the back of each to accommodate the ¼″ ply backing.

Cut the base, center divider, and electronics shelf out of ¾″ ply. Cut the drawer fronts along with the front and rear spacers out of ¾ ply. Cut and dado the drawer boxes out of ½″ ply and then cut the drawer bottoms and dresser back out of ¼″ ply.

If desired, dado out the center divider to accommodate the front spacers. The spacers should be centered between the top and bottom of adjacent drawers.

Optional: Make a cutout at the bottom of the dresser side to provide a "leg-like" effect.

Step 4: Assembly

The fun part! If you are using edge banding, add it now to any edges that you wish to veneer.

Use the pocket-screw jig to drill out all the screw holes for the dresser frame and faces. Align the pieces carefully and start gluing and screwing! Using clamps to hold the pieces makes this easier and more accurate.

Build the drawer boxes. They should be both glued and nailed. A brad nailer is handy if you have one.

Install the drawer slides on the frame and drawers. Test the drawers.

Don't attach the drawer faces until after they have been finished.

Step 5: Finish

Sand any surfaces that will be exposed. Then varnish, sanding lightly between coats.

Install the handles on the drawer faces and the attach the drawer faces to the drawer boxes.

Refinished Lamp

By Anthony Michael (english tea)
http://www.instructables.com/id/Refinished-Lamp/

These twenty-year-old brass-plated lamps used to be popular, but now they adulterate the bedrooms, lounges, and home offices of young people's first homes everywhere.

I resolved this plight by turning my old lamp into a delightfully modern and stylish lamp.

Step 1: Paint the Lamp

Take off the shade and any other parts you don't wish to be painted and lightly sand the metal so that the paint will adhere well. Clean off any dust thoroughly and apply many thin layers of spray paint.

Warning: If your knowledge of electrics is limited to only how to change a plug, I recommend putting the screwdriver down and masking off the light fitting and wire rather them removing them and rewiring the lamp later.

Step 2: Fabric Shade

Tear a sheet of fabric (I used an old bed sheet) into strips about 3" (7.5cm) in width. Wrap the strips tightly around the shade. Each wrap should slightly overlap the previous one. Use safety pins to hold everything in place.

Optional: Add a single white stitch line around the top and bottom. I thought this subtle addition really finished it off well.

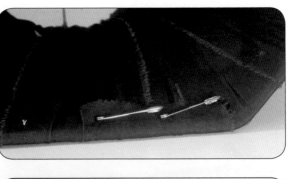

Step 3:

Warning: Use an energy-saving bulb rather than an incandescent bulb. They aren't as hot and will minimize the risk of fire. Please don't blame me if you burn down your house, as I was only trying to make it look prettier.

Reassemble the lamp, and when your generous donor asks for their lamp back (because it's so awesome now), you can politely refuse.

Tips

- Automotive paint is by far the best. However, it is expensive. If you can afford it, you won't regret it.
- Spray painting is not easy to do well and is a good skill to learn. With practice you will get a better finish.
- Use etching primer if you want a more durable and flawless finish.
- Clean metal surfaces with methylated spirits, alcohol, or nail-polish remover to clean thoroughly. (Don't use nail-polish remover on the painted layers. It will remove the paint!)

Hang Your Bed from the Ceiling

By Command-A

http://www.instructables.com/id/Hang-Your-Bed-From-the-Heavens/

In this Instructable I will show you the basic, easy process of hanging your own bed from your ceiling. This is a great way to get that extra POW factor in your room. The reason I finally did this project is my bed spring wouldn't cut the last corner downstairs into my bedroom.

When I was making it I wasn't sure if people would go for it or think I was a freak, but it turned out to be great. The weight limit is 600 pounds if done properly, so you have about 500 people pounds after the mattress and wood weight. This is enough for almost any couple to safely sleep, and with proper safety it should never fail sans advanced warning.

This bed is also adjustable. I can make X's with the cable to raise it around 5 ½' above the floor. Also, making the wire loops "longer" lowers the bed. Please buy plenty of cable so you too can adjust your bed to the right height. I am just short of 6' tall and I can crawl up just fine, but most need a stool or chair; keep this in mind along with the added risk of having a bed 4' off the ground.

There are a few requirements for your dwelling you need in order to make this happen. I would hate for you to start chopping up your place to find no trusses to hang from. Before you begin you should know you will probably only be able to do this is you live in a house (duplex, town home, etc.) and not an apartment. From my experience of building homes and living in apartments those of you will be out of luck.

Step 1: First Step Is Gathering Supplies

The hardest thing I had to do was to make the (economical and safety) choices to ensure the best way to DIY. The trip to Home Depot should only take one try. I bought everything I needed from there and spent about $90.00.

- 8" wall or ceiling hooks (×16)
- ³⁄₃₂" coated wire (×60')
- ³⁄₃₂" wire clamps (×16)
- Same-thread safety nuts (×32 to ensure the clamps do not slip)
- 2" × 4" board (×4; about 84" long Boards)
- 84" × 60" plywood sheet
- Drill of choice

I wanted this project to be safe as well as fun. It puts me to sleep faster than Ambien and Scotch. It should be noted this bed moves with your natural body movement. Until I slept in this bed it wasn't something that was clear to me. When suspended you are able to move forward backward and side to side without much resistance, and this is what can make some folks feel motion sickness. To my understanding it is just a false sense of security many beds provide that this one does not. It moves exactly reflective of your own movement.

When I said this project was rated to 600 pounds that is the amount the weakest link can safely ensure. The weight rating on the hooks is 75 lbs. per on a vertical load. (That drops to 35 for a horizontal load.) This means that with eight hooks the vertical safe load is 600 lbs. The cable is doubled over and rated at 320 pounds, so each loop is viable at 640 lbs. The clamps have a rating of 200 lbs., and since we are using two clamps per loop of cable this is overall a very safe setup.

Hook Load   (8 × 75LBS = 600lbs)
Cable Load   (640 × 8 = 5120 lbs)
Clamp Load   (200 × 16 = 3200 lbs

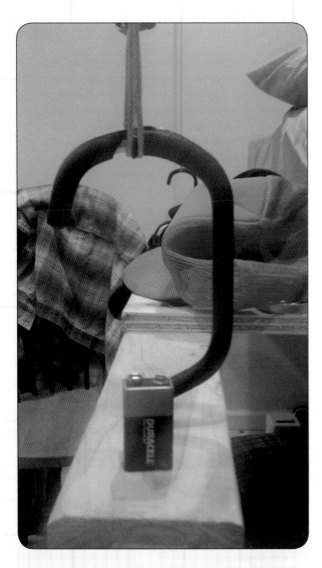

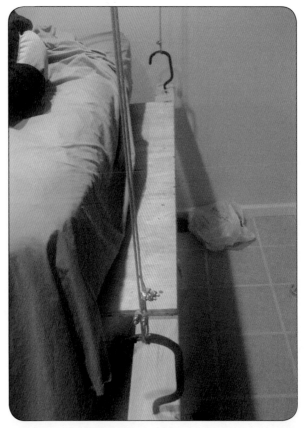

Step 3: Getting Hooked

This is the most important part of the project. If you get this wrong, or install this bed into a ceiling that is not load bearing, you could seriously injure yourself. Please understand you just might not be able to install this bed. If you are, test each hook individually for hanging the bed.

Use a stud finder to locate the trusses.

I would suggest finding any trusses in an unfinished part of the house (attic or furnace room) where you can actually see and measure them without having to cut sheetrock from the ceiling first. As I learned, and as you can see by the photo, I figured they would extend across the basement from the unfinished room to bed placement. My drill holes tell a different story, and that's when I realized they were not the same boards.

Measure your drill holes in conjunction with where the eight 2" × 4"s terminate. You don't want the bed to pull on the hook except for downward. This could possibly work a hook loose after time.

Using your stud finder locate the sides of each truss, so as to measure your hole in the middle.

I went ahead and cut all the sheetrock so I could visually see the hole in the wood. You might run the risk of drilling off-mark in the middle of the wood if you don't verify hole placement, especially with a cheap stud finer.

I drilled out most of the size of the hook's screw. The truss wood is very strong, but without pre-drilling

Step 2: Assembling the Frame

The next few steps could be done in any order; this is just the order I choose.

1. Place the 2" × 4"s evenly along the length of the plywood sheet. They should be roughly ¼ of the length apart. They do need to be spaced evenly to disperse the weight, balance, and load. The easiest way is to place the starter board at the beginning and the end board at the other end. Then divide the distance for the remaining two 2" × 4"s.
2. Screw four screws into each board using four 2" wood screws.
3. Do this for each board so you have four evenly spaced boards. This ensures the best weight distribution.
4. Clip off any screw heads on the opposite side of the board to prevent scratches on walls, floors, etc.

I know the frame looks pretty weak, but I am broke and in college. I would love to have made this from exotic wood with polished stainless hooks, but plywood and deck screws will have to work.

I was certain the truss would crack. The threads are what hold the weight.

Repeat process 15 times for all your contact points.

To install the hook into the 2″ × 4″ the process is the same.

I did use a smaller bit for the 2″ × 4″s because the wood is much softer than the truss word and has more give.

You want the hooks as tight as possible for maximum tension.

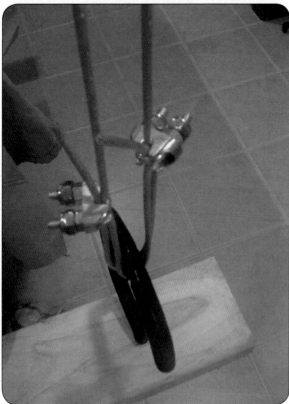

Step 4: String It Up, and Let the Sway Begin!

This is the step that is the biggest safety issue for the bed. These wires and clamps must be done right!

How high you want your bed will determine the length of wire you will need to cut for each hook set.

Mine were 5′ apart, so each cable needed to be 126″ long. We're looping the cables and need a few extra inches for the clamps.

Cut the wire to desired length.

Loop cable with a few extra inches for double cable clamp crimp.

Make eight total and tighten them just enough to bear 20 pounds or so. The friction of the plastic on the cable was enough to keep it snug without being too tight. You will waste much time if you over tighten and lock too quickly. This is the only part of the bed that is adjustable, so you must complete this step later on after hanging the bed.

Hang all eight loops over installed ceiling hooks.

Hang bed hooks into cable loops. Presto!

Now you can begin the process of making your bed level. This is done by pulling more or less cable through the clamp to adjust that loop length with the others. Once you have made your bed level, tighten down on the clamp bolts and then add the safety washer.

Step 5: Get Down

Now that you have the coolest bed in the city, (unless you have the bed that floats on magnets) you will have no problem finding dates for Valentine's Day, or opposition to watching a movie on your laptop and cuddling.

Now you have your heavenly bed!

Folded Cardboard Window Blind

By Mimikry

http://www.instructables.com/id/folded-cardboard-window-blind/

I live in northern Sweden, and in summer there's no sunset as it never gets dark.

Our house has many big windows, and I'm simply too cheap to buy that many window blinds.

I came up with this inexpensive, easy, and yet decorative window blind.

It takes about 30 minutes to make one.

Step 1: Materials
You'll need:
- A big sheet of cardboard (the one I used was kind of sloppy and had a lot of holes in it; you should choose a nicer one)
- Drill
- Some twine
- A long, straight piece of lumber or anything else to use as a straightedge

- A knife or cutter
- Two hairclips or clothespins
- Two hooks or heavy stones
- A big needle for the twine (works without but it'll much easier with the needle)

Step 2: Measure Your Window
Measure your window and add about 20" to the height. Cut your cardboard the same size. You'll need to know the depth as well.

Step 3: Impress the Cardboard
You measured the depth of your window - right? Let' say it is 5" deep, in which case you'll make your folds about 2 ½".

Mark lines with 2 ½" distance, then take the straight piece of lumber (or whatever you use) and place it on the cardboard. Now take the *back* of your knife or cutter and impress every second line. *Don't* cut through the cardboard, as the lines are only a help for folding the blind. you won't need much pressure. See the pictures.

127

Step 4: Folding

Now fold the cardboard in every line—all in the same direction! Press the fold hard with your hand. See the pictures.

Now turn the sheet around.

Step 5: Impress Other Side

Impress the remaining lines on the other side, and fold them too. You'll end up with a zig-zag-folded cardboard.

Step 6: Drill a Hole and Thread It

Now take your drill and drill a hole through the folded blind. Take the twine and thread it through the holes. If you have a big needle, life will be much easier. Make a knot on one end (see the pictures). Now repeat this on the other side.

Step 7: Mount the Blind

Mount the side with the knot on the upside of your window. I chose to clamp it between the window and the frame; for a more permanent solution, you may use screws.

Secure both pieces of twine on the bottom of the window. I used two heavy stones; for a more permanent solution use hooks.

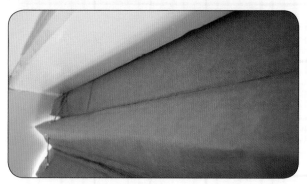

Step 8: Adjust Length

To adjust the length of the window blind, use the hairclips or clothing pins as shown in the pictures.

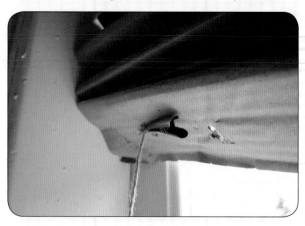

Our master walk-in closet was all white wire shelves. It's not only lack of space for hanging cloth, but also lack of storage we really need. So we wanted to design and build a couple of three cabinet build in units for two sides to solve the problem. We checked out the home center pre-build units, they are not very budget friendly, plus they are made from particle boards—not our favorite. So we decided to build our own from scratch.

Step 1: Design And Material

We have a 9′ × 7′ closet with 9′ ceiling, and we decided to not make the cabinet to cover from floor all the way to the ceiling, we still wanted to be able to vacuum the carpet in the closet every week, so the cabinets will be hanging from the top to a certain height from the floor. I figured everything in my head, but I did draw the rough dimension to show the design. I believe every closet would be different, so if you decide to build your own, most likely you are going to have to resize them to fit your need. Four of these are double hanging closet and two shelves—as they all have two hanging bars; two of them are just a closet with one bar but three shelves—we don't have much of longer stuff, so these are narrower with more shelves. The miter angle cut on the bottom of the side panel is there because of two reasons, one is to avoid straight corner at body level so that we don't run into it, and two is for static, I think it looks better and the closet will look bigger that way.

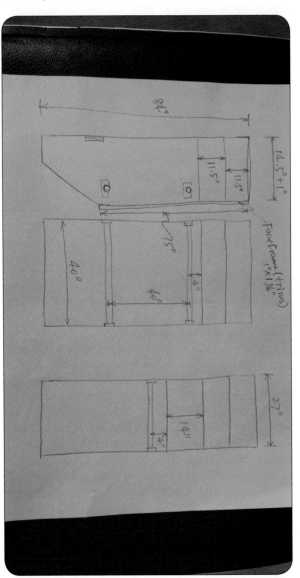

Step 2: Plywood Ripping And Preparation

First, rip 6 of full sheet of ½" Birch plywood to three 14.5" strips with my shop made ripping jig, and have a 4 ¼" left over. We will need 18 of wider 14.5" strips for side piece of six cabinets and their shelves. The leftover smaller strips will be used for cross braces on the top and bottom of the cabinet. Second, make miter cut on all side panel pieces with circular saw, and cut all shelves to length. I cut a notch at the back side of the side panels for mounting strip, and it will be ¾" plywood with 45° bevel cut—it's called "French cleat." If you Google it, you can find more information. I took one of the pictures on the internet just to show what it looks like. Third, cut all cross braces into length. Then use router and straight edge to cut ³⁄₁₆" deep dado on the inside of the panel. The size of the dado should be the same or just a hair wider of the thickness of the plywood that is using. This is an extra step, because the dado is not only going to help for aliment, but also increase the rigidity of the structure. After the machining is done, everything get sanded and sealed with primer, then painted before assembly.

Step 3: Cabinet Assembly

Since the cabinets will be mounted side by side, so the outside will never be seen, everything could be put together with glue and screws straight through. Pre-drill all the holes at the dado side to provide an exact location of the screw holes, and cabinet get assembled piece by piece with glue and screw, make sure to pre-drill and countersink holes from outside before drive the screws in. Tip here is to use two hand screw clamps at the end to set two side panels up for assembly, because it's very difficult to hold panel and shelf together, align them square and drive a 1 ⅝" screw through with just two hands, that's where the dado and clamps come in really handy. Before the glue set, measure two corners diagonally to make sure the cabinet is square.

Step 4: Hanging Bars And Mounting Cleat

Hanging bar mounting cleats were made from a strip of ¾" plywood. Cut them at 4" × 3" pieces, chamfer on one side for the better look. Drill an 1 ½" through hole at the center, sand them on all edges, cut them into two halves, and that will become the brackets at two side. Spray paint them and they are ready. Bars are made from 1 ¼" EMT conduit cut to length with sawzall and bi-metal blade, they are rigid enough and very economical. Just make sure to remove the burr and sand the edges.

Step 5: Hanging Bar And French Cleat Installation

Mounting the hanging bar brackets uniformly is a little tricky and requires a jig. I went through all the cloth hangers we have and measured all of them for the clearance needed from top to end of the hook, and found that 3" would be plenty from bottom of the shelf to the top of the bar for easy access. The brackets top edge will be sitting ¾" below the top of the bar (with 1 ½" OD), plus some needed room for face frame, thus, a piece of 4" × 4" scrap was used as the positioning jig. Two pencil marks were 1 ½" at top and bottom from one edge of the jig. Place the jig on the outside panel with top edge align to bottom of the shelf, side flush with front edge of the cabinet. Position the bracket below the jig with one corner align to the pencil mark, trace the shape onto the cabinet - providing an exact location that it will be inside the cabinet, then repeat the same process from inside, clamp the bracket onto the panel without tracing the shape, pre-drill and counter-sink the mounting holes from outside, and drive 3 screws in. Clean the closet wall, patch the holes and repaint it as you like. Find all the studs on the wall, and place pencil marks for the locations. Use cabinet mounting screws (pan head 2 ½") to secure mounting cleat onto the desired location. I left 2 ½" gap from ceiling to the top of each cabinet for crown moulding.

Step 6: Hanging The Cabinets

Hang cabinets onto the wall with French cleats. I made some special notes on the pictures. Make sure to shim all sides in order to hang them plumb and level. Screw cabinets together at the hanging bar locations so that they won't be seen after installation.

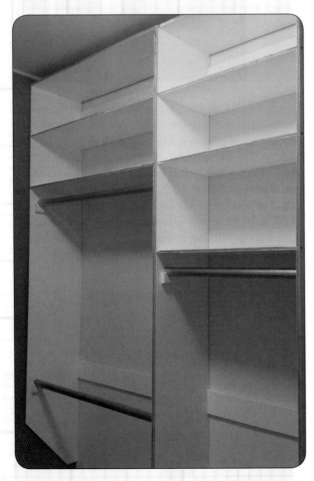

Step 7: Face Trim

I ripped some 1x pine boards to 1 ⅛" wide, and dressed them up on one side using router and chamfer bit, they were then sanded, primed and painted. I used 1 ½" long 18 Ga nails to secure them onto the front of the cabinets. Nail holes were patched, sanded.

Step 8: Crown Molding Installed And Finished

Crown molding was installed all around the top, then I painted face frame and crown molding last for two more coats. There are many ways to cut and install crown molding, I will provide some of the aspects at next Instructables when we update our daughter's rooms. Overall, we spent about $350 on all the materials, including plywood, paint, 1x pine boards, crown molding and other necessary stuff. I spent some weekends and some nights on and off, and the whole project took about three weeks long.

Now we have a much better functional walk in closet and great appeal as well.

I created underbed storage using IKEA EXPEDIT bookshelves. This is a super easy project with no sawing needed. And, surprisingly, the bed is completely stable. Since I already had a bed and frame, it cost about $400.

Step 1: Parts Needed

- Three IKEA EXPEDIT Bookshelves ($90 each)
- Two IKEA OBSERVATOR Cross Braces 393 Version ($5 each; be sure to select the 39" version, not the 28")
- Queen-size mattress
- Queen-size bed frame or 80" × 58 ⅝" sheet of wood

Optional items:

- IKEA LEKMAN boxes ($12 each; eight fit in each bookcase; I only put eight LEKMAN boxes in the bookcase at the foot of the bed; IKEA has many storage options for the EXPEDIT bookcases)
- Three mat shelf liners sized at least 15.5" × 59" ($5 to $8 each)

Tools needed:

- Drill
- Phillips-head screwdriver

Step 2: Build the EXPEDIT Bookshelves

Build the EXPEDIT bookshelves as IKEA instructs. Place them spaced evenly on the floor as shown.

Step 3: Install Cross Braces

On the two end-unit bookshelves, drill and screw in the IKEA OBSERVATOR 39" cross brace as shown. This will keep the bed from swaying left to right. Just with one cross brace, the bed was stable. I added a second one to be careful. I chose to install the cross brace at the foot of the bed on the inside (under the frame) so that it would not interfere with reaching storage from the outside. At the head of the bed (touching the wall), I installed the cross brace on the outside so that it would not interfere with reaching the storage under the bed.

Step 4: Place Frame and Bed on Top

In order to protect the shelves from scratches and provide some grip, consider placing a mat liner at least 15.5" × 59" on top of them (mine are 16" × 62", so I had to cut a few inches off the end). Then place the bed frame or 80" × 58 ⅝" sheet of wood on top of that. For this project, I lined up four narrower sheets of 80" s 14 ⅝" wood. Because the bed is around 3 ½' high, kids and those under 5'10" will need a chair or stool to climb into it. But if you need the storage, this provides lots of organized space.

Murphy Bed with Sliding Doors

By newfangled

http://www.instructables.com/id/Ikea-Hack-Murphy-Bed-with-Sliding-Doors/

We have a spare bedroom that is long but also fairly narrow. With a queen bed there wasn't much space for anything else, but we wanted to make the room more multi-functional. The obvious solution was a Murphy bed.

We spoke to some of the local suppliers, and for a basic Murphy bed and cabinet with no additional storage space the price would have been about $3,500. That's a little steep, but the bigger problem is that we didn't like the style of any of them.

Step 1: Arrange Two PAX Wardrobes

Space two IKEA PAX 100x236cm wardrobes about 172cm apart. If I were doing it again, I would probably increase the spacing to 180cm, just to get a few more inches' clearance.

Step 2: Assemble and Install the Bed Mechanism

After some searching online I decided to use the Next Bed kit for the Murphy bed hardware.

Here it's shown assembled and installed. It rests on the floor and is attached to the wall at the baseboard level with eight screws.

Just for reference, the mattress is a 12" pillowtop, with a mattress pad on top of that. It's currently set up so that it's tight to the wall, but there's enough clearance that I could move the bed further out from the wall to hang a picture on there.

Overall I'm really impressed with the quality of the Next Bed kit and would recommend it to anyone. The instructions are clear, and they have several helpful assembly videos available online as well.

Step 3: The Bottom Section

I did the bottom section in two parts.

There is a reinforced "L" section that gets screwed into the wardrobes.

Then a cover gets screwed on top of that. The exposed edge gets hidden by the track for the sliding doors.

The material for this comes from cutting up a third PAX wardrobe.

This doesn't take much load, but I made it fairly strong because I didn't want it to break if someone stepped on it or kicked it.

Step 4: The Lower Track

Each track is about 198cm long. The total width of my assembly is only about 372mm, so I shortened each track by about 12cm using a Dremel and hacksaw.

The lower tracks are notched for the sides of the wardrobes, but since I wasn't using standard dimensions I had to cut an extra notch with the Dremel.

Step 5: Assemble the Top Section

This is the top section, showing the underside and the top.

The material for this comes from cutting up a third PAX wardrobe.

The "fingers" are there so that after the section was lifted up it would hold itself in place.

Once it's in place there's no way to run cabling, so all of the lighting had to be installed first.

After it was in place I added a stiffener at the front, because it was flexing a bit too much under the weight of the doors. Refer to "Step 11: Lessons Learned" for some more details on that.

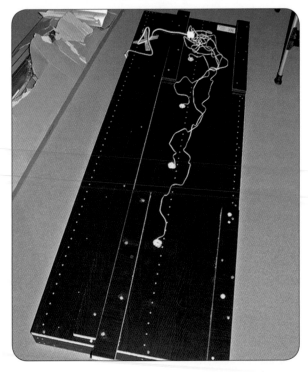

Step 6: Install the Top Section

The top section is lifted into place and is supported by "fingers." I then connected it to the wardrobes with screws.

I ran an extension cord from the left wardrobe to provide a power connection in the right wardrobe. This had to be done before the top section was in place.

Step 7: The Upper Track

Each track is about 198cm. The total width of my assembly is only about 372mm, so I shortened each track by about 12cm using a Dremel and hacksaw. The plastic piece is easy to remove, and then I re-drilled new holes on the shortened track and moved the plastic piece over.

Step 8: Joining the Track

IKEA tracks are not meant to be connected together (usually they're too short for that to work). But the IKEA hardware still does a pretty good job of joining them together.

I used pieces of an aluminum can as a shim to get the alignment just right. When the doors cross the joint there's a little bump, but they roll very smoothly otherwise.

Step 9: Little Details

I replaced the switch from an IKEA ANSLUTA power supply with a pushbutton switch that I ordered from eBay. I ran the wires in the through the bottom instead of the sides and then mounted it on the sidewall to control the overhead lights.

One of the PAX wardrobes was in front of an electrical outlet. I cut a rough opening in the back panel and then finished that by gluing on a typical cover plate.

From start to finish the project took about one week—that was one solid Saturday of work, with everything else being done in the evenings.

For the most part all of the work was done by one person, but there were a few steps where a second set of hands was needed: initially assembling the PAX wardrobes, lifting the top piece into place, and lifting the doors onto the rails.

Next step: buy new comforter cover.

Step 10: All done!

After that you just follow IKEA's instruction for installing the doors, and then you're done!

Materials:

- 3 IKEA PAX 100x236cm wardrobes (one was cut up and used for materials)
- 2 sets IKEA PAX LYNGDAL 200x236cm sliding doors
- 1 set IKEA INREDA LED spotlight
- 2 IKEA INREDA LED light strips

IKEA Cost: $1,010 (We waited until IKEA had a bedroom sale event. We bought the PAX stuff, got $150 gift card back, and then used that to buy the lighting).

- 1 Next Bed Murphy Bed hardware kit
- Lots of 2" and 1 ¼" particle board screws (different lengths depending on the type of joint)
- 1 roll of dark brown cabinet edging tape.

Total Cost: $1,650
Total Width: approx. 372cm (12' 2")

Step 11: Lessons Learned

As mentioned, I spaced the two wardrobes about 172cm apart. With the bedding and sliding doors installed this is a little bit tight. It's still workable, but if I were doing it again it would be nice to have a bit more clearance so I would space them at 180cm, for a total overall width of 380cm.

Also, with the doors installed, the weight causes the center section to bow down a bit. The deflection is only a few millimeters, but it's enough to throw the angle of the doors off. They stay on the tracks and move freely, but there's a little gap at the bottom when they're pushed together. This really isn't a big deal, but the photo shows a stiffener that I added to the top section to lessen the bending. It is just one of the end-cap channels that came with the sliding doors—I have two sets, but I only need one, so I cut down one of the spares and attached it.

Bookcase Door That Replaces Your Door

By THE GOOSE

http://www.instructables.com/id/
BOOKCASE-DOOR-THAT-REPLACES-YOUR-
DOOR/

Note: 90 percent of these books were water damaged to begin with, as I don't condone destroying books.

I've wanted to build this door for years but didn't want to ruin a bunch of books. I finally found some water-damaged books that no one would want to read. I cut all the books then sunbathed them for a few days to dry them and take any smell out. You could just go to a library book sale and get bags of books for about $2 a bag, but people frown upon destroying books, so try to find damaged ones if you can.

You can reuse your door or build a new one like I did. If you reuse your door it's a matter of adding more wood and books to it.

Step 1: Cut Your Wood

Cut 1 ½" × ¾" pieces to make a frame around your door. Make sure you leave enough space on the latch side so that the door will shut and will not hit on the jam. Measure the books you get to determine where you put the next piece of wood.

Step 2: Cut the Books

Cutting the books is not fun! If you have a table saw, shop vac, and dust mask you can do this fairly easily. Set your fence on the saw to 1 ¼" and hook up your shop vac to the saw. Put on your dust mask and start cutting the books with the binding of the book facing the fence. You will have to empty the shop vac about five times depending on the size of the vac. If you try to cut these in a closed area without a shop vac and mask you will not be able to breathe. I know because I did it.

Step 3: Stain Your Wood

Stain or paint all your pieces of wood and then attach them together with glue and nails. If you're building a new door, stain everything. Make sure you match the stain or paint of your door jam. Next, coat your wood with a varnish or polyurethane.

Step 4: Glue the Books on the Door

Glue the books on the door, making sure to dry-fit them first using pl400 or some other very good glue. I used a lever handle, so I could simply hollow out the book I wanted to use as the handle. I then drilled the handle and attached with screws. If you don't have a lever handle, you could get creative with two books.

Step 5: Hang the Door

Now you can rehang the door, but keep in mind that your door will be much heavier and you may need to add a heavier duty hinge. It should look something like mine, or better! The inside of your door will look just like a door.

Step 6: Handle in the Wall

My bedroom is very small, and after hanging the door I hit my arm on the book handle a few times. I came up with this idea to make the handle go into the wall, gaining me about 3" of walk space. I just marked the wall were the inside handle hit the wall and built a box that fit around the handle. I cut out the wall and slid in the box, securing it with a little glue. I then mounted a wall bumper on the wall down low. This feature could be added to about any door.

Laptop Stand for Bed

By profpat

http://www.instructables.com/id/Laptop-stand-for-bed-my-design/

I have seen lots of laptop stands here on Instructables, but none that suited my needs, so I decided to build my own. I motored down to the nearest lumber yard and purchased a clean 1" × 2" × 8' white pine and, checking my hardware scraps, came up with this one-day project.

Step 1: Cutting the 1" × 2" × 8' Wood

Tools needed:

- Electric drill with different sizes of wood bits
- Jig saw or hand saw
- 2 pcs. 120- to 150-grit waterproof sandpaper (to smooth the wood)
- Screwdrivers

   Note: You need to make two of each of the following items. Cut your 1" × 2" × 8' as follows:

   footings = 16"

   legs = 14"

   table top support = 11"

   angle stopper = 7"

Step 2: Inserting the T-nut

Before assembling, you need to insert the T-nuts.

Step 3: Assembling the Legs

For the holes' dimensions and spacing, I will leave it to you for your own project. They are not critical, and I have found the table to be well balanced.

Step 4: Table Top

For my table top, I used a Plexiglas I saved from my broken 19" LCD monitor. The 1" × 1" wood is wood-screwed from the bottom, which will keep your laptop from sliding down if your table is angled steeply.

Step 5: Complete the Other Legs and Screw in the Table Top

Complete the other legs and attach the table top with wood screws (three per side).

Note: If the table top keeps moving, insert a folded piece of sandpaper between the legs and table top support, before screwing in the big knob.

Hanging Jewelry Organizer from Utensil Holder

By Color Me Blue

http://www.instructables.com/id/Hanging-Jewelry-Organizer-from-Utensil-Holder/

This is functional, took some crafty thinking, is totally doable, and will last for quite some time. I'm always looking for new and better ways to organize my jewelry. I've gone from putting them in a plastic grid box from the Container Store, to displaying them in vintage bowls, to storing them in a drawer, but none of these methods really satisfied me. I like being able to see all my jewelry displayed in an organized, uncluttered way. And this little project does just that.

So let's get started. . .

Step 1: Supplies

- One wooden utensil holder (I used one from Bed, Bath, and Beyond)
- Four packs of small solid brass screw eyes (⅝")
- Three packs of solid brass cup hooks (⅝")
- Picture hanger set
- Measuring tape (optional)
- Pencil
- Hammer
- White spray paint

Step 2: Mark Where Your Screws Will Go

Mark where you want to put your screws. I put two in each column (for necklaces), and as many as I could fit in the smaller horizontal shelves (for earrings). You can use a ruler if you'd like to space them out evenly.

Step 3: Twist in the Screws

Twist all of the screws into place. This step can be a pain in the butt, so here is what I recommend: use an ice pick or a bigger screw to start each hole. If your hands are sweaty or shaky, try using a paper towel to get a better grip on the screws as you're twisting. Push down hard so they really go in and go slowly with a steady hand. A glass of wine is recommended.

Step 4: Attach Picture Holder

Attach the picture holder. On the back of your jewelry organizer, twist the two screws in towards the top so they are evenly spaced out in the center. Secure the wire by twisting it around itself. Cut with pliers.

Step 5: Spray Paint

Spray paint! Go outside and put newspaper down. Follow the directions on the can and let dry.

Step : Hang and Add Jewelry

All done!

Iron Pipe Shoe Rack

By alextardif

http://www.instructables.com/id/Iron-Pipe-Shoe-Rack/

Step 1: Empty Space!

Have lots of open space under the staircase? Time to get busy!

Step 2: Dimensions and Layout

The first step was to measure the closet space: each wall length and their angles. Next I found it helpful to outline a layout with masking tape to help visualize the final product.

Step 3: Shopping

All connectors, pipes, and flanges are available at Lowe's. Black iron pieces are cheaper than galvanized ones, but you will need to clean them of oil to prep for paint (household vinegar works well).

Step 4: Spray Paint Time!

Two coats for each part was plenty.

Step 5: I Can't Control My OCD

Sort of like Lego pieces, no?

Step 6: Shelves

I used pre-cut, 1" × 8" × 8" pine. I sanded it to get rid of any imperfections. Two coats of wood stain were brushed on. Two coats of satin top coat were sprayed on.

Step 7: Assembly and Installation

Yep, everything fits.

Step 8: Done and Done

Shoes live here. . .

Bathroom

There's only so much you can do to a bathroom. While they may all appear different, each one has the same function . . . or should. That's what we're here to guarantee.

So, what needs fixing? Do you need to start from the bottom up and learn how to remove and install a toilet yourself? Or do you just want to save some money and make that old shower curtain last a little longer? The authors at Instructables can show you how to do these things and much more!

Quick Shower Curtain Fix

By ezman

http://www.instructables.com/id/Quix-Shower-Curtain-Fix/

Is your shower curtain sagging? Is your floor sopping wet? Sure, you can fix your shower curtain with scotch tape. But, here is a minimalist suggestion for a quick shower curtain fix. With only one tool and three to five minutes of work time, you really cannot go wrong.

Tape Method

Over time the tape loses its adhesiveness. The bathroom environment does not lend itself to the tape approach. Steam will work its way under the tape, and once that happens the original issue, the rip, has not been dealt with effectively. My option saves using tape and will give you an extra hole to hold the curtain.

The overarching issue is that the shower/bath tub curtain rod is not solid—it is two rods. The rings have to move over the lip where the two rods overlap, and half the time they become hung up. When that happens, people, unintentionally, pull down harder (instead of lifting up and over), adding more stress to the plastic to overcome the obstacle. The benefit of my design is the extra weight of the user pulling down on the curtain is distributed over more of the plastic surface via the extra holes. So change the behavior and spare the shower curtain or add extra holes to some of the loops. This issue occurs the most with the two hanger holes at either end of the curtain.

Objective

The intent of this Instructable is to:

1. provide an alternative to the premature replacement of the shower curtain
2. encourage you to engage in a do-it-yourself franchise and community.

Step 1: A Poem

T'was the night before Thanksgiving, my life was a stir,

for days before had been no less than a blur.

The guests had arrived in droves and by number.

Now they were settling down for a pre-T'day slumber.

But what to my wondering eyes I did spy,

the sagging shower curtain, and I began to sigh.

"Why didn't I remember. . ." no sooner had I said those ill-fated words,

than I looked around in vain,

so no one would see me complain.

I sprang to my workbench with such a matter,

before I could get any madder.

More rapid than eagles my ideas they did come,

I whistled, and whispered, moving on to something more fun.

From the top of my workbench;

to the bottom of my tool wall.

Dash away, splash away, need not fret at all.

I bound down the hall with a twinkling eye,

my feet barely touching as if I could fly.

I surveyed my task with relish and delight.

With the tool in my hand and the curtain in sight.

I went to work as a matter of fact

with this simple shower curtain hack.

Step 2: Tool

- Hole Punch
- Skill Level: Easy
- Time to Complete: 3 to 5 minutes

Step 3: Procedure

Fold the curtain with the hole as the center.

Step 4: Align the Hole Punch Off to the Side

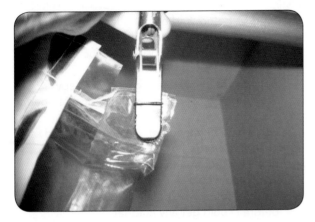

Step 5: Squeeze the Handle and Rotate

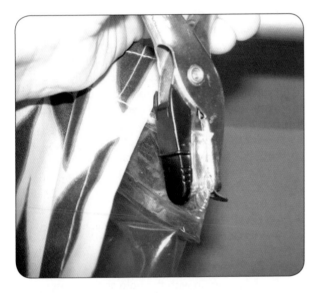

Step 6: Remove the Hole Punch and the Plastic Chad

Put the curtain hook through the two new holes. Repeat for each hole if necessary.

Step 7: Observations Summary

1. The benefit of this design is that the weight of the curtain is distributed over more plastic surface via the extra holes.
2. The plastic is strong around the new holes, not weak by the existing rip as is the case when using the tape method.
3. The areas that are most susceptible are the two hanger holes at each end of the curtain. If you add a second hole at each of those hangers, then you should push the inevitable off for awhile, if not avoid it entirely, before you replace the curtain.

Step 8: Summary

The shower curtain has stood up for more than eight months and is still going. I am satisfied with these results.

Step 9: Addendum

I have a favorable update. During the evaluation period I found the shower curtain hole next to the original repair ripped. I had done a visual inspection of each of the shower curtain holes for signs of stress or rips. There were no visible signs. So I did what any minimalist would do and only fixed the broken part.

This incident has given me a chance to test the durability of the repair. So what does that say about the strength of the repair? I would have to say it passed with high marks.

Judge for yourself. You could wait until you replace the curtain or prolong the current curtain. At any time you can double up on each of the shower curtain hanger support holes. In any case it is at your command to implement this quick shower curtain fix.

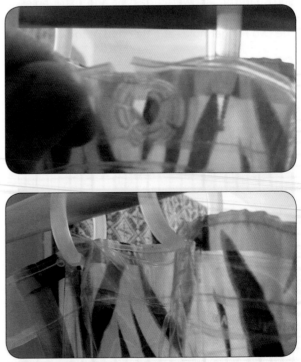

Sharpen a Nail Clipper

By Phil B

http://www.instructables.com/id/Sharpen-a-Nail-Clipper/

Many years ago when this nail clipper was new I needed to cut a couple of fine copper wires. I had nothing else at the time and I used my nail clipper. The wires made nicks in the cutting edges of the clipper. Eventually I learned a way to sharpen the clipper's cutting edges evenly and did so. (Ignore the surface rust that has appeared in the years since.)

Step 1: Remove the Actuating Lever

The jaws will need to be held in position for sharpening. You need some precision difficult to obtain by using the actuating lever alone. Remove it by squeezing the jaws together with your thumbs or thumb and first finger, or with a pair of pliers as shown here. The lever falls out of the pin. Remove the pin.

Step 2: Bring the Jaws Together

Insert a screw into the hole for the pin and put a nut onto the threads. Tighten the screw and nut to pull the cutting edges on the jaws lightly together or nearly so. They could be even closer together than shown here.

Step 3: Sharpen

The nail clipper has a flat face at the cutting edges on the front of the jaws. Grinding this flat surface will sharpen the cutting edges equally. This clipper has a mildly convex surface, so it is easy to grind on a flat sharpening stone. Some clippers are rather sharply concave on the front of the jaws. Light passes with a very fine grinding stone in a Dremel tool will work nicely.

Continue grinding lightly until all nicks in the cutting edges disappear. You may need to tighten the screw and nut a little as you go to keep the cutting edges close to one another while you grind. When you are finished, you will have two factory-new cutting surfaces, and your clippers will work great once again. When finished grinding remove the screw and nut. Insert the pin. Squeeze the jaws together a bit and attach the actuating lever. Wash the clipper to remove any grit from grinding the cutting edges.

Fix a Sink Stopper

By Phil B

http://www.instructables.com/id/Fix-a-Sink-Stopper/

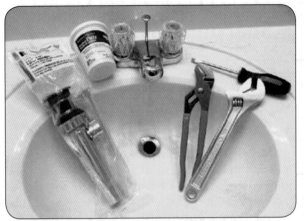

A sink stopper with a push/pull rod control at the faucet is a great modern convenience. But sink stoppers fail. When they do, they are often unsightly and an irritation. This is a repair you can do yourself.

Step 1: Materials and Tools

The photo shows a typical array of tools and supplies that may be needed to replace a stopper.

When you go to the store to buy a replacement stopper, you want to look for a pop-up assembly. Most are 1 ¼" x 12". They come with a lift rod and linkage. Often you can buy the linkage rod with ball and a stopper without buying the whole pop-up assembly. I chose to replace the whole pop-up assembly. The cost is very little more, and I am beginning with all new parts.

Slip-joint pliers are a good tool to have nearby. An adjustable wrench and a screwdriver may be needed, but it happened that I did not use them on this project. A sealant of some type will also be required. Shown is a container of plumber's putty. As I was in the middle of replacing the pop-up assembly I discovered that my plumber's putty has a warning label that says it is not to be used with marble or plastic. I ran to a store to get some silicone sealant formulated for use in the bathroom, including with plastics.

Step 2: What Goes Wrong

It is tempting to think something merely separated from another part and you can restore the function of the stopper by manipulating the operating rod while holding the stopper in place or twisting it somehow. See the photo. In reality parts have either broken or badly deteriorated from rust and will need to be replaced.

Step 3: First Steps

There are instructions on the pop-up assembly package, but I learned some things I wish I had known at the beginning. The instructions on the package I bought for this project say to shut off the water supply to the sink. That is not necessary, but a pan under the pipe connections and some paper towels nearby are a good idea.

In the photo I am removing the top retainer nut on the P-trap. I do not know why it is named that, but it always contains water in the low bend of the trap. That makes a seal to keep sewer vapors from coming into the house. If a house is left unoccupied for a long while, you may smell sewer gas. Just run water for a minute or two wherever there is a drain for water, and you will solve the problem.

The parts on this P-trap are plastic, and I really did not need the slip-joint pliers to loosen them. Some P-traps are chrome-plated brass, and pliers or a wrench would be necessary to loosen the retaining nuts. With a catch pan under the P-trap, loosen both retainer nuts and place the P-trap in the pan.

Step 4: Disconnect the Lifting Rod Assembly

Pinch the ends of the C-shaped retainer clip together and slide off the end of the linkage rod. See the text boxes.

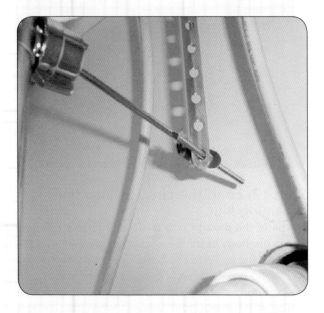

Step 5: Loosen the Pop-Up Assembly Retaining Nut

The old pop-up assembly is metal and has a brass retaining nut under the sink. Loosen it with the pliers.

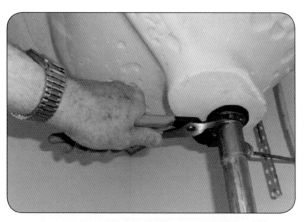

Step 6: Remove the Finished Flange

Once the pop-up assembly nut is loose a few turns, rock the pop-up assembly back and forth to loosen the old sealant below the finished flange at the bottom of the sink. Push up on the pop-up assembly and grasp the finished flange with a pair of pliers. Hold it and turn the body of the pop-up assembly below to unscrew it from the finished flange.

Step 7: The Old Sealant

This is what you will see when the finished flange is unscrewed from the body of the pop-up assembly. The old sealant cracks and breaks away easily. Remove all of it. The old finished flange will not be needed. Discard it.

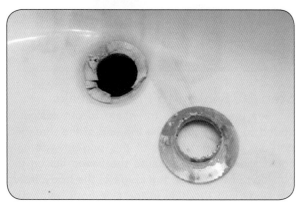

Step 8: Surprise!

Something will always be as it should not be. The old metal finished flange screwed into threads on the inside of the body of the pop-up assembly. But, the new chrome-plated plastic finished flange screws onto threads on the outside of the pop-up assembly. The diameter of the threaded area on the new finished flange is too great to slip into the hole for it in the bottom of the sink. Fortunately, there is a plastic ring molded into the bottom of the sink. I trimmed it with a sharp knife and then the finished flange fit the hole just fine.

Step 9: Apply Sealant to the Flange

Apply a bead of sealant around the finished flange where it will contact the sink. Press it into the hole and down on the sink. Check to be sure there is enough sealant and no gaps or air pockets. Add more sealant if needed. You will need to clean away excess sealant later. Do not use more than necessary.

Step 10: Sealant to Prevent Leaks

See the text boxes for where to put sealant. I added some sealant at the top end of the threaded portion, too. The design of this pop-up assembly could allow leakage because the flange fits on the outside rather than on the inside of the body. Insert the body into the hole in the sink from below the

sink. Screw the body onto the finished flange without disturbing the finished flange and its seal. Hold the body of the pop-up assembly so the fitting for the linkage points toward the rear of the sink—that is, the side toward the wall.

Step 11: Tighten the Body Nut

Tighten the nut on the pop-up assembly body. This plastic one is made to tighten sufficiently with fingers only and no pliers. Tighten the body nut as tightly as your fingers can tighten it. Be careful that the body of the pop-up assembly does not rotate out of its position. Hold it firmly while tightening.

Step 12: Load the Linkage into the Retaining Nut

Slide the linkage into the nut. There is a Teflon ring in the body of the pop-up assembly that is a seal between the ball and the body. Feel to make certain it is still in place. It has a concave indentation to fit the ball on the linkage rod. There is also a piece of similar white plastic that falls out when the linkage retaining nut is removed from the body. You can just see it inside the nut visible in the photo. If your pop-up assembly is metal, be careful not to tighten the nut too much with a pair of pliers. Part of the metal nut is a thin washer mounted in the nut and it can push out.

Once it does, you will have difficulty making the nut hold the ball on the linkage rod so there are no leaks. In some ways, the plastic pop-up assembly kit is an advantage over the metal.

Step 13: Assemble

Drop the new drain plug into the hole in the finished flange from the top of the sink. Place the linkage rod into its hole and catch the loop at the bottom of the drain plug with the rod. Screw the linkage retaining nut onto its place on the body of the pop-up assembly. With the end of the linkage rod in its most downward position, choose the hole in the lift-rod assembly that best fits it. Slide the hole over the end of the linkage rod with the springy C-retaining-clip. (There was nothing wrong with the old lift-rod assembly, not even a scuff on the chrome. I chose to save some work and leave it in place. I can save the new lift rod assembly parts or use them as raw materials in some project.)

Pull up on the lift-rod knob as if you were using the sink. Does the stopper in the sink pull down as far as it can go to seal? If not, slide the springy C-clip toward the body of the pop-up assembly until it does pull down and seal.

Step 14: Install the P-Trap

Remove the plastic compression washer and nut for the P-trap from the old pop-up assembly. Place the nut and compression washer on the new pop-up assembly. Fit the P-trap and screw both of its nuts in place. Tighten appropriately.

Step 15: Finish

Remove the blue protective film. Clean up any extra sealant around finished edges. Check for leaks under the sink. Enjoy your new, working drain plug.

Removing a Toilet

By PaleoPunk

http://www.instructables.com/id/Removing-a-Toilet-Home-Improvment/

When your toilet is out of date or you're updating your bathroom, replacing the toilet can be huge barrier for the do-it-yourself home improver. This particular bathroom is in desperate need of an update.

Step 1: What You Will Need

The only tool you NEED is a crescent wrench or a pair of pliers.

Optional tools. . .
- Gloves (promoting cleanliness)
- Plastic grocery bags
- Paint scraper (for scraping wax seal)

Step 2: Empty the Bowl

First, you need to turn off the water supply to the toilet. There should be a knob connected to a hose connected to the toilet tank.

After the water has been turned off, disconnect the hose from the shut-off knob. There will be a nut connecting the two pieces. (After the nut has been removed you may have to pull hard to get the hose out.)

It is easier to see the next step if you remove the top of the toilet.

Now, flush the toilet. The tank should be mostly empty after flushing.

The nasty part is ladling/scooping out the remaining water in the bowl. Any residual water can be absorbed with a sponge.

Step 3: Detach from Floor

In this step you will need a wrench to unscrew bolts. These bolts will be at the base on either side of the bowl. Unscrew the nuts. The bolts themselves will remain upright, connected to the floor.

Step 5: Preparing for the New Toilet

First you need to scrape off the old wax seal. Don't get it on your hands or clothes, because it is really hard to clean off.

To protect your tools, pets, etc. take a wad of old plastic grocery bags and fill the top of the hole. (This is removed before you insert the new toilet.)

Step 4: Rock the Bowl

Straddle the bowl and rock side to side until the wax seal under the toilet breaks. When the toilet rocks freely, the seal is broken.

To remove the toilet, lift it straight off the bolts. You will be left with a disgusting wax seal, a metal collar, two bolts, and a big hole.

I am completely remodeling my bathroom, and the old toilet was ugly and wasted a lot of water, so I decided to replace it with a new, water-efficient model. Water-efficient models may be a little more expensive on upfront costs, but the long-term savings for the planet and your water bill are worth it.

Step 1: What You Need
- A toilet with any nuts, bolts, etc. that come with it
- A wax toilet seal (it's round, made of wax, and is usually easy to find in the plumbing section of any store that also sells toilets)
- A crescent wrench
- A toilet seat/lid (if your toilet doesn't come with one. Toilets usually have very standard sizes, just remember to check what type of bowl your new toilet has)

Step 2: Setting in the Bowl
Carefully turn the toilet upside down. Squish the wax ring around the hole, being careful to make sure it seals all the way around. This is important if you

don't want the contents of the toilet flowing over the floor.

Around the drain hole there will be a metal ring attached directly to the floor with two bolts sticking up. If you are replacing the toilet, it is usually fine to reuse those bolts.

Being careful not to drop the toilet, turn it back over, setting it on the bolts (there will be holes in the base of the toilet for them).

Now, put the nut and washer on the bolt. Do not over tighten or the toilet will break. Tighten nuts until snug. Repeat on the other side.

Step 3: The Tank

On many modern toilets the inner workings of the tanks are pre-installed, so all you have to do is set the tank on the bowl and attach the hose for water. The water hose is attached to a valve that will be off. It should be fairly obvious where to attach the hose on the back of the toilet (it will just screw on). Turn the valve on.

Congratulations, your toilet should work now.

Step 4: The Lid

Installing a toilet lid is quite simple. Set the lid on the bowl of the toilet. The holes in the hinge of the seat/lid should line up with the holes in the toilet. The lid should have two bolts that fit in the holes previously mentioned. Screw on the nuts snugly but not too tightly. Snap the cover over the head of the bolt.

If you've done everything right, your toilet is now fully functional!

Add a Shower to Your Toilet

By jeff-o

http://www.instructables.com/id/Add-a-Shower-to-your-Toilet/

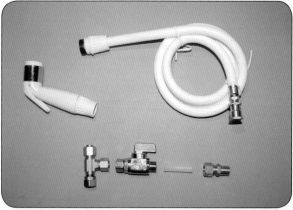

Have I got your attention? It's not what you're thinking, and if you have kids in diapers you may wonder why you didn't do this sooner! Disposable diapers are very hard on the environment. That's why my wife and I use cloth diapers. Instead of sending pounds and pounds of soiled diapers to the dump every week, we simply wash the diapers in the washing machine. However, you can't just dump the dirty diaper directly into the machine! That would be truly nasty. You have to clean off the majority of the solid waste before it goes into the laundry. So why not spray it off—directly into the toilet?

Step 1: Parts and Tools

If you've made it to the first step you must be a parent, or plan to be. For those who have never had to change a baby poop, it ranges in texture from a thin paste to a solid lump. What we're going to do is splice a hand-held kitchen sprayer into the water line that feeds the toilet. The sprayer can be used to wash the larger chunks of poop into the toilet, where they can be flushed away. The diaper can then be put into the wash.

Here are the parts and tools you'll need:
- T-junction with one male ⅜" compression joint and two female ⅜" compression joints
- Valve with ⅜" compression joints (optional)
- ⅜" compression to ¼" threaded pipe joint adapter
- Kitchen sprayer wand with a ¼" connector
- 2"-long piece of ⅜" OD plastic tubing
- Stick-on hook (optional)

Step 2: Assembly, Part One

I had a heck of a time trying to find an adapter that converted a compression fitting to a regular threaded pipe. In the end I had to settle with using a short piece of tubing. If you can rig up the splice using fewer parts, then do so!

The first few pieces can be put together "on the bench." Take the T junction and remove the nut from both the long and short ends. Set them aside for later. Compression fittings don't need plumber's tape, so screw the valve directly on to the short end of the T junction. Tighten it with a wrench. Make sure that the valve lever is pointing up, as shown. Take one of the nuts and slide it onto the end of the short piece of tubing. Tighten the nut onto the output of the valve using a wrench. Remove the nut from the compression fitting to ¼" adapter and slide it onto the free end of the tube. Next, tighten the nut onto the adapter. You may need to use two wrenches, turned in opposite directions, to properly tighten the nut.

Now it's time to use the plumber's tape. Wrap a few layers onto the free end of the adapter and screw on the kitchen sprayer hose. My hose actually had another adapter; seal this junction with plumber's tape as well, if there is one. Finally, screw the sprayer head onto the other end of the sprayer hose.

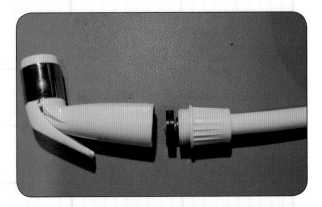

Step 3: Assembly, Part Two

It's time to move things to the bathroom. Locate the short piece of flexible hose that carries water from the valve to the toilet. Turn off the valve (turn it fully clockwise) and then flush the toilet. This will drain the water from the tank. With a rag under the valve, unscrew the hose from the valve and allow any remaining water in the hose to drain out. Grab the splice you created in the previous step and screw it onto the output of the valve. Make sure it's good and tight. Since this is a compression fitting, you won't need to use plumber's tape. Now screw the hose from the toilet onto the top of the T-junction.

That's it! You'll probably want to add a hook somewhere for the sprayer. It will help make everything a bit neater, and you won't trip over the hose when you stumble half asleep into the bathroom in the morning.

Step 4: Using the Toilet Sprayer

With everything hooked up, turn on the main valve that comes out of the wall. Check to make sure there aren't any leaks. Now, turn on the valve for the sprayer and again check for leaks. Obviously, if there are any leaks you should track them down and fix them—usually by tightening things up a bit more.

Using the sprayer is pretty straightforward. Simply hold the poopy diaper inside the toilet bowl and spray it off. Always aim downward, and work from the top to the bottom. You may want to wear gloves, but I don't. I just wash my hands after I'm finished. When the diaper is rinsed off, plop it in a bucket with all the other rinsed diapers. Flush the poops down the toilet and rinse off the sprayer head in the sink. Close the valve for the sprayer each time you're finished using it. (The valve is technically optional, though I do recommend it. If you have a toddler, they will almost definitely find the hose and try to use it. The valve will hopefully prevent them from filling the bathroom with a foot of water.)

And there you have it! No wiping, no scrubbing, and no garbage bins filled with guacamole poop.

Hack a Toilet for Free Water

By gregorylavoie

http://www.instructables.com/id/Hack-a-Toilet-for-free-water./

This is a step–by-step description of the process of adding a sink to the top of a toilet, thus allowing the use of the clean water before it goes into the bowl.

Motivation

Water is a precious resource, and our everyday lives are immersed in consuming it. The average toilet uses excessive amounts of water. This hack allows you to minimize some of that water consumption. I wanted this Instructable to be simple enough that anyone could build it with basic tools and materials. I also tried to be material conscious with this project in that many of the materials are recycled from other things (sheet wood and copper tubing) or second hand (metal bowl), and that it is put together using screws and friction fittings, so when the sink has finished serving its purpose it can easily be taken apart and the parts can be recycled.

Step 1: Materials
- 9"×20" piece of sheet wood
- Small plastic funnel
- Copper tubing with ½" outside diameter

- Metal bowl approximately 8" diameter
- Four feet of vinyl tubing ⅛" inside diameter
- Four "L" brackets and small wood screws
- Scrap paper
- Silicone latex caulking glue
- Steel binding wire

Tools:
- Hand drill
- Jig saw
- ½" spade drill bit
- ⅛ " drill bit
- Center punch
- Sharpie
- Hole saw 3"
- X-Acto knife

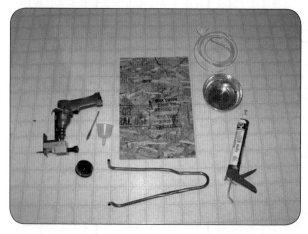

Step 2: Locate the Parts and Trace

Remove the lid from the toilet tank. Locate the overflow tube and gently remove the rubber tube going into the top of it. Take the small plastic funnel and stick it in the tube. Now take a straight edge and span it across the walls of the tank next to the funnel; mark the edge on the funnel. Now remove the funnel and lay a piece of paper of the tank. Trace out the walls and the location of the overflow pipe in relation to them. Next take the lid from the tank and trace it onto the sheet wood.

Step 3: Cut Out the Lid

Cut out the shape of the lid from the wood with a jig saw and clean up as necessary with sand paper. Now take the paper tracing off the tank and cut on inside wall line with scissors. Now center the tracing on the new wood lid; take the center punch and mark the center of overflow tube on the wood lid. Using this mark as center, drill a 3" diameter hole with the hole saw.

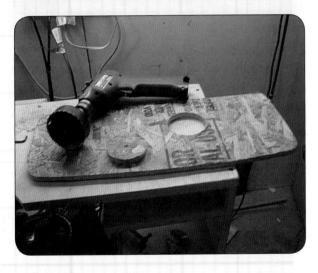

Step 4: Making the Sink

With a marker, extend the line on the funnel so that it goes all the way around and then cut on the line with an X-Acto knife. Now take the metal bowl and create drain holes in the center with a small drill bit, making sure the final drain is no bigger than the top of the freshly cut funnel. Next place the funnel on the bottom of the metal bowl and apply liberal amounts of caulking glue on the crack between the bowl and funnel.

Step 5: Faucet

The faucet is made from copper tubing bent into an upside down "J". To bend the tubing without kinking it, tightly wrap the wire around the section to be bent and carefully bend it with your hands, retightening the wire occasionally. Trim off the extra tubing with a tubing cutter. Drill a ½" hole with a spade bit, 3" away from the large hole in the wood lid. Force the long end of the copper "J" into the hole; friction should hold it in place.

Step 6: Bracket in Place

To keep the wood lid from sliding around on the tank you can attach brackets. To figure out where the brackets need to be, flip over the lid and center the paper tracing of the tank on it. The brackets should be against the outer edge and attach with small wood screws.

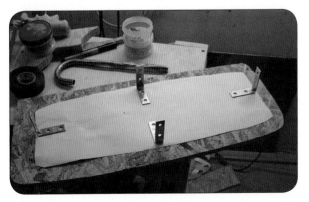

Step 7: Installation

Back inside the toilet tank, locate the rubber tube that was inside the overflow tube and follow it back to the float valve; pull it off. Now attach the 4" vinyl tubing. Push the other end of the vinyl tube through the bottom of the wood lid's ½" hole and up though the copper tube until just before it sticks out the other end of the copper tube. Now lower the new lid onto the tank making sure the vinyl tubing does not interfere with the internal mechanisms in the tank. Take the metal bowl with the funnel attached and make sure the glue is dry. Now look down the 3" hole in the lid and you should see the overflow tube. Take the bowl and funnel and lower it onto the hole; the funnel needs to go into the overflow tube.

Step 8: Finished

The sink is now complete. I would recommend putting some kind of waterproofing on the lid to protect the wood.

Shower Rack for a Claw Foot Tub

By Ronny Kraft (RonnyK)
http://www.instructables.com/id/Shower-Rack-for-a-Claw-Foot-Tub/

It's hard to find a shower rack that works for a claw foot tub because they generally are made to go around the shower neck. The shower neck on my claw foot is completely vertical so most racks just don't work. I had used the kind of rack that fits in the corner, but it got rusty, so I decided to have a go at making my own. It turned out to be a relatively cheap and easy alternative. The cool thing about this rack is that you can add whichever shape and type of basket you want and reposition at will.

Step 1: Supplies and Tools

Supplies:

- Four yards of chain: I got coated white to match the shower and in the hopes it wouldn't rust (about $6)
- Two U-clamps (about $1.50 each)
- Four quick links (mini carabiners; $.89 each)
- Two eye-and-hook turnbuckles (about $3 each)
- Nine feet of bendable wire (I used this to secure the back of the rack, if you find baskets that have a back, you don't need this; $3)
- And, of course, baskets! I searched high and low for the perfect baskets and ended up not finding quite what I wanted for the amount I wanted to spend (under $20 total) so I ended up settling for some kitchen racks from Home Depot. They were $7 and $4.

Tools:

- Pliers
- Adjustable wrench

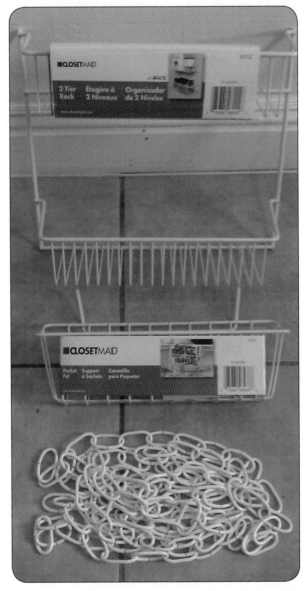

161

Step 2: Secure the Back of the Rack

If you find baskets that already have a back to them you can skip this step.

String the bendy wire around the back of the rack so that your shower things won't fall out. The wire I got was pretty stiff and stayed however I bent it, so this step was pretty easy.

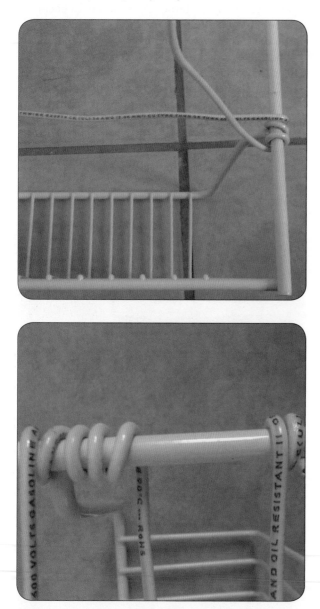

Step 3: Attach the Chain to the Curtain Rod

My shower rod forms a full rectangle and is anchored securely to the wall and ceiling. I attached the two chains to the bar that is opposite the shower head. If you wanted, you could really place it anywhere, such as in the corner. Just be sure to place the chains the same width apart as the basket/rack that will hold your shower stuff.

Use the two U-clamps to attach each end of the chain to the curtain rod.

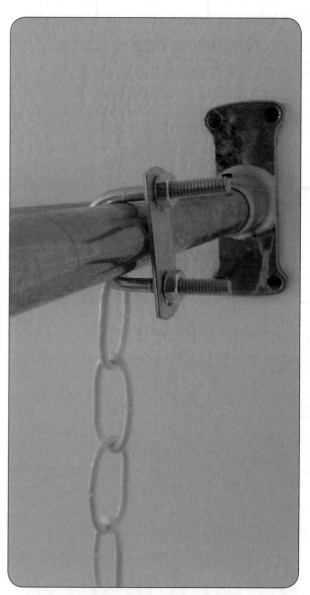

Step 4: Attach Chain to Tub

Now you're going to use the hooked turnbuckles to attach the chain securely to the lip of the tub. When you turn the middle part of a turnbuckle the eye loop and hook either unscrew or screw tighter at the same time. Start with the turnbuckles almost fully expanded as shown in the first photo.

Now put the hook end of the turnbuckle underneath the lip of the tub and hold it up so that you can see where you will need to separate the chain. See second photo. Do this for both sides of the chain. My shower rod is crooked so my chains ended up being different lengths.

Now it's time to pry open the chain links. I used pliers, an adjustable wrench, and my muscles. There are probably other ways to open chain links that won't scrape off as much of the coating as my method, but it worked. See third and fourth photo. Pry open the chain just enough to slip on the eye loop of the turnbuckle.

Slip on the expanded turnbuckle to the opened link. Now it's time to close the link back up. This is actually a little harder than opening it. I used pliers to squeeze the top and bottom of the chain together. See fifth photo. Do this on the other chain.

Put the hook under the lip of the tub and twist the middle part of the turnbuckle so that it tightens. Twist until the chain is taut, but no need to crazy. Do this for both chains.

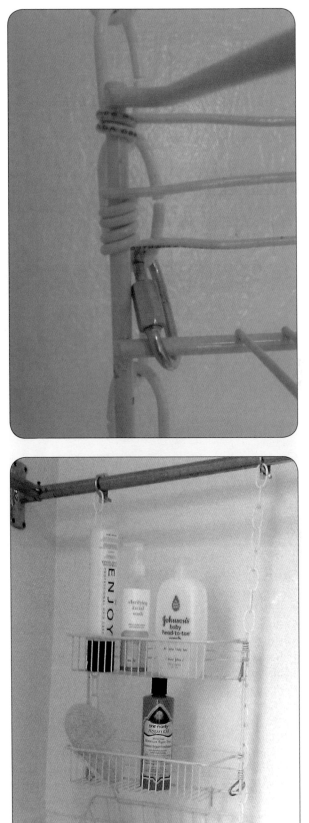

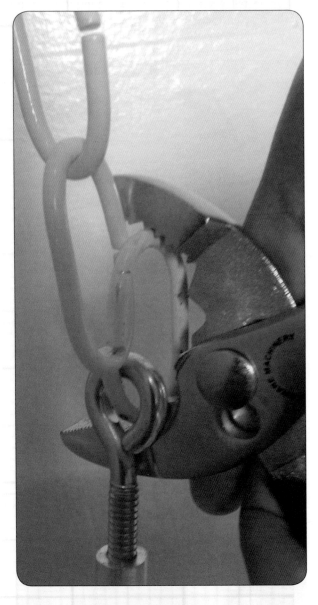

Step 5: Hang Up the Baskets/Racks

Last step! Attach whatever basket or rack you're using to the chains using the quick links (mini carabiners) shown in the first photo. The cool thing about this set up is that you can place the basket/racks at whatever height you want.

My little basket actually had hooks at the top, so I just attached it to the bottom of the bigger rack. Shown in second photo.

And, you're done!

Removing a Sink and Vanity

By PaleoPunk

http://www.instructables.com/id/Removing-a-Sink-and-Vanity-Home-Improvement/

This outdated bathroom is getting fixed up, and I decided to do it myself, gaining experience and saving money. Taking out the sink and vanity was very difficult, so this Instructable is to help any other do-it-yourself home improver's.

Step 1: What You Will Need

Tools you need. . .

- Crescent wrench
- Bucket
- Utility knife
- Screwdriver or electric drill

Tools you may want. . .

- Pry bar
- Hammer and chisel

Step 2: Shut Off Water

First, you need to shut off the water. This is important, unless you want your bathroom full of water. To shut off the water, there should be a knob (right tight = no water; left loose = water flowing). On most sinks there are two. Both need to be off.

Next, disconnect the hose from the shut-off valve. It will be connected by a nut; a crescent wrench works well for this.

If the valve leaks it is probably time to replace it. Also, if one leaks, the other will most likely start to leak soon too, so it's best to replace both.

To replace the valve you first need find the main water valve that shuts off the water to your entire house. The second picture below shows my house's valve.

Now, all you have to do is unscrew the nut and take the old valve to your local hardware store to find a new one. Either you'll be able to tell or a hardware store employee will be able to tell you which one is correct. You'll also need to buy plumber's tape.

To install, wrap the tape twice around the threads of the pipe and screw on the valve. Now, you can turn on your house's water.

Step 3: Disconnecting the Drain

To prevent a large puddle, place a bucket under the drain pipe.

Now, unscrew the nut at either end of the catch pipe.

There will a "drain assembly" that needs to be disassembled. There is a screw that needs to be loosened, and then the plug can be removed (see the second picture).

Step 4: Removing the Sink

First, cut away any caulk around the sink.

Then, remove the screws and brackets from under the sink. Be careful because the sink will fall through.

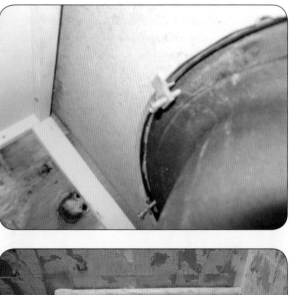

Step 5: Removing the Vanity

Start by unscrewing every screw in sight.

If the vanity doesn't fall apart, use a hammer or pry bar to tear it apart.

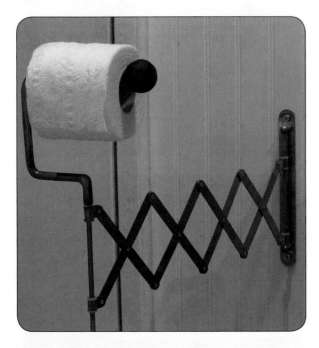

Step 1: Supplies and Tools

Supplies:

- 1 x IKEA FRACK extendable mirror
- 1 x thick fender washer, about ⅛" thick with a 2" to 3" diameter. Mine was 2 ¼".
- 1 x coupling nut, size 6.5mm. One that is ¼" will work in a pinch, but it is slightly smaller than the IKEA bolt on the base rod. You can reuse more of the mirror unit by snapping the swivel part of the mirror off of the nut attached to the mirror. It is only compression riveted on. I tested it myself and it was rather simple to pop out with a punch and hammer.
- 1 x screw that fits the coupling nut; this will be used to prevent slag from entering the nut. If you are careful you can skip this step, but slag loves to land in threaded components.
- 1 x length of steel rod ⅜" by at least 1 ½" long. The extra length facilitates in the bend, if done by hand. If you are frack'n strong or have a steel bender, go with the absolute minimum of 1".
- 1 x steel ball bearing, diameter of 1 ¼". You could go larger but it has to be able to slip easily through a roll of toilet paper.

Tools:

- Wire feed welder, MIG, TIG, or stick welder. I use an el-cheapo Princess Auto wire feed welder. I would recommend a MIG welder with full gas. None of that pesky slag to deal with.
- Bench clamp
- Angle grinder with a zip-cut abrasive cutting disk and a grinding disk. Ideal is a flap disk—it grinds but leaves a smooth finish. They are worth it!
- You may need a drill and drill bit that matches your rod diameter.
- A Dremel with a drum bit will help get in to the those tight spots to grind out some of the welds.
- And, of course, safety gear. A good welding mask, full face shield, ear protection, thick leather gloves, non-flammable hat if you like your hair, and a suitable location. Ventilation is key; welding makes nasty fumes and all that grinding can start a fire real quick. So be careful!

Step 2: Pre-Sanding and Bending

I started by removing the mirror with its swivel base from the extending base. It just un-screws. If you have bought this new, it is already off in the flat-pack and you're good to go!

Next I took my piece of metal rod and sanded it by hand with some sand paper till shiny smooth. If yours is nasty rough, rusted, or painted then grind it smooth with a grinding wheel or flap disk.

Your bar probably doesn't have a bend in it already like mine did, so this is what you will need to do: Insert about 2 ½" into the clamp, then tighten and bend it down hard and quick. The actual curved bend will use about ½" of length, making your first intended section 3" long.

Next move the rod in the bench clamp as shown in the pictures below so that at least 3 ½" is in the clamp. Tighten it up and grab hold, bending it down quick again. This bend will also use up about ½" of length. Trim the long piece down to about 5 ¼".

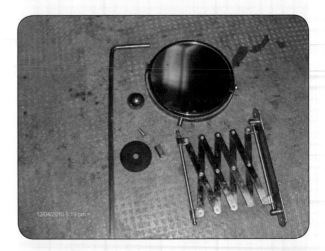

Step 3: Welding on a Fender Washer

Now grab your fender washer; if you are lucky like I was the hole was ⅜" already, same diameter as my rod. If you are not so lucky, throw it in a clamp and drill it to receive the ⅜" rod!

Next sand the washer till it is all shiny. Mine had that black protective coating on it.

Slip it over the long section of the rod just shy of the end by about ¾". The toilet paper end should have a minimum of 4".

Once in place, you're ready to weld. Just make sure to weld it on the side that faces the toilet paper. God forbid you weld kind of sketchy like, the toilet paper will cover it up.

Now tack weld it in place. You can weld all the way around the rod, or just use three simple tack welds. I did this to minimize the heat scoring on the other side. You can grind this off, but it is tricky at such a tight corner. Grind down the weld till acceptable to you, as well as any nasty, slaggy bits that have stuck to your nice shiny washer or rod. For those inner corners a Dremel with drum bit works great!

Step 4: Welding on the Ball

Put your bent rod in the clamp and center the tip on the ball as in the picture. Pressing the ball up against the rod, do a single tack weld. Take a look and make sure it is centered. If not, break the weld and repeat. Now weld all the way around. Grind it smooth.

Step 5: Welding on the Base

Insert the screw into the coupling nut to keep out rogue slag bits! Put the coupling nut into the bench clamp. Either hold the rod yourself or, safer and smarter, clamp it to the work table. Put a large tack weld to hold it in place. Now weld every seam! Grind it smooth.

Step 6: Put It Together for a Test Run

Screw the welded coupling nut on to the extension post. Screw it on to the wall, keeping in mind how it moves and how far it can extend. Slip a roll of toilet paper on and test it out! Nice, huh? Hey, what about the Sugru?

Go to the last step.

Step 7: Complete, with a Sugru Twist

Last, you may have noticed the proximity of the ball on the dispenser to the sink. Now I don't really think the steel will mar the porcelain, but it is possible, especially with kids around. The simple solution here is to wrap it in Sugru. Any color will work.

Take a small wad of Sugru out, about the size of a 1" ball. Flatten it smooth. Wrap just the ball end in the Sugru. Pat it smooth; a thin layer is all that is needed. Allow to dry 24 hours.

The Sugru also makes it easier for small hands to grab. Although it has not been tested, I thought this would be great in someone's bathroom that has to be wheelchair accessible. So much extra space is required for the manipulation of a wheelchair in a small area, I thought this would make things easier.

Foot Flusher

By Evan H. Nass (reykjavik)

http://www.instructables.com/id/Foot-Flusher/

Here's what you need:
- 2 paper towel rolls
- 1 wire hanger
- 1 Kiwi Express Shoe Shiner (or similar)
- 1 package of 3M (I used the "Utensil Hooks" but technically any one of these Command Strip products will work—more on that later)
- 1 to 5 rubber bands
- Some tape or glue

Optional things:
- Spray Paint to paint the paper towel rolls
- Some Goo Be Gone will help
  And that's it!

This is a simple little project that will allow you to easily and quickly set up a foot flusher. A foot flusher is a pedal that attaches to *any* toilet, thus allowing the user to flush the toilet with his foot only—allowing for a hands-free flush.

Step 1: Gathering Materials

This is an amazing thing. I thought it would just be a neat novelty but it turned out to be something that I can't imagine my life without now (especially with how cheap and easy it is to make). This will take you anywhere from 20 minutes to 2 hours to make depending on tangential issues (like aesthetics and how detailed you want to be). What I like most about this project is that you will most likely have all the pieces you need to make this, or, at most, you'll need to buy one $5 item that can be found almost anywhere.

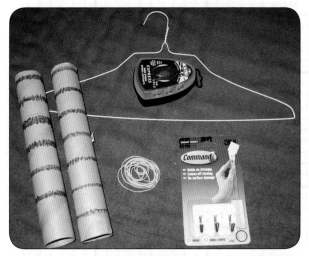

Step 2: The Paper Towel Rolls

Let's first work on the paper towel rolls because most likely, you will want to paint them so they look nice in your bathroom next to your toilet.

Note: Technically you do not have to use paper towel rolls. You can use a hollowed-out broom stick, shower curtain rod, or whatever you may have depending on your ambition. I like the rolls because they're cheap, easy, and paintable. However, you technically don't have to use anything, as the only purpose this serves is to hide the hanger. If you don't care that the hanger is visible then forget about this step and move on.

Assuming you do not want the wire hanger to show, you're going to want to cover it up with something nice. Take the two paper towel rolls and shove them into each other so you have one long tube. Squeezing it and mishaping it is fine, and you can technically glue it on the inside for extra support, but you don't have to as the spray paint is sticky and when drying will stick them together. Do this step first as the spray paint needs time to dry and will require numerous coats; each coat must dry before spraying a new one. This whole process will take maybe an hour, but you can do other things while waiting for it to dry. Spray paint is dangerous! Only use it if you are an adult and know how.

Step 3: The Wire Hanger

This step depends on how high up your toilet is. Remember that this project can be done on any type of toilet. I use a flushometer, but it will work on flush handles as well. Find the approximate distance between the floor and the handle and, using pliers, keep bending the hanger back and forth until the piece is straight and the excess has been taken off. Mine was approximately 22". It doesn't have to be exact as you can always bend it a bit later on. Also, it doesn't have to be perfectly straight either, as once the paper towel rolls are over it, you won't see the hanger at all.

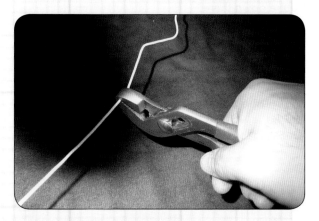

Step 4: The Foot Pedal

Okay, this is the most important part. You need to get a foot pedal. I had a hard time trying to figure out what would make a durable, yet cheap, foot pedal, and then I came across this Kiwi Shoe Shiner. I took the plastic case cover off and threw the rest away. I was left with a perfectly foot-shaped, durable piece of plastic. What's so great about this is that it costs approximately $4, and the tip of the foot pedal has a plastic ring meant to be used for placing on store shelves. We'll be using it to attach the wire hanger.

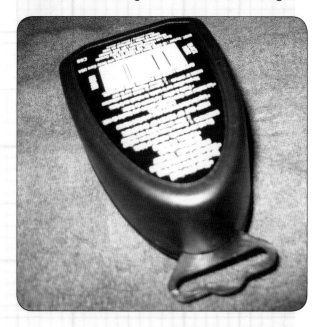

Step 5: Attaching the Wire Hanger to the Pedal and the Rubber Band

You're going to need some pliers or some really strong hands. What you need to do is place the wire hanger around that plastic ring and then close it off with some pliers. Take a look at the picture and you'll see exactly what I mean. In the picture there is still a bit of a gap. Don't have this—do as I say, not as I do. Make sure the hanger is entirely closed off.

On the other end of the hanger, place the strongest, thickest rubber band you have around a hook. Double up the rubber band as much as you can because it needs to stretch, but it also needs to pull. That is the key. This rubber band will be pulling the handle of your toilet. Once done, use pliers again to close it off.

Step 6: Almost Done!

This next step isn't necessary, but it makes everything look nicer. This step involves taking the sticker off the pedal. This is by far the hardest part of this hack. I suggest using something taken after refinement from a petroleum plant, like Goo Be Gone. This stuff is toxic, smells like crap, and within the next few years will probably develop brain-like tissue and take over the world. But for now, it's unbelievable stuff and really works. So go for it, but again, you don't have to do this step.

Step 7: Attaching the 3M Hook to the Pedal

This can be tricky, but fortunately there are numerous ways to do this. You must pop a hole in the back of the pedal to attach the 3M hook. This hook will be what sticks to the floor in your bathroom. Technically you don't have to use this. You can use glue or Velcro or whatever. But I like the fact that these can easily be stripped and taken off so if you mess up you can easily take it off and try again (you won't mess up, trust me).

To pop the hole you can either get a drill and drill through it really quickly or use a pin and then increase the size of the hole. What I did was I placed a screw driver in a flame until it got hot and then simply pressed it against the pedal. This melts the plastic so you can push it right through. Only do this if you are an adult and can handle it. It can be very dangerous so I don't recommend it—especially since there are other ways to achieve this. And remember that Goo Be Gone is probably flammable, so make sure you clean it off really well before putting it near any flame.

Once you have the hole, pop the 3M piece through it. Feel free to use a small piece of tape to hide the strip handle (see the pictures).

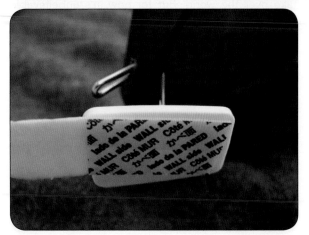

Step 8: You're Done—Last Step

Now you just have to put it all together. First place the paper towel roll over the wire hanger. Then go to your bathroom and attach the rubber band to the handle. This part is a bit tricky. You need the perfect compromise, and it may be tricky to find. What you need to do is make this pedal far away enough so that you're putting strain on the toilet handle, but not so far away where it becomes obtrusive and in the way of your daily bathroom routines. Play around with the area before sticking it to the ground, using your hand to see if it works from each position while you're down there.

Finally, once you have a nice, happy spot, follow the directions that 3M provides (cleaning the spot a bit, waiting an hour etc. I didn't follow those directions and neither will you, but I feel like I must say it.

TADA! You're done. You now have a $5–$10 foot flusher. Set them up in each bathroom. Once the lid is up you won't see the wire hanger, so it looks nice.

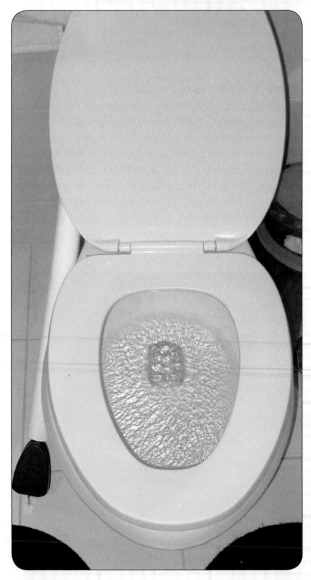

Sugru Toothbrush Holder

By andrea biffi
http://www.instructables.com/id/Sugru-toothbrush-holder/

Do you know how troublesome it is to try to make a toothbrush stay upright on a plane so that bristles don't touch the surface? I try to do that every morning and I still can't do that! So I usually keep my toothbrush in a cup, but it hardly fit into the bathroom cabinet, and it has to be cleaned very often. If you're accustomed to buy always the same toothbrush you can make this useful holder.

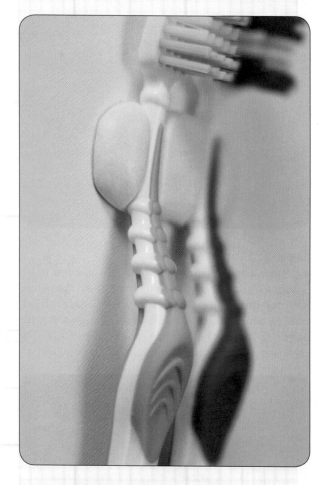

Step 1: The part list

You don't need too much tools, but maybe you've to steal in secret your girlfriend toothbrush, wait to trash your last one, or to open another brand new one, so to have two of them. Then of course you need a little package of Sugru. I've used white because is one of the last left ones from the eight coloured mini packs.

Step 2: The kneading

Open your Sugru pack cutting all around, and roll it until it reach a cylindrical shape about one inch wide. Work on a flat surface which you can keep wet and wash after removing it.

Step 3: The molding

Dampen the two toothbrushes and push them on the cylinder so it wrap the two handles in the narrow segment. The material has to cover the handles for about 10–15 percent of the width, so to keep them tight. If the handle are wet they shouldn't stick on the Sugru.

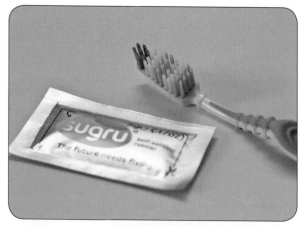

Step 4: The drying

Before the Sugru dries himself off, transfer everything on the vertical surface and push it so it will stick. If it will not stay still due to the toothbrush weight, wrap it with a tape, leaving toothbrushes in place, until everything is dry. pay attention it will not interfere with the internal shelf, as it almost happened to me ;-) After some time (I waited some hours) you can remove the two toothbrushes and verify the joints work properly. Now you've a very handy toothbrush holder, you don't need to become a professional tightrope walker to let the toothbrush remain clean, and you neither have to clean your bathroom cup every day!

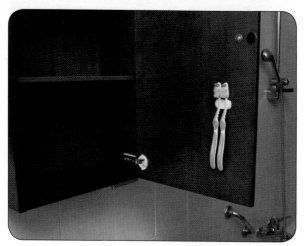

In this Instructable I'm going to show you how to make rainforest shower head in 10 minutes, with only a few simple things that you probably already have in your house. It doesn't require special skills. Be careful while working with stuff that gets hot, because it can be painful!

Step 1: Things You Will Need

Things used may vary; I used things that didn't have any purpose, but you can find other stuff that can work as well.

First of all, I used a 10-CDs box. Then you'll need a hot glue gun, some hose, one shower head (the one you use right now will work), needle, ruler, scalpel, candle, and some ordinary tools.

Step 2: Drawing Grid

What you need to do is draw a grid of circles and lines. The number of circles is not strictly defined, so it's up to you. The lines don't need to go deep into the plastic, since they are there only to guide you in making the holes in some order.

Step 3: Piercing Holes

Now when you have the grid, all you need to do is light a candle and heat up the needle on the flame. (Do not hold the needle with your fingers!) Then, quickly, while needle is hot, pierce through the clear plastic to make a hole in it. Repeat the process until you have made as many holes as you like.

Step 4: Making the Base

To make a base, you first need to cut off the piece on which the CDs go (the spindle). The black plastic is soft enough to do this with a scalpel. Then you'll need a piece of pipe, plastic or copper, or something else. Put that pipe through the hole in the black base and glue it so it is watertight. Be careful not to make it too long, because if it is too long you won't be able to close the CD box, and water won't be able to flow.

Step 5: Close the Box

Now you need to merge the clear plastic part and the black base. Just close them as a regular box and then glue them together, making sure it is waterproof.

Step 6: The Hose

I used a 1 cm diameter hose, but you can use other sizes, under condition that its inner diameter isn't smaller than your shower hose is. Attach it to the rainforest head on one end. On the other end, you need to cut the regular shower and use its lower part, since it has screws on it and can be screwed on to a regular shower hose. Once you cut it, glue together the hose and the part of regular shower you just cut. It should be watertight.

I did this so I can put my rainforest shower head on and off, and can choose between regular shower and this one.

Step 7: Structure

Only thing left to do is to add some structure to the project, since it needs something to hold it in position. I found a metal tube that I used, but anything else that can hold the weight of the shower will work. Glue it to the part of the regular shower and to the head. You might want to use something that is both strong but bendable, because you might want to adjust head's position.

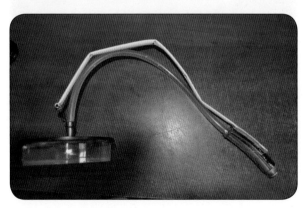

Step 8: Result

That should be it. You made a rainforest showerhead for free. Now you can beat the heat of the summer with long, relaxing showers. I hope you like it!

Copper Pipe Towel Rail

By Matt Jackson (flambewomble)

http://www.instructables.com/id/Copper-Pipe-Towel-Rail/

This is my method for building a new towel rail for the bathroom.

Time: 1.5 hours cutting pipe; 1.5 hours soldering pipe; 1 hour cleaning and polishing; 0.5 hours fixing to wall; total time was 4.5 hours

Step 1: Materials
- 6m of 15mm copper pipe
- Blow torch (for soldering)
- 26 elbow joints
- 18 T-joints
- Wire wool
- Flux
- Metal polish
- "Pacman"-shaped copper pipe cutter
- Ruler

Step 2: Cutting

The first thing to do was pipe cutting. I wanted to hold 10 towels, so that would mean 11 shelves. Using the 15mm pipe cutter, I cut 42 x 10cm sections and 11 x 20cm sections of pipe (this took about an hour).

Step 3: Dry-Fitting

I then dry-fitted the whole thing to check that the design would work and that all the sections lined up.

Step 4: Soldering

I then soldered the upright/vertical sections (which were 10 x 10cm sections joined by T-joints and an elbow at each end) on some very flat slate tiles and made sure they were very straight. I inserted the 10cm pieces that came out of the right angles of the T-joints, being very careful to make sure it was all true. I then soldered the joints.

Next I did the other upright, making sure it lined up with the first one (and was straight).

Step 5: Assembly

I then inserted the 20cm pieces (the "shelves") to join it all together, checking for straightness along the way. The soldering was pretty easy—just clean pipe ends, add a smear of flux, flux the joint, insert shelving pieces, and apply copious heat!

Then I had to let it cool naturally, and I checked the joints. If yours are still loose, try again!

Step 6: Cleaning

I finished it off by cleaning up the oxidization from the blow torch with wire wool and then gave it a quick polish.

Note: As predicted, the copper tarnished pretty quickly, and although I liked this look, I decided to treat the metal (to avoid any contamination getting on clean towels). I bought a stainless steel kit. This is a very easy fix. Polish the metal, wipe with the supplied degreaser, then wipe on the self-annealing polymer coat.

174

Here's a very simple project anyone can do with very few tools and materials. Although many of you will think this tube shape is not really practical for a shelf, and you wouldn't be wrong, it's very eye catching and most certainly won't go unnoticed. It's kind of "anti-shelf," meaning it is modular and personalized. You can make them in pairs like I did, but you can also play with assembly and composition in any way you like. I chose bathroom and toilet, but it can be "installed" all around the house—the kids' room would definitely be a good choice.

Step 1: Tools and Materials

I've done the whole project without the power tools, but if you have access to bigger circular saws (table ones) you'll slice your tube faster, cleaner, and more precisely. Many of you will ask where to find this cardboard tube thingy—mine came as a packaging case for decorative aluminum picture moldings. You can also use plastic water pipes or something like that.

Tools:
- A really good hand saw (or electric table one)
- Scalpel
- Paint brush
- Sandpaper

Materials:
- A cardboard (or plastic) tube 22 cm (or bigger) in diameter
- Concrete paint
- Stronger mounting glue (kit)

Step 2: Paint and Assembly

I cut my tube into 8 cm and 16 cm slices, but you are free to adjust this to your needs. Then I sanded the edges, but I did not bother to much—I wanted to get that rough metal look, like the one you can see in shipyards. The color inspiration also came from the same place. Also, two to three layers of concrete paint took care of surface roughness.

I also tried to get that "metal weld"–like connection between two tubes. I used Pattex strong montage glue to make that "weld" long lasting and durable.

Step 3: The Final Result

The final result is this here. Most of you will say it's not practical, but others will love this abstract anti-shelf. Enjoy and geek on!

Living Room

Fix Your Couch

Make an Armchair out of a Coffee Table

Make a TV Cabinet Fit Its Electronics

Fix a Snag in a Rug

How to Fix a Broken Slat on Blinds

Refinishing a Hardwood Staircase

Fix a Weak Battery-Door Catch

Upgrade Your Old Ceiling Fan

Four Lives of a Modern Side Table

Hack a Mattress into a Couch

Home Theater Projector Screen
on a Budget

Coffee Table Upgrade

Build and Upholster an Oversized Couch

New Living Room Pallet Table
for Letting House

Rain-Gutter Book Shelves

3D Hardwood Floor

Corner Hammock Shelf

What is the main thing that defines a living room? The furniture, and more specifically the seating! If you have too many tables, you can learn how to fix that by turning one into a comfy chair. And don't forget to clean up all that clutter and get some shelving in place!

Make sure you don't ignore what's in front of you. Fix up those snags in the carpet and quit turning over your cushions to hide tears and stains when you can just fix them!

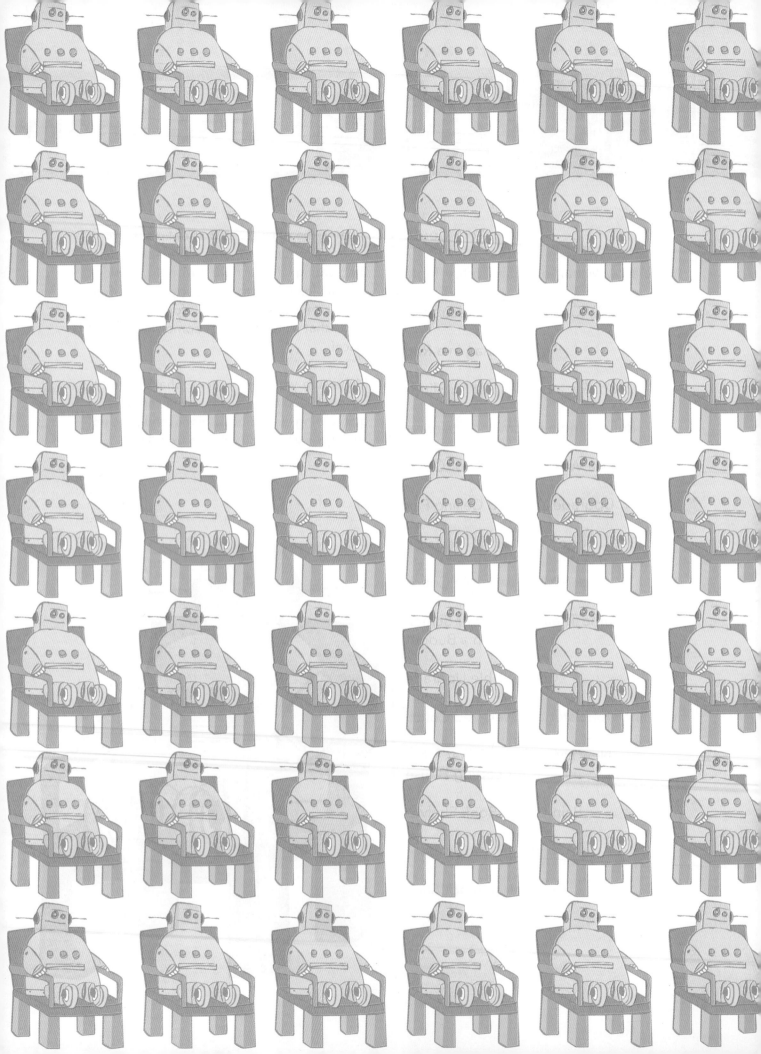

Fix Your Couch

By wizgirl

http://www.instructables.com/id/Fix-Your-Couch/

Sometimes bad things happen to good couches . . . very, very bad things. Reupholstering is awesome, but hard. If your couch cushions are ripped, but the rest of your couch is intact, why replace everything? This Instructable offers an easier solution.

Note: O Skylos Rex (pictured) is innocent. He was used for re-enactment of a crime committed by another dog.

Step 1: Damage Removal

The level of destruction exerted on your couch is will determine how much must be replaced. In this case, only the tops of the cushions were . . . eaten. First, remove the cover from the cushions. Next, using a seam ripper, remove the damaged portions of the cushions. Set the removed portions aside, as you will use these as a pattern for the replacement fabric.

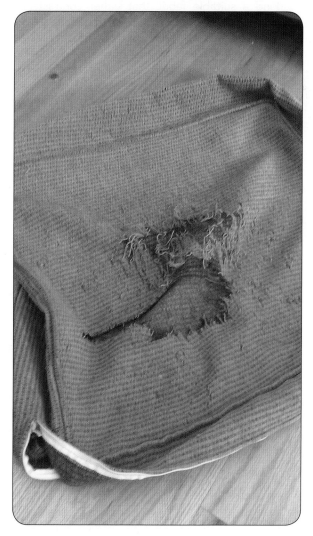

Step 3: Good Job

You kept your couch out of landfill! There is rarely a reason to buy something new; you can fix what you've got and make it cooler than something you could find in the store.

Step 2: The Cover Up

Find a suitable fabric that either contrasts or matches your couch. Use your imagination. If you have enough undamaged fabric from the old pieces, consider sewing some of the new and old fabric together to create an interesting pattern. This is a great opportunity to customize your couch. Using the removed, damaged fabric as a pattern, cut new pieces of fabric. Turn the couch cushion inside-out. Pin the replacement fabric in place and sew around the edges. Be sure that patterns face the same direction when fixing couches with multiple cushions.

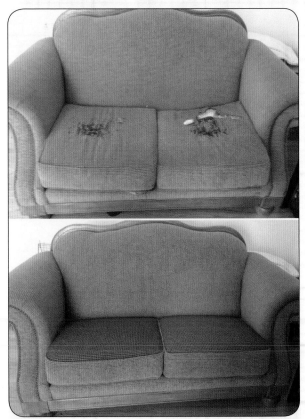

Make an Armchair out of a Coffee Table

By Linda Bellosi (lindarose92)
http://www.instructables.com/id/Make-an-Armchair-out-of-aCoffee-Table/

Some days ago I was visiting a local store when I noticed a beautiful octagonal chair that almost looked like a hand. At first I didn't even think that I could make one, but a few days later I found a ruined coffee table in my basement. I'd had it in the living room for years but I had since completely forgotten about it. Because of its octagonal shape, it immediately reminded me of that chair I saw in the store. I knew this would be one of the hardest things I had ever tried to do, but I thought, "Why not?" So I took advantage of this hot weather to spend some time in the basement working on this chair, and this is the result!

Step 1: Prepare the Table

My coffee table has a triangle piece at the bottom of its legs, and as you can see from the picture, the edges are a bit beat up. I thought that it would have been useful to keep this level on my future chair, so I removed it for a while and cut its edges a little to give it a regular shape again, then I put it back where it was once I'd painted it.

The first thing I did was putting a layer of primer for wood on the triangle and on the legs of my table. This paint helps the final color hold on a very smooth piece of wood. You could actually sand it a little with sandpaper instead, but doing this on a very curvy surface is not easy at all. For this reason, I used this special paint for wood and let it dry. I didn't do this on the whole table because I knew that I was going to upholster the rest later.

Step 2: Paint the Table

Once the primer is dry, you can remove the excess and make it smoother using a fine steel wool. You could use a fine sandpaper but, again, steel wool is much easier to use on curves. After doing that, you can finally paint on the white paint with a regular varnish—I used a beige/cream color. You may need to use more than one layer of paint this time; it depends on how well your varnish covers the wood. In this case, always remember to wait for the previous layer to dry before painting on it again. When you finally decide that the wood is completely covered, let it dry for the last time!

Step 4: Glue the Foam

Before covering the seat, we need to secure the foam to the table to make sure that it doesn't move. What you need here is a specific glue for foam—I think it's *epoxy* in English, but I am not too sure about this. Anyway, I didn't have this glue the day I worked on my chair so I tried to use white wood glue. I spread it on the table and placed it upside down on the octagonal foam that I had cut. I let it dry for a night . . . It worked!

Step 3: Cut the Foam

It's time to begin the upholstery part! Lay a big piece of thick upholstery foam on a table. It must be bigger than your coffee table because this will become the seat. Mine was 10cm thick (3.93") but you can use a thicker or a thinner one. It doesn't really matter except for one thing: the thicker it is, the harder the stapling of the whole seat will be later. Now place your coffee table upside down on the upholstery foam and trace its outline on the foam, making it about 1cm bigger (0.39") than the table. Remove the table and cut the foam following the outline you traced. I used a special foam cutter, but you can use whatever you have or you feel more comfortable with. I don't recommend using scissors (even big ones) because the cut will not be accurate on thick foam. You can normally use them if your foam is thin.

Step 5: Cover the Seat

It's time to cover the seat. I used red artificial leather, but this can be done using any other kind of fabric. Cut a piece of fabric big enough to cover the whole foam and reach the wood behind. Lay your piece of fabric upside down on a table and place your coffee table in the middle of it with the foam facing the back of the fabric. Start stapling the opposite sides of the fabric to the wood, always pulling it enough to keep it tight. If you are using artificial leather like I did, be careful not to pull it too much because it can easily break where the staples are. In case you are using another kind of fabric, pull it as much as you can: the result will be better. Continue to staple all along the eight sides.

Step 6: The Seat Is Almost Ready . . .

After stapling the sides, there are all the angles left . . . don't panic! Actually, the angles that need to look better are the ones that will be at the front of your chair, and there are only two of those! The others will be hidden later. Because my coffee table has three legs, I figured that the front side of my chair would be the one that has a leg right in the middle. This way the chair will be steady when I sit on it. So, considering your front side, continue to pull the fabric around the two angles from the adjacent sides and staple them. Now fold the left fabric at the front and staple it too. I am sure it's much easier to understand while looking at the pictures. All this would have been easier if the upholstery foam was thinner. Continue to staple the other angles the way you prefer; as I said before, they will be hidden so it doesn't matter too much. When you are finally done, cut the excess fabric. The seat is done!

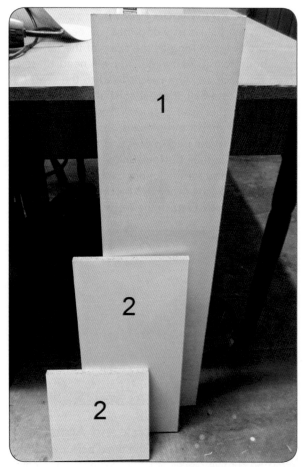

Step 7: The Back and the Arms

Let's start to prepare the back and the arms of the chair now: you need three pieces of wood for the back and two for the arms. As I've already said, my coffee table has only three legs, so I decided to make it more stable adding a fourth "leg" in the back. My idea was to make the central back part of the chair long enough to touch the floor. I wanted to make the whole back this way, but the chair would have become way too heavy. I wanted the back of my chair to be 40cm tall (15.74"). Plus I had to consider about 4cm (1.57") for the seat height because these pieces would be fixed to the back of the seat—you'll understand better later. So two pieces of the back are 44cm tall (17.32"), and the longest one is exactly like that plus the distance to reach the floor. It's much easier to do than to explain! The arms are shorter than the back, so I made them 24cm tall (9.44")—20cm + 4cm for the seat bottom they will be attached to. Their width is as long as the coffee table sides.

Step 8: Foam for the Back and Arms

Just like you did for the seat, you need to cut pieces of upholstery foam for the back and the arms. So cut three big foam rectangles of the same measures of the back plus 1cm (0.39") on each side (a little more at the top, if possible), and remember not to consider the 4cm (1.57 inches) in excess at the bottom—these must remain foam-free. Do the same for the arms. When you finally have all the pieces of foam, spread the glue on the wood and glue the foam to them. Do the same for the two arms. I used a thinner foam for them, but you can continue to use the thick one if you prefer. After everything is dry, staple the tip of the foam to the top of the wood back to give it a round shape.

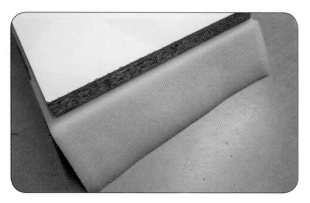

Step 9: Extra Wood Pieces

The last pieces of wood that you need for your chair are strips as long as the sides of the table and are about 2cm (2.78") wide. You will need these to keep the back and arm pieces fixed to the seat. Cut the edges as a half triangle so that they can easily face each other (see pictures). You'll need five of these. Now make three holes through them and attach them to the back pieces and arm pieces using screws, right at their bottom, on the same side where the foam is. And for the longer back piece, you need to place it near the other two pieces to know exactly where you have to attach the wood strip.

Step 10: Cover the Back and Arms

Now you have to cover the three back pieces and arms. So cut five pieces of fabric, big enough to cover each of the backs and arms. Lay one of them upside down at the center of the fabric and start to staple all around it, always pulling a little, and proceed just like you did for the seat. Do this for all your pieces. The only difference for the arms is that I decided to cover one angle of the bottoms too because they will be visible once they will be fixed to the seat. Make sure that they are opposite angles because one arm will be facing the other. I covered the left angle for the left arm and the right angle for the right arm. I admit that this step is a little hard to do if you, like me, are not a real upholsterer. You need patience because artificial leather easily breaks as you staple it, plus you need to make sure that there are no bad looking "waves" at the front. You may need to remove staples once in a while (I often did actually), but I can assure you that it's not impossible!

Step 11: Put Everything Together!

The hardest part is over . . . It's time to assemble the chair! The first thing I did is to temporarily attach all pieces to the seat using long nails in the back at the bottom. I started placing the longest one of the three backs on the opposite side of where the front of my seat was. After that, I added the other two ones next to the first one, and finally, the arms facing each other on two opposite sides. When you've finished placing all the pieces the way they should be and you are satisfied, secure them with screws at their bottom, where you added the extra wood strips, turning the chair upside down. I also added four iron bars that join the pieces together in the back, always using screws. This way I am sure that they can't move anymore. Your whole chair is finally steady!

Step 12: The Arms and Back

The last big thing you have to do is to cover the back of the chair with more fabric. Cut a big piece of fabric that will cover the whole back, including the central back/leg piece, and two smaller pieces to cover the back of the arms. Make sure to cut them bigger than the actual measure, especially the pieces for the arms, as they must be much larger than they actually are.

Let's start with the arms. Staple one edge of the fabric upside down at the top of the arm back, as you can see in the picture. Cut two strips out of cardboard, just a little shorter than the arm's width. Now staple one of these strips to the fabric you just stapled, but make sure that it's straight and parallel to the top of the arm. Fold down the fabric, pull it a little, and staple it to the bottom of the arm, where nobody can see it. The fabric on the side that meets the other back piece must be stapled on the back of it so that it will be hidden after you cover that other part too. The other side doesn't meet any other piece so just staple on the side. We will hide it later. The trick of the cardboard gives a good and finished effect so that the staples will be hidden. Do the same for the back of the other arm.

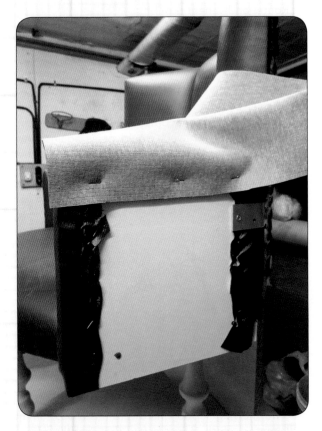

Step 13: The Back's Back

Cover the rest of the chair just like you did for the arms, except that it's one whole piece of fabric this time. Staple into the back when it's possible, and when it's not, simply staple on the side. Look at the pictures to understand how I covered the back and leg. You will have to fold the excessive fabric on the sides of the leg and staple them on the back (I actually cut some out too because it was too much).

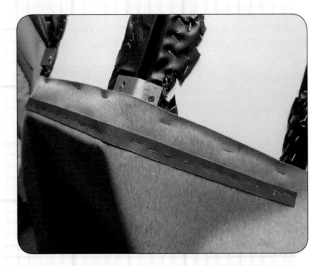

Step 14: Cover the Leg

You probably have noticed that the inside of the leg has still not been covered. You could leave it that way if you prefer, but it's visible, so it's better to cover that part too. Simply cut another piece of fabric, lay it on the wood and staple all around it. When you are done, cut all the excessive fabric on the sides, trying to keep the cut as close to the staples as possible. It will be easier to hide this way. Do the same on the whole chair if you still have excessive fabric left.

Step 15: Finishing Touch . . .

Now the last part . . . Hide all the visible staples by gluing strips of trimmings on them, all along the sides. Remember to do this on the back of the leg too. It will become just like a frame all around it. I used hot glue for this and it worked perfectly. I am proud to announce that your chair is finished! All you have to do now is try it. I can't tell you enough how comfortable it is!

Make a TV Cabinet Fit Its Electronics

By Phil B

http://www.instructables.com/id/Make-A-TV-Cabinet-Fit-Its-Electronics/

- Lead pencil
- Tape measure
- Masking tape
- Hole saw
- Hot-glue gun
- Router and veneer trim bit
- Workmate
- Belt sander
- Sandpaper

This is the only TV cabinet my wife could find to match the other furniture in our living room. She wants all of the electronics components behind the doors on the front, but the DISH receiver is too wide for the shelves inside. This Instructable will show how I moved the center divider to one side and changed the sizes of the shelves.

Step 1: Materials and Tools

This photo further illustrates the problem. The shelves are a bit less than 16" in width. The DVD player in this photo is almost 17" in width.

Materials:

- ¾" oak veneer plywood 2" x 4"
- Solid oak sliced thin for a finished edge treatment
- Yellow wood glue
- Drywall screws
- Stain and varnish
- Masking tape
- Old newspaper

Tools:

- Phillips-head screwdrivers
- A block of wood for hammering on finished surfaces
- Hammer
- Chisel
- Table saw
- Electric drill
- 7 ¼" circular saw
- Straightedge
- "C" clamps
- Squares

Step 2: Remove Hindrances

I began by laying the cabinet on its back. I wanted to open the two doors completely, but the pulls on the DVD storage drawers would press against the glass in the doors and could break it. Remove the drawer pulls and set them aside.

Step 3: Remove the Shelving Hardware

The shelving support hardware has a post 5mm in diameter, which is just a few thousandths of an inch larger than ³⁄₁₆". These have a couple of ridges, which make them difficult to remove. I had to run a screwdriver shank through the screw hole and pull with both hands. I needed more shelving hardware, so I bought more conventional 5mm hardware.

Step 4: Remove Screws Securing the Center Divider

The photo shows a view inside the cabinet looking at the underside of the cabinet top. The center divider is attached to a cleat by three short drywall screws. I removed them, but left the cleat in place.

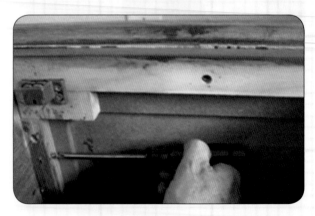

Step 5: More Screws to Remove

The photo shows the bottom of the cabinet under the center divider. There are three drywall screws that go through the bottom and up into the center divider. They are also short.

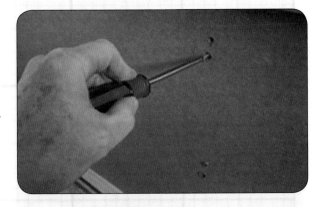

Step 6: Knock Center Divider Loose

I removed the left side magnetic door catch and its mounting block. A chisel knocked the block loose. See the green arrow. Compare to the right side magnetic catch mount. Hold a wooden block against the finished surface on the side where the wooden cleat is located. The divider is glued to the top of the cabinet, so I had to strike the block fairly hard to break it loose.

I discovered later that there are two $^{5}/_{16}$" dowels that keep the bottom of the divider in place. It is also glued. When it did not respond to my hammer blows, I decided to tip the upper end of the divider to the left to break it loose.

Step 7: Repair Any Damage

The center divider is MDF (medium density fiberboard) covered in oak veneer. It fit quite tightly, and cracks appeared in the top end when I forced it to the left. I worked glue into the cracks and clamped them to repair the MDF as much as possible. This is a blemish, but the cabinet is rustic and has a number of blemishes, so this is not a big problem. Plus, we hope to keep the doors on the front of the cabinet closed as much as possible. I did use my circular saw and a

straightedge clamped to the divider to trim less than $^{1}/_{16}$" from both ends. Not only did that make for a better fit later, but it also cleaned up the old glue and fragments of MDF for better mating of surfaces. (The two dowels in the bottom of the divider were not glued and pulled out fairly easily before I trimmed with my circular saw.)

Step 8: Mark the New Position of the Center Divider

I decided the optimum amount to move the divider to one side is 1 $^{1}/_{16}$". I used a square and a pencil to mark the new location for the center divider.

Step 9: Add a 1 $^{1}/_{16}$" Spacer

I ripped some ¾" pine to 1 $^{1}/_{16}$" and cut it to length. Here you see it clamped and glued to the original cleat that had supported the center divider. I also drilled and added drywall screws 1 ½" long from the left (through the spacer and into the cleat) to hold it securely.

Step 10: Drill New Dowel Holes

I very carefully measured 1 1⁄16″ laterally from the centers of the old dowel holes and drilled new holes. Dry-fitting the center divider gives a clue to any adjustments that might need to be made so the dowels slide into their holes.

Step 11: Check for Proper Positioning

In this photo the bottom of the divider is anchored in the new dowel holes. The top of the divider is pushed firmly against the cleat and spacer. The square indicates everything is close enough to be good.

Step 12: Edge Treatment

We recently moved and my radial arm saw is still not assembled and ready to use, but an improvised bench saw based on a wood lathe is ready to go. I decided to cut thin strips from solid oak and use them to make a finished edge on the new veneer plywood shelves I am making, as well as to cover a damaged area on the cabinet's bottom interior.

To set my saw's fence, I used my framing square as a shim between my saw blade and the fence I am using. A couple of pieces of scrap from the thin strips I cut can be seen in the photo.

The bench-saw attachment for my lathe can be seen in detail here. It was nostalgic in a good way to do real work with this tool again. I was very careful and did it very safely.

Step 13: Glue Down a Strip of Oak to Cover the Damage

The first strip I cut included a finished face that matches the wood in the cabinet quite well, so I utilized it. The surface below the strip was quite rough because bits of MDF and veneer tore away when I removed the divider. I decided to use hot glue to fill in the gaps and to attach the oak strip without needing to clamp it in place.

I used a hole saw to make an extra set of holes in the back of the cabinet for routing cables and for allowing heat to escape.

Step 14: A Little Problem

The orange arrows point to two retainers for the glass and fabric cover. The new position for the center divider means these bump into the divider and need to be moved to the positions shown by the green arrows.

In this photo you can also see that I have cut the original shelves to fit the narrower left half of the cabinet. Where there was one shelf there now are two.

Step 15: A New Position for the Left Magnetic Door Catch

The location of the magnetic catch on each door is not critical; the only requirement is that the plate aligns with the magnet. I did need to install the wood block again that is part of the support for the magnet assembly. I decided I needed only two screws to hold the magnet assembly, even though there were originally four.

Step 16: Edge Treatment on the New Shelves

In step 12 I described making thin strips of oak for the edge treatment on the plywood. Here you can see how I glued the strips to the front edge of the new plywood shelves with a yellow or white wood glue. I used strips of masking tape to hold the glued strips in place. Then I put down newspaper and placed the glued end down over carpet to provide an even pressure on the strips. The shelf pieces stood vertically while the glue dried so their own weight would assist in clamping during the time the glue dried.

A veneer trim bit in a router will make the edge treatment strip flush with the shelf surface so that only a little sanding is needed to give the shelf a nice finished look.

Step 17: Stain, Varnish, and Install

I used some golden oak stain to match the new shelves to the rest of the cabinet. Here you see all of the electronics components in place. If heat builds up too much inside the cabinet, I will cut some circular holes in the shelves to facilitate the movement of air from below upward and out the holes in the back of the cabinet. Time will tell.

Step 18: The Final Product

My wife has a good eye for decorating. She was very disappointed after the DISH installer left us with a piece of electronics too wide to fit the only cabinet she could find. But, now her TV cabinet again has the uncluttered look she wanted to achieve.

We did a little experiment and found the signals from our remotes pass through both the glass and the fabric in the doors. We can use our equipment with the cabinet doors closed.

Your TV cabinet may be much be much different from ours, but the inner construction may be very similar, and that means you could modify a cabinet that does not quite fit your electronics, too.

The only remaining problem: we can receive 120 channels, but often there still is nothing we want to watch.

Ghost images on the glass are reflections from the rest of the room.

Fix a Snag in a Rug
By Johnt007871
http://www.instructables.com/id/Fix-a-Snag-in-a-Rug/

This is a fix I made on a "medium grade" rug, made with rows of stitching. Nicer plush rugs may not work for this technique.

Step 1: Required Materials
- Scissors
- Flexible fabric glue (I opted for some that dries clear and flexible)
- Straight pins (or something similar, for the large pulls that yield long pieces of string/yarn/fiber)
- Scotch tape (as needed)
- Wax paper
- Something heavy like a text book

Step 2: Trim

First, cut some of the snag away. Be sure you leave enough to cover the void that it created. Many times the snags fluff and fray and will never be the same shape they were originally.

Step 3: Glue

Gently pull the snag aside and, using the fabric glue, place a small bead in the bottom of the hole.

Use the tip of the glue pen or your finger to work the snag into the hole.

If possible, work the surrounding fibers into the hole to help cover it and make it look more full.

Step 4: Set

Place the wax paper over the glued snag and place a textbook-like object on top of it.

My glue required two to four hours' dry time, so I just left it overnight.

Now for the large snag . . .

Step 5: Oh No . . . a Big One

This snag was about a foot long, and the yarn-like fibers came to be about a couple feet long (hard to tell as they're stretchy). It unraveled along a single row of stitching. It has an orange and green straight pin at either end in the first photo.

I placed the straight pins at either end and wound the yarn about the pins until it looked like it filled in the void nicely. I taped off the excess in case I needed more, as you can see in the second photo.

I pressed the tip of the fabric glue pin between the wound section and the normal, carpet section and applied a line along both ends for the entire length. I also added a generous amount around either pin because I was paranoid of it coming undone when the pins came out.

I also had to add some glue here and there because the top layers weren't touching any glue. I basically created a semi-flexible patch in the rug using the pulled out yarn. While it doesn't feel exactly like the rug around it, it is flexible and won't stab bare feet or anything.

I put wax paper and a book on top as stated before and inspected my results the next day. Trim excess as needed, and remove tape and pins.

My wife and I purchased our first house in August. One of the minor problems we noticed when we moved in was a broken slat in the blinds. I had never thought about blinds as being something repairable, but realized something such as this shouldn't be trashed based on a single broken slat.

This fix is very simple and the pictures may not be necessary, but I know I would've gone into it with more confidence than I had if I'd had photos to follow.

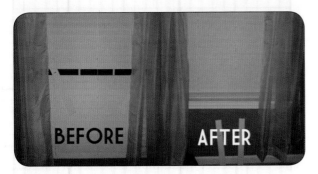

Step 1: Identify the Problem and Intended Solution

My problem is obvious. The slat is broken right in the center. Fortunately, the blinds are too long for the window and there are a few extra at the bottom. The plan is to remove the broken slat and replace it with one from the bottom.

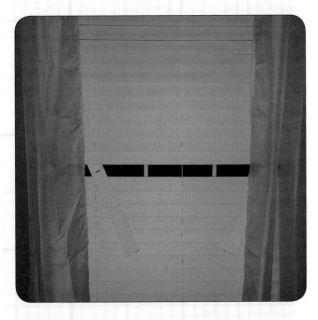

Step 2: Find and Remove the Plugs

On the bottom of every set of blinds are at least two plugs holding and covering the lift strings. These are easily removed with a flat-head screwdriver. You can then pull the lift string through the hole and either untie or cut off the knot. If you're removing a slat you will have plenty of extra string and can afford to cut the knot off as I did.

Step 3: Remove the Lift String

Once you have the knots removed from the lift string you can begin removing it. You only need to go as far as the slat you need to remove. In my case this is the broken slat; however, if you're just adjusting the blinds for a better window fit you will only remove the necessary bottom slats.

Step 4: Replace the Broken Slat

Now you will put the replacement slat in place of the broken one. You will also move the base of the blinds up by one space so there are no gaps when fully extended.

Step 5: Rethread the Lift String

Check how the lift string is threaded and follow the same course with it through the slats and bottom.

(It was at this point that I realized this would've been a little easier if I had left the blinds open.)

Step 6: Thread the Base

You can use tweezers or other means to push the string through the base. You will not see this once done so it doesn't matter how it looks. For two out of the three I was able to trim the frayed string and slip it through; I had to use finishing nail to push the third through. Tie each one off as close to the same length as possible.

Step 7: Replace the Plugs

Now you will replace the three plugs removed at the beginning. Make sure these go over the rungs of the other string, securing it in place.

Step 8: Finishing Up

Trim the excess string from the bottom and return the blinds to their original place.

Refinishing a Hardwood Staircase

By KittyJ

http://www.instructables.com/id/Refinishing-an-Hardwood-Staircase/

This is an adventure in refinishing my hardwood staircase, told by an amateur artist and homeowner. This may not be how the pros would do it, but it was done for about $150 in materials and a few days of my time.

I floundered a bit in figuring it out, but here I'll share the things I've figured out. Most of this uses low-odor, quick-drying options because I'm working in a house with small children in wintertime. (They're not home while I'm working, but they need to sleep here at night.)

Step 1: Tools and Materials
- Orbital hand sander (or two)
- Plastic drop cloth
- Safety goggles
- Dust masks (buy a multi-pack)
- Ear plugs
- Vinyl-palmed work gloves
- Vinyl or latex disposable gloves
- Cheap throw-away paintbrush for chemical paint stripper
- Paint scraper
- Screwdriver
- Hammer
- Small wood chisel
- 2.5" angled natural-bristle paintbrush
- Small paint tray
- 40-grit sanding pads (be sure to get the right size pads with the right number of holes—they're for ventilation, and your sander will overheat without the right ones). I used about 15 pads for 14 steps and a landing.
- 40- or 60-grit sandpaper and a sanding block, if desired
- 2" wide painters tape
- Spool of cotton twine
- Hi-speed ready-strip citrus paint and varnish remover (this project used one half-gallon jug)
- MinWax wood finish (this project uses two quart-sized cans of golden pecan stain)
- Low-odor mineral spirits
- MinWax water-based polyurethane for floors (this project uses one gallon of clear satin-finish poly)

Here you see the old staircase. Someone had painted that beautiful wood a chocolate brown when the house was built. It was old and dingy and banged up. The dark color robbed the stairwell of all light, making it a dark area even in midday.

Step 2: Stripping the Old Paint, Part One: Chemical Stripper

After spending too much time on the first step, trying to sand away many layers of 30-year-old chocolate-brown stairs, along with the nicks and dents in the wood, I got smart and used a chemical paint stripper. Many of the "safer" ones say they work in as little as four hours, but I chose Back to Nature brand Hi-Speed Ready-Strip, which says it works in about a half an hour. The half-gallon container was more than enough.

1. Open your windows and turn on a fan. It might be "low-odor and environmentally safe" but it still stinks.
2. Shake the bottle really well—it's very separated.
3. Pour some liquid onto the top step. Using a cheap paintbrush, spread over the step in a thick layer. Make sure to get the corners and edges well.
4. Move down the steps to the bottom and throw away your paintbrush, then find something else to do for about two hours. I started the bottom step after a half an hour, and worked my way back up. But during the rest of the paint removal process, the upper stairs that had had the stripper on them for about three hours took a third of the time it took to remove the paint from the lower steps.

193

5. Using a paint scraper, scrape across the step with the grain of the wood. The old polyurethane comes up with the stripper goo. Wipe the goo off of the scraper and continue (don't bother trying to rinse it off). I scraped it into an old shoe box, but where doesn't really matter. Scraping takes off most of the stripping agent, I didn't bother to wipe off the remaining.

These steps are old and dinged up, and the dark stain penetrated into the wood and its imperfections. I was removing the many layers of old poly with the chemicals in order to get closer to the wood and to get started. The picture here shows the stairs after the chemical stripper was scraped off. It was only the first step of removing the old color, but it made the rest of the project move much more quickly. The time (a day) and cost of the stripper was less than the time and cost of using sanding pads to get through that old poly. Not to mention, it was much easier on my back. I wore work gloves for all of this step, though I really didn't get any on myself.

Step 3: Stripping the Paint, Part Two: Sanding

Now comes the sanding! Before getting started, I cut strips of plastic drop cloth and pinned them across the entrances at the top and bottom of the stairs. It wasn't a perfect system, but it kept much of the sawdust in the stairwell. After the first day, I found out how important it is to turn off your central heating system when you're sanding if there's an intake vent in the stairwell. My house is covered in a fine layer of sawdust now. But after changing the air filter and learning from my mistake, that didn't happen on sanding day #2.

It wasn't lead paint, but it was still a loud and messy business. Full safety goggles, a dust mask that I had to change several times, and ear plugs were necessary. On sanding day #2, I added a kerchief for my hair.

I was working through the color and into the wood to remove dark spots and chips and dings. This was labor-intensive. I actually have two orbital sanders, and used one in each hand for most of this process. My Roybi wiggles back and forth while it sands, so it muscles through the old stuff faster. It also gets closer to the wall than my other one. My DeWalt doesn't wiggle, so it gives me more control. I used it to do around the front edge of the steps and under the lip. But both are powerful. So when I wasn't sanding out edges or front curves, I had both going at the same time. It doubled my productivity.

Nice and slow, back and forth, longer on dark spots. The upper stairs where the chemical stripper had stayed on longer were much quicker to sand off. You can't muscle your way through it. Pressing on a hand sander will overheat your unit. It takes the time it takes; you can only use the large grit and be patient.

I'm something of a perfectionist, so this took me a long time. There are still some spots where the old stain permeates deeply. On several of the lower stairs, there are lines of dots where the staples under the stairs opened the wood to the stain. They will always look "refurbished" rather than new, but they look nice and have character.

An important note: You'll notice that I never use a sanding grit finer than 60 in this project. Most DIY sites, and the poly container, and the stain container, all say to do a rough grit first and then go back over the wood with 100 or 120 grit. The guy in the hardware store even recommended 180. But here's the thing: everyone in my house has fallen down my stairs. They were very slippery. Over the two years we've owned the house, we've even considered painting sand onto the stairs, like you do on exterior masonry stairs. So in refinishing them, I just let the texture of the wood remain. No one's going to want to "risky business" slide across the stairs in their underwear, anyway. There's now a slight roughness to the steps. There's a picture toward the end. It may mean that they'll have to be redone again in 10 years rather than 30, but maybe no one will break a leg between now and then, and that's worth it.

Step 4: Stripping the Paint, Part Three: The Little Details

Finishing up the removal. I actually removed the old color in several sweeps. This photo is after the initial sanding. My husband used his chisel to carve out the edges. It took out a bit of wood in a few places, but for the most part, it just brought up the paint that had been loosened by the chemical stripper.

I did another pass with the sanders after this, and mostly used those to get in close. In a few places, and in the square corners where my round sanders couldn't reach, I used the chisel. Just a little tap-tap-tap with the chisel angled to take off the tiniest fragment of wood and pigment. The second picture shows the before-and-after of removing the paint.

Then I used a sanding block and sandpaper to smooth out the chiseled areas and to remove the last of the color. Here you see my daughter "helping." She lasted about three minutes before she ditched me.

Finally, you see my naked stairs.

Step 5: Prep Work

Before getting started, I decided to pull up the little edging border around the landing that no one had ever bothered to paint. It made getting to the edges much easier. I had worried that dark color edging the landing would always look dirty. I started at the edge of the edging and tapped a screwdriver (with a hammer) first behind and then under the border, slowly working it loose. Before I replace it, I'll paint it the same white that I'm going to paint the rest of the trim.

Then I taped carefully around the wood. I'm a great believer in good taping. I've never done a floor before, but I've painted many things, and taping well can save a lot of trouble down the road. That being said, I didn't worry about the odd drop of stain or polyurethane, as I'm going to repaint all the molding and trim soon.

The most involved part of the prep, however, was remediating the landing.

Step 6: The Landing

The landing was one of the most challenging parts of this project. And this brings in the fact that I'm an artistic person and not a contractor.

The floor was old hardwood. There were gaps in between the boards. Some were completely joined together, some had gaps of 3 mm to 4 mm. Most had gaps of 1 mm to 2 mm, and they were all uneven. I saw a website that suggested the use of rope to fill in a space or two in wide-plank hardwood floors, and I decided to make the plan my own.

First, I used a screwdriver and a vacuum to scrape years of crud out of the spaces.

Second, I stained the floor.

Third, I cut lengths of cotton twine. For 15 row spaces, I cut eleven 8' long pieces and four 12' long pieces. I dipped them into the stain I would use on the wood and hung them outside on the fence to dry overnight. We were concerned they might get stiff, but they were not stiffened at all in the morning.

Then, I started using the string to fill the gaps. After experimenting, I settled on the following technique:

1. In the widest/deepest gaps, I cut a length of twine the length of the deepest part, laid it in the gap, and pressed it down using the back of a razor blade (I had a blade holder you see in the photo—you could use a screwdriver). Then I started a length of twine near the wall, with a bit

of an overhang (~1cm) tucked into the gap. Then I ran the twine down the gap, pushing it gently into the gap with the blade as I went along. In spaces where the string fell too deeply into the gap, I pulled it out and pressed another short piece into the gap, then brought the long piece back over it. I was careful not to let the string come up higher than the floorboards.

2. It wasn't until I was almost to the back wall that I encountered a problem. A couple of boards were very close together, too close for the string, and the adjacent gaps were extra-wide. I had noticed when I was scraping out between the boards that they could wiggle back and forth a little. I used a probe, and very gently tapped at the crack until the board moved. It looked so much more even, and so much better, that I decided to use my string method to fix the floor. I used the probe to open the boards, then pressed a piece of twine deep into the crack, holding the boards apart. Then I ran the top piece of twine to finish it. The evened gaps were such an improvement that I went back over the floor and repaired a few other sections as well.

In the pictures here, you see the big, uneven gaps in the old floor. Then you see the stained floor with the dyed twine in place. Then you see the polyurethaned, finished floor. The color of the floor and the color of the twine are very similar after being polyed. There are still a couple of small gaps, but I think it looks great. It was a certain charm to it.

It turned out to be a great solution to a problem.

Step 7: Staining the Wood

Staining the wood is quick, easy, and gratifying.

I used MinWax Golden Pecan #245. The color was nothing like it looks on the can. It actually turned out a golden red color. It's very pretty, and I like it, but my original plan was more gold and less red.

1. Start early in the day, open all of your windows and doors, and turn on your fans. This stuff

smells so bad. Really—much worse than the chemical stripper or the polyurethane. It smelled *terrible*. I had closed the bedroom doors and turned off the central heating to keep the smell out of the sleeping areas, and the lack of circulation certainly didn't help. I did have a fan at the head of the stairs, but only later thought to pull down the steps to the attic and let the roof vent pull out some of the chemicals. The can says to paint on, wipe off any excess after 15 minutes, allow to dry for four hours, do a second coat, and then allow at least eight hours of dry time before painting. But really, you want to have a good six hours of having the house open before you bring kids back into the house.

2. Wear safety goggles and disposable gloves. Make sure stairs (and walls) are vacuumed and wiped down to remove the sawdust. I also kept an old sock next to me as I worked. I wiped down each step before I moved down, and if the paintbrush pulled up an errant splinter of wood or speck of dirt, I picked it up with a gloved finger and wiped it right on the sock.

3. I painted on the first coat and watched as I moved down the staircase. There wasn't really any pooling, so I just leaned over the steps and used the paintbrush to spread out any thicker areas before I started the landing, and again as I moved from the landing to the lower stairs, and again as I finished the lower stairs.

4. I played Skyrim for three hours.

5. The stairs were mostly dry, but still a little damp, so I sacrificed a pair of my husband's old socks to wear to go up and apply the second coat. I didn't want to get dirt or sneaker prints on my wet stairs. My toeprints were definitely visible as I worked my way back down the steps, and I had to make sure to cover them well with the second coat. It underlined the fact that you can't walk on stained steps till they're really dry.

Two coats of stain made the color rich and even. I didn't need a third. It was already a darker color than I had planned. I rinsed the brush out with mineral spirits and used it again the next day for the poly.

Then I sat in my living room, bundled up in coats and a hat and gloves with the windows and doors open at night in the end of December. It was not the high point of the project. I had started staining at 3 p.m. I'd suggest 9 a.m. as a better start time. When the stain was mostly dry to the touch (just the tiniest shade damp), my husband took a dry cloth and wiped the last of the damp stain off of the steps. There wasn't much; we were just trying to get rid of the smell. I really couldn't have done it sooner. Think toe marks.

Step 8: Polyurethane

Oil-based polyurethanes are recommended for floors and stairs. Apparently, they hold up better, age to a desirable yellowed color, and only require two coats. The downside is that they give off terrible, noxious fumes and need to dry for 12 to 18 hours between coats, and may need a couple days after the last coat before you can walk on them.

But I live in this house, as do my husband and three children, and that was not an option.

So I did some research and found MinWax water-based polyurethane for floors. I bought it at a local Duron paint store, rather than going back to the big hardware store, and it cost me $49.99 plus tax, rather than the $65 I'd seen it for online.

I cannot tell you how fantastic this stuff is! I kept seeing reviews online about how water-based polys bead up on oil-stained floors and cause the wood grain to come up, and that you have to do *so* many coats (one review said up to a dozen!) for it to be done.

They were so wrong.

This stuff was great! It brushed on smoothly and easily. There was no trouble at all with beading. It's a little milky going on, but they said it would dry clear, and it did. By the time I was half-done with the landing, the upper steps were dry to the touch. There was very little smell. I opened all the doors and windows in the house, and I left the central heating on this time, since I had a good eight hours before the children would be home. (I used the disposable gloves for this step, too.)

On the landing, I used a lot of poly and painted sideways across the boards first to get plenty of poly into the cracks with the twine. Then I went over the wood again, painting with the grain.

I had read warnings about water-based poly drying too quickly and brush marks being visible. I had even bought a small foam roller to run over it and take the brush marks out. I had no such problems. I painted it on with a brush, painting with the grain, starting at the edges and working toward the middle. Then I painted the front edge of the step, and then I used the roller brush to paint the underside of the lip of the step. It's the only thing I ended up using the foam for, and could really have used a $0.49 foam brush rather than a $5 foam roller. I tried the roller on the steps, but it left a textured look I didn't care for at all. Before moving down to the next step, I went over the whole step with the brush, just gently dragging it over the paint with the grain of the wood, including the front edge. The paintbrush only needs to be rinsed out with water to clean it, which was nice and easy.

It worked great and looks terrific.

I plan to use the same poly when I redo the dining room floor. It will be necessary to move quickly so it doesn't dry on me, but it was so easy to do, with so little odor, that I'm not worried about it at all.

I let the poly dry for a solid two hours before doing the next coat. It was completely dry as I walked up the stairs in my socks. The only part not entirely dry was the gaps between the boards with the twine. Two coats look good, and the wood is sealed. The one-gallon container easily did two coats, and could do a third, which I think I may go ahead and add on the next time I have some time off again. But I'm comfortable with it the way it is.

Again, the directions do say to sand in between, but I wasn't going for a smooth finish, so I didn't. I'm including here a picture of the texture I ended up with. It's nothing like my in-laws' unfinished staircase in their mountain cottage. There's just a very slight texture underfoot. If you didn't know to look for it, I don't think you'd really know the difference.

Step 9: Repainting Backboards and Molding

After finishing the polyurethane, the backs of the stairs and the trim looked all the worse. We still had some paint left from painting the chair rails recently. We decided that, since the stairs ended up darker than planned, that a nice coat of shiny white paint around it would lighten it right back up.

The paint I used was Olympic brand latex paint, "ultra white," in semi-gloss. I have the "environmentally preferred—zero VOC" premium paint. I didn't even open any doors or windows. It dries fast, and it doesn't smell.

First, we taped over the freshly-refinished wood and the wall above the trim.

Here I got to use that small foam hand roller that I really didn't use while applying the poly. I rolled most of it and cut in the corners with a brush.

I gave it one good coat all over and then went back a half hour later and gave a few spots a little extra, where old scuffs were showing through the paint.

Finally, I painted white that trim that I had pulled up. It had never been painted, so it took three coats of paint. It only needed about 10 minutes to dry between coats.

Just walking up and down my stairs is so exciting now. It looks beautiful! Our stairwell has gone from a dark, dirty hole in my house to a beautiful, shiny, clean staircase that I can be proud of. I love our little house, and now I love the hardwood staircase, too.

Fix a Weak Battery-Door Catch

By Phil B

http://www.instructables.com/id/Fix-a-Weak-Battery-Door-Catch/

This is the battery door for an MP3 audio player I have. The "V"-shaped catch on the battery door has lost its spring-like quality, and the battery door sometimes falls off of the player. I tried heating the bottom of the "V" and bending the catch, but the plastic is weak and it does not hold its position.

Step 1: Open the Catch a Bit

I pulled the catch open to spread the "V" so it would hold itself within the player if this position could be maintained. Be careful not to break the plastic by pulling too much.

Step 2: Test for Thickness

I folded a new rubber band over and stuffed it into the "V" to see how many layers of rubber band I would need to fill the "V." Two should do the job if I can get them to stay in the lower portion of the "V" opening on the catch. Do not use an old rubber band. Those have already lost some of their elasticity.

Step 3: Cut the Rubber Band

I cut two pieces of rubber band each as long as the catch is wide.

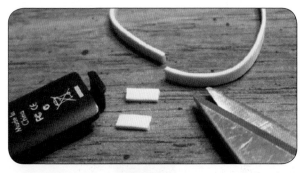

Step 4: Glue the Rubber Pieces in Place

I glued each piece of rubber to the plastic surface it touches, but did not glue them to each other. I used a fast-setting epoxy glue and a toothpick. I tried to push the pieces of rubber as far as possible down into the "V" opening of the catch. Then I waited for the glue to set.

Step 5: Finished

My battery door once again closes with a reassuring "click," and it stays in place.

Upgrade Your Old Ceiling Fan

By tinawina

http://www.instructables.com/id/Upgrade-Your-Old-Ceiling-Fan/

Cheap fans with phony shiny wood grain and "brass" parts are pretty ugly, and pretty prevalent. Since I couldn't find a great looking replacement that didn't cost a gazillion dollars, and since my fans still worked fine, I decided to just change their look. This project is easy to do and doesn't require any electrical work (unless you want it to). Plan on taking 2-3 hours to tackle the first 6 steps, and another 30 mins to reassemble your fan and turn it on.

Step 1: Materials
- Primer paint
- Finish paint
- Rustoleum oil based paint or the like
- 2-3 paint brushes
- All purpose cleaner and towels
- Screwdriver (flat and/or Phillips depending on your fan)
- Ladder

Step 2: Remove Fan Blades from Motor

I have done two fans. For the first I removed the entire fan from the ceiling requiring me to turn off the power to the fan at the circuit box. While this did allow me to fix a problem with the fan (it's a 3-speed but was only one was working), it made painting the motor housing difficult.

For the second fan I just left the motor on the ceiling. This made painting the motor housing really simple. Removing the fan blades is very easy to do. Seems pretty standard that the blades are attached to the motor by a couple of screws and that's it. Just remove the screws and the blade and connector will separate from the housing.

Step 3: Separate Fan Blades from Connectors and Clean All

Unscrew the blades from the connectors. These screws came out very easily in both my fan projects.

Fan blades get super grimy and dusty, esp if near a kitchen which was the case for one of mine. I used all purpose cleaner and rags and went over the blades a few times to get them clean. Same with the connectors.

Step 4: Put a Primer Coat on the Blades

You only have to paint one side of the blades since no one will ever see the top side. Prime the edges of the blades first and then work a thick coat onto the face of the blade. Any good quality primer will work. I used Zinsser water-based primer.

I did one coat of primer and that seemed to be enough. But two coats wouldn't hurt, and primer paint dries pretty quickly.

Step 5: Paint Metal Parts—No Primer Needed

I used Rustoleum oil-based black satin paint. If you use an oil-based paint wear gloves as the paint likes to stick around. For the connectors I did a nice thick coat with a cheap brush. Even if you splat it on, the paint sorta smooths itself out as it dries and has a spray-paint finish to it in the end, very smooth and even. One coat was all I did, with a little touching up on the finished product. For the motor housing, I positioned a 6-foot ladder on one side of the housing attached to the ceiling and painted one half then moved to the other side to paint the second half. I used a much thinner coat on the housing since I didn't want drips -- that Rustoleum is nasty stuff to clean up.

Step 6: Paint Blades with Two Coats of Finish Color

By now the primer coat is dry enough to do the first color coat. I used left-over water-based latex paint from the paint job recently done in my living room so that the fan blades match my walls. You'll need to do at least two coats if you are going to a lighter color on your fan blades.

Step 7: Reconnect Blades to Connectors and Connectors to Motor

Wait overnight for everything to dry and then put the fan blades and connectors back together — reverse what you did in steps 3 and 2. Be careful when handling the connectors because the paint can scratch off pretty easily. Not really a problem later since you will probably never touch the connectors, or if you do it will be with a soft cloth when cleaning.

My fans have two rows of screw holes so that I can choose to use four blades (inner row of holes) or five blades (outer row of holes). I went with four to minimize the fan even more. With the nice white paint you can hardly see the fan when it's on.

Step 8: Touch Up and Voila!

You may need to touch up your paint job, especially the paint you use on the connectors and motor housing—it's tough to paint those shiny surfaces thoroughly in one go around. Regardless, I found touch-up to be minimal.

I chose to ditch the horrible glass globes that come with these old crappy fans and invested in these Satco light adaptors. They work like adjustable track lights. I picked these up online for around $12 each, so $72 for enough for the two fans. (I bet you could do something awesome and super cheap with little Ikea light fixtures!) And the six 50w halogen narrow floodlights set me back about $30. But even with these accessory costs, I got two great looking, great working fans for well less than half the cost of one replacement fan.

Four Lives of a Modern Side Table

By modhomeecteacher

http://www.instructables.com/id/Four-Lives-of-A-Modern-Side-Table/

When thrifting at Goodwill or other vintage shops, it takes a keen eye to choose furniture wisely. See how this laminate-topped modern side table was strong enough to live four lives. Each look brought the table closer to its final form.

Step 1: Original Table from Goodwill

Nice legs make this table a piece worth having. The laminate top was not so pretty.

Step 2: Second Life as a Painted Tiered Table

A coat of primer and two coats of paint help disguise the laminate, but it doesn't hold up to everyday use.

Step 3: Third Life as an Upholstered Felt Table

After giving up on the painted table, I decided to upholster it with felt.

Step 4: Smashed to Smithereens by Mr. Mod

After a trip and a stumble, the table's middle supports came undone. It could have been repaired but it had one more life to live as an upholstered ottoman.

Step 5: Add a 2" Foam Top

Trace the base circle shape on a piece of foam and cut it out with an electric knife.

Step 6: Sew the Ottoman Cover

Cut out a circle ½" larger than the table top. Also cut out a strip of fabric 5" deep and 3" larger than the circumference of the table. Stitch cording to the circle top and then stitch the band on to the corded circle. Fold fabric over and pin and stitch the band closed, using topstitching if you want.

Step 7: Upholster the Ottoman

Add a layer of batting over the foam-topped ottoman. Slip the sewn cover on top of the ottoman and pull evenly all around while securing with staples, keeping the cover smooth all the way around.

Step 8: The Fourth Life

Modern, sleek, and jazzy ottoman for use in the closet, the bedroom, the living room, or kitchen.

Hack a Mattress into a Couch

By zurick

http://www.instructables.com/id/Hack-a-Mattress-into-a-Couch/

For years we've had a sitting area made out of cushions (sort of a Middle Eastern vibe) but wanted something a little higher, so I decided to see if I could convert the mattress into a sitting area/couch.

What follows is just my experience. Your mattress and situation will be different, so think of this as a sketch and use it as a jumping-off point. If you have a better idea, that's great.

The overall plan is to cut out a middle section of both the mattress and the box springs, leaving two ends for each of the same size. Then you close up the ends and sew covers for them out of canvas and upholstery fabric. The basic idea is pretty simple, but it is a bit of work and requires both a Dremel tool (or something to cut the metal springs) and a sewing machine.

Purchasing the fabric is the most expensive part of this project. I used remnants I already had, so this project cost me nothing; your situation will probably be different. Note that upholstery fabric can run $30–$40/yard, so keep your eye out for sales.

Note: Don't forget to use goggles, ear protection, and gloves.

Step 1: Tools Used

- Scissors
- Dremel tool with a fiberglass reinforced cutting wheel
- Hand saw
- Staple gun
- Sewing needle and upholstery thread
- A lot of straight pins
- Sewing machine

- Pliers
- Thimble
- Hand clamps (the ones that look like industrial clothes pins)
- Bee's wax (to wax hand-sewing thread)

Step 2: Cutting through the Box Springs

Calculate size of sitting area

I measured the cushions on a regular couch to find out where to cut the two ends of the box springs. I wanted an L-shaped sitting area formed by two sections, but you can create any configuration you like. Look at the bottom of the box springs and see where the wood cross pieces fall. It's important to cut it so that one is left to form the new back line. This maintains the box's integrity. In my case this made the bottom section slightly narrower than the mattress section on top of it. But in the end the overhang made it more comfortable to sit down and stand back up.

Cut through outer covering and padding

Use a regular pair of scissors to cut through the covering right down the center. This was my exploratory cut. See how yours is constructed before you open it up too much. Peel the covering back. You will now be able to see into the box springs. Measure the two ends and mark the cut on the springs themselves with a Sharpie pen (I used blue so I could see it better). Remember to make this mark longer so that you can bend the cut end over. You don't want the metal rod poking straight out through the fabric.

Cut springs

Using a Dremel tool with a fiberglass reinforced cutting wheel, cut down the line of springs (see photo). Make sure to wear eye and ear protection and gloves because the sparks smart. Hold the tool steady because any jerky movement will break the wheel. Depending on your mattress you may want to cut the springs longer (the height of the box springs) and then use pliers to fold the wire down, forming the back wall of the new section. I tied the folded-down wire with cotton rope to give it more support.

Cut wood

If it is possible, cut the wood leaving a supporting crosspiece to form the back line of the new edge (see photo). If this isn't possible nail a crosspiece along the back edge.

Close ends

Close up ends by pulling covering and padding back into place. Wrap it around to the bottom of the wooden crosspiece. Staple in place and trim excess. Then pull the bottom thin fabric (looks like interfacing) and staple it back on and trim excess.

Repeat on the other end of the box springs to form the two lower platforms.

Step 3: Cutting through the Mattress

Cutting the mattress is pretty much the same as cutting the box spring, except there is no wood in the mattress. So cut through the outer covering, cut the springs, and sew the ends to form the two mattress sections.

Use short pieces of thread to lessen the tangling, and knot often. You don't want the thread to break and a large section of your seam to unravel. It is easier to have a second person help you hold the mattress and the seam as you sew. I also folded the seam part over to have a more finished look.

Step 4: Sewing New Coverings
Measure and cut panels for the mattress

Lay the fabric on the sections to measure and cut. I wanted a contrasting color for the sides so I sewed strips of brown fabric together to form one long wrap-around piece. On one short side hem a slit that will create the opening to get the cover on and off. You can see this in the third photograph in this section. I allowed the slit to wrap around the long sides about 3". You can test this to make sure the mattress will fit through this slot.

This is where all those pins come in. I anchor-pinned the brown wrap-around piece (inside out) on the mattress and laid the decorative fabric on top (also inside out). I then pinned that fabric to the wrap-around piece. Depending on the stretch of the fabric you might want to pull it taut as you're pinning so it's not baggy when you finish. I had a ½" seam allowance. Make sure that as you are pinning you are not pinning to the mattress itself (other than the anchor pins, which you will remove later to take off the cover for sewing). I then trimmed any excess fabric. Off to the sewing machine. At the ½" mark

I did a straight stitch all the way around. Then I went back with a zigzag around the edge. I snipped the curves to make sure that when I turned it right side out the corners were smoothly curved.

I took the cover back to the mattress (still inside out) and put it on the mattress. I flipped the mattress over and anchor-pinned the sides on to hold it in place. Then I pinned and trimmed the second side, remembering to keep the fabric inside out. This is when you use the slit in the side. After you've removed the anchor pins that are holding the side panels in place, slide the cover off the mattress as you would a pillow case.

Back to the sewing machine and repeat for the second side.
Slip cover over mattress

Turn the finished cover right-side out and slide it onto the mattress. If you made it nice and snug this may take two people. Straighten it all the way around and begin sewing up the slit.
Sew ends

I used a thimble and needle-nose pliers to sew the ends. I also used a glover needle that has a pyramid point, which is a little stronger and a little easier to grab with the pliers. You might want to pull the seams together and clamp. I used those clamps that look like industrial clothes pins. Butt the two hemmed edges together (don't overlap) and hand stitch. Wax the thread with bee's wax to both strengthen it and help it glide through the fabric. As with the mattress, use shorter pieces of thread to lessen the tangling, and knot often. You don't want the thread to break and a large section of your seam to unravel.
Measure and cut panels for the box springs

The idea is the same for the box springs except the bottom is just wrapped around and stapled. I didn't do a bottom panel. I also only used a heavy cotton for the top panel instead of upholstery or decorative fabric since it isn't seen. Since the box springs cover is dropped on and wrapped around there is no need for the end slit.

Pile them up, throw on some pillows, and you're finished. Take a well-deserved break.

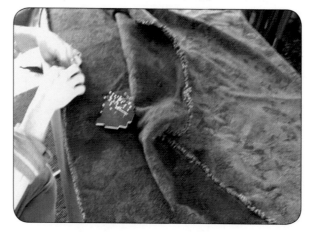

Home Theater Projector Screen on a Budget

By tracydanger

http://www.instructables.com/id/Home-Theater-Projector-Screen-on-a-Budget/

If you want to make a good looking, good quality projector screen and you don't want to spend a lot, this is one good way to do it. My total cost for the screen was around $50. I learned little nuggets of wisdom along the way that I will share with you. I shared my particular measurements throughout as an example. Yours will likely vary, but you can use the same basic principles.

Step 1: Preparation

Before getting started, here's a list of supplies you'll be using:

- Tape
- Staple gun, staples
- Wood glue
- Hammer
- Measuring tape
- Pieces of 1" × 3" poplar (you'll get the measurements in the instructions)
- 1" pieces of plastic trim
- Paint roller, Paint pan
- Primer paint
- Paint for the top coat
- Sandpaper
- Chalk
- Drywall anchors
- Screws with O-rings
- Screws with hooks

Here we go . . .

1. Install the projector where it will be.
2. Measure height and width of the screen while the projector is on (mine was 45" x 102 ½").
3. Pick your paint. For the higher end, you can use screen goo. I plan to use that some day (when I get more Christmas money). It sounds like a great solution. If you want to be cheaper, like me, for now, you can select a normal paint.

I went to Home Depot and picked several paint chips from white to light grey. Some AV forums suggested Behr "Silver Screen" paint (770E-2). This is what I ended up using. When you have grey, it appears to be a better contrast ratio than white does. Also, I used a matte finish because it's less reflective, and that's what you want.

I suggest picking up several different shades (make "Silver Screen" one of the options) and get a small stack of each individual color. When you get home, tape all of the chips of one color together so that it makes a square that is about two to three square feet in area.

Slap them up on the projector wall. I used painters tape as an adhesive so that it wouldn't mess up the walls. Now, watch part of a movie. Find one with good colors and sections with good blacks. Do your best not to compare the white to the greys, because you may think, "Oh, the white looks better compared to the grey." But remember that when the whole screen is one color you won't notice that. The white may have "popped" better in my test, but I think I'm better off with the grey (because of contrast ratio). With the black border (very important and addressed later) it looks great.

Step 2: Plan Your Cuts, Buy Supplies

You want to plan for a border of 2" to 3". I chose 2", so in my example, I have a screen height of 45", so I add 2" on each side for a total of 4", meaning my "outside" height will be 49" and the inside will be 45" (length is 106.5" and 102.5" respectively).

You'll be cutting your wood at 45 degree angles, assuming you want it to look good. I bought pieces of 1" × 3" for my frame. I highly suggest using poplar wood. Look at each piece lengthwise to make sure they're all straight. Plan to have enough for some corner supports.

If you already have your paint color picked out, you might as well buy it at the same time. Make sure to get some primer paint if you don't already have some, as you will be needing some for the first two to three coats.

You want something like a canvas material for the screen and some black non-reflective material (thick is preferable) for the border. I went to Walmart for the cloth. Any fabric store will do. Make sure to check the discount bin first. Also, talk to a worker. I described what I was looking for (a smooth, canvas-type material), and the employee found the perfect cloth for me that I would not have found. It was pretty sturdy/stiff and smooth—not like a potato sack. You may find a material that works better for you than canvas, like the back side of some pleather. The screen material only cost me a $1 per yard (I got about three yards' worth), and the black material for the border was only $2/yard.

Make sure to measure the area of the screen PLUS 2" for EACH side PLUS about 3" to 4" for overlap on EACH side. Remember, you'll be wrapping this around 1" × 3" slats and you want leeway on each side.

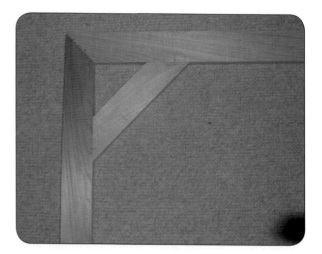

Step 3: Build That Frame!

Make your cuts according the measurements you figured out. Don't forget the corner support pieces. Double check your measurements before cutting. I accidentally cut one of my pieces 45" instead of 49" and had to go back and buy another piece. If you were using the same measurements as me, it would be 49" from tip to tip and 106.5" from tip to tip as in the diagram from the previous stage.

Sand any rough edges. I poked little dents on the portions being glued together so that the glue had that much more surface area to touch. It may have been pointless. You may know better. Before you start to glue, put all the pieces together to make sure you have true 45 degree angles and that it makes a rectangle correctly.

Set the four pieces on the ground in the rectangle. Glue the adjoining faces of two corners and stick them together. Spread any excess glue around (and know that there will probably be some coming out the back). Staple. Use a hammer to lightly tap the staples all the way in. Repeat this with the other three corners.

Carefully flip the whole frame over and staple the back side on every corner. Now, glue and staple the corner supports that you cut. Hammer-tap again. Staple the other side.

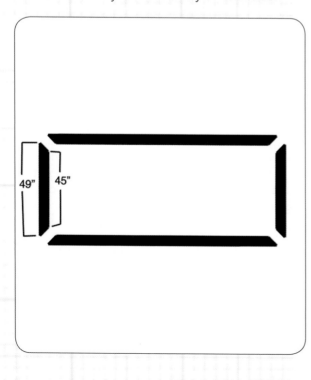

49"   45"

Step 4: Attach the Screen Material

After your frame has had time to dry, you're ready to add the screen material. If need be, iron your material. Lay the material out flat and put your frame on top.

I suggest using some help for this part. I did it by myself and it was tedious stretching it out so it was taut. If you get it pulled as taut as you can and there are still some wrinkled looking areas, do not fear. At least for me, I had some wrinkled looking areas, but after I painted, they disappeared.

With the frame centered, fold one side of the material over and staple away.

As a side note, I used longer staples to staple the wood, shorter ones to staple fabric, and longer ones for a later step of adding the plastic trim.

Pull the opposite side as tight as possible and staple it down the same way. I started at the center of the other side and, as I pulled tightly, worked my way, stapling, towards the outer edges.

Finish off the other two sides of the rectangle.

Step 5: Paint the Screen

If you use canvas material like I did, you will need to put at least two coats of primer on. When getting rollers for this job (you want to use rollers), ask a sales clerk which ones are best for a smooth surface that also will not leave bits of fuzz. I used one roller for primer and a different one for the final paint coat.

Even if you know how to paint well (always roll over the painted surface lightly after you finish an area to make sure it's smoothed out), painting on canvas is not as easy as a wall, so expect that. Follow the can for instructions on how long to wait between coats. I put two coats of the Behr Silver Screen on after the primer and then still added touch-ups after that (always going over touched-up areas lightly with the roller for an even surface).

If you're not used to painting, don't worry when you get done and it looks splotchy, because once it completely dries it'll be more even. You will do the same basic thing if you use the Screen Goo.

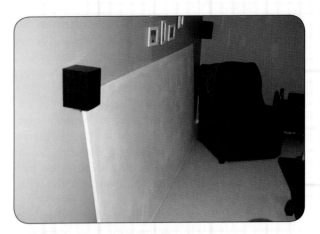

Step 6: Add the Border

Once you've painted, you are to add your border. This is probably the most complicated step to explain. You may come up with a better idea. The schematic picture is my best depiction of how I laid out the plastic 1" trim if the black material were not there.

In the picture, black represents the wood frame, white represents the plastic trim pieces. Cut the black material into strips that will cover the border area. I cut mine lengthwise into thirds and cut one of those pieces in half, which gave me four pieces the right size for what I needed. Do your own measuring. It's better to have too much that will just end up folded on the back.

I folded my black material in half to make it thicker. This is where it kind of gets tricky in the explanation. With this, again, I'm using the measurements for my screen. If you want a bigger border, you may do it a little differently. It's important to look at the progression of the pictures along with the following steps.

Start on one of the sides (the 45"/49" sides). With the screen (painted area) facing up, lay your black material about an inch inside the screen with the excess laying inwards toward the middle of the screen. Staple along the edge of the black material, which will be about 2" inset.

Next, measure and mark all along the side at exactly 2" in with chalk. Also, measure 2" in from the top and bottom. Take a piece of 1" plastic trim and cut it to 45" long. Place the inside edge of the trim to the outside of the chalk line (so that 1] from the edge of the frame to the other side of the trim equals 2" and 2] from the inside of the trim on one side to the inside of the trim on the other side—once it's all done—equals 102 ½" for the length [or 45" for the height] of the screen). You'll also want the trim to be 2" from the top and 2" from the bottom.

Now staple this trim piece down on top of the black material, basically on top of where you stapled the black material already. I stapled one direction for the material and then perpendicular to that for the trim so that I didn't hit any staples when I was stapling down the trim. Through this whole process, always make sure to tap the staples down with a hammer to make sure they are flush. You can go ahead and do this whole process to the other side as well.

Next, flip the screen over so that the back is facing up, then wrap the black material around to the back. In doing so, you are wrapping it over the 1" trim, covering it up. Make sure the material is taut. Start this same process for the length (ultimately, the top and bottom of the screen). The only difference is that this time, you cut the trim to go all the way to each edge (each side). It's okay if you have to use more than one piece of trim for the length since it's all going to get covered up by the black material anyway.

The last picture in this step illustrates what this will look like once the material is stapled and you put the trim down, but have yet to wrap it around to the back. Once you complete this for the two sides and the top and bottom, you're just about done.

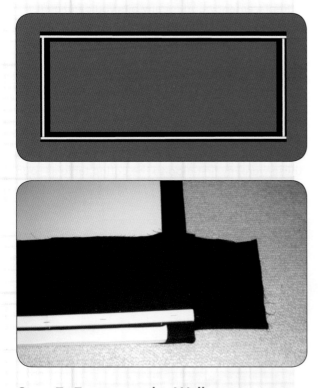

Step 7: Fasten to the Wall

I'm not putting much here because there's many ways to do this. You may want to have yours permanently affixed to the wall. I put the finished screen up to the wall centered exactly, then measured from the edge of each wall to the middle of the 1" × 3" on each side (this should be the same on each side if you want it centered). Then I screwed in a screw with an O-ring to the back of the frame, making sure that the screw portion was short enough that it wouldn't protrude out the front of the black border area (that would be ugly).

On the ceiling, I used screws with open-ended hooks. I made the holes and used drywall anchors to give it enough strength to hold up the screen (trust me, if you're not screwing into studs, you need drywall anchors). Remember, if you're hanging it close to the ceiling, you need enough wiggle room to get it hooked and unhooked.

Like I say, you may find a solution you like better for hanging yours. This way works for me and I can easily mount or dismount it from the wall when not in use.

Step 8: Enjoy Your New Screen

Here are some pictures of my finished product.

A note about aspect ratio: To get the measurements for my screen, I chose a movie with the 2.35:1 aspect ratio (movies like *Matrix*, *Star Wars*, etc.) and blew the picture up to the size I wanted. When I watch content with 16x9 or 4x3, there is white showing on both sides of the screen not being used. To address this, I added black curtains (along with a black skirt) so that it covers up any unused portion of the screen. The result is that the entire wall is either the movie or black. Another way to address the aspect ratio variation would be to create a 4x3 screen that was much taller, but still as wide as possible. Then you could have a black skirt that you raise up for 16x9 content or 2.35:1 content. This way, regardless of the aspect ratio, your content will be as wide as possible on your wall.

Make sure to have a party for the inaugural movie viewing.

Coffee Table Upgrade

By Matthew Thomas (lofgren)

http://www.instructables.com/id/Coffee-table-upgrade/

Create extra storage and a top that raises up to meet you—and your needs!

What's the job of a coffee table these days? To rest your drinks on? A stable surface for the odd TV dinner? To rest your feet on? How about storage? What about for using laptops? Ever bent over your coffee table to use your laptop? How about sitting on the floor and using it as a desk?

Several years ago, we bought a coffee table that was pretty much what we wanted. It was large, rustic-looking, and solidly built . . . but a bit high! We'd find that we'd sit back on the couch at the end of the day and put our feet up, only to find the coffee table was so much higher than the seat of the couch that it would soon be biting into our Achilles' tendons. It was the last day of my holidays and I found myself sitting back, watching *Hot Fuzz*. After shuffling my legs about on the table trying to get comfortable, I thought it was about time to put a long-held plan into action. So, I checked with the boss, and she liked the sound of my idea—mod the coffee table or get a new one!

My goals were to lower the coffee table, add storage, and add some kind of funky lid to get to the storage areas.

Step 1: What You'll Need

Tools:

- Screw drivers (electric driver/drill makes this more fun)
- Hammer
- Pinch/wrecker bar (or something similarly thin and strong to prevent you bending your screwdriver)
- Old blanket to catch splintered wood, screws, scraps, and keep the boss happy
- Ear protection (hammering the pinch bar and smacking at the wood from the underside of the table generated a fair bit of noise and caused my ears to ring before I grabbed the earmuffs)

Materials:

- A similar table to start with (something with a fairly heavy base if you are going to make it open up)
- Bolts
- Nyloc nuts
- Hardwood for the cantilever hinge
- Any extra wood required for shelves, etc.
- Replacement wood for any bits you damage (I had to sacrifice the top routed edging as it was nailed and glued to the table and the table top)

Step 2: Dismantling the Old

After gathering my tools I began to dismantle the table. I started by removing the drawer. I then removed the black steel edging pieces by unscrewing them with the electric drill and a Phillips-head #2 bit. Next I took out the wheels (these were my first mod to the coffee table as soon

as I'd gotten it home). Next up were the legs—I unscrewed the 4" screws and smacked them off with the handle of the hammer to break the glue. The bottom routed edging was glued and nailed, so it got interesting here—patience was the key. I used the pinch bar to gently pry them off, starting at one end and moving along. For the top surface and the top routed edging, trying not to break the wood, I pried the table top away from the base and did the same with the routed edging. In the end I got impatient and frustrated and kicked at the table from the underside. I can't recommend this as it split the wood of the table top. Fortunately I noticed before I kicked a hole straight through.

Step 3: Now That You've Broken It, What Is the Plan?

Time to make some choices. Hinge the table top from one side? I chose not to. You'd either have to remove everything off the top or tip everything off. Also, in my case I had design issues with the routed edging at the top making any kind of simple hinges difficult.

Mount the top on a slide? That could work with some kind of drawer rails. It would probably require a commercial kit, but it could look cool.

What about splitting it in half and hinging both halves? Or having both halve slide open? What about a cantilever hinge? Cantilever (like the hinges on the toolboxes below) means the top will be flat while it is closed/open and while it is opening.

Now, what about storage options? I had considered storage bins on either side of the existing drawer. After looking at how the cantilever hinges would work I realized there wouldn't be much room for storage bins after all. I also figured that bins wouldn't be so practical. So I took some measurements and considered a tray above the drawer. I went with this option.

Step 4: Working Out the Hinges

I didn't take photos of the scrap wood I used to get rough measurement, but you will get the idea. I used the scrap wood to confirm my assumed knowledge and workings of cantilever hinges without wasting the hardwood in testing. I didn't do much measuring, other than working out the maximum size

I could make the hinges and have them fit in the table. I can't give you much more of a guide than to say look at the pictures below. Note that the shorter bits of wood are the parts that move. All the bits of wood that are touching make up one hinge. The moving parts are attached to the long parts at the same distance apart and at the same height. The moving parts are all the same length. Follow these two statements and your tabletop should remain level whether it is open/closed or moving between the two positions.

The first picture is working out where the holes will be drilled. The second is illustrating how the hinge will look when open and confirming that my placement of the holes is correct. The third is countersinking the bolts, and the fourth is the roughly completed hinges (I later added nyloc nuts after discovering regular ones unscrewed with the hinging motion).

Step 5: The Storage

I next added supports for the tray shelving above the drawer and placed the three-ply wood into position. By this stage I had already chopped the top and bottom off the coffee table (notice how the unstained part where I removed the routed edges is no longer as big? It is ½" instead of 3"). To do this, I very carefully ran the whole box over the table saw after very carefully checking that I'd removed all nails and screws. This was a little awkward due to the size and weight of the box shape that makes up the table. Though it was not as heavy as it had been with the routed edging and table top.

Step 6: Surface Preparation

The structure is there, now it's time to prepare all surfaces and put it back together. I used a belt sander to remove most of the previous stain. Incidentally, it was "old teak" and the original manufacturer was quite rough in putting it together, slopping it around in some parts and only sanding roughly to give it that "rustic" look. Sanding the whole thing gave it a more finished look in the end, and removed old coffee rings! I think I used something like 80- and then 120-grit sanding belts. I also filled any holes and dints with wood filler. The table is pine, so I bought pine!

Step 7: Reconstruction

Put it all back together and check out how it works.

Step 8: Stain and Seal It

I bought a Wattyl product that both stained and sealed in one go, as it was cheaper than separate stain and seal products. Unfortunately, the finish on that wasn't so great, so I went back and bought a second Wattyl clear sealer product that was much better. Both were water based "for easy clean up."

I painted two coats of the stain on everything. Because the surface is the main part of the table that everyone will interact with, I paid special attention to that. I then added the second clear seal product (three coats). I gave a light sand between coats with black, wet, and dry sandpaper that is something like 800 grit (if I remember correctly). The routed edge bits were the hardest to prepare for painting. I used paint stripper on them in the end. To scrape off the paint stripper and old stain gloop, I used the hook-like can opener you find on a Swiss army pocket knife (the shape fitted nicely into the routed edging).

Step 9: The Final Product

The table is finally done and we love it. Closed, the table is lower than it was, like a regular coffee table. At the end of the day when you put your feet up, it is relaxing—not uncomfortable. Open, and sitting at the table while on the couch, it is a little higher than a standard table would be if you sat down to it on a chair, but it is great. We have the extra storage and can sit up to it quite comfortably to eat. I would definitely measure the overall open height against the couch seat if I was going to do it again. Having it be a tad lower would be slightly more practical.

Build and Upholster an Oversized Couch

By liberty5-3000

http://www.instructables.com/id/Build-and-upholster-an-oversize-couch/

I built this in the showroom of the handbag company where I am a designer. Space was limited, but with a lot of improvisation, I was able to make it work.

Step 1: Gather Materials

Materials are given for the specific size and shape of the "couch" that I built, and any variation will affect the supply needs.

- Three sheets ¼" × 4' × 8' lauan plywood (wood type doesn't matter; I went with the cheapest option. In hindsight, I also would have used ½" thick wood, to prioritize strength rather than lighter weight.)
- One 2" × 4" × 96"
- One 2" × 4" × 92 ½"
- Two 2" × 4" × 75"
- One 2" × 4" × 56"
- Three 2" × 3" × 16"
- One 2" × 4" × 15" (I did purchase and use additional 2" × 4"s for reinforcement. If you start with the ½" plywood, you may decide this is unnecessary.)
- Three pre-made Queen Anne French-style chair legs (Make sure that if you order online, you are

accurate about the height of the legs. The site I ordered from included the tenon height in the overall height, which none of the other websites had done. This is why some of the tenon is visible on each leg.)
- Three sheets of 4" × 40" × 72" foam
- Two packages of 81" × 96" batting (as thick as possible)
- Seven yards poly/velvet fabric
- One package crystal upholstery buttons (24 to a pack)
- Spray mount adhesive
- A couple yards of ribbon or string

Tools:
- Power drill
- Jig saw
- Staple gun and staples (the serious kind, not the office kind)
- Long piece of wire
- Electric turkey knife (cuts foam like butter!)
- Utility knife

Step 2: Measure, Re-measure, and Cut

I laid out and marked all my 2" × 4"s (which I had delivered precut from the lumber yard). I also laid out some of my other supplies, in a mock-up, just to check that I had enough of everything.

I had drawn the curve shape for the back in Illustrator, so I was able to print and piece the pages together. I used this printout as a template for drawing the topline of the back. You can freehand it or use various drafting tools. Once I had traced the template, I used the jigsaw to cut out the shape. I also cut the plywood rectangle to fit the seat part of the piece.

I painted the front three legs that I had ordered premade and the back three legs, for which I used the 2" × 4"s.

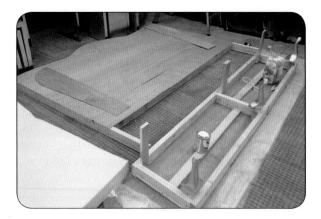

Step 3: Drill, Baby, Drill

Screw your frame pieces together for the back and the bench. Attach the premade legs and the 2″ × 4″ legs and double check that everything is square and level. (Do not attach the back to the bench yet.)

Screw the plywood back piece to the back frame, and the bench portion to the bench frame. I used an additional "wing" piece on each side of the back to get the curve shape.

Step 4: Glue and Cut the Foam

Lay the foam pieces out for the bench and the back and plan your arrangement. Use the spray adhesive (or any strong glue) to attach the foam to the plywood. Then use the electric turkey knife to cut the foam to the shape of the back and bench. (I glued and then cut; however, if you can manage, I would recommend cutting first. The glue gummed up the knife and it eventually died.

Step 5: The Batting and the Fabric

Lay out your batting on the back piece and the bench. Cut roughly around the shape, allowing yourself lots of extra to wrap around and staple at the back.

Do the exact same thing with the fabric, on top of the batting.

At this point, if you wanted to use a few staples to temporarily tack the fabric and batting in place, you could. However, I found that the texture of the foam and the batting, and even the fabric, meant that everything stayed pretty well in place.

Step 6: Tufting

This part you definitely need two people for. Plan out how many and where you want your button "tufts." This took a lot of measuring and remeasuring for me.

Using a small drill bit, drill through the plywood where you want the first button. Take the wire—it doesn't matter what kind, it just needs to be soft enough to work with, but firm enough to force its way through the foam—and fold it in half. Poke the bent center (not the two loose ends) through the hole you just made and through the foam and batting. Don't feed the wire all the way through; hold on to the loose ends from the back. You will need to use a utility blade or scissors to get through the fabric. From the front, thread a button onto a foot or so of ribbon and then feed both ends of the ribbon through the bent wire—like threading a needle. Pull the wire back through, bringing the thread with it. Have someone stand in front and help you gauge how tight to pull the ribbon. Once your tuft is how you like it, use the staple gun to attach the ends of the ribbon to the back of the piece. Repeat for as many tufts as you desire. There are probably easier or better ways to do this, but I chose to do it this way so that I could easily remove the buttons and change the fabric if I decided.

Step 7: Finishing

Now it's time to attach the fabric and the batting. Choose a starting point and pull the fabric and batting tight, wrapping it around the edges and stapling it to the back. Work your way around the whole back piece, pulling and smoothing as you go. After you've gone around once, you may need to go back around to neaten the ends of the fabric by cutting or adding more staples.

Once you've completed the fabric on both pieces, you can attach the back and the bench pieces to each other.

New Living Room Pallet Table for Letting House

By Kyriakos Simou (D0itYourself)
http://www.instructables.com/id/NEW-LIVING-ROOM-PALLET-TABLE-FOR-LETTING-HOUSE/

I had to build a better-looking table for my letting-house living room. The house is near the sea, and the idea was to build a table that gives you a sense or remembrance of the sea.

Step 1: Materials Used

The materials used are as follows:

- Wooden pallets (found around)
- Makita multi-tool
- Sandpaper
- Primer
- Paint
- Screws/nails
- Plastic feet
- Silicon base
- Glass (ordered)
- Sea rocks
- Star fish (from SCUBA diving)
- Anchor, scuba helmet, wooden barrel and an amphore

Step 2: Sanding the Pallets

This was the second wooden pallet table I did. When I finished the first one I said that it would have been better to disassemble the pallets so it would be easier while sanding, painting, and cutting the pallets to make them the same size.

Step 3: Disassemble the Two Bottom Pallets

I disassembled the two bottom pallets and I cut them to be 100cm x 60cm. Then I sanded them and applied woodworm. After that, it was time for primer and sanding again. Then I painted them white. After a day once the paint had dried, I assembled them.

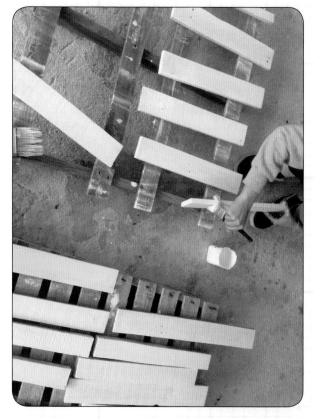

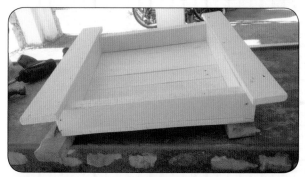

Step 4: Design the Pallet with the Drawer

So, the idea for this table was to make a "drawer" on the top and fill it with sea rocks, star fish, anchor, and other things so it refers to sea. We have decided that the drawer will be at one side of the pallet and not in the middle. I disassembled the pallet, cut it in the right dimensions, and started designing the drawer.

216

Step 5: Decorated
My fiancé did it!

Rain-Gutter Book Shelves

By Biodynamic

http://www.instructables.com/id/Rain-Gutter-Book-Shelves-1/

Believe me, I was skeptical too! When my wife mentioned that she wanted me to install some book shelves I was psyched. I thought I was going to be able to break out my new compound miter saw that I got for Christmas. When she told me they would be made of vinyl gutters . . . I cried a little on the inside.

After a few weeks, I can honestly say they have been a great addition. The kids who can read are reading more, and the kids who can't yet read are asking to have books read to them way more often. The rain-gutter book shelves don't look like I anticipated they would. They look ten times better. Depending on how high you install them, they can take on the appearance of a chair rail, can be used to keep things out of the reach of inquisitive younger siblings, or make an attractive shelf that can hold a multitude of things.

The gutters can be cut to size, be painted just about any color, and are super easy to install. Please check out the pictures.

Step 1: You Are Going to Need . . .

- Vinyl gutters (they come in 10' sections).
- Mounting brackets
- End caps
- Screws
- Screw driver or drill
- Level
- Measuring tape

I used a laser level that made things a whole lot easier. I'm pretty sure anyone can do this.

Step 2: First

Plan out how long your shelves are going to be.

Step 3: Second

Decide how many brackets you will need. I used one gutter bracket for every 24", give or take a few inches. I tried to space them evenly for the length of gutter I was going to hang.

Step 4: Third

Calculate how many end caps you will need. You will need a left end cap and a right end cap for every shelf you plan on hanging. We decided to eliminate the caps in the kids' rooms to save on cost. We knew we could always go back and add them if we didn't like the way they looked. So far, no complaints.

Step 5: Fourth

Start hanging gutters. I didn't bother drilling into the studs because I knew we weren't going to add that many books.

Step 6: Fifth

I don't know how to instruct beyond this point. Check out the pictures to see what you think.

3D Hardwood Floor

By Vyger

http://www.instructables.com/id/Make-a-Hardwood-Floor-that-looks-3D-from-your-OWN-/

I have cut a lot of logs over the years and I have always been impressed at how beautiful some of the wood looks inside. I always wondered if there wasn't something I could do with it besides burn it for firewood. But how can you make anything from trees without the large scale professional tools and a mill? I discovered there is a way, but I warn you, it's not an easy project.

A perfect project for this idea is to make a hardwood floor with wood from locally grown trees. There are three common hardwood trees in northeast Montana: they are the Ash, the Siberian Elm, and the Russian Olive. Russian Olive wood is probably the most distinctive, being almost chocolate colored, and it is a very beautiful wood. However, virtually no one uses it for anything other than burning. Though it is the softest of the three woods it is still a hardwood, so it will work for a floor. Russian Olive trees are usually not very big. They do not produce large straight trunks, and they often grow crooked in many directions. This makes it a very poor candidate for milling or for even getting large pieces out of it.

The Siberian elm is often thought of as a junk tree, a nuisance, and/or a weed tree. It puts out huge amounts of seeds in the spring, which sprout everywhere, and the seedlings are tough to remove once they get a foothold. There are many types of elms, and elm wood is known to be a beautiful wood, but also a difficult wood to work with. It has the tendency to split, crack, and warp so it is not used that often for wood projects. The only tree in the group that has a good reputation is the Ash.

Almost all of the wood floors that you will come across are made of long boards. That's nice, but it is a near impossibility to get long lengths from these trees, especially without any kind of mill. So what can you do with short pieces? I finally found an answer to that while looking up yet more information on hardwood floors. There is a tiling method that uses a rhombus (a diamond or squashed square) and requires small pieces of three different types or colors of wood—a perfect fit for what I have.

Cutting up logs and turning them into 2" diamonds—yep, a crazy idea. That's what I am going to show you how to do in this Instructable.

Step 1: The Chainsaw

For this job you have to start with a chainsaw. For cutting these logs the way we are going to you should use a gas one. The electric ones just don't have the RPM to cut this much. You could do it, but it would take you forever. I am using my old reliable Craftsman.

One thing about chain saws to remember: the bigger they are, the more tired you get using them. You can cut all day with a medium-size one and not feel that your arms are going to fall off. So unless you have really large logs and can afford an expensive saw, a medium 16" or 18" one will work great.

I have two kinds of logs for this project—big ones and really big ones. Logs under 3" in diameter won't really work for getting finished dimensions of 2". Anything over 4" or 5" will work pretty well for this, but the way you cut the medium logs and the really big logs is different. Big logs can be cut into slabs. Since my finished size is going to be 2", I try to cut the slabs in 3" thick pieces. Small logs you can cut into 2" pieces. The size you need to cut them to depends on how large a piece your band saw can handle.

A key to cutting straight is to have a sharp chain and a good bar. If some of the teeth on your chain are dull on one side, it will cause your saw to cut in an arc, which means you're cutting firewood and not wood for the floor.

Cutting in the snow has its benefits. You can use the snow to brace the logs to keep them where you want them. And if you cut all the way through the log and into the snow it doesn't dull your chain.

A Y or fork or branching produces some of the more interesting grain patterns. Cut it straight through the center to make it manageable for your band saw. Don't try and cut from the top down straight through. The saw will wander all over. Start by cutting a line all the way down where you want your cut to go. That gives you a guide of sorts. Often when you cut like this the saw will cut out stringy wood. This is because you are cutting with the grain and rather than producing little flakes it scrapes out long strips, much like a hand plan does. It can clog your saw, so if it gets jammed up stop and clear it out. If you get too much of this shredded wood jammed around the saw sprocket it can cause your chain to fly off.

Step 2: Cutting Slabs and Blocks

These pictures make it look easy, but it's actually pretty difficult to cut straight lines through large tree trunks. You might want to practice on some firewood ones before you try any that you want to use for lumber.

Start by measuring where you are going to make your cuts. You can just guess, but in my experience you often will guess wrong. It's easier to use a tape measure.

My finished size is going to be 2", so I am making 3" cuts. That sounds like a lot of waste, and actually it is, but any chain saw is going to take out a pretty wide cut because the bar is not narrow. In addition, the cut is not going to be completely straight up and down. Even the best chain saw moves around while it's cutting and takes out extra wood. Finally, this slab is going to have to be processed further. It needs to be run through a planer in order to make the cut sides parallel, so you will lose wood there too.

Start the cuts across the top following the lines you made. After getting these started—and I usually cut them as deep as the bar is—angle the saw down and cut lines down the front. These serve as guides so you can stay on a parallel cut.

Rock the saw between the cuts across the top and the cuts on the front. This allows you to keep both lines straight as you work down through the wood. You might notice that my trunk is sitting on top

of another piece. This gives me clearance to cut the front lines. Often you will find your saw at about a 45 degree angle, cutting both top and front at the same time. Take your time and let the saw do the work.

Cut all the way down but don't cut a piece off until you have all the slots cut almost all the way. This gives you the weight of the whole log as a stabilizer until you get them all cut. Having another log underneath also prevents you from cutting into the ground and dulling your saw when you get to that last little bit. After you get through these you are ready to take them inside for the next step.

Step 3: Logs Are Imperfect but There Are Ways to Work Around It

A lot of times logs will rot from the center outward. In these the core is not going to be any good. When you run across these try to cut the good wood on either side of the bad part. How can you tell if it's bad? Looking at the end you will see that the core wood is different, soft, and spongy looking. It also doesn't leave sharp lines when cut, kind of like cutting warm butter.

Wet Versus Dry:

This is a good place to talk about wet wood versus dry wood. You can't use wet wood for your floor, it has to dry out first, but wet wood cuts easier than dry wood (usually). An exception here is really wet wood that is frozen solid, which is like cutting rock. But dry wood is stable, and it's usually done cracking and warping. You can cut a parallel slab of wet wood, let it sit for the summer to dry out, and find that its warped into a U while drying. I prefer to let the wood dry for several years before I do anything with it. When the bark peels off of it and leaves just the bare wood then it's close to being ready. Of course you take a chance of it rotting in the meantime, but at least you can work with it without it changing shape and shrinking, which is what wet wood will do. This means you have to plan way ahead or find trees that are already dead and dried that are of the type of wood you are looking for.

The main goal with the band saw is to cut logs down into blocks that are small enough to fit on the table saw.

Step 4: A Finner Cut

Now that you have your slabs and dissected logs done you can move indoors and work with power tools. Smaller logs can go directly to the band saw. Why not go straight to a table saw, you may wonder. Table saws are great tools but they have their drawbacks. The maximum height of the cut of the blade of my old Craftsman table saw with its 10" blade is 2 ½". Also, table saws can't handle any kind of twisting or rocking of the cutting stock. If the material does anything except move in a straight line it will usually bind up the blade. The blade has no flex to it. On the other hand, band-saw blades are just fine with the wood moving a little, and they can usually handle much thicker wood.

My band saw cuts wood almost up to 5" thick, so I cut all my logs to be just under that. The saw comes with a ⅜" blade, but it's worthless for cutting anything thick like these logs. You need to get a full ½" blade for it. Actually, several blades. I found that dry, rock-hard ash wood dulls the teeth on these pretty fast.

Note: In the end I bought a carbide-tipped blade for this saw. They cost almost six times as much as the regular blades but they cut through the hard wood much faster and easier. They also last a lot longer, as the tiny carbide teeth don't get dulled from the hard wood. When these bands break you will want to repair them, as the teeth will probably still be sharp. You may want to invest in a splicing kit.

Step 5: Planing Slabs

The reason you have to plane these slabs is so they can run flat on the table saw and not bind up the blade. I tried cutting both planed ones and unplaned ones. The planed ones were much easier to work with. The unplaned ones rocked around on the high spots and were very difficult to move through the saw blade without binding it up. Also, when the two sides of the slab are not parallel and it's too thick a piece to cut all the way through, you cannot flip it over and cut it through from the other side. The saw blade is pointing in a different direction because the surfaces are not parallel, and the two cuts won't match up. So, it's a little extra work to plane them but it saves later on.

Raise the plane above the work piece and slowly lower it down as you run pieces through it. I usually work with only one piece at a time rather than trying to run multiple pieces through one after the other. Be very careful doing this. If you go too fast the planer blades can impact on a high point and actually break them. You want it to shave the high points down gradually. It might take many passes to accomplish this. After you get a flat side, turn the slab over every two or three passes so you shave down both sides evenly. Keep going until the chain saw marks are mostly gone. If your slab is too wide to fit your planer you might have to cut it in two with the chain saw.

Planing produces a lot of saw dust and chips. I bagged up a lot of mine and gave it to a friend, who used it as bedding for his dog. It is soft and warm and smells great (depending on the kind of wood), and when it gets dirty you can dump it in the garden to use for compost.

Step 6: Finally, the Table Saw

Once you get blocks small enough for your table saw, you begin to get results that look more like lumber and less like logs.

To cut the slabs you might need to free cut them through the middle. If the slabs don't have flat edges you can't run them along the rip fence. You need to get a flat face to glide along the rip fence. If the slabs are too thick for your saw blade to cut clear through, you can flip them over and cut them again from the backside. Another option is to run them on your band saw. The band naturally follows the partial cut and glides right through.

After you get a stack of rough-cut sticks you are ready to move on to the final cut. The reason for making a rough cut first is to make certain you get the right size. You can't uncut a piece of wood, so even though it seems like a waste of wood you need to do a rough cut before you move on to the final cut. The rough-cut size I am working with is 1 ¼" by 2 ¼". The intended finished size is 1" × 2".

I found it to be a good idea to let the rough-cut pieces "rest" for several days. A few weeks would be even better. If they still have moisture in them it lets them dry out more. In addition, if they are going to do any warping or cracking now is the best time for it before you start finished cutting. An even bigger problem is shrinking. As wood loses moisture it shrinks. If it shrinks below your target dimensions you will not be able to use it.

Step 7: Making the Final Cuts

To do the finished cuts I used a fine-tooth saw blade. The blade I have been using up until now is a 40-tooth general-purpose blade. Now I am moving to an 80-tooth blade. The larger number of teeth make a smoother, finer cut. This is where we need to get exact, so precision becomes the priority.

To measure for these cuts do not go by the markings on the rip-fence guide. Those were fine for the rough cuts but not now. Measure from the edge of the saw tooth to the rip fence. Actually, put the measure under the tooth so you can see it line up. Don't use a tape measure; it's not accurate enough for this. Use a good ruler that is accurate.

I made four cuts on each stick. I cut them first to 1 ⅛" and 2 ⅛". This way I cut every side of the stick with the fine-tooth blade. This blade actually puts a little shine on the wood after it cuts because of the fineness of the blade. This might seem like a lot of cutting, and it is. I made a really big pile of sawdust, but the final goal requires that you get the individual pieces all as exact as you possibly can.

Step 8: Sanding

You need to decide which side is going to be the top for each stick. Then each top needs to be sanded. You should do this now because it's a lot easier to sand a stick than it is to sand a little rhombus piece. You could wait and sand them after they are in place in the floor, and you may need to do that anyway, but it's easier to take out any flaws and saw marks now while you have a chance.

A stationary belt sander would be nice to have for this job, but I don't have one. What I do have, however, works just as well. It's a Craftsman 3" belt sander, and I got the stand to go with it when I bought it long ago. The stand turns it into a stationary sanding machine. Bolt it down to a portable work bench and you are all set for mass production.

I started with a 50-grit, fast-cutting paper and ran everything through to take out the flaws. I followed it up with a fine 80-grit, which didn't leave behind any sand marks.

Just a suggestion: by now you should have invested in some dust masks, and this is a good place to use them.

Step 9: Spline

Rather than just gluing my pieces together in a flat butt joint I decided to use a spline to join them. I could have used the traditional tongue and groove method, but that would have involved a lot more cutting, and I would have lost even more wood. A spline can work just as well as, if not better than, most other methods for joining surfaces.

A spline is a small, flat piece of wood that fits into a slot in order to help hold jointed pieces together.

One of the advantages of using this method is that the spline will help with any cracks in the wood like you see in the pictures. The spline together with the glue will reinforce the piece at the same time that it holds it together.

I needed to switch saw blades for this. I used my 60-tooth Craftsman blade. The teeth on this blade are narrower so the slot that it cuts is smaller. I have a lot of thin plywood pieces called door skins that fit perfectly in this slot, so I don't need to cut any wood specially to use for the spline.

Set your blade height to what you plan to use. I cut mine ½" deep. Cut the slots on both sides. I ran all my pieces twice to make sure the slots were clean. Cut them with the face towards the rip fence. By doing this you make sure that all the tops of the boards will line up level with each other even if a piece's thickness is a little off.

Cutting these now is a lot easier than after the rhombuses are cut. You will still have to cut a slot into each side of those, but you will already have half of it done by cutting these now.

You might notice that I put a finish on these pieces. Normally you would wait until after the floor is in place to put a finish on them, but because I was planning on taking pictures of the pieces and showing the possible designs I put a couple of coats of finish on them after I sanded them.

Step 10: The Last Step—Make a Jig and Cut the Rhombus

A cutting jig is a saw accessory that helps you make complicated cuts that turn out the same every time. To cut the angles for the rhombus you need to make a jig. It's not hard to do if you follow the steps.

First you need a piece of wood (or plastic) that will fit into the miter guide slot in the saw table. This stick has to fit tight to keep the jig from moving anywhere except back and forth, but be loose enough to slide freely in the slot.

Next find a big enough piece of plywood to fit the saw table and cut at least two sides square. The square corner will be at your lower right-hand position. Set your rip fence for 2", the final dimension of your pieces, and use your ruler to measure it. Then slide your plywood up the rip fence and make a cut in it about halfway down. Stop and turn off your saw but don't move the plywood.

Now, with the plywood still in place and not having moved, screw the plywood to the stick in the miter guide slot. This fastens and locks your jig in place square with your blade. It should now be able to slide back and forth along the rip fence but not bind with it or the saw blade.

Now you need a good protractor or angle guide. Move the rip fence out of the way and put the protractor on the saw blade. You need to measure and set your angle with the blade, not the edge of the jig. It's the blade that counts. The angle you are setting is 60 degrees. Be exact. Mark your board as to where this angle is. Then take a straight piece of wood and place it along the line; check it again with the protractor. When you get it dead on then screw it down to the board. This is the guide for cutting all your sticks. You may have to (very likely) adjust this angle to get it correct. I was ½ a degree off in my initial setting and my rhombus pieces would not fit together correctly. This is a very exact angle, and it needs to be as close to 60 degrees as possible. You can adjust the angle of the guide stick by loosening the screws, all but the one nearest the blade, and pivoting it on that screw. Once you get it right don't ever move it.

Make a push stick with the front cut to the same angle as your rhombus pieces and make it as thick as they are. A rejected stick from your cutting makes a perfect push stick. Screw a piece of wood to the top so it reaches over your cut piece. The idea is that once you cut off that little diamond it's going to vibrate from the saw blade running. If it turns even a little bit sideways and a tooth of that blade catches it, it will launch straight back at you. Your push stick keeps it straight against the rip fence and allows you to push it on past the blade, and the top prevents it from popping up out of your slot.

I added a bumper board to the front once I had tried the jig out and had it all correct. The bumper actually works really well. You hold the stick to be cut against your guide with your left hand, hold your push stick in your right and then just push the whole thing into the saw blade with your hip. After a very short time you develop a rhythm and it's almost like a machine cutting. All your little rhombus pieces slide out the back and make a nice pile.

You will have short pieces left over from your sticks that you can't hold to your guide with your fingers because the pieces are too short. Save them and cut them at the end using a clamp to hold them to the guide. You won't waste them, as they *can* be cut, but don't try and do it by hand that close to the blade.

our brain is used to seeing in 3D, and when it sees something like this it tries to interpret it as such.

Now make three boxes and push them together, then add three rhombuses to the blank edges, and you are once again back to a six-sided figure. But now it looks like three boxes inside of another corner of a bigger box, or does it? Take six pieces of all the same color and make a star out of them. It's the same pieces, just in a different arrangement, and it looks completely different until you notice that it actually has boxes in it like the other one. The more you play the more fun it gets. The patterns that emerge are amazing, and your eyes keep trying to make sense of it.

Getting this far, to the finished floor pieces, is as far as this Instructable is going to go. I need to make a bunch more batches of rhombuses until I have enough.

You can make these pieces out of conventional wood stocks. Left over scraps would work perfectly. I started out with logs because I wanted to do something with my own wood. That is optional. You will need to make a cutting jig though even if you use different wood.

Have fun with it.

Step 11: The Results

Finally, from a tree to a rhombus. Now sit down at your table or on your floor and start playing with your pieces. Put three different colored pieces together and look at it for a moment and you will see a box. It can either be a solid box with the outside corner towards you or it can be an open box with only the two back sides on it. Your eyes might flip back and forth between the two. Since we live in a 3D world

Corner Hammock Shelf

By okurt

http://www.instructables.com/id/Corner-Hammock-Shelf/

Let's make a shelf that seems like a hammock. You can store your books or other small things. At the same time, it can be a cute furnishing to decorate corners in your room.

There are always a lot of books in our homes, especially frequently used books that must be stored. We sometimes squeeze them into places in our rooms. Maybe what you need is a knitted shelf with chain.

Step 1: Materials
- Needle-nose pliers
- Thin metal wire
- Scissors
- Chain (about 15 meters)
- Two metal rings
- White plumbing pipe (two pieces about 30 cm long)
- Transparent corrugated plumbing pipe

Step 2: Preparing Pipes

We need an electric drill to drill the pipe with holes at equal spaces. Put the white pipe within the thicker, transparent pipe and then start to drill. These holes will use chains to connect to each other.

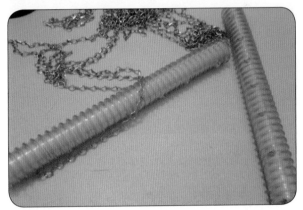

Step 3: Knitting the Chains

To start to knit chains, first divide your chain into two equal pieces for the two sides of the shelf. The first chain piece must open from his unity and connect with the metal wire to carry it through the pipes. You must twist the wire after the connection. Then start to knit the other chain lines toward the center.

Step 4: Knitting

Combining the chains must be done diagonally. To combine the chains use the needle-nose pliers. Open the chain's wire and close after the combining. When finished with the line connect it using metal wire again and pass through the other side of the pipes.

through the pipes must connect with the hanger chains, and then they connect to the rings at an appropriate point on the chain. Cover the end of the white pipes with stretch film.

Step 5: To Finish Knitting

After you finish combining all lines, the next step is connecting hanger chains. The wires that we carry

Step 6: Final

Now your corner hammock shelf is ready for hanging! Hang it on your corner wall and throw your books on it.

Kids Room

Fixing things makes life easier, and when it comes to your kids room, it can become essential. One missed step on the bunk bed ladder could prove disastrous. Don't put off fixes that you can do now yourself. Make sure you keep everything in working order with these fixes for around your child's room and inside their toy chest.

I was looking for furniture for my kid's room at a local Goodwill when I stumbled upon two little mismatched school chairs and a beaten up drawing table. Despite their poor cosmetic appearance, they were stable and in good condition. I decided to cover the top of the table with pictures of books my children love, art quotes, and some random puzzle pieces, and to paint the chairs to match. I'm really happy with the results of my "fix"!

Step 1: Here Is What I Used

- Fine sandpaper
- Towel to wipe dust away after sanding
- Rust-oleum Painters Touch spray paint (I needed a paint that would work on plastic)
- Color printouts and puzzle pieces for decoration
- Mod Podge
- Foam brush
- Krylon Clear Acrylic Spray

Step 2: Start with the Right Piece of Furniture

I had a clear idea of how I wanted to decorate the table. So, I got to work with the sandpaper to remove the old crayon and pencil marks. It didn't take too long to sand, and I would suggest using a face mask to prevent breathing in any lead paint from old furniture.

Once I sanded down the tabletop, I wiped it down to remove all of the dust. I used a wet towel for this step. You need to remove as much dust as possible in order for the adhesives to work.

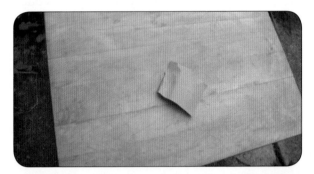

Step 3: Arrange and Glue

I printed off the book cover photos using a color printer and cut off the excess white margins. I played around with the arrangement until I was happy with the result. Then I took a picture of it so I wouldn't forget the layout.

I used a foam brush to put Mod Podge onto the back of each photo and then onto the spot it would cover on the table. Don't be alarmed if the Mod Podge shows up white at first; it will dry clear.

I worked slowly so that I could reposition the photo if needed before the glue fastened. I didn't get any photos of this part of the process because my fingers were pretty sticky! Once I finished positioning everything on the table, I slowly brushed Mod Podge on top of the entire table top to cover all of the items. I smoothed out any wrinkles in the paper and bubbles that formed during the drying process or the surface would have been bumpy.

Giving it about 15 minutes to dry in between each layer, I covered the table with another three layers of Mod Podge.I had a lot of edges sticking up so I pressed them down for a few minutes with my fingers, and that seemed to work pretty well.

I let my table dry for three days (because it was pretty humid here). I then used a clear acrylic spray made by Krylon, and in a back and forth motion, sprayed it over the entire table top.

Now for the chairs! I wiped them down with a wet cloth to prepare them for the paint. Once they dried off, I used the spray paint to cover each chair completely. This is where the face mask would come in handy again because you do not want to breathe this in! Allow for drying time.

Step 4: Acrylic Spray

The clear acrylic spray leaves a glossy finish and makes it weather (and hopefully crayon) resistant. All in all, I spent less than $20 and created a special table for my little artists!

Bunk Bed Ladder Fix

By jdevine1

http://www.instructables.com/id/Bunk-Bed-
Ladder-Fix/

My daughter *loves* sleeping on the top bunk of her bed, except for one thing: It is a metal bunk bed and the ladder hurts her feet when she climbs up and down. After doing some pondering, I came up with an idea.

Step 2: Cut the Noodle

I just lined the noodle up with the step and cut the noodle to the length I needed. Then cut the noodle lengthwise so you can slip the noodle pieces over the ladder steps.

Step 1: Grab Your Supplies

• Pool noodle. Choose a pool noodle in any color. Noodles come with various sizes of center openings, so just choose one closest to the size of your ladder rungs.
• A pair of decent scissors. You know, not a pair your kids have been messing with.
• Decorative duct tape

Step 3: Place It on the Ladder

Open the noodle where you just cut it and slide it onto the ladder step.

Step 4: Repeat

Repeat this process for each step of the ladder.

Step 5: Wrap with Duct Tape

Wrap each step with decorative duct tape to hold the noodle on the step. This step is optional, but without it, the noodle will pop off of the ladder, and you will constantly be putting it back on. Plus, it has the added benefit of looking cool. My daughter reports that the ladder no longer hurts her feet. This solution literally cost me $3 plus tax: $1 for the noodle and $2 for tape.

Fix a Classic G.I. JOE Figure

By Mario Caicedo Langer (M.C. Langer)
http://www.instructables.com/id/
Fix-a-classic-GIJOE-figure-using-
a-condom/

Last Saturday I was invited by a couple of friends of mine to their home. They have an awesome collection of classic G.I. JOE action figures. Some of them were damaged because the inner rubber band that put them together was broken. Luckily, they keep the parts. Then I took one of the apparently good figures and accidentally broke its rubber band. Now I have in my hands the legs, hip, and chest of another dead JOE.

They told me I didn't need to blame myself. After all, it was normal age damage on the classic JOEs. Maybe one day they would buy some rubber bands for the action figures. Or maybe not.

I didn't want to leave without making amends for my fault. But what could I do? I didn't have any rubber bands, nor my Dremel or my Sonic Screwdriver. So I used something everybody has: a condom. It worked so well my friends asked me for help fixing other figures. It's a simple solution and you can give a new life to your old G.I. JOEs. You can even reuse expired condoms.

And here I am, using condoms near Valentine's Day, repairing some old toys . . .

Step 1: Materials
You will need:

- A classic G.I.JOE action figure, with the inner rubber band broken
- A condom
- Scissors
- Tweezers (or anything for grabbing the rubber band, like a paperclip)
- Small screwdriver

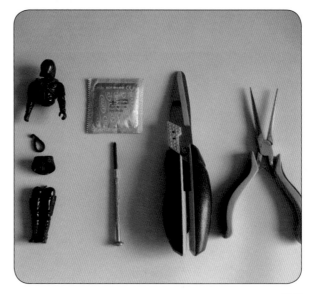

Step 2: The Condom

First, transform the condom into a rubber band. Unroll it and cut the base ring. Wash it.

Please, for God's sake, use a NEW condom. The rest of the condom will become useless for its original purpose. So please, again, please don't try to use it.

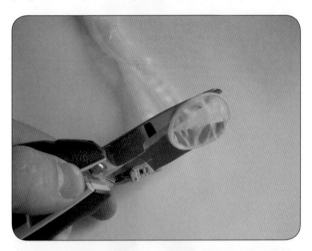

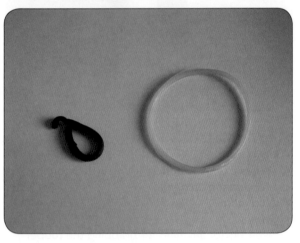

Step 4: The Legs

Hook the condom's rubber band (use it in two loops) on the legs hook and pass it across the hip.

Step 3: The Torso

With the screwdriver, remove the screw. Remove the chest. Watch out for the correct position of the arms.

Step 5: Arm It Again

Put the rubber band in the center of the chest. Make another loop for reducing the elasticity. Put on the head, arms, and chest and screw it. It's done.

How to Fix a Cassette Tape

By ke4mcl

http://www.instructables.com/id/How-to-fix-a-cassette-tape/

This Instructable takes for granted that you can use basic hand tools and have good dexterity with small parts. The only items required are the tapes, a small screwdriver set, a pair of needle-nose pliers, and Scotch tape.

For all those folks still holding on to a cherished but broken cassette tape, here's how to properly fix the common ailments. We'll cover transplanting the tape from a busted shell to a good shell, how to get into a welded shell cassette, how to splice a tape, and how to fix squeals.

The lowly cassette… If you were a kid of the '80s you knew them well. Littered around the car's glove box, piled around a boombox, or crammed in your pocket on your way to school, cassettes were everywhere. It's how an entire generation swapped music or impressed their partner with their ability to create a mix tape. Thanks to the iPod and its huge storage capacity, the mixtape has become a lost art. Swapping music went from being a very social activity to something as mundane as checking email. Despite the advances in tech, millions of cassettes still survive as do the machines to play them on. Granted the music on many tapes is available in digital form, but not all is. Lots of folks used hidden recorders to make bootleg tapes at concerts. Just look at the huge online community that still swaps Grateful Dead recordings. Many of those bootleg recordings were initially made on cassette. There are also mixtapes that were made with a personal touch that a playlist on an ipod can never come near.

Enough reminiscing, let's dig in!

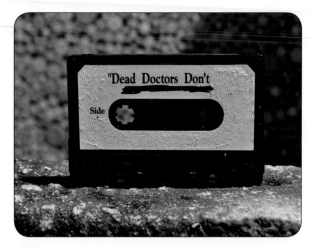

Step 1: What Kind of Shell Do You Have?

Cassette shells basically come in two types: welded together and screwed together. The screwed together shells will have from one to five screws holding them together. The welded ones have no screws. Both halves are joined using a process called *sonic welding,* which makes repair a little difficult but not impossible.

Welded-shell tapes must be cracked open. Screwed-together tapes come apart easily once the screws are removed.

Step 2: What Repairs Require Getting into the Tape?

Before touching any magnetic tape, wash your hands with dish soap and dry them thoroughly. You don't want to get grease, grime, oil, or dirt on the tape itself.

If your tape has snapped and wound itself up so you have no tape in the access hole, you need to open the case to fix it. If your tape is mangled or broken but both ends are still hanging out of the shell, you can fix that without opening the shell. Mangled tape can be straightened out and carefully wound back up by turning the hubs on the cassette. Broken tape in which both ends are hanging out of the shell still can be spliced without opening the shell. See the step on splicing tape.

Cassettes that are squeaky, binding, wrapped on themselves, or on which the shell is just in very poor shape will require disassembly. Some DIY articles mention using vegetable oil to cure squeaky tapes and that is 100 percent wrong. Do not do that as it will gum up the works on your tape machine and ruin the tape over time.

Step 3: Getting into a Screwed-Shell Tape

On a screwed-together shell, you remove the screws and the shell comes apart. Your best bet is to perform the whole operation without lifting the tape off the table so you don't spill its guts all over the floor. You should be able to remove the top half of the shell while leaving the bottom half and its contents lying on the table.

Make sure you use a *non*-magnetized screwdriver for this. Magnetized tools will cause drop outs in your tape. Remember this is magnetic media; do not use magnetized tools for any of this work.

Screwed-shell tapes make great donor shells. If you have any screwed-together cassettes that don't interest you, don't toss them. They are perfect for transplanting the guts from a welded-shell cassette that had to be cracked open for repair.

Step 4: Getting into a Welded-Shell Tape

If you are going to be repairing a welded-shell cassette, you will need a donor shell to move all the guts into. Even when they snap open in a clean fashion, welded-shell cassettes never go back together properly no matter how much crazy glue you have. Old cassettes are cheap at flea markets. Get some screwed-together donor shells if you plan on fixing old tapes.

It's destroy-stuff-in-a-vise time! (And who doesn't like destroy-stuff-in-a-vise time?)

There are two well-known ways to get into a welded-shell tape. One is to use an X-Acto or other knife to pry your way around the seam, snapping the welds as you go. I have tried this and impaled myself too many times.

My preferred method is the vise. Insert cassette into vise as pictured and squeeze till you hear the seams pop. Turn the tape 90 degrees and repeat. This should cause enough breakage for you to be able to carefully pull the tape apart without spilling its contents all over the floor.

This doesn't always work as planned. The tape in the picture turned out to be made of a very brittle plastic and it just exploded its guts all over the floor. Yup, safety glasses are a good idea here.

Just about all pre-recorded tapes will be in a welded shell.

Step 5: You Dropped the Tape and Made a Mess...No Biggie

Take the fullest spool and get it back into what remains of the shell that is useable as pictured. Place finger on the edge to keep it from unwinding further and slowly wind the tape back up. Slow, tedious, and hard to do at first, but once you get the hang of it, it becomes easy.

Step 6: Components of a Cassette Tape

To explain what's inside a cassette, we'll use the one that came apart peacefully.

Picture 1: inside a cassette with half its shell removed

Picture 2: the slip sheet. This reduces friction between the tape and the shell. These can be clear.

Picture 3: the pressure pad. This provides even contact between the tape and the heads on the machine that read the tape. This is an important part and without it most cassette players will have poor audio reproduction. There are some high-end machines that don't require the pressure pad, but about 90 percent of machines made need it.

Picture 4: the Mu metal shield. It has nothing to do with cows. It's a magnetic shield required by older tape machines.

Picture 5: the rollers. Most cassettes have two of these. Really cheap cassettes may have just a plastic peg here. These can squeal. The only fix is a minuscule amount of nylon-safe lubricant on the metal shaft of the roller. We are talking a very small amount as you don't want any lube getting on the tape.

Picture 6: the tape "pancake"

Step 7: A Word about Slip Sheets

Those little plastic sheets are important. They lower friction between the tape and the sides of the case. They also help keep the tape evenly wound. On very old or cheap cassettes, the slip sheets can be made of inferior material that wears out easily, causing tape squeal. Replacing old and worn slip sheets cures some squealing issues on cassettes.

In the picture there are two slip sheets from the same cassette. The shiny side faces the shell; the dull side is coated with a dry lubricant and it faces the tape pancake. Sometimes these can be easily interchanged from one shell to another. Worst-case scenario is that you may need to do a little trimming so they fit.

In picture 2 there's a closeup of a little plastic peg the slip sheet has to fit around. Notice there's a "V" cut in the slip sheet. When swapping sheets from one tape to another, keep in mind you may have to do a little trimming to make it work.

Some tapes used a clear slip sheet. Those make it harder to keep track of which side is up, so try to keep them lying in the shell in proper orientation. If you do drop it, there's still hope for figuring out which side is up. Note in the first picture that the dull slip sheet has its indentations facing up. That's the side that's supposed to go against the tape.

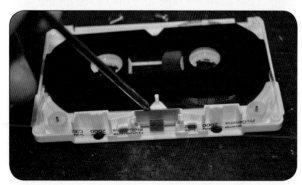

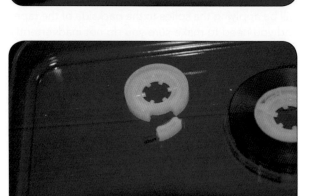

Step 8: Tape Popped Off Hub: How to Fix

A common failure on very old tapes is that it will pop off the hub on fast wind (see picture 1). This is an easy fix. On the ends of the tape you will usually have a leader. The leader is a non-magnetic bit of tape and it's what's attached to the hubs. The leader attaches to the hubs using a snap-in plastic clincher.

The clincher can be opened by sliding it off the hub (see pictures 2 and 3). Remove the bit of leader left on it. Take the leader from the tape pancake and snip off a small piece so you have fresh plastic to work with. Lay the leader in and insert the clincher end first facing the rest of the leader (see picture 4). Pinch clincher shut with needle-nose pliers. It should click in.

If all went well, it should look like picture 5.

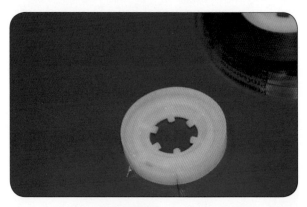

Step 9: Snapped Tape: How to Fix

Snapped tape can happen. Oftentimes it's caused by a poorly functioning machine that ate the tape. A machine that eats tape is malfunctioning. It's likely to be extremely dirty inside, or the belts are failing—two things outside the scope of this Instructable but not impossible to fix.

Do not keep putting tapes into a machine that eats them!

A snapped tape can be fixed, but keep in mind that you will lose that little bit of music that got mangled.

Pull out enough tape from each spool so you can work. 6" is generally enough to work with and not have it blow around from your breath. Yes, cassette tape is that light. It's very important that you keep sight of the proper orientation of the tape here. You will be applying the splice to the backside of the tape, and you need to make sure you do not inadvertently flip the tape. The easiest way I have found to do this is use a Post-It to hold the tape in place while working.

Snip the ends of the snapped tape so you have nice square cuts. Lay the Post-It down on the table sticky-side up. Lay one end of the tape down. The side of the tape that touches the play heads (faces outside of the tape) should be what is stuck to the Post-It. Use tweezers or needle-nose pliers to lay the other end of the tape down, making sure it's lined up, facing the right way, and has a very minimal overlap.

Use a piece of trimmed, invisible Scotch tape to hold the splice together. Scotch tape should NOT overhang anywhere on the magnetic tape. Any overhang will mean that there's adhesive tape waiting to catch on the mechanism and bind things up.

Once done, carefully pull tape up off Post-It sheet. Pull one half up first, then pull up the second half. Trying to yank it all at once may ruin the splice.

This same process can be used to re-attach a leader to a tape. On very old cassettes, the factory splice that attaches the leader to the magnetic tape can fail. This is common in really old Sony tapes from the '70s.

You may be asking yourself, "Is scotch tape the right stuff?" Nope, it is not. In reality you are supposed to use splicing tape. Splicing tape was at one time a common item at Radio Shack and music stores. It is no longer easy to find. It can be ordered from tape specialty places, but for the average Joe just wanting to listen to an old tape, the expense far exceeds the attention span. Quality Scotch Magic tape, the kind that disappears when stuck down on something, will suffice.

Step 10: Reassemble

Once done with your repairs, put the contents back in. Don't forget the slip sheets, metal shield (if tape had one; not all do), pressure pad, and rollers. While reassembling, make sure tape is properly threaded in the case. It's easy to munch the tape up while trying to fit the case halves together.

Step 11: Enjoy Your Tape!

You did it! You just took part in a forgotten art, that of repairing a cassette tape. Now try doing it 1980s high-school style on the glove box door of a moving Camaro while trying to make it back from lunch before your buddy finds out your deck ate his tape!

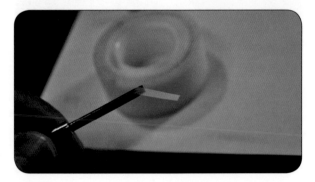

This Instructable will show you how to fix a broken action figure using a small bolt and no glue, so as to not restrict movement.

Step 1: Materials
You will need the following:
- Broken action figure
- Small bolt or screw
- Drill with fine drill bit
- Pair of pliers or side cutters
- Hacksaw

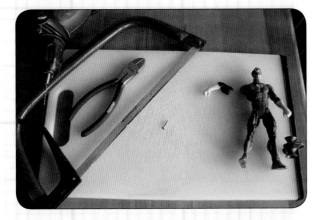

Step 2: Drill Holes in Action Figure

Taking the drill (the bit should be a wee bit smaller than your bolt thread), carefully drill a guide hole into either side of the break. In our figure, the humerus was broken, so we wanted to drill in towards the shoulder and down into the arm.

Make sure you don't drill too far so as to avoid creating problems with other moving parts.

Step 3: Cut Bolt to Size

Using a hacksaw or side cutters, remove the head of the bolt. The required length depends on how far you can screw the bolt into your action figure without the bolt obstructing other movement.

Step 4: Insert Bolt into First Guide Hole

Using pliers, carefully screw half of your bolt into your first guide hole. In our case, we replaced the distal humerus.

Step 5: Screw on Limb

Carefully rotate the limb, screwing it into your action figure's second guide hole. Make sure you don't strip the guide hole by screwing it in too tightly.

Step 6: Your Superhero Is Now a Man or Woman of Steel

Hopefully, you now have your action figure again in one piece. You might even find that he or she is slightly stronger!

Kid's Rocking Chair Moroccan Makeover

By modhomeecteacher
http://www.instructables.com/id/Kids-Rocking-Moroccan-Makeover/

My usual Goodwill perusal turned up a $6.99 kid's rocking chair that had seen better days. In comes the Moroccan look, or you may even call it Anthropologie-inspired. Either way, it's an easy style to adapt for a nursery or kid's bedroom.

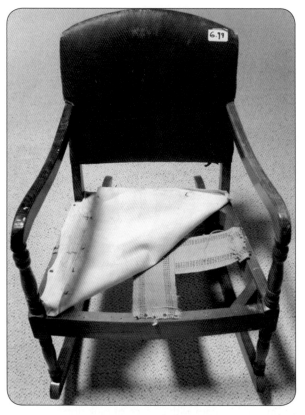

Step 1: Teardown

Here's the worn-out, saggy seated rocker throwing a tantrum for a makeover. The first order of business was to strip it down to the bones and sand off the shiny finish.

Step 2: Freshen Up the Frame

White primer and white glossy spray paint worked just fine. It's always a pain to wait for the paint to dry thoroughly.

Step 3: Attach a Fresh, Tight Foundation and Padding

Here is where you need to re-do the base that will hold the padding. You need to add jute webbing strips, burlap, padding (fluffed-up straw-like material taken out of the old upholstery), new

243

batting, and a new dacron covering. Then you'll be ready to upholster.

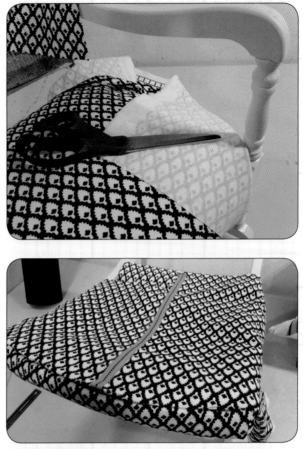

Step 4: Upholstery Time

Once the padding is ready, you can upholster the seat or back in whichever order you choose. I happened to have run out of fabric for the outside back (OB), so I had to stitch two pieces together and cover up the seam with a piece of pink ribbon. Clever disguise, if I do say so myself. Then, just make a cute little pillow to add some pizazz.

Canvas Pocket Bookshelf

By ncurrier
http://www.instructables.com/id/Canvas-Pocket-Book-Shelf/

Around my house summer means kicking back with a good book. My three-year-old granddaughter loves books, but her bookshelf was a mess—books stacked and falling over, and she could never find the one she wanted. So I took the bookcase out of her room and made a "Pocket Book" shelf that hangs on the wall. She can see the covers, books are easy to take out and easy to put back, and it looks great in her room! It turned out so well I have been "commissioned" to make one for my niece's daughter.

This project takes minimal carpentry and sewing skills.

Step 1: Materials and Tools

Materials:
- Four pieces 1" × 4" pine
- 2 ½ yards canvas or other heavy fabric
- Five dowels of ⅜" or ½" diameter
- Wood screws - #6 × 1 ¼"
- Wood screws - #8 × 2 ½"
- Wood glue

Tools:
- Sewing machine
- Scissors or rotary cutter
- Drill
- Drill bits
- Saw
- Stud finder

Step 2: Making the Frame

Cut the 1" × 4" into four pieces—two sides and two crosspieces. Mine is 33" wide × 33" long. I had a specific space in mind for hanging the bookshelf, so my dimensions match that. You can adjust the size to make your shelf taller or wider to accommodate more pockets—use your "Instructables" creativity. And it doesn't have to be square. That's just how mine worked out.

Place the pieces on a flat surface and check for square. I set my crosspieces down a couple of inches from the top and up from the bottom so they don't show. Mark on the sides where the crosspieces go and where you will pre-drill the screw holes.

Step 3: Marking Dowel Placement

Next I decided where to place the dowels. They need to be about 6" to 7" apart and on a diagonal line along the side to allow space for books to fit in. I marked the line in masking tape and placed colored dots where I wanted the dowels. "X" marks where I will drill. I clamped the two side boards together and drilled through both boards at once so the holes would line up perfectly. The hole marked furthest down on the side board will be the TOP of the shelf.

Step 4: Assembling the Frame

To assemble the frame, I used the "glue and screw" method. Drill the holes slightly smaller than the diameter of the screw. (This helps prevent splitting the wood.) I used three screws in each crosspiece. Apply wood glue to the raw end of the crosspieces and insert screws. Do *not* screw dowels to frame yet. (That was the voice of experience!) Cover screw head with wood filler, sand the entire piece, and put two coats of polyurethane on it (or paint yours to match the room).

Step 5: Measuring the Fabric

Since my shelf is 33″ wide I cut the canvas to 34″, allowing 1″ on each side for turning under and hemming and a half inch clearance from the side frame. I cut the length to 90″. (I may adjust this after I've laid out all the dowel sleeves.)

I wanted each of the pockets to be 6″ to 7″ deep to hold some of her bigger picture books. Each dowel sleeve takes 4″ of fabric. The first and last sleeves take an extra inch for hemming. The math would look something like this: 1 + 1 (inches for top and bottom hemming) + 6 ½ (inches between pockets) × 4 (the # of pockets) + 13 (the length of a 6 ½″ pocket folded) × 4 (the # of pockets) + 4 (inches for each sleeve) × 5 (the # of sleeves) = 88″

Step 6: Hem the Sides

Along a long edge, on the back side of the fabric, fold under ½″ of fabric, iron, then fold over ½″ again and iron. Sew along the edge to create a hem. Repeat for the other long edge of the fabric. Double check your overall width (32″ for mine) after you iron, but before you sew the second side.

Step 7: Top Dowel Sleeve

The top dowel is going here. Iron under ½″ of fabric then fold under another 2″ and iron.

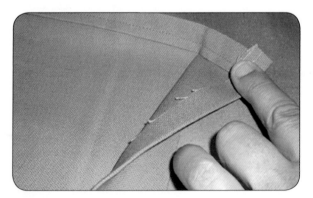

Step 8: Sewing the Top Dowel Sleeve

Sew ¼″ from the edge all along the top.

Step 9: Measure Out the Rest of the Dowel Sleeves

Measure down from the top edge the distance you are putting between dowels (for mine, it's 6 ½″). Mark it on the fabric (I used plain old school chalk. It wipes off later with a damp cloth). From this mark measure down twice the depth you want the pocket to be and mark again.(My pockets were 6 ½″ deep so I measured down 13″). Now measure down 4″ from this and mark again. This is your next dowel sleeve. Match up the last two chalk marks, pin, and sew across the fabric, making another sleeve.

Repeat this step for each of the dowel sleeves. I used five dowels, so I sewed four more sleeves.

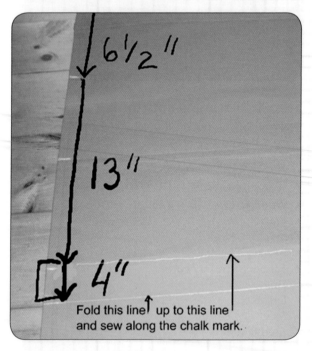

6½″
13″
4″
Fold this line up to this line and sew along the chalk mark.

Step 10: Finished Sleeves

When you have all the sleeves sewn, the fabric should look something like this.

Step 11: . . . and with the Dowels Inserted

Step 12: Assembling the Dowels and Frame

Now cut the dowels one at a time to fit into the frame. Pre-drill the ends and slide the dowel into fabric "sleeve." Screw into place. Repeat this step for each dowel. Photo shows my frame with the top two dowels in.

Step 13: Fill 'er Up!

Time to hang it on the wall. Since the shelf is 33" wide it will span two studs. Mark where the studs are. I used two screws in the top and bottom crosspieces. Pre-drill the holes in the shelf. Attach to the wall using 2 ½" wood screws.

Fill with good books, pour some lemonade, and find a hammock in a shady spot where you can share a story with your best friend.

How to Build a Safe and Strong Baby Gate

By trevormates

http://www.instructables.com/id/How-to-build-a-Safe-and-Strong-Baby-Gate/

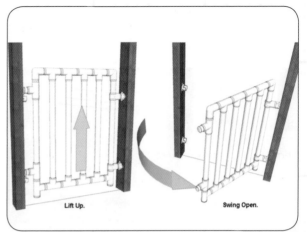

Lift Up.   Swing Open.

Like a lot of parents, our house if full of baby gates. We have one in practically every doorway, hallway, and entrance. One of the things that my wife and I found out early is that baby gates are expensive if you want quality (around $75 to $100 per gate).

This particular model is pretty simple and uses just PVC components to work. There are two "slip tees" in the structure that allow the gate to slide vertically just slightly so that you can lift it up and over the "table caps" that it will snap into. Once over the table caps, just press down and it is as secure as can be.

1. It's made from furniture-grade PVC and fittings, obtained from formufit.com, which is non-toxic, contains no dioxins (the nasty stuff they make plumbing PVC with), and is impact- and UV-degrade proof (it won't break down in sunlight).
2. The slats are all 2 ¾" apart, which is below the required 3" of distance between slats.
3. It is extremely strong. I can put my entire weight on it (215lb. male) closed and it will not budge.
4. All corners and edges are rounded, so no snagging.
5. There are no pinching mechanisms in the gate once closed.

I tried to make it with features that other baby gates incorporate, such as being attached to a wall or door frame, removable, and swings. I built each gate for around $48.00.

Step 1: What You Need
Parts:
- 12 × 1 ¼" PVC Tees
- 2 × 1 ¼" PVC 90 degree elbows
- 2 × 1 ¼" PVC slip tees
- 2 × 1 ¼" PVC fitting caster inserts
- 4 × 1 ¼" table caps
- 2 × 1 ¼" internal domed end caps
- 3 × 1 ¼" 5' furniture-grade PVC pipe

I also had some spare 1 ¼" plumbing-grade pipe to make the connecting inserts, which are not exposed. Fairly inexpensive, a 10' section will run you $3.00 at Home Depot or Lowes. They will cut it down for you if you need.

Hardware:
- 2 × ¼" × 2 ½" or 3" hitch pins
- 1 bag ¾" wood screws (full thread)
- 1 can of PVC cement

Tools:
Normally I would have used a miter saw to make all of the cuts, but I chose to use a hacksaw, as it was just as fast (a little deburring was needed). I did need a ¼" drill bit to make holes for the hitch pins. Everything else is screwing, so just a power drill, a couple of drill bits, and a Phillips bit should get you through this.
- Power drill or power screwdriver
- Phillips-head bit
- Hacksaw
- Measuring tape
- ³⁄₂₂" drill bit
- ¼" drill bit
- Countersink bit
- Knife or deburring tool

Step 2: Design
I designed the gate in Google SketchUp using the PVC components. I built it with a 32" doorway in mind, as that is what most of mine are.

In order to accommodate larger doors, you will need to add another "T-Section" (or more than one) for an additional 5" in width. An example is shown below in one of the SketchUp diagrams.

To accommodate doors between 33" and 37" you can increase the parts that connect to the wall by an inch on each side, but do not go over 2" or you will make the span between the frame and the doorway more than a 3" gap, which is not recommended under baby-gate standards.

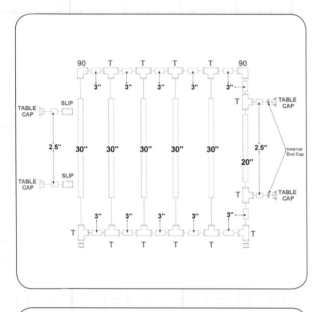

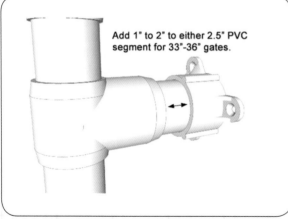

Add 1" to 2" to either 2.5" PVC segment for 33"-36" gates.

Step 3: Cutting

You will need to make cuts to the furniture-grade PVC, but they are pretty straightforward. The most difficult part is cutting the plumbing-grade PVC into little 3" bits; again, I suggest a hacksaw as these parts might fly off of a miter saw.

One benefit of miter-saw cuts over a hacksaw: deburring. You will need to debur each of the PVC segments using a pocket knife, razor blade, or if you have one, a deburring tool.

I've provided a cutting template for all of the lengths of furniture-grade and plumbing-grade PVC pipe below. I've tried to maximize usage, and it has

worked out pretty well for me. Make each cut as straight as possible.

You'll need a total of each of the following for the furniture-grade PVC pipe:
- 5 × 30"
- 1 × 20"
- 4 × 2.5"

You'll need a total of each of the following for the Plumbing Grade PVC pipe: 12 × 3"

Once the cuts are made, throw the parts into a box so they don't roll away on you.

Step 4: Table Cap Modification

You will need to slightly modify two of the table caps to allow them to act as a catch mechanism. I created the cut so that it just barely, but securely, holds the door in place.

It's a little difficult to explain the cut, and I will let the diagrams below do most of the work, but basically you make one horizontal cut right above where the top of the tab meets the cap and one vertical cut with a hacksaw along two of the supports of the table cap. This will remove a small crescent-shaped section that you can throw out. You could also perform this with a Dremel tool, if you are so inclined.

Tip: When cutting the table cap, secure it with screws to a table or piece of lumber to make it easier.

Once your cuts are made, sand down all sharp edges with sandpaper or a sanding block. We don't want any spikey edges!

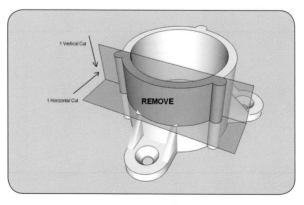

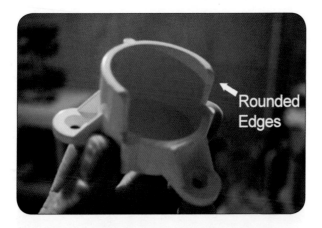

Rounded Edges

Step 5: Assemble the Top

Important: I chose to use ¾" wood screws to keep the pipe and fittings in place. I drilled a small hole into the fitting where it meets the PVC and used a Phillips bit to put the screw into place. It is just as strong as PVC cement, and the friction of the pipe into the fitting keeps it together anyway. Plus you can avoid the noxious odor and other concerns that come with PVC cement. Also, this way you can perform a "dry fit" of all of these items and then attach screws.

I like to use a countersink bit attached to the drill so that it makes a nice indentation for the screw head to go into. It keeps it clean and won't allow snagging of clothing or little fingers.

I do use PVC cement for a couple of items later.

Should you choose to use PVC cement, remember: PVC cement essentially melts the PVC to merge the pipe and fitting together, in about 30 seconds, so make sure that the parts are lined up and going in the right direction when connecting them.

We'll start assembling the top of the gate. For this you will need two 90 degree fittings, five tees, and six pieces of the 3" plumbing-grade PVC segments.

Simply assemble the fittings as shown in the diagram below, with a 90 elbow first, followed by the four tees using a 3" plumbing-grade PVC segment between each fitting, then another 90 degree elbow. You'll put another tee facing outward off of the final 90 degree fitting.

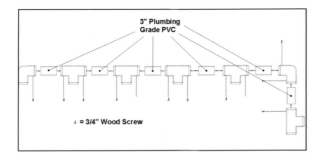

3" Plumbing Grade PVC

⊥ = 3/4" Wood Screw

Step 6: Assemble the Bottom

Now for the bottom of the gate assembly: For this you will need seven tees and six 3" plumbing-grade PVC segments.

Assemble the fittings as shown in the diagram below, with a tee vertically positioned and followed by four tees facing upward, with another tee vertically positioned. Use the 3" plumbing-grade PVC segments to connect them all together. Attach another tee vertically positioned facing outward to the top of the final tee.

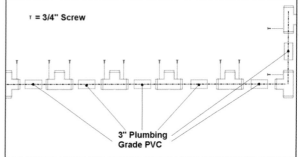

⊤ = 3/4" Screw

3" Plumbing Grade PVC

Step 7: Insert Pipe into the Bottom

In this step, we are going to add the vertical pipes to the top and bottom gate segments.

Insert the five 30" segments of furniture-grade PVC into the bottom section of the gate that we just assembled. Secure the pipes in place with screws. Insert the one 20" segment of furniture-grade PVC pipe into vertical tee that is off to one side.

Slip the two slip tees over the 30" segment of PVC pipe at the far end. This will be our hinge mechanism. We'll get back to these later.

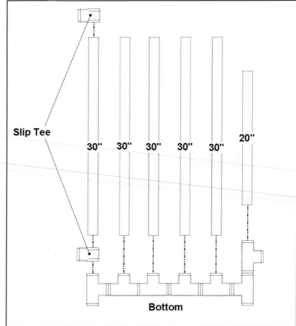

Slip Tee

30" 30" 30" 30" 30" 20"

Bottom

Step 8: Attach the Bottom to the Top

In this step we will start to put together the main gate by attaching the bottom segment with pipes inserted into the top.

Line up the top of the gate with the pipes already attached to the bottom of the gate and make sure they are all in place by pressing down hard on them. Then attach with screws to secure the whole deal.

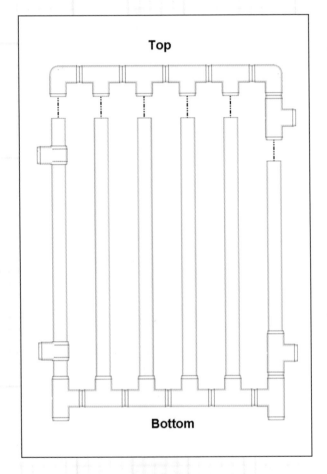

Top

Bottom

Step 9: Make the Gate Removable

You will need two of the 2 ½" furniture-grade pipe segments and two table caps. We are going to drill ¼" holes through both the table cap and pipe inserts. This will accept the hitch pins to make the gate removable.

Screw the table cap into a table or piece of lumber to secure it. Push the 2 ½" furniture-grade pipe segment into the table cap. It should be *slightly* loose. Next, drill through the table cap and furniture-grade pipe around ½" from the end of the table cap, through both sides.

Push in the hitch pin (it should be slightly difficult at first, as you have to get by the ball). It should go all the way through. You will see in my picture I used a 3 ½" long hitch pin. I suggest a 2 ½" or 3" at most.

Using the ¾" screws on the outside of the slip tees (that are on the 30" pipe segment), secure the 2

½" segment of pipe to the slip tee. Do this for both slip tees.

Step 10: Add the Catch Mechanism

Using PVC cement, lightly coat the inside of the remaining 2 ½" furniture-grade pipe segments and insert an internal end cap inside of it. Wipe away any excess PVC cement that may come out. Next insert the other end (uncapped) of the 2 ½" furniture-grade segments into the two outward-facing tees on the gate structure. Attach with screws or PVC cement.

Step 11: Installation

Important: When installing the gate, make sure that you are installing into a stud, door frame, or other solid structure. Sheetrock alone will not hold up *any* baby gate. If you cannot install directly into a stud (when putting into sheetrock), use a nice piece of hardwood to span between the studs or wall.

Slip the two caster fitting inserts into the two tees on the bottom of the gate. These will act as feet. I recommend for hardwood floors to add a couple of felt pads, available at most stores, to make it easier on your floors.

Line up the slip tee/table cap combos with the wall or inside of the door that you want to install onto. Line up the slip tees with the tees on the opposite side of the gate so that the whole thing looks symmetrical. This also allows free travel of the slip tees, which is part of the catch mechanism. Attach table caps to the doorframe, studs, or wood structure with 2" wood screws.

Once attached, the gate should swing freely. Insert the two "modified" table caps onto the "catch posts" and line them up on the opposite wall or door frame. Make sure that the section that you cut out of the table caps faces up. This is critical. You want them positioned so that the gate will snap into them. Screw these into the studs or door frame with 2" screws.

Enjoy!

Children's Growth Chart

By Ben Hollerbach & Jake Tompkins
(hollerback.tompkins)
http://www.instructables.com/id/Childrens-Growth-Chart/

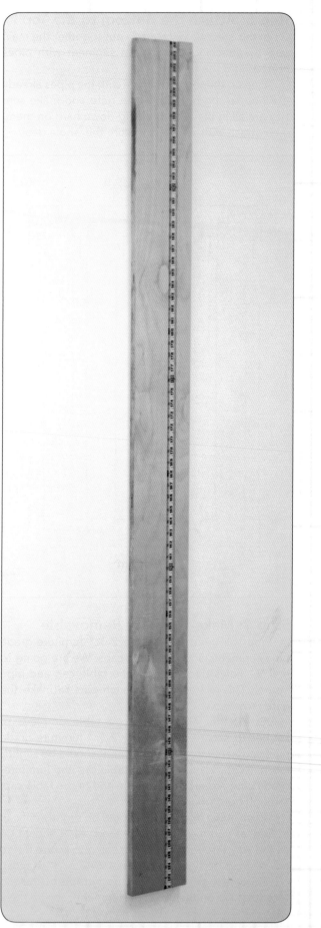

In my childhood home, the wall next to the laundry room door was covered with a series of marks and dates. A few times a year my mother would tell me to stand up tall with my shoulders back up against the wall, a cereal box would be placed on top of my head, and a line would be drawn where it touched. Each line was dated and another addition to the history of my growth was created. When I was 12 my family moved out of that house, and all that history was painted over by the next inhabitants. While at the time it seemed like more of a nuisance to have my height marked regularly, today it's a missing piece of my personal history I would love to have kept.

A broken tape measure may be the end of the tool as a whole, but not of its parts. Not wanting to throw away a perfectly good piece of measured steel, it struck me that a piece of tape measure would be perfect for recording the growth of children.

Step 1: Materials and Tools

Materials:
- 6" × ¾" board 5' or longer
- Tape measure
- Wood glue
- Picture hanger
- Felt pads

Tools:
- Table saw
- Chisel
- Screw driver
- Scissors
- Sand paper
- Polyurethane
- Hammer
- Picture hanger
- Pads
- Chop saw or hand saw

Step 2: Take Apart Tape Measure

Disassemble the tape measure carefully. Begin by removing the five screws that hold the casing together. Make sure to keep a hand on the case so it doesn't pop open. Open the casing slowly to make sure it doesn't pop out. Remove the coil from the casing (that's the white part) and put a finger on the tape to keep it coiled up. Slowly unroll the tape in a safe place (remember it's as long as the tape says it is, so it's best to do this in the garage or outside).

Step 3: Cut Tape Measure

Using your scissors cut the tape into more manageable pieces. We recommend leaving about 6" on either side of the 6' you want to end up with just to make sure you have it right. You can easily cut

the rest of the tape into manageable-sized pieces and save it for more fun projects later.

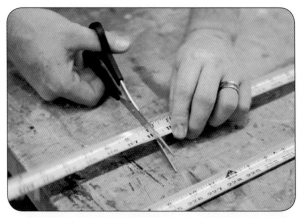

Step 4: Cut a Groove

Next we head to the table saw. We're going to be making a dadoe (or a groove) in the wood that is ½" deep and $^{15}/_{16}$" wide. If you have a dadoe blade it's simple to set it up and do this; if not it'll take a little longer but isn't too difficult. Set the height of your blade to ½", and if necessary remove your safety cover. Set the fence on your saw at 1 ½" and run your first line. Set the fence to 2 $^{5}/_{16}$" and run your second line. The second measurement is a bit smaller than what the groove actually is because the blade width adds the additional smidge of an inch. (We messed up our first board trying to add $^{15}/_{16}$" to the first measurement.) Continue to bump the fence in a bit at a time and run lines till the gap has been mostly cleared out. This takes seven to eight passes, and if you want less cleanup you can do it in $^{1}/_{16}$" increments. Make sure to wear safety goggles and use a push stick when using the table saw.

Step 5: Clear Out the Groove

Using a chisel clear the remnants out of the groove. This may take more work depending on how many passes you did. Once the groove is cleared out you're ready to cut to length.

Step 6: Cut to Length

Measure to 6' on your board and using a chop saw (or hand saw if desired) cut the board to length.

Step 7: Sand the Board

Take a square of 150-grit sandpaper and run it along all of the edges of the board (this is called breaking the edges). This should remove burrs and also make the board more pleasant to touch. When you're done with the edges give the whole front and back a good rub with the sandpaper (or use an electric sander if you have one).

Step 8: Polyurethane It

Wipe all the dust and dirt off of the board. If you think your board is particularly dirty you can use a rag with a little mineral spirits on it to get it clean, but make sure to wait till it fully dries before beginning the finishing. Brush or rub the wood with a light coat of polyurethane (or paint, lacquer, or your preferred finish), making sure not to get it into the groove.

Once the poly (or whatever) dries, lightly sand with 220 grit to remove the raised grain, and then recoat. You can coat the back if desired, but it isn't necessary. You can recoat till you're happy, but a slightly rougher finish will take pen marks better than a glossy one. You can decorate the board any way you want, but remember you'll have to change what you use to write with depending on color and finish.

Step 9: Insert Tape Measure

Once the finish is dry it's time to insert the tape measure. Make sure the tape is the same length of the board and trim accordingly. (We put the tape over the groove and trimmed it there.) Run a bead of glue down the center of the groove. Place the tape over the center of the groove and press it firmly into the groove. The tape should flex into the groove and then hold itself inside (the glue is so it won't move after you're done). Make sure to start with one end in the right spot because it's hard to move once it's in there. Allow the glue to dry overnight with the board horizontal so the glue doesn't drip out.

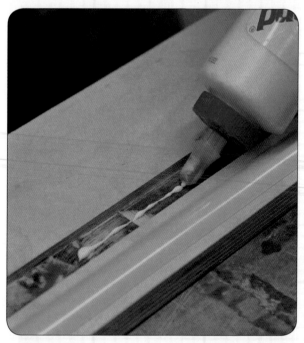

Step 10: Attach a Hanger

Once the glue has dried you can attach a picture-frame hanger to the back side. Measure up 5' from the bottom of the board and make a mark, then use a piece of tape to make a mark in the center of the board. Attach your hanger around this center point. Add the two pads at the bottom of the board so the base doesn't mark up your wall.

Step 11: Hang It Up

To hang on the wall, measure up 6' and put a nail or other hanger in the wall (since the board starts at 1', and the hanger is 5' from the bottom, this should mean your board is hanging in the right spot). Double check it with a working tape measure.

Step 12: Measure Away!

Once it's hung begin documenting your family's growth. Kids around 12 months should be able to stand (with help), and you can begin recording their progress. Many styles of marks exists, but I prefer name and date (when you have a second child the name is really necessary, and sometimes it's fun to give each child their own color too). Lighter colors work well with regular pens, darker colors require paint pens or metallic Sharpies. Pencil will possibly wipe away, and ink needs to be left to dry depending on the finish.

Office

When you are working from home, you need to make sure your home office is free from distraction. Having a busted mouse or cords tangled around your feet can make it difficult to get your work done. A clean desk means a clean mind, and we have projects to help keep everything neat and tidy. Fix that CD that won't stop skipping, keep computer cords up and out of the way of harm, and prop up that keyboard that just won't stay stable.

Also, don't forget to fix your feng shui with a miniature zen garden right on your desk!

Fix a Keyboard Key
By fungus amungus
http://www.instructables.com/id/Fix-a-keyboard-key/

I found a great keyboard in our junk pile, a Microsoft Natural Ergonomic Keyboard. It has a comfy layout, but there was just one problem: the "N" key wasn't too responsive. You had to really bang on it to get it to register.

Naturally, this wasn't going to work for regular typing, but the fix for it was easy. Here's how to do it.

Step 1: Pop Out the Key

Use a flathead screwdriver to get the key out. Just get the tip of the screwdriver under the key and push down on the other side. With a bit of leverage, the key will pop right out.

Step 2: Get a Piece of a Straw

Cut off a little more than an inch of a clean plastic straw.

Step 3: Fold and Insert

Fold the straw in half lengthwise and insert it into the bottom of the key. It should now be sticking out quite a bit.

Step 4: Trim to Fit

Cut off the straw so that a few millimeters are sticking out. You now have an enhanced key that sticks out more and will be better at engaging the button inside the keyboard.

Step 5: Put Key Back in the Keyboard

On most keyboards, this is just a matter of placing the key in the right place and pushing down. You'll know when you get it right.

Test out the button and see if it's responsive now. If it's working, but it feels a little stiff, then pop the key back out, trim a tiny bit more of the straw off, and put it back in. Done!

Quick Fix for Broken Laptop Hinges

By lampshade74

http://www.instructables.com/id/Quick-fix-for-broken-laptop-hinges/

The hinges on my Inspiron 300m are worn out. Being cheap and not wanting to fork out $100 for new hinges, I came up with this simple workaround with Velcro strips and a brace. It might not look the best, but it works!

Step 2: Attach Brace

Use an old brace or get one for $1.50 at the hardware store and secure it onto the laptop using the strips. Voila, the screen now stays up!!

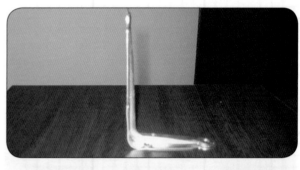

Step 1: Attach Velcro Strips

Get some Velcro strips and attach to the bottom of the laptop and to the back of the screen. In retrospect I would probably go for wider strips than I have now.

The USB cable on your mouse can get pretty knackered. Rather than buy a whole new mouse, why not give soldering a go and fix your old buddy, who has been with you for thousands of clicks? If you follow this guide, you can't mess it up, even if you're not a great solder-er.

Why sugru is good for this hack:

- It's an electrical insulator
- It bonds to this particular plastic

Sugru comes in to play because it fits perfectly into the inner cavities to hold the cable. It will also protect the newly repaired cable from coming loose and unwinding.

In this Instructable, we will cut the USB cable, open up the mouse, and re-solder the cables. Then we'll put some sugru into the mouse cavity to help keep the cable in place. We'll also add a protective layer on the outside of the mouse to future-proof the USB cable.

Let's get started!

Step 1: What You'll Need

This is what you'll need to fix your mouse:

- Soldering iron and solder
- Scissors
- Flat-head screwdriver
- Small Phillips-head screwdriver
- Sugru
- Scalpel / small knife
- Wire strippers / cutters
- Angled pliers / normal pliers

Step 2: Cut Off the Wire

Use your scissors to snip off the wire. Try not to waste cable so snip it as close to the mouse as possible!

Step 3: Take Off the Ring Mount

Carefully wedge your Phillips-head screwdriver between the mount ring and the side button of the mouse. Please be careful here, otherwise you might damage your mouse. Don't force it. Work your way around the mouse slowly and steadily, using the scalpel to lift up the ring slightly before you go in with the screwdriver. On old mice, the little hooks might be more prone to breaking. If they break, don't worry. You'll have some sugru leftover to fix them!

Step 4: Pop Off Inner Hooks

Use your flat-head screwdriver again to unhook the top of the mouse's moving part (the bit that clicks). You should be able to see the two little hooks keeping the moving part from swinging outward. Go ahead and unhook them both, and the moving bit of the mouse should swing outwards.

Step 5: Pop Off Swivels

You'll notice that the moving part of the mouse is swinging around at two points on the other side of the mouse. Go ahead and use your friend, the flat-head screwdriver to pop off the swively bits on the bottom side of the mouse. Be careful, 'cause when you do this, one half of the mouse will pop off, but will still be attached to the top with little ribbon wires, which you'll see in the next step. You don't want to rip these!

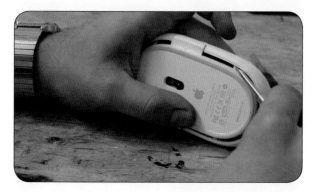

Step 6: Unplug Capacitive Sensors and Scroll Wheel

First, take a mental note (or even more sensibly, a photo) of how the two ribbon cables are attached to the circuit board. Then, use your pliers to unplug the ribbon cables. Be gentle with them. If you damage these cables, you probably won't be able to solder them!

Step 7: Unscrew the Circuit Board

Next, pick up your Phillips-head screwdriver and take the three screws off the circuit board. This will enable you to get underneath it so you can re-solder your USB wire. All three screws have exactly the same length, so there's no need to replace the same one back into its original position.

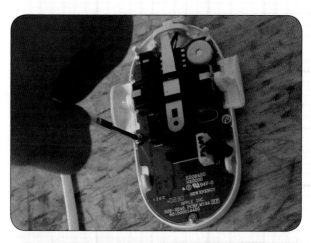

Step 8: Chop and Strip Your Wires!

First, chop off the white plastic bit that held the cable in place before you unscrewed the circuit board. Then, strip both the USB cable that you chopped off in the beginning, as well as the black cable that was sitting under the circuit board.

You might have to use your scalpel to strip off the heatshrink on the black cable.

USB cables have five wires in total:
- The crazy, exposed, silver-braided wire.
- D-, which is the green-striped wire.
- D+, which is the white-striped wire.
- Ground, which is the black wire.

Strip them all and prepare them for soldering by twisting the multicore (the tiny wires that make up each individual wire) round slightly so that they stay together.

Step 9: Solder the Wires

Before you solder, please make sure that you've passed your cable through the gate on the mouse mount! If you don't do this, you're going to have to chop off your wire and start over!

Solder each wire to its corresponding brother on the other side. So red-striped goes to red-striped, green-striped goes to green-striped, etc. Take your time whilst soldering, making sure you create a sturdy joint, because you don't want to open that mouse up again.

After you do that, make sure you use some insulating tape to insulate the wires so that they don't touch each other when you close the mouse. This is very important, otherwise your mouse will just short circuit!

When you have the top back on, I'd give the sugru one last check to see if it's moved out of place, or if it needs a bit of pushing around to fully engulf the cable.

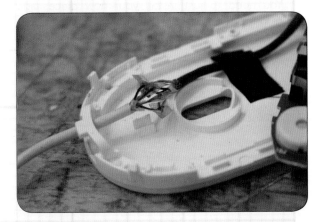

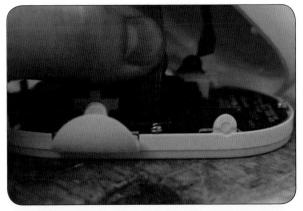

Step 10: Insert Sugru

After you reattach the circuit board back onto the mouse, open up your sugru pack. Take ¾ of the sugru contained in the pack and push it into the space between the circuit board and the plastic. Push it firmly so that it doesn't exceed the height of the black button. You want it to cover the wires underneath and mold into their shape so that they can't go anywhere once the sugru has cured.

You also want to make sure that the cable has some sugru underneath it too at the point where it comes out of the mouse enclosure.

Just make sure that the sugru has engulfed the cables and let it do its job. It should hold the little cables in place, as well as insulate them. It should also hold the USB cable so that it doesn't damage itself whilst moving.

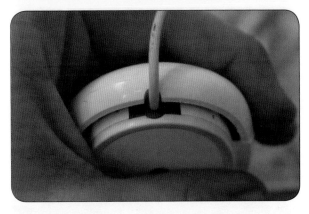

Step 12: Close and Seal the Mouse

Once you're satisfied with your inner sugru work, put the ring back on. Use some of your leftover sugru to seal the cable and secure it nicely onto the main housing of the mouse.

Now, if you've broken the mount ring in the process of popping it off, no worries! Use your leftover sugru to create little balls and stick them around the ring. That'll hold it in place for at least one eternity.

Now admire your beloved mouse and click away at it; it will hold itself together for years to come. And, if not, open it up and fix it again!

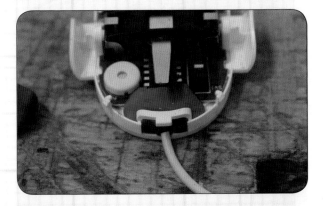

Step 11: Put the Top Back On

Remember how those ribbon cables were plugged in? Good, 'cause you're going to have to put them back in their happy place. You can either do this with your fingers, or you can use the pliers again.

Once you've plugged them back in, go ahead and click the top back on. It's easier if you pop on the swivels first and the hooks last.

Many keyboards have nice, flimsy feet that like to venture out into the world on their own, leaving us helpless without them. These feet are disrespectful little buggers who have do not deserve the home you gave to them in the first place!

This quick guide will show you a quick recovery with a new (keyboard) foot.

Step 1: What You Will Need
- A band saw
- Some wood

Step 2: Size Matters!

Maybe the old keyboard foot was too small, maybe it was too big, maybe it was just right . . . Whichever way it was, lift the back of your keyboard to an appropriate height and then measure this distance. Next, measure the size that your new piece will need to have along the bottom edge. This created for me a triangle with a height of 1" and a length of 4".

Step 3: You Don't Have to Change, He Does!

Next, draw your measurements onto some wood. Then, cut along your drawing with the band saw. I do not personally own a band saw, so I used the band saw at TechShop San Jose. Once your cuts

are finished, feel free to sand the piece to make them smooth (or not if you like it rough).

Step 4: Enjoy Your New Toy

You need to just install your new pieces and you're done. This is simply sliding the pieces under your keyboard.

How to Fix a Power Adapter

By StumpChunkman

http://www.instructables.com/id/How-to-Fix-a-Power-Adapter/

As much as I enjoy Asus, I am currently incredibly irritated with the power adapter that came with my current Eee PC. The front plate of the adapter has always been a bit flimsy, and yesterday when I pulled the adapter out from the wall, the faceplate decided to remain embedded in the outlet, while the rest of the adapter rested quite comfortably in my hand. Since I was already running short of time, I grabbed the bit stuck in the wall, threw everything in my bag and ran off to school to fix it later.

While this is built around my specific plug, these techniques should be applicable to any plug that has inexplicably pulled itself apart for no reason what-so-ever.

Safety warning: Before unplugging any exposed wires from the wall, please ensure that you turn power off to that outlet. Your life is more important than fixing this plug.

Step 1: Issues

Getting to school and needing a computer, I set to the task of figuring out exactly what was wrong and how to fix it.

My first impression was that there was absolutely no solder on either the cables that were ripped from the back of the plug, or the plug itself. There were small holes on the back of the plug, but they were too small to get any more than two strands of the threaded wire through. I currently have no idea how the wires could have been connected. I also find it awkward how much bare wire was exposed without any proper shielding, but that's just me.

All in all, it seemed an easy fix—I'd just solder the wires back on to where they popped off and call it a day!

Step 2: Not So Simple

No stranger to solder, I tried soldering wires straight to the plug to no avail. No matter how hot I got the plug, it was too polished and the solder just wouldn't stick. It was more difficult than trying to solder something to the bottom of a can of soda.

Plan two: Try to force a separate wire through the tiny holes in the back of the plug and solder the cables to that. Sadly, the holes were too small to get any sort of wire to pass through.

Tired of burning plastic and making no headway, I decided I didn't care about keeping the plug pretty and went with plan three!

Plan three: Get a different plug, cut it in half, and solder the two sets of wire together. Having no two-prong plugs sitting around, I opted to go for a three-prong and just ignore the third prong.

Step 3: Figuring Out Connections

So the first thing after cutting the new cable (which was left over from some old component) was to figure out which prongs of the plug went to which wires. Since the plug to my computer only used two prongs, I needed to make sure I used the same two prongs on the three-prong plug.

I set up a multimeter to test resistance and checked for continuity between each of the three internal cable wires with the three prongs.

It turned out the green cable went to the ground prong (which I've been told is standard), and black and white went to the other two prongs. Since my computer didn't care which way it was plugged into the wall (neither of the prongs was larger than the other), it didn't matter which way I soldered the black and white wires to the plug. I did do my best to look at where the cables wanted to be, and soldered them to the plug that they would have wanted to go to, but I don't think that mattered at all.

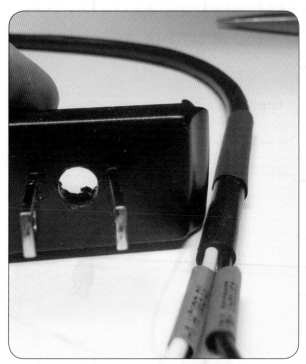

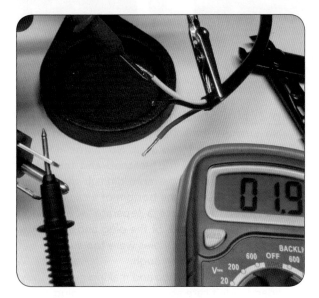

Step 4: One Last Thing before We Put Everything Together . . .

Right before I started soldering the cables together, I noticed that if I'd kept going, the power adapter would have had a large exposed side. To keep this from happening, I decided to drill a hole right in the center of the faceplate for the adapter. If my fellow classmate wasn't asleep, I might have taken a Dremel to the prongs to keep the faceplate clean. Looking back, I'm very glad I didn't, as the final look of the plug is perfect.

To pick a drill bit, I compared the width of the bit to the width of the wire I had previously cut in half. I picked the smallest drill bit I thought the cable would just manage to fit through.

You can use a punch to center the drill bit, but I was in a hurry and eyeballed it.

Step 5: Putting Everything Together

Now that everything was ready, it was just a matter of getting everything set up, soldered, and adding finishing touches.

Make sure you add any heat shrink and the faceplate over any cables that are going to be soldered. Solder the two cables together. Heat the heat shrink (or cut it off and apply electrical tape as I had to do). Prep the faceplate and internals for final closings.

Step 6: Wrapping Up

Snap the faceplate back in place and enjoy your new plug. If your plug doesn't have a snap, a little extra tape on the outside will work just fine. I did my first power check not plugged into my computer. I plugged it into the wall, and ensured the "I'm plugged in correctly" light came on. After that, I set up my computer for a presentation, plugged it in, and had it running for six hours. I've yet to have any problems with my fix.

As a side now, this is now my absolute favorite plug.

After falling in love with my new (used) Kindle, I sat on the screen and cracked it. Strictly adhering to my DIY, minimal-waste ethos, I found a YouTube video made by the good people at PowerBook Medic with clear instructions on how to replace the screen instead of dumping the whole Kindle.

It struck me that Instructables had no such guide so I set out to make a step-by-step guide for other people with the same problem. I ended up learning an important lesson in the process.

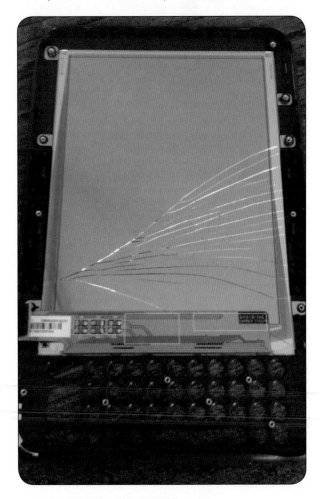

Step 1: Order a New Screen

Where can I get a new screen? What will it cost?

I found no e-ink screens for less than $50. After some careful perusing, I ordered my new e-ink screen from eBay.

Fifty dollars was worth it to me considering the price of a new Kindle and my desire to fix rather than trash. Everyone will have to evaluate this for themselves because as you will see, the repair process is not for the faint of heart.

Step 2: Tools Required

- Set of electronic screwdrivers, both flat-head and Phillips (I highly recommend the Stanley set I used, which has spinning tops, magnetic tips, and comes with a sturdy case)
- Soft plastic pry tool, aka Spudger

Step 3: Begin Disassembly: Pry Off Rear Cover

Pry off the plastic rear cover. The best tool for this is a flat-head electronic screw driver because the cover fits very tightly in the back of the Kindle. This step requires a surprising amount of force, but be courageous because you are not in danger of damaging anything . . . yet.

Step 4: Remove Battery

You will immediately see the large black battery, which has "Amazon.com" labeled on it along with the other disclaimers. This is the first component to remove and is held in place by two Phillips screws at the top left.

Step 5: Disconnect Four Cables and Wires

Disconnect four cables and wires that originate from the screen and keyboard and are plugged into the logic board. I have labeled them in the picture with red circles. Also remove the red and black speaker wire with white socket, which easily unclips.

Some are held in place with a brown lock bar. The lock bar can be released with the flat-head screw driver but is sometimes easiest done with your finger!

Each cable will simply slide out of the socket they are plugged into with a little help.

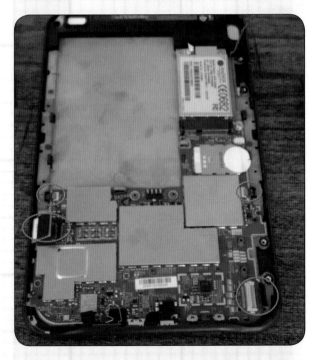

Step 6: Remove Grounding Mechanism and 3G Card

Remove the two screws that hold the small ground piece down and then remove the two screws that hold the silver 3G card down. Next, unclip the

black cable that is plugged into the 3G card. These are all circled in red in the image.

Step 7: Undo Screws Holding Logic Board

Begin by removing this black component with four screws on the corners. Next, look for approximately 12 screws holding the logic board to the midboard. You will be sure you have removed all of them only when you can lift the logic board off. This takes some trial and error and some prying.

Step 8: Remove Midboard

Now that the logic board is out, the midboard is exposed and can be removed. This also requires some patience and experimentation but can be removed with the (black) speaker module still attached.

The keyboard will likely fall out at this step.

Please pay attention to the rocker knobs for the on/off switch as well as the volume because they are not permanently attached and can simply fall out without being noticed! See picture.

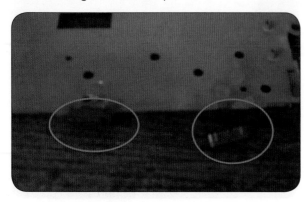

Step 9: Replace the Screen!

Congratulations, you've taken the Kindle totally apart and you're ready to replace the broken screen with a new one.

CAVEAT: You must be very careful during this step because the e-ink screens are surprisingly delicate. The back of the screen is made from a very thin piece of glass, and any torque or torsion will crack it. Normally the case of the Kindle will prevent this kind of damage but when it is out as a separate piece it is extremely vulnerable. Actually, the first time I did this procedure, I broke it!

Step 10: Reassemble

Now that you have replaced the screen, you must do the whole ordeal backwards, which will be much easier.

A few things to keep in mind:
1. Don't forget the keyboard
2. Don't forget the volume rocker
3. Don't forget the on/off slide switch

When you put the midboard back onto the screen, be careful—be delicate or it could crack the screen. I can't emphasize this enough or the whole repair will be botched.

Before you screw down the midboard, make sure the cables are sticking up and are clear of their respective holes in the midboard or you won't be able to connect them later. The lock bars can be replaced onto each of the cables.

Have an old, scratched-up CD that won't play anymore? That CD probably held many memories for you, and you wish you were able to play it, if only it wasn't so scratched up. But now you can re-live those memories using the magic of peanut butter!

Step 1: What You Need

- Peanut butter (You need only one tablespoon of peanut butter. Please, use common sense and DON'T use chunky peanut butter. Please.)
- Scrubbing utensil (You also need some way of rubbing the peanut butter. Use napkins, paper towels, polishing cloth [it's recommended you don't use a good one], or even your fingers.)
- Water (Now, most CD warnings say to not submerge the disk in water. But you need SOME way of getting that peanut butter off, right? Besides, we're not "submerging," we're "washing." I used water to get it off, and it worked fine.)

Step 2: Start the Cleanest Mess You'll Ever Have!

This step is really messy. I advise you have some way of cleaning up messy stuff nearby. Now, take the peanut butter and start scrubbing it into the CD using small, circular patterns. It's awkward, I know, but in the end, it all works out. Continue scrubbing for about two minutes, then wash off the peanut butter. Make sure you have as much of it off as possible, because you don't want a peanut-butter and Walkman (or Playstation) sandwich.

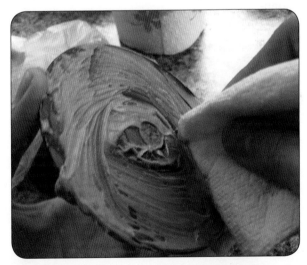

Step 3: Finish Up, Clean Up, and Play!

Now, once you have all the peanut butter off, dry your CD and put it in its respective player. It should work fine, and most of the scratches will be gone; however, minor scratches will still be visible but won't hinder its performance.

I hope this helps!

A file cabinet is a great organizational tool and a necessity for most people, but let's face it: it's a big eyesore! Some people buy their file cabinets from secondhand stores, so they are typically pretty beaten up. Mine was actually brand new when I got it, but it came in this ugly putty color. I recently decided that I needed to do something about it. So, I covered it in woodgrain-looking contact paper to make it fit in better with the bedroom decor.

Step 1: Materials
- Contact paper (I used woodgrain, but I also think a crisp white would have looked nice.)
- Scissors
- Plastic card, like a credit card, to smooth out bubbles
- Screwdriver
- X-Acto knife
- Tape measure

Time: Approximately six hours

Step 2: Measure the Width and Length of the Drawers
Add about ¾" to each side and then cut four pieces of contact paper that size. (FYI: I didn't need to take the drawers out to apply the contact paper.)

Step 3: Remove the Hardware from the Front of the Drawers
This actually took more time than I thought. If I had taken the drawers out, I bet it would have been an easier and quicker process.

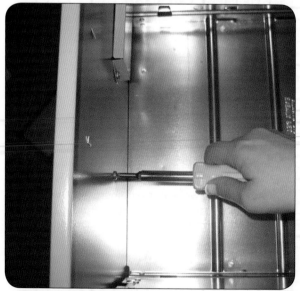

Step 4: Apply the Contact Paper, But Do So Slowly

Peel away part of the backing and start at the top of the drawer. Simultaneously, press the plastic card against the cabinet and push downward inch by inch, starting from the center, to smooth out the bubbles before you unroll more paper.(FYI: In my experience, it is impossible to get rid of all bubbles. Don't worry, though, because people will only be able to see them if they're closely inspecting your work.)

Note: The point of this photo is to show you how to hold the plastic card as you are smoothing away the bubbles.

Step 5: Cut a Hole around the Latch on the Front of the Drawer

I wasn't able to remove the little silver latch thing that is used to open and close the drawer, so I had to use the X-Acto knife to cut a hole around it. Do this when you have smoothed the paper about halfway down the drawer. Cutting a hole will allow air to escape and prevent more bubbles from forming. (FYI: If you cut too far around it, no need to panic because adding a few slivers of contact paper around it will blend right in.)

Step 6: Repeat Steps 4 through 5 on the Other Drawers

Then, replace the hardware.

Step 7: Apply Contact Paper to the Remaining Sides

You can relax; the hard part is over. Now, repeat the process of applying the contact paper to the rest of the sides of the file cabinet. Remember to keep the woodgrain pattern going in the same direction.

Step 8: Step Back and Admire Your New and Improved File Cabinet!

And now for a picture of the finished faux-wood file cabinet. That's all there is to it! Happy filing!

This will show you how to clean up that cable mess below your desk. I believe this method is extremely flexible for various cable paths and is extremely cheap!

Step 1: Materials and Tools

Materials:
- Large (2") binder clips (under $4 for a box of 12)
- ¾" wood screws (under $1 for a box)
- Washers (under $1 for a box)
- Velcro straps (optional)

Tools:
- Screw Driver or Power Screw Driver

Step 2: Unplug, Untangle, and Gather the Supplies

Unplug all the devices and separate the cables from each other. Gather your supplies. I am using ¾" screws because my desk is 1" thick. It is important that you take the time to measure your desktop. Pick a screw length that is at least ¼" shorter than the thickness of your desktop. A surefire way to ruin your day is to finish the project and find that you now have eight screws sticking up through your desktop.

Step 3: Mount the Hardware

I would recommend mounting your power strip first. Mount the power strip in a centralized location. I typically place it closer to the wall in the middle of the desk. Use a pencil and scrap paper to make a map (rubbing) of the mounting holes on your power strip. Then when placing the screws, screw them right through the paper into the desk. When you are finished placing the screws, rip the paper away.

I like to place multiple clips around the power strip because this is going to be an area with lots of cables. Then place other clips where you need them.

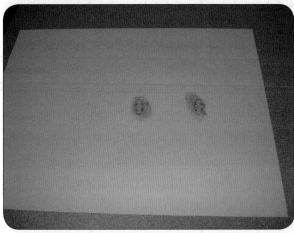

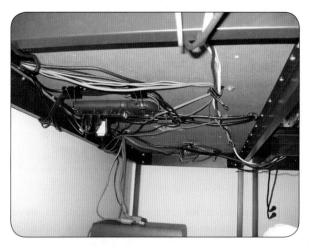

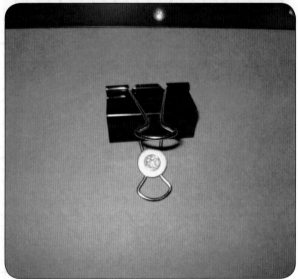

Step 5: Route Cables to Designated Areas

I routed my cables to designated areas. In this case, I am routing cables for my PC and an Xbox 360. I have mounted a clip in the back above these areas. This grouping of cables allows for a cleaner look.

Step 4: Routing the Cables

Now you can route the cables through the mounted clips. If you are a purist, you can take the time to mount enough clips to separate out your power cables. This might keep your power cables from causing distortion in your other cables. I didn't do this because I have never found it to be an issue.

Step 6: Finished Product (Comparison)

After I plugged everything back in, I added some Velcro straps to keep the bundles tight.

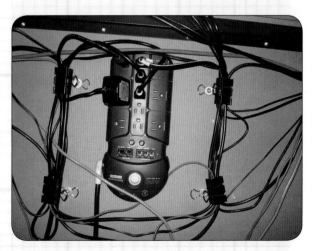

How to Build Your Own Desktop Zen Garden

By obbitz

http://www.instructables.com/id/How-to-build-your-own-desktop-zen-garden/

There are a lot of people that like to have something special on their desk. There are also a lot of people that like gardening, but they simply don't have a place to practice it. This little desktop garden will make them all happy. It's built from recycled scraps and other easily found stuff.

Let's start building our own desktop Zen garden, for those moments that we look away from the papers or the computer.

Step 1: Required Tools and Materials
Materials:
- Wood scraps (planks and sticks)
- Some nice rocks you can find (maximum 10 cm in size)
- Small pebbles
- Sand
- Some separating material (plastic, rubber, fiber) so the pebbles don't mix with the sand
- Old newspapers
- Some old paint (I found some water based)

Tools:
- Measuring tool (tape or meter)
- Right angle
- Screwdriver (manual or electric)
- Sharp knife or cutter
- Stapler
- Clamp
- Hand saw
- Scissors
- Screws
- Pencil
- Metal file
- Paint brush or roller

That's about it . . . Let's start working!

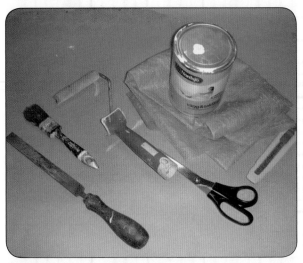

Step 2: Cut the Wood and Start Making the Box

You need to measure the planks you've found. Mine was 84 ½ cm long and 14 ½ cm wide, so I cut two pieces of 42 cm each.

The sticks I found were of different lengths, so I cut out two pieces of 29 cm for the box legs and another four pieces to make the perimeter of the container.

I used the file to smooth all the edges of the planks and the sticks.

The box legs hold the two planks together side by side, so it's easier to mount the perimeter sticks afterwards.

Attention: Please be careful not to split the wood if you have large screws. It's better if you drill the screw holes and afterwards you screw them in. It's the safe way to do it.

276

Step 3: Insulation and Paint

I used a fiber cloth to insulate the wood from the sand and pebbles. It's not really necessary, because it's a dry garden, but I like to keep materials separated.

I stapled the material tightly to the inside of the box.

I then stuck newspaper pieces to the wood with the water-based paint. I chose to do this so I could hide the defects on the sticks, the screw holes, and the spaces between the wooden parts. If you have good quality wood you don't need to do this.

Personally I like the texture the paper gave the box.

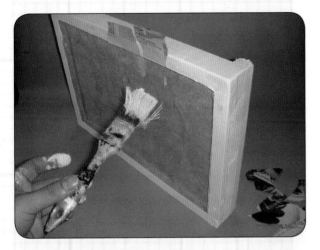

Step 4: Adding the Fillings

After the paint dried, I stapled some canvas strips about 2 cm from the sides as a barrier to create a sort of moat full of pebbles. This is important because you don't want the pebbles to mix with the sand.

After I added the pebbles, I added the sand and leveled it with a flat stick.

Then I chose my bigger stones and positioned them as I liked.

Afterwards I scraped the sand with a screw tip (you can use anything sharp) from one side to the other to create straight lines. This gives the sand the impression of water. Also I scraped the perimeter of the rocks with three to five lines that emulate water ripples.

There you have it! Your desktop Zen garden!

Angry Birds Cable Holders

By Christine Nast (ChrysN)

http://www.instructables.com/id/Angry-Birds-Cable-Holders/

I needed a way to organize the USB cables that connected my iPod, Kindle, and other devices to my computer. I definitely had cable management issues; they are usually tangled and often hard to find, not to mention that I've seen bite marks on the ends from where my cat has been chewing on them. I wanted to make something that was functional and also looked nice, since it would be sitting in a conspicuous spot on my computer desk.

Step 1: Materials

To make the three characters, I used four packs of Sugru, one of each of the following colors: red, green, white, and black. If you want to make this for larger cables such as power cords you may need to use more.

- Sugru
- Soapy water and cling wrap (Sugru doesn't stick to either of these; soapy water is also good for smoothing it out)
- Scissors
- A permanent marker
- The cables you want to hold

Optional (to dye the Sugru):
- Food coloring
- Corn starch
- Spoon
- Shallow dish

Step 2: Dyeing the Sugru

I really wanted to make the red bird, but unfortunately Sugru doesn't come in red. I tried using cornstarch and food coloring, which actually worked quite well and was fairly easy to do.

In a small plastic dish, measure out about ¼ teaspoon of cornstarch.

Add a drop or two of red food coloring and mix with a spoon.

Add a drop at a time while mixing in between until the cornstarch has turned completely red, but is still dry.

The cornstarch should absorb the liquid from the food coloring so it forms a red powder.

Step 3: Red Bird, Part One

Protect your work surface and cable by covering it with cling wrap.

Mix some soapy water and put some on your hands and whatever else you don't want the Sugru to stick to.

To make the red bird, open a pack of orange Sugru.

Save a portion of it to be used for the beaks (of this bird and the black one).

Dip the larger portion of orange Sugru into the red powder you made in the previous step, mix it in (you may want to use gloves for this), and add more powder as needed until you get a nice red shade.

Save a small bit of the red Sugru to be used for the top feathers.

Form a ball from the larger portion and press the cable down across the lower half, then remove the cable and pinch the lip of the trench together. When the Sugru has cured, you want the cable to fit snugly into the trench so that it holds it securely in place, but you also want to remove it if needed.

278

Step 4: Red Bird, Part Two

Place the remaining small bit of red on the top of the bird to look like feathers.

Open a pack of white Sugru and make the eyes and the white belly.

Mix some of the remaining orange with the white Sugru to form the beak and place it just above the trench.

Open the black pack of Sugru and take a bit of it to form eyebrows (remember to make them look angry).

You can affix the finished bird to the spot where you will be using it (Sugru sticks well to wood, glass, computer monitors, etc.) or, if you want, you can leave it on the cling wrap and use double-sided tape to affix it where you want it once it dries. Allow the Sugru to cure overnight.

Step 5: Black Bird

To make the black bird, use the remaining black Sugru.

Save a small portion of it to be used to make the grey belly and the feather on top of its head.

Form a ball and press the cable down across the lower half, remove the cable, and pinch the lip of the trench together.

Take a bit of the black to form the top feather

Mix part of the remaining black with some white Sugru and place the grey on the lower part of the bird (the belly).

Form the eyes with the white Sugru.

Take some of the orange left from the previous bird to make the eyebrows.

Take the remaining orange to form the beak and place it just above the trench, saving a tiny bit of orange to put on the tip of the top feather.

You can affix the finished bird to the spot where you will be using it (Sugru sticks well to wood, glass, computer monitors, etc.) or, if you want, you can leave it on the cling wrap and use double-sided tape to affix it where you want it once it dries. Allow the Sugru to cure overnight

Step 6: Pig

To make the pig, open the pack of green Sugru.

Save a small portion of the green to be used for the snout and ears.

Form a ball and press the cable down across the lower half, remove the cable, and pinch the lip of the trench together.

Mix the remaining green with white Sugru and form the ears and snout

Place the snout just above the trench.

With a pencil or other sharp object, form the nostrils on the snout.

Form the eyes with the white Sugru.

You can affix the finished pig to the spot where you will be using it (Sugru sticks well to wood, glass, computer monitors, etc.), or, if you want, you can leave it on the cling wrap and use double-sided tape to affix it where you want it once it dries. Allow the Sugru to cure overnight.

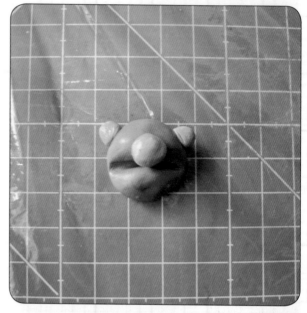

Step 7: Finishing Up

Once the Sugru has cured, draw in the eyes with a fine-point Sharpie. Then draw in the front of the pig's ears and eyebrows. Since I didn't actually stick the cable holders where I needed them before the Sugru cured, I had to add some double-sided tape to the bottom.

Wraparound Desk

By Bob Klepfer (themostbob)
http://www.instructables.com/id/
Wraparound-Desk-Made-From-One-Sheet-of-
Plywood%2c-2-/

Five years ago I wanted a desk. When I was a kid my mother made a desk out of an interior door and two filing cabinets. I already had one filing cabinet about 29 inches tall, so I bought another the same height and tried the desk out.

It was ugly, tended to slide by itself, I hit my hip on the corners occasionally, and I heard disconcerting cracks and creaks when I put my 20" CRT in the middle where I wanted it. So I thought again.

My specifications were, in order of importance:
- Elegant - I liked desks that wrapped around you
- Easy to Make - Minimize tools and time
- Cheap - Ideally made out of one piece of plywood
- Movable - I 've moved too many times to set myself up with a cumbersome desk

I like corner desks as a rule, so I drew up a design with 6' legs from a corner, with a couple of curves. 6' on a side was a good size not just aesthetically, but because with judicious cutting I could cut all the structural pieces out of one piece of good, double-sided plywood. In my book, elegance of design is something you enjoy long after you've forgotten the monetary cost.

This project took an morning for the woodwork, plus the rest of the weekend for staining and poly coats.

Step 1: Gather Materials and Tools
Materials:
- Two (2) short filing cabinets of equal height
- One (1) 4' 3 8' piece of ." double-faced plywood. Just make sure both sides are pleasing to the eye,

since you will have to flip one half over to marry it with the other.
- One or two (1-2) table/trunk/whateveryoucallem-latches. You know the kind—two pieces, one with a loop and a level thing to grab onto the other side. (see picture below)
- Four pieces of ½" radius quarter round trim, 18" long.
- Metal strapping or corner brace for extra support in the center. I used a corner brace because I had one handy, but a straight bracket would make more sense.
- Paint or stain plus polyurethane for finishing
- Optional: ~12 feet of real wood edging with heat-sensitive glue on back.

Tools:
- Jig saw
- Screwdriver
- Optional: circular saw and long straightedge
- Optional: Clothes Iron or possibly curling iron
- Sandpaper of varied grits
- Paint brush/drop cloth

Step 2: Cutting the plywood
- Make the long diagonal cut all the way through the sheet from a point 2 feet from the corner along one long side to a point 2 feet from the opposite corner along the other long side. (it's the long straight cut diagonally side-to-side in the drawing) Use a circular saw with a long straightedge clamped into place, if you have such. The straighter, the better.

281

- If you have a long enough cutting blade for your jig saw, clamp the two pieces together, lining up all the sides (rotate the top cut piece 180 degrees to line up with bottom piece).
- Using a pencil on a non-stretchy 12" string and anchoring the string at point "A" in the diagram, draw an arc from the short edge of the sheet around through about 120 degrees. Point "A" is 18" from the (previously) long side of the sheet, 12" from the end. (see drawing)
- Lengthening the string to 18," draw an arc centered at point "B" in the diagram from the edge you just cut around until it meets the other arc centered on point "A." Point B is 6" from the shortest edge of the quadrilateral you're left with after the diagonal cut, and on the cut diagonal edge (actually 30" from the end of the sheet). (see drawing)
- Cut along the long curved line you just drew.
- Take the pieces left over and cut a 12" × 30" shape and a 12" × 12" right triangle shape from them, in the manner shown on the diagram, outlined in orange and blue respectively. These will form the corner support stand.

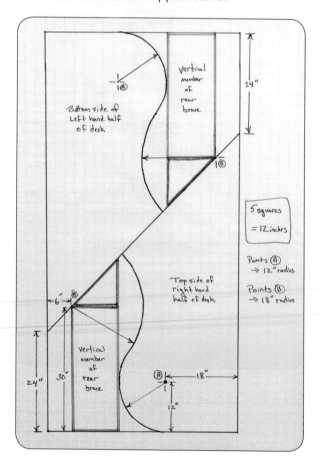

Step 3: Corner Support Assembly

Trim the long leftover rectangular pieces to the height of your filing cabinets, in my case, 29" tall. You want the final height of the stand to be the same as your filing cabinets. Use glue and screws to assemble the corner support. I used 1.25" drywall screws, just because I had them around. Since you're screwing into the edge of plywood, pilot holes are a good idea. These are all just lap joints, nothing fancy. It's not very visible anyway.

Step 4: Surface Prep and Finish

Clamp the two halves of the top together again and sand the edges to try to make them as symmetrical as you can. I used a mini-drum sander bit for my electric drill, but sandpaper on a curved surface should work well, if slower.

Orient the top pieces in the way they will be assembled (one top piece has to flip over and join with the other at the diagonal cut). Mark or somehow assign which is the top side and sand with progressively finer grits of sandpaper until it's as smooth as you like it. You may wish to sand the bottom to a medium fineness—the stain applies easier to a smoother surface.

I didn't do this to mine before I stained it, but if you want the edges to match the top, apply the wood edging to the exposed edges with a heat source, either a clothes iron or (possibly—I didn't try this) a curling iron. The curved surface of the curling iron may work better on the concave curves.

I really liked the look of colored stain for this, so I chose a blue-tinted Minwax stain. I stained the bottom sides first, the the tops, and repeated for a total of 2 coats each side.

I then applied 3–4 coats of water-based polyurethane, sanding between each step. I poly'd each of the surfaces which would be seen, including the "front" of the corner support stand.

Step 5: Assembly

Note: *I did not then nor have I yet attached the desk tops to the corner support. I had planned to do it, but when I place my monitor on the desk in the corner, with the file cabinets in place, nothing seemed to move, so I didn't bother. Feel free to attach them if you wish—I'd use 1.25" screws from the bottom.*

Turn the desktops face down on the floor, diagonal cuts together. Place the two-piece latches, closed, on the joint and mark and drill pilot holes for their screws. Be careful not to drill through the top side. Attach the latches. Unhook them and separate the pieces.

Place the corner support in the corner and the file cabinets to either side of the corner in their approximate positions. Place each desktop half, top side up, where it's supposed to go supported by the file cabinets and corner support. Latch the two halves together with the latches you just installed above. Hopefully both halves will move as one now.

Line up the file cabinets along each wall, maybe moving them 1–2 inches out from the wall to allow cords and such to go behind them. Put them under the fattest part of the outer curves and mark the undersides along the sides of the cabinets. Unlatch the desktop halves and turn them over. Align the pieces of quarter round along those marks, flat sides toward the underside of the desktops and toward the filing cabinets. Make sure they're short enough to not be seen when the desk is right-side-up. Pilot drill and screw them down with 1" screws.

Place the desktops back up on the cabinets where they belong and latch them together. You most likely need a little more support in the middle right under your arms since the latches are the only things holding the top together and they occasionally become uneven. I used a corner bracket screwed into each side. In elegant perhaps, but each half is level with the other and there is plenty of support for my hands, keyboard, forearms, yada yada yada.

Step 6: Done!

It's ready to use—enjoy. I have. Mine has been great, even with my honkin big desk chair (see picture). The center sitting area is about 32" wide—plenty of room in general, and there is a metric buttload of deskspace to fill up, as I am want to do. Have fun.

Optional: If you want an easy cord pass-through the desktop, you can cut the tip of the corner off each desktop half prior to staining.

Pac-Man Cork Board

By dominator24

http://www.instructables.com/id/Pac-man-
Cork-Board/

Upon arriving at college, I realized that I had forgotten my cork board back at home. Instead of having my parents mail it to me or even (gasp) going a whole term without a cork board, I decided to make a cheap, geekified version of my own! For less than $10, I made an eye-catching art piece that also has a functional purpose!

Step 1: Tools and Materials

Tools you will need:

- Scissors or box-cutter
- Tape measure or ruler
- Markers
- Straightedge (if you don't have a ruler handy)

Materials:

- Cork board tiles (I bought a pack of four on Amazon for $6.79)
- Tape or other means of sticking the boards to the wall

Step 2: Come Up with a Design!

Pac-man is only one of many designs you could put on here. When choosing what you want your cork board to be shaped like, keep in mind that the image cannot be too detailed because it will be too hard to cut out (unless you have a laser cutter, in which case, go for it!). Also keep in mind that it is a lot easier to cut out straight pieces than round ones.

Once you have chosen a design, create an image of it using your image editor of choice; I used GIMPshop for my design. To make it easier to transfer

the design onto the cork board, scale the image so that the longest side is 12" (or whatever length your cork board is.)

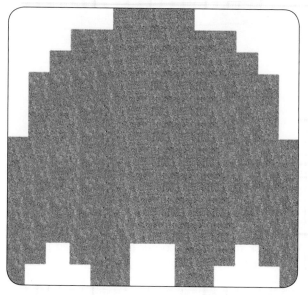

Step 3: Put the Design on the Boards!

Once I had created my templates, I reset the rulers in GIMP to show inches instead of pixels (see picture below). Using the templates as a guide, I then used a straightedge and a tape measure to draw the image on the cork board. To do this is very simple; for example, if the first corner on the image is 1 ½" from the left in the image, then make a mark 1 ½" from the left on the board. If your design is simple enough, you can make all the marks on two edges of the board, then use a straightedge to draw the lines in.

Step 4: Cut Out the Images!

This part should be pretty simple; just cut along the lines that you drew in the previous step. I used scissors for my cutting, which worked pretty well unless I had to make tight inside corners. The part I had the most trouble with was the bottom of the ghosts, but I think it turned out pretty well. I'm not sure how well a box-cutter (or any other knife) would work, but I would imagine that it would be easier to use.

Step 5: Put It on the Wall!

Now all you have to do is put the cut-out pieces on the wall! I used painter's tape to put mine up. The cork boards also came with some double-sided foam tape that you can use.

Now all that's left to do is fill your new cork boards with all of your papers that need organizing! Enjoy!

Floating Multi-Use Wall Storage

By voodooduck

http://www.instructables.com/id/Floating-Multi-Use-Wall-Storage/

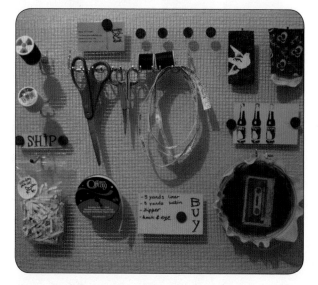

This Instructable will teach you how to make a floating metal grid that can be used as a magnetic bulletin board, a place to display artwork, a jewelry organizer, craft organizer, or whatever else your crazy little heart desires! I originally came up with this idea in my freshman year of college to display pictures. In the dorms we were not allowed to put holes in the walls, so I instead stapled some wire mesh behind an old ladder that we had sitting around. The picture ladder was perfect for us because we could just rearrange our pictures whenever we wanted by moving the magnets.

Realizing the many things that we were able to do with the wire mesh, I decided that I should reincarnate it once more. This time I went to Home Depot and let myself go crazy finding all sorts of goodies to pimp it out to its full potential. The new and improved floating multi-use wall storage is a great addition to any room of yours. It makes a particularly good gift because it can be used in so many different ways. If your friend is a crafty individual, it could easily be used to store his or her craft supplies. Use it to display pictures and memories, or even to showcase products for retail stores—the possibilities are endless! And, best of all, you can constantly rearrange and recreate it with minimal effort!

Step 1: Gather It Up!

Get in your car and go to Home Depot. Then gather these things.

Note: You may want to look ahead to the final steps and decide how you want to use your board before going to the store.

Materials needed for basic construction:
- The mesh
- ¼" hardware cloth (the smallest size you can get is 2' X 5.' That is sufficient.)
- 4 rod-coupling nuts (⁵⁄₁₆"18" × ⅞"; the package only has three . . . Sorry, you have to buy two packs.)
- 4 pan-head Phillips-head screws (#10 × 2")
- 8 washers (¼ SAE washer; the size of the washer isn't that important, just make sure that the screw fits through the washer and the head of the screw will be larger than the hole in the washer.)
- 1 nail (pretty much any nail that is a good bit skinnier than the screw will do. It's just used to make the pilot hole for the screw.)
- Pencil
- A friend for step 6

Things to gather up at home:
- Gardening shears or some sort of wire trimmers (I have used scissors before to cut the wire, but it is a little more difficult.)
- Drill
- Phillips-head screwdriver bit
- Hammer
- Yard stick
- Level

Step 2: Prep the Mesh

Open up the package of hardware cloth (wire mesh). Usually it is tied up with some wire—use your wire cutters to snip this wire until you can unroll the mesh.

We are going to cut a piece that is 2' × 18." Since the mesh is 5' × 2', we are going to use the existing 2' width and make a cut 18" into the 5' length. The mesh will want to stay rolled, so weigh down the edge with some heavy books.

Now that the mesh is secured, measure out 18" of mesh. Grab your wire cutters to cut the mesh. Cut the mesh along the wire line that is closest to 18." The wire is *very* sharp after you cut it, so keep your fingers away from it. Make sure you are cutting as close to the wire line as possible so as not to leave any prickly pieces of wire along the edge (see image).

Now you should have a free piece of 18" × 24" mesh. The mesh will probably roll up. Try to roll it the opposite direction to bend it into a somewhat flat sheet. It doesn't have to be perfect.

You should now have a rectangle just like the green one in the drawing! Measure the difference between the top and bottom lines. Make sure it is 12 ¼". Then, measure the difference between the left and right lines. It should be 18 ¼". Now erase the lines, leaving only little plus signs at each corner of the rectangle.

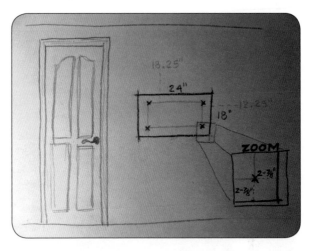

Step 4: Nail Time

You will now create pilot holes for the screws. Hammer the nail into the center of one of the X's. Be sure to keep the nail as close to perpendicular to the wall as possible. Pull the nail out and repeat the process for each of the X marks. This should leave you with four holes.

Step 3: Measure It All Out

Okay, our piece of mesh is 18" × 24"; the screws that will hold it in the wall will be placed 2 ⅞" into each corner. That means 2 ⅞" horizontally from the corner, and 2 ⅞" vertically from the corner (see the drawing).

Once you decide where you want to place your floating mesh piece you will need to mark it out as follows. Start by making one small light pencil mark to indicate where the top edge of the mesh will be. Then measure 18" down and make another mark. Now measure down 2 ⅞" from the top mark and make another light mark. Then, measure up 2 ⅞" from the bottom mark and make another mark. You can now erase the first two marks you made.

Place your level horizontally at the top mark and draw a light, level line that will function as the top green line in the first image below. Now repeat with the bottom mark. Now you need to make the vertical lines. Measure out where you want the 24" width and make a mark at each end of it on the top line. Measure 2 ⅞" to the right of the left-most mark and make another mark. Measure 2 ⅞" to the left of the right-most mark and make another mark. Place your level vertically and draw a vertical, level line for each of the marks. These lines will serve as the vertical green lines in the first image.

Step 5: Prep for Screws

First, you have to understand how the screw-and-bolt combination will work. Look at the first picture to understand the order. It should go like this: screw head, washer, mesh, rod coupling nut, and then another washer, then the remainder of the screw will screw into the wall.

Grab your Sharpie. You will end up having four marked squares to indicate where the screws will go in the mesh. You are going to mark the square that is 12th from the top or bottom of each corner and 12th from the left and right of each corner. When you measure vertically and horizontally in from each corner, the center of that marked square should be 2 ⅞".

Step 6: Screw It In!

Now you should have the mesh marked where the four screws will go and have four pilot holes in the wall. Plug your drill in and get the Phillips-head bit locked in place. Grab a buddy and have them hold the mesh in place so that the marked squares line up with the pilot holes. Thread a washer onto your first screw and then put the screw through the mesh in the marked place.

Place a coupling nut behind the mesh and then another washer behind that (see image to make sure you have it right). Now, with your friend holding the mesh in place, set the point of the screw in the pilot hole, making sure you are holding the drill level, and screw that sucker in!

Be careful not to keep drilling after it is tight because it may strip the dry wall. If you hit a stud it will be more difficult to screw into. Make sure you apply enough pressure into the drill to keep it from stripping the screw. Repeat this until all of them are

screwed in, and then you should have yourself a floating wire mesh thing to use however your happy little heart pleases!

Step 7: Jazz It Up

Congrats! You are done with the tedious part! Now for the fun! Here are some different ideas for things to do with your mesh board and a list of extra things you could use for each.

1. Jewelry storage uses a multi-tool rack (light duty for six tools is what I used), double-prong straight peg hooks (I used ⅛" × 2"), and some ¾" S-hooks (you can get larger ones if you have chunky jewelry that may not fit within the curve).
2. Craft storage uses multi-tool rack (light duty for six tools is what I used), double-prong straight peg hooks (I used ⅛" × 2"), some ¾" S-hooks, sewing pins, and magnets (I got the basic ones from Wal-mart).
3. Photo collage uses some ¾" S-hooks and magnets (I got the basic ones from Wal-Mart).

These are just a few starter ideas—the possibilities for this mesh are endless. Be creative with it, and have a blast!

Yard

When it comes to outside your home, it really comes down to curb appeal. You need to make a good first impression and you can't do that with cracked and uneven sidewalks or with chairs falling apart at the seams. Take that sidewalk and replace it with a functional and beautiful wooden sidewalk and get those chairs fixed up before someone falls right through them!

When you've got that done, better check out your water hose and lawn mower. Can't have them falling apart on you too!

How to Repair a Rusty Wheelbarrow

By AngelLifeLearning
http://www.instructables.com/id/How-to-Repair-a-Rusty-Wheelbarrow/

My school garden class had a rusty wheelbarrow out in the backyard that needed to either be thrown away or be repaired. The rust was so bad that stuff would fall through. It was both inconvenient and dangerous to use. We came up with an idea to fix it without having to go out to the store and purchase a new one. In this Instructable I will show you how you can repair a rusty wheelbarrow. Hope you enjoy it!

Step 1: Materials Needed

- Safety glasses/gloves
- Pop rivets
- Pop rivet tool
- Tin snips
- Pliers
- Electric drill
- ³⁄₁₆" drill bit
- Aluminum sheet metal (aluminum flashing from a hardware store will work)
- Marker

All these items are easy to find at any hardware store.

Step 2: Make a Pattern

First, find old cardboard and cut the right pattern for your wheelbarrow. Make sure you make the pieces much bigger than the rust holes so that you can attach it to metal that is still solid. The area near the hole will be too badly rusted for the rivets to hold. You will use the cardboard cutout later to trace it on to the sheet metal.

Step 3: Trace Pattern

Trace the pattern that you cut out onto the sheet metal. Once you trace it use the shears or tin snips to cut it out.

Step 4: Rivet Sheet Metal with Pop Rivets

Place sheet metal where damage is. Use a electric drill to drill holes through wheelbarrow and sheet metal using ³⁄₁₆" drill bit. Now attach the sheet metal with the ³⁄₁₆" pop rivet. You can use the back-up washers on the back side of the rivet to make sure the rivet does not pull through.

Step 6: Ready to Use!

Now that all sheet metal is in place covering up the damage, the wheelbarrow is ready to be used again.

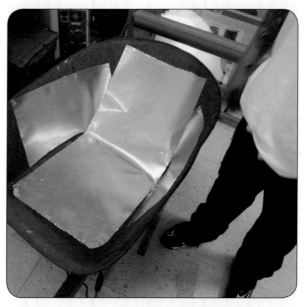

Step 5: Riveting

Now repeat the same process by riveting and making sure the other pieces of sheet metal are attached to the wheelbarrow and cover the holes.

Garden Hose Repair
By AT
http://www.instructables.com/id/Garden-Hose-Repair/

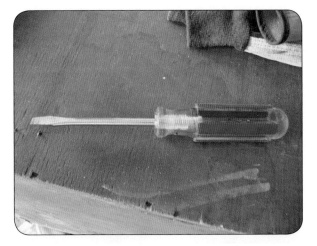

I know that garden hoses are not that expensive, but I can't bring myself to go out and buy a new one when I can fix the one I have. Both the ends and middle of a garden hose can be replaced. This Instructable will go through how to replace the end of a garden hose.

Step 1: You Will Need
- Broken garden hose
- ⅝" replacement end (male, in this case ⅝")
- Hose clamp
- Utility knife (or some other thing that will cut the hose)
- Screwdriver

Step 2: Examine Hose and Cut

When you find that your garden hose has gone bad, check to see if where you found the problem is the only place. In my case, there were three places near the end and the rest of the hose was still good. If there are several bad places along the entire length of the hose, then maybe it is time to go get a new hose. After the third place at the end where the hose is going bad is where I am going to make my cut. I cut the hose a couple inches back from the last bad spot to ensure I will be working with good hose.

Step 3: Put the Hose Clamp On

After you have cut the hose, you can put the hose clamp on the good part of the hose.

Step 4: Insert New End and Clamp

Insert the new male end into the hose. You should be able to push the new end into the hose by hand. Once it is all the way in, secure with the hose clamp. The new end should stay in place without the clamp, at least until you put pressure behind it. If the new end falls out, you have the wrong-size piece or your hose is worse off that you thought.

Step 5: Done!

You are now done with the repair. The hose should be ready for use. Typical garden hose comes in two sizes: ⅝" and ½". Most longer hoses are the ⅝" type. The ½" hose is usually a shorter hose. If you are not sure which size your hose is, get replacement parts for both sizes and then return the one that is the wrong size.

How to Change a Lawnmower Blade

By wilbur34

http://www.instructables.com/id/How-to-Change-a-Lawn-Mower-Blade/

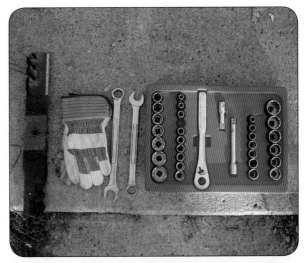

After a certain amount of time of using a lawnmower, the blades will need to be changed. Due to the cutting of the grass and mowing over the occasional rock, the blades will begin to dull and chip. This leads to blades that do not cut grass well anymore, and the only way to fix this is to switch the blades with some sharp ones. A person will know when the blades are dull when either the engine sounds like it is working harder than usual to mow the grass or when there are patches or lines of grass in areas that have just been mowed.

Changing lawnmower blades is a simple procedure that will take less than half an hour if the right tools are already owned.

The tools needed for this project are sharp blades, work gloves, and a ratchet and socket (or a wrench).

Notes: Sharp blades are not needed. If there is no spare sharp set of blades, the time to change the blades will increase significantly because time will need to be added in order to sharpen the dull blades once they are taken off.

The ratchet and socket will be easier to work with than a wrench, but a wrench will work in the absence of a ratchet and socket.

Step 1: Finding a Place to Change the Blades

Finding a proper place to change the blades can make the process easier. For example, in the mower pictured in the first picture, the deck raises from the front. The mower was driven to the top of a raised piece of ground to give even more room while working.

Depending on the type of mower being used, different places will be better than others. For example, a small push mower can just be flipped on its side on top of a cement pad after the oil and gas has been drained.

For a mower parked on top of a raised piece of ground it is mandatory to use the parking break.

1. Find a place to park.
2. Switch the parking brake to the "On" position as seen in the second picture.
3. Turn the engine off and let the mower cool if it is hot.
4. Place a block in front of and behind a tire as seen in the third picture.

Warning: If steps 2 and 3 are not followed the mower could roll down hill and cause injury.

295

Step 2: Find What Size Tool Is Needed

To find what size tools are needed you can either look it up in the user's manual for the mower or on the Internet if tools need to be bought. If the proper tools are on hand and only the proper size is left to be determined, it is easiest to put the socket or wrench onto the bolt to find the proper size. It is recommended that when crawling under the deck of the lawnmower to place an old rug or sheets down to protect against minor scrapes and scratches as seen in the picture.

1. Place the socket onto the ratchet as seen in the third picture.
2. Crawl under the deck and put the socket and wrench onto the bolt like in the fourth picture. If the socket does not fit onto the bolt try a bigger socket. If the socket fits onto the bolt but does not catch when turned, try a smaller socket. When the socket fits snugly onto the bolt, the right socket has been found.

Step 3: Taking Off the Blade

Taking off the blade is a simple and quick process. It is important to wear gloves while doing this to protect your hands from getting cut. Wearing gloves will also protect your hands from getting grease on them.

1. Once the right socket is found, turn the ratchet's switch to the right as seen in the second picture.
2. Place the ratchet and socket on the bolt and grab the blade with the other hand as seen in third picture.
3. Twist the ratchet counterclockwise to loosen the bolt. Once the bolt is loose enough, loosen the bolt by hand, continuing to turn counterclockwise as seen in the fourth picture.
4. Skip this step if there is only one blade. Crawl out from under the lawnmower deck and place the pieces in a safe location, where they will not be lost, as seen in the fifth picture. Repeat steps 2 and 3 until all the blades are off.

Step 4: Switching the Blades

Once done taking the blades off, the next step is to switch the dull blades with the sharp blades. If there are no sharp blades on hand, the dull blades will need to be sharpened.

Caution: Some lawnmowers that have more than one blade will sometimes have blades of different lengths. Pay careful attention to make sure the spare blade is the same length as the blade it is replacing.

1. When done taking the blades off, crawl out from under the lawnmower deck and place the blades onto a cement or gravel surface as seen in the first picture.
2. Take the blade off as seen in the second picture
3. Put the new blade on, making sure that the side with the long edge is facing the sky as seen in the third picture. A way to check to make sure the blade is oriented correctly is to have the sharp edges be doing the cutting if the blade turns in a clockwise motion while looking at it from the top, as seen in picture one.
4. Repeat steps 2 and 3 until all the blades are changed.

Step 5: Putting the Blades Back On

After replacing the dull blades with sharp ones, the next step is to place the blades back onto the mower.

Caution: Because some blades are different lengths, when putting the blades on, make sure to place the same length blade where it was originally.

1. Crawl under the lawnmower deck with the correct length blade and insert the bolt into the hole.
2. Hand-tighten the bolt clockwise. Once the screw is hand-tightened you will need to use the ratchet or wrench.
3. Flip the ratchet switch to the left as seen in the third picture.
4. Place the socket onto the bolt and grab the blade with your free hand and turn counterclockwise until you can no longer turn the ratchet, as seen in picture four.
5. Repeat steps 1, 2, and 4 if there are additional blades to put on.
6. Turn the mower blades in a circle a few times to make sure the blades do not catch each other. If they catch, the proper length blades were not installed and the blades will need to be replaced with ones of the correct length so that the blades can freely turn.

Step 6: Clean Up

After the blades are switched, all that is left is to clean up the small mess.

1. Crawl out from under the deck of the lawnmower.
2. Pick up the blanket or rug if one was used.
3. Place tools back into the tool box or tool chest.
4. Remove the blocks from the tire as seen in picture one.
5. Turn the parking brake to the "off" position. The "off" position for the parking brake can be seen in picture two.

Block Base for a Fire Stand

By Michael F. Quinn
(the_Magnificent_Macak)
http://www.instructables.com/id/Block-Base-for-a-Fire-Stand/

I got tired of burning a brown spot into my yard, so I decided to pick up some materials and make a nice block base to put my fire stand on. You can do it with a few hours and under $100, depending on the type of brick you choose.

Step 1: Select Location
Find a nice flat spot away from the house and neighbors to place your fire stand. Choose wisely, because this is permanent.

Step 2: Planning, Supplies, and Tools
Depending on the size of your stand, first decide how large you want the base to be. This will determine how much material you will need. I did not want to cut any blocks, as I do not have a chisel or brick saw. Based on the 6" X 6" and 9" X 6" blocks at the store, I settled on a 3' X 3' area.

One deceivingly complex task is to figure out the block pattern you want to use. Try drawing it out first to see what you like. Once you have the pattern, count the blocks and sizes you need to purchase. My pattern required 16 9" X 6"s and 12 6" X 6"s.

Now go get some drainage rock for the foundation. I wanted a 3" stone base, so 3' X 3' X ¼" = 2 ¼ cubic feet. I also wanted 1" of sand to place the bricks on and make them level. 3' X 3' X .083" = 0.75 cubic feet.

Materials:
- Sixteen 9" X 6" blocks
- Twelve 6" X 6" blocks
- Five bags of drainage rock at 0.5 cubic feet per bag
- Three bags sand at 0.5 cubic feet per bag

Tools:
- Spray paint (not necessary but makes it easier to keep your cut straight)
- Spade shovel or edger
- Digging shovel
- Tape measure
- Length of wood (to help screen out sand)
- Gloves
- Mallet
- Level
- Broom
- Tamper (if you have one; not completely necessary)

Step 3: Get Diggin'
I spray painted the outline of my location and used the spade shovel to cut the outline of the base. Cut the square just a little smaller to get the blocks in nice and tight. You can also cut away more soil later if you need to.

I then pried the grass outline with the shovel and rolled up the lawn like a carpet. You don't have to save the grass, but it's a good piece of sod that you can use somewhere else.

Next, start digging to the depth you need. Just add the stone thickness, sand, and block height to get the required depth (3" + 1" + 1 ½" = 5 ½"). I needed to go 5 ½" down. Make sure to measure often, as you don't want to go deeper than you have to, otherwise you'll need more stone and sand. Tamp the soil if you have a tamper. I do not, so I dropped a bag of the unopened stone into the hole. You do this to make sure your new base doesn't settle over time.

give each block a few whacks with the mallet to set it in. My square wasn't quite large enough, so I had to use a hoe to cut the edge just a little bigger.

Step 6: Sweep in the Sand

Sweep in extra sand in between your blocks. Sprinkle some water on the blocks and sand to compact it and then add some more. I also had to put some soil along the outer edge of my blocks.

Step 4: Add the Stone

Add the drainage stone. Again, make sure you compact the stone with your tamper; in my case I used a block of wood and hammered it with the mallet over the entire area of the base. A compacted base is a happy base!

Step 7: Enjoy

Place your fire stand on top and start enjoying the summer nights with your campfire. The total cost was close to $55 in materials and took maybe two hours on a Saturday.

Note: I may have gone overboard with the three inches of stone. You might not even need to use the stone at all, or as much, depending on the drainage and soil conditions in your yard.

Step 5: Add the Sand and Blocks

Add your sand. Try to level out the sand with a piece of wood and a level. This is where your blocks will go, so the more level the better. I had a really hard time getting everything exactly level, so I gave up and just eyed it up.

Now insert your blocks onto the sand. Use the mallet and level as best as you can. Level it up and

How to Make a Tire Swing

By adlabens

http://www.instructables.com/id/How-to-make-a-tire-swing/

This explains how to build a tire swing. On the surface, a simple tire with a rope would seem to be a good tire swing. After all, it worked for us when we were children. But, these days, just tying a rope to a tire is not good enough. For purchased play sets, tires are now mounted horizontally instead of vertically, and that presents an entirely new set of challenges. Here is how I succeeded in building my children a professional-looking tire swing for half the cost!

Let me note at the onset that this Instructable is not a joke. It is long and detailed, with lots of pictures. If you're really not interested in building a tire swing, then don't waste your time looking through it. But, if you are truly interested in building a tire swing, then this provides serious and detailed instructions that ought to give you every tool to be successful. Good luck!

Step 1: Pick Out a Tire!

First, pick out a tire. Thinking "Bigger is better" will only get you in trouble here. Without being indelicate, consider the size of the derrieres that will be riding the swing. For smaller children, a big tire just won't do. For large adults, a smaller tire should be fine—as long as it's bigger (the tire, not the derriere) than the one on your wheelbarrow! I was looking at a tire from a pickup truck, but realized our 2 ½-year-old twins wouldn't get near it. So, I settled for the tire I'd just taken off the 15" rear wheel of my motorcycle. Perfect!

Once the tire is chosen, look at both sides of it and determine which looks better. This will be the top side. Flip the tire over and drill holes in the bottom sidewall. To do this, set the tire on a surface that will be at a height appropriate for drilling without straining your back. I used our new picnic table and it did the job perfectly. Use about a ½" drill bit and drill holes around the sidewall, every few inches. The holes don't have to be perfectly spaced, but it'll drain better if the holes are more evenly spaced. I used the tread pattern to space the holes. Here's a picture of the bottom of the tire with the drain holes already drilled.

Step 2: Attach the Eye-Bolts (Part 1)

Next, flip the tire over so that it's top-side up. This is where we're going to attach the eye-bolts that'll attach to the chains that will support the tire swing. Since a triangle is the most stable plane, you'll want to find three spots, equally spaced around the sidewall, for the eye-bolts. You can use all kinds of geometric formulas for determining the ideal spots. I simply picked an arbitrary spot for my first hole. I went ahead and drilled it with a drill bit just barely big enough for the shaft of the eye-bolt. I put it in a spot where the fender washer won't stick out over the curvature of the tire.

this process, because you'll have to do it on all the S-hook attachments.

Step 3: Attach the Eye-Bolts (Part 2)

Then take a string and approximate where the second hole would be, then use the string to see if the third hole would be equal distance from the first two. Finding that it wasn't, I adjusted the string and tried it again. This process took three attempts before I hit the perfect distance. I drilled the other two holes. Then, I threaded the eye bolts with one nut and a fender washer. Next, I threaded the eye-bolt through the tire. On the inside of the tire, I placed another fender washer on the eye-bolt, then the lock washer, and, finally, the second nut, which I tightened down. I've included a few pictures of the hardware, in the sequence in which they are to be attached.

Step 4: Attach the Eye-Bolts (Part 3)

The tire sidewall is now being squeezed between the two big, flat fender washers. This prevents the smaller nut from pulling thru the sidewall as it gets stressed by the weight of the person swinging.

Step 5: Attach S-Hook

Next, take an S-hook and put it through the eye-bolt. Using a pair of big pliers, squeeze the attached side of the S-hook so that it eventually is closed around the eye-bolt. This takes several squeezings of the pliers to make it happen. Adjust the pliers so they are open pretty wide and squeeze them, closing the S-hook just a little bit. Open up the pliers and tighten down the adjustment bolt, making them a little smaller, and squeeze them tight again, closing the S-hook a little bit more. Repeat this process, making the pliers smaller each time, until the S-hook is completely closed around the eye-bolt. Remember

Speaking of doing it again, do it again for the second S-hook on the second eye-bolt and for the third S-hook on the third eye-bolt.

Step 6: Attaching the Chains

Now that the S-hooks are attached to the eye-bolts, it's time to attach each of the 3' chains to each of the attached S-hooks.

Step 7: Attach the Top S-Hook

Next, take the fourth S-hook and attach the tops of all three chains to it, clamping it tight with the pliers just like the first three.

Step 8: Top Attachment Hardware (Part 1)

There are three pieces of hardware to attach to the top of this last S-hook that will complete the tire swing portion of the project. Their purpose should be obvious once you see them. The ratchet is in the picture for size reference. Going from left to right is the order that the items will be attached to the S-hook.

First is the swivel. This will allow the tire swing to swivel freely. The second piece is the connector link between the swivel and the clip hook. The clip hook is in the sequence so that the height of the tire swing will be adjustable. If you don't want or need it to be adjustable, then either use the connector link to attach it directly to the hanging chain, or use another S-hook. The S-hooks came in packs of two, so I had four of them, using three at the tire and one at the top of the chains. Instead of getting another two-pack of S-hooks, I got the connector link (I didn't want any leftover parts).

Step 9: Swivel to the S-Hook

Here are three shots of connecting the swivel to the top S-hook:

Step 10: Top Attachment Hardware (Part 2)

Here's a shot with the clip hook connected to the connector link connected to the swivel connected to the S-hook connected to the hip bone connected to the knee bone! Well, you get the picture. Tighten down/up the screw closure on the connector link, and the Tire Swing is now ready to hang.

Step 11: Long Chain

Here's a picture of the 12' of chain that I strung from the tree branch.

Step 12: Hanging the Chain

Here's a picture of the 12' chain hanging loosely from the branch in the back yard:

Step 13: Connector Link on Hanging Chain

Here's a picture of the connector link I used to close the hanging chain:

Step 14: Completed Project

And here's the final picture of the finished project:

Step 15: Final Notes

The whole thing, except for the tire, cost about $60.00. You could buy the kit from one of the play set manufacturers. The kit runs just a hair under $100.00. Doing it this way gave me the flexibility to do what I wanted and hang it how I wanted, and saved money along the way.

304

Copper Rain Chain

By Tool Using Animal

http://www.instructables.com/id/Copper-Rain-Chain/

This is a copper rain chain I made for my wife. I guess I should mention what a rain chain is! It's an alternative to a downspout, as it guides the water and breaks up the flow. They originated in Asia.

Step 1: Materials
- ¼" soft copper tubing 3½ times as long as you'd like the finished chain
- 2" PVC pipe
- Diagonal cutters
- Lead-free solder

- Blow torch
- Heavy leather gloves
- Flux
- Pliers

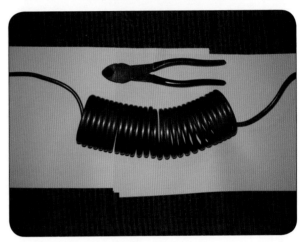

Step 2: Coiling the Copper

In this first construction step you'll only need the copper tubing and the PVC. Grip the end of the copper tubing and the PVC tightly in one hand. Now start wrapping the copper around the PVC while pulling on the copper to prevent kinking. You should end up with a nice coil that looks like it belongs on a still.

Step 3: Separating the Rings

Take the pair of diagonal cutters and snip the coil into rings. That was easy.

Step 4: Making the Chain

First we need to adjust the rings. Carefully adjust them until the two ends line up. If your snipping was consistent, you're ready to solder; if not, then pliers can be used for less delicate adjusting.

Step 5: But Don't Solder Yet!

You need to link the rings before soldering.

Now that they're linked, brush each joint with a little soldering flux, heat it in the torch, and flow in some lead-free solder. This is where you need the gloves, as copper is an excellent conductor of heat.

Step 6: Hanging

Hanging is simplicity itself. Remove your old downspout, feed the topmost copper ring up through the hole, and insert a spare piece of straight copper to span the downspout through the topmost ring. Now just wait for rain. With our drought I simulated it with the hose.

Pallet Adirondack Chair

By captianoats

http://www.instructables.com/id/Pallet-Adirondack-Chair-1/

There seems to be a movement of people trying to make all kinds of new stuff out of used pallets. There are several reasons I wanted to jump on this bandwagon:

1. I'm a tightwad, and pallets are free.
2. It's an earth-friendly way to repurpose something that would otherwise end up in a landfill.
3. I like making stuff.
4. It's a challenge.

So here is my chair. This is a very simple build based on other chairs I found online, and I adapted this to the lumber sizes I had. If you have a saw, a drill, and a pallet you can make this. I designed it so it is easy to modify to your own needs. You could easily fan the back, build it with curving back and seat, or make it bigger or smaller based on your lumber, skill, and taste.

Step 1: Pallets

This was made out of a single 42" × 60" pallet. It was constructed of 1" × 6"s and 2" × 4"s. You can easily build this out of other sizes. I'm not going to spend much time on how to disassemble a pallet; there are some great Instructables on this. However, I did it with a pry bar and hammer. I had the pallet apart in under half an hour.

I did it by driving a pry bar between the boards. Pry slowly so you don't break the boards. Once they're apart drive out all of the nails.

Step 2: Get Everything Together

Lay out all of your boards (this is two pallets). You'll have some splintered boards, and some aren't going to be as nice as others. If they're all spread out you can easily pick and choose which boards to use. Keep all of them! Some pieces will be fairly short, and even if something is splintered badly or warped, it has use if you just cut out the bad parts.

I used 1 ½" drywall screws to put everything together, as well as a circular saw and cordless screwdriver.

307

Step 3: Cut the Rails

This is the hardest cut you'll make (and it's not that hard). Cut two pieces of 1" × 6" 33 3 × 4" long. Now, measure 32 ½" and mark. Draw a line from this mark to the corner of the board. Make a cut; this should be about a 15 degree angle. Now measure over 2" from your new 75 degree angle, and cut it off to make another 90 degree angle.

After you make the cuts, sand everything. It's much easier now than once it all gets put together. You can see sanded and unsanded boards.

Notes: Don't trust the maker of the pallet to cut everything at a 90 degree angle. I try to cut the end off the board first; that way I know it is even, plus now it's smooth.

If that cut description is hard to follow, or if you're just wanting to make it a little easier, use these rules instead. Cut two pieces of 1" × 6" 33 ¾" long. Now go to one corner, measure over 2" and up ½". Make a mark and cut that little corner off (like what is in the top left of the picture). This won't give you the nice parallel legs once it's all done, but will still sit stable on the ground. It's not very noticeable, however, since this cut is at the bottom rear of the chair.

Step 4: Make the Seat

Cut four more pieces of 1" × 6" 21" long.

Screw one to the front of the runners. Now measure back 19 ½" and spread out the rest of the boards so they're evenly spaced; screw them in. Make sure that the pieces of the runner that you've cut the 2" corner off of is facing the ground. Sand everything.

You can easily use different size boards for the seat, just make sure you have at least ½" between the boards. This helps everything feel level and will let water run between the boards if the chair will stay outside.

Step 5: Make Back

Measure your gap between the runners (mine was 19 ¾") Cut two 2" × 4"s that length. Now cut three 1" × 6"s 30 ½" long and screw it all together. Start sanding.

Again, use whatever width board you have. This is flexible.

Step 6: Front Legs

Cut two 2" × 4"s 20 ¼" long. Now cut a 15 degree angle off of each one. (If you can't measure angles, don't worry and keep reading)

Now measure up 15" and screw the top of the front of the chair to the leg.

If you couldn't measure the angles, just screw the board on. Then you can see how the corner sits on the ground, draw a line parallel to the ground and cut it off. Now cut the top off parallel to the ground.

Step 7: Add the Back

Screw the back on at a 90 degree angle to the seat.

Step 8: Arms

Now measure the length from your front leg to the back parallel to the ground and cut a 2" × 4" for the arm. I used also cut a center brace and ran it across the center of the back to make it feel more sturdy . . . this is completely optional.

Step 9: Braces Under Arms

Another optional step: You can put braces under the arms. Just cut a square of 2" × 4" and screw it under each corner of the arm. Now paint if you wish, or keep it rough, the choice is yours.

Woven Patio Chair

By Katherine Lewis (katvanlew)
http://www.instructables.com/id/Woven-Patio-Chair/

A friend of mine had some metal frames for round patio chairs. The canvas seats had fallen apart a long time ago and he was trying to think of a way to use them again. The frames were a bit rusty but still quite sturdy. At the same time, I was trying to think of something to make out of dog food bags. I purchase dog food in these 20 pound plastic, woven bags that I hate to throw away. They are quite strong and imposible to tear. This chair should not be left out in the sun for long periods because the plastic will eventually crack and weaken, I keep my colorful chair under my porch.

Step 1: Supplies Needed

You will need several dog food bags The bags are made out of plastic looking strings, tightly woven together, a metal chair frame, scissors, sewing machine, thread, spray paint, sandpaper, clothes pins, and measuring tape.

Step 2: Preparing the Frame

The metal frame I used was still sturdy but it was a bit rusty so I got some sandpaper and sanded it. Then I spray painted it outdoors and allowed it to dry for a couple of hours.

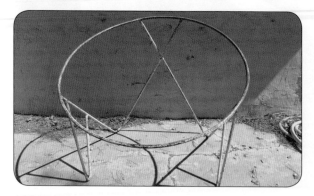

Step 3: Cutting Up the Bags

Cut the bottom off of the bags. Locate the seam on the side or back of the back. cut the seam open. Open the bag and wipe the inside with a damp cloth. Cut each bag into 4" strips.

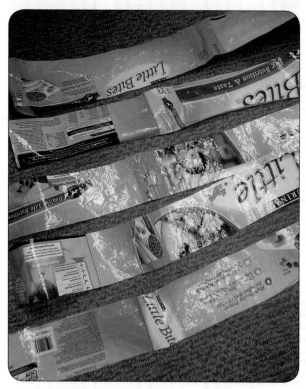

Step 4: Sewing the Strips Together

Cut the ends of the strips at a diagonal. Sew the ends together with a ½" seam allowance. This step distributes the bulk better when folding.

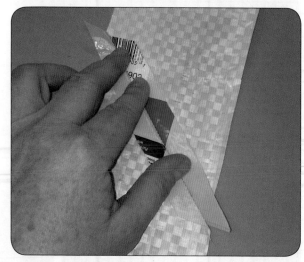

Step 5: Folding and Pinning the Strips

Fold the strip in half lengthwise, crease with your finger. Open the plastic and fold both sides toward the center crease. Fold in half again. This hides all of the raw edges. Pin the folded strip.

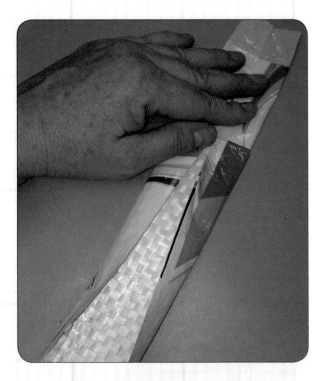

Start in the middle attaching 2 or 3 strips vertically and then 2 or 3 strips horizontally, and work your way to the edges. Use Clothes pins to hold them in place until you achieve the desired length. Hot glue the ends to the back to hold in place until you can sew each one.

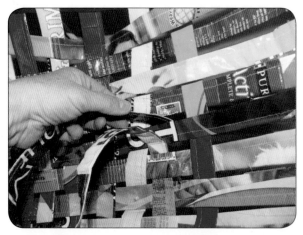

Step 6: Sewing the Plastic Strip

Using a sewing machine, stitch the strip folded. Sew 5 or 6 strips together and leave about a foot unfolded so you can add more as you need. I wound my strip on a piece of cardboard until I was ready to weave the chair.

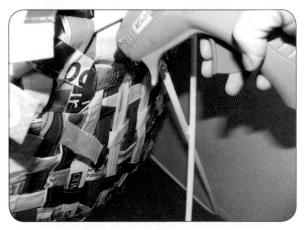

Step 8: Hand Sewing Plastic Strips in Place

When you have the strips woven and glued in place, hand sew with strong embroidery thread or crochet string.and a large yarn needle. Go around entire frame, securing each end.

Step 7: Attaching the Strips to the Frame

Now you can place the plastic strips to the metal frame. If you are working with a round frame, don't pull the strips tight, but if it is a sqaure frame with a seat and a back, it does need to be pulled tightly.

My friend and I were given the task of creating outdoor furniture from a total of four wooden pallets. After some many days in the lab we decided to do something out of the ordinary and create a pallet swing. We designed it from the ground up based on a picture we found online. In the next couple of steps we show you a brief step-by-step rundown of how to get to the finished item.

Step 1: Items You Will Need

- Jig saw
- Chop saw
- Nail remover
- Hammer
- Screw gun
- Four wooden pallets
- Sufficient amount of screws
- Patience
- Metal chain and U-bolts
- Carriage bolts and nuts

Step 2: The Tear Down

The first step to any project using pallets is the actual breakdown of the wooden pallets. For our project we found it simpler to cut the pallets apart using a jig saw, as it was quicker and easier and there was less of a chance of split wood versus using a pry bar to pry the wooden pallets apart. The down side is we lost a lot of longer pieces of usable wood that we could have gotten if we attempted to pry apart the pallets. In the end it's whatever you feel most comfortable doing.

Step 3: The Seat Bottom

So for the business end of the chair we took two of the pallet sides, which are shaped like compressed m's, and attached them together by the 1" × 4" pallet wood we had collected. We made our seat bottom about 14 ½", but you may size it as you wish to fit the different-sized bottoms there are in the world.

Step 3: The Seat Back

For the back on which you rest your body we expanded on what we had created on the bottom, but instead of using two of the pallets sides we used three and connected them again by 1" × 6" planks that we collected for this. We made ours to about 22", but, again, it can be varied from spec to what you would feel comfortable with.

Step 4: Seat Back, Part Two

The picture below should be what your finished seat back should look like from the rear.

Step 5: Connecting the Seat Bottom and Back

Here is where it begins to get tricky. To attach the bottom and back we engineered a system by fitting two more pallet sides to both the bottom and back perpendicular to the ones already there. From there we attached to the bottom and back by connecting the two with carriage bolts, allowing us to create

a hinge and allowing us to create an angle we were looking for.

Step 6: Almost Done!

Because we ended up running out of time we ended up finding the angle we wanted and securing it using extra pieces of wood, but at this point if you would like, armrests are a very nice touch and can also provide structural support for the swing. The last step is to sand and stain the chain and attach the chain. Depending on how large you made the chair, attach the chain using bolts so that is balances correctly for how you would like it to look.

Step 7: Finally Finished

At this point you should have a finished project worthy of accepting your hind quarters. Congratulations!

Here's our Reclaimed Wood Flat-Pack Picnic Table with Planter (I know. It's a mouthful). There is a gutter running down the center below the tabletop surface that can be filled with ice to put your beers in on a hot day, or for planting herbs (reach across the table to get the freshest seasoning for your food) or decorative plants. Making this table flat-pack was an easy decision: neither of us has a truck. The table was made in pieces: two ends that provide the structure for the table, two center pieces with the tabletop slats, the trough, and the removable legs that simply screw in place. Disassembly and reassembly take minutes, and everything can be fit in the back of a compact car.

All the wood in this project is reclaimed except for the table legs, which were purchased from Discount Builder's Supply in San Francisco. As always, the design was influenced by the materials: we would have made the slats go lengthwise, but most of the beautiful pieces of reclaimed redwood we had were short, so they're widthwise instead. At the time we made this table, we didn't have access to a jointer or planer, so we sanded our reclaimed wood with palm sanders. The whole project took us about a week, but it would take far less time with a jointer and planer.

Note: this Instructable is for the table only.

Step 1: Materials and Cutlist

The tabletop is 60″ × 41″. Our trough is 5″ wide.

The tabletop uses wood of varying widths, enough to cover a tabletop that is 60″ × 41″, accounting for small gaps between each slat. These pieces will all be cut in half, and end up being 1″ × any width × 17″. There are also two tabletop end-pieces that are longer. These are listed below, under "Outer Aprons."

Two Inner Aprons use:

- (4) 1″ × 4″ × 64 ½″ (long apron pieces)
- (4) 1″ × 4″ × 10″ (short inner endpieces of the apron)
- (4) 2″ × 4″ × 10″ (table leg supports)

Two Outer Aprons use:

- (2) 1″ × 4″ × 25″ (outer end pieces of the apron)
- (2) 1″ × any width × 41″ (long tabletop slats)

[Note: 1″ and 2″ mean wood that is "one inch" thick and "two inches" thick. However, that is their nominal size. A 1″ board is usually around ¾″ thick when measured. 1″ boards all used to be one inch, but in order to make them flat, a sawmill had to remove some of the thickness. Generally, when naming the size of a board, the thickness comes first, then the width, then the length, as in 1″ × 3″ × 11″. The x-es stand for "by", so you would say, "One by three by eleven".]

Salvaged length of gutter or trough: 6′. You can also use any old bendy sheet metal if you have it.

Table legs and leg attachment hardware: Throughout our project, we looked for some beautiful old table legs, but weren't able to find any. We bought ours from a hardware store. They were screw-in legs with metal top plates that attached to the table top. They were easy to install, but not as sturdy as we'd like. If we were to do it again, we would come up with an alternative way to attach the legs to keep them removable, but still sturdy.

Hardware:

- Screws: a box of 1 ¼″ and a box of 2″. Make sure your screws are outdoor friendly: I used decking screws.
- A nail gun with 1 ½″ nails and wood glue to attach the top slats to the tabletop supports. If you don't have that, I recommend using screws and a screw gun.
- (8) ⅜″ bolts, with one nut and two washers for each.

Step 2: Reclaim Some Wood

This part is an adventure. We met many really lovely and interesting characters on our search. We like to find free stuff on Craigslist and Freecycle, and also really enjoyed going to salvage yards. In the Bay Area, we recommend The Re-Use People, Heritage Salvage, Whole House Building Supply, and OhMega Salvage. For the look of this project, we used all different kinds of wood.

Step 3: Lay Out the Tabletop

Before cutting anything for the final time, lay out the order of the wood you'd like to use for the tabletop. If you're looking to use a random pattern, like we did, try a lot of different orders before settling on one. It's quite difficult for humans to create random patterns, so don't stress too much about exactly which pieces are next to what. You're the only one who will ever notice. Label the boards in the order you want them to go on the tabletop. Since all these boards, except the two end boards, will be cut into two pieces to make room for the trough, it's okay to use two short pieces. Just make sure they look like they come from the same board. Continuing grain across the trough is a slick move. Make sure you have enough wood to go across the entire length of your tabletop plus some extra. In our case the length of our tabletop is about 68", with spaces between each board of ⅛".

Step 4: Cut Tabletop Slats to Size

In order to cut our tabletop slats to all the same size, we set a stop on the chop saw by clamping a piece of scrap 18" from the edge of the blade. (The blade of the chop saw has a thickness, or kerf, of maybe ¹⁄₁₆". Therefore, we don't want to cut down the middle of our line we drew on our wood, because then we would lose ¹⁄₃₂" to the chop saw's blade.) With a chop saw, as with many wood-cutting devices, it's a good idea to also sacrifice a piece of back-up wood behind the wood you are keeping in order to prevent tear-out. Make sure your back-up wood has

equal thickness and is pushed up all the way against the fence: if it isn't, what you cut will not be a right angle.

Step 5: Sand Tabletop Slats

You can decide how much you want to sand your reclaimed pieces and how much "character" (i.e., scratches, machine marks) you want to leave. In the first and second pictures, you can see how different the reclaimed wood looks after just a few seconds of sanding. When you are sanding, make sure all your pieces are the same thickness. [If the tabletop pieces are several different thicknesses, it's a good idea to run them through the jointer and planer if you have access to one. This will also save you a lot of sanding time! With reclaimed wood, be absolutely certain there are no nails or other bits of metal in your wood. Run them through the jointer and planer before cutting to their final length.] To sand the faces of the wood, we used a random orbital palm sander at 80 grit. We did the edges with the belt sander and the ends with the disc sander to make things quick, but if you don't have access, you can certainly do all your sanding with a palm sander.

Step 6: Cut the Rest of the Pieces You Need for the Table: Aprons and Supports

Use the same technique for setting a stop on the chop saw outlined in step 4. Look at the cut list from step 1 and cut the pieces for the two inner and two outer aprons.

Step 7: Put On Your First Coat of Finish

If you are planning on putting finish on your table to protect it from the elements and to give it nice depth and shine, I recommend putting a coat of finish on everything now, before anything is fastened together. That way, even if moisture gets in between hard to reach spaces and joints, there will be finish on it. The next two-plus coats of finish will be after everything is fastened. We chose to use a spray-on indoor-outdoor finish that dries in ten minutes. The can needed shaking often, and worked best vertically, so if you have somewhere to spray your boards vertically, I'd recommend it. We sprayed inside a decommissioned chicken coop because there was a beautiful tree dropping its flowers all over the yard and lots of wind that day. Make sure you are in a well-ventilated area, use a mask, and take breaks often in the fresh air.

Some tips for spraying: First, I sprayed one edge of all the boards, then after our ten-minute drying time, turned each board to spray the face, then the other edge, then the other face, and finally, each end. Make sure you are turning every board in the same direction so you don't lose track of what surfaces you have sprayed and what you haven't. In order to ensure the finish is being sprayed evenly, picture the spray coming out of the can as a cone. The cone has a top edge, a bottom edge, and a middle, which is a straight line out of the nozzle. If you are spraying the face of a board, start by spraying the center of the cone at bottom of the board, all the way with the grain, starting and finishing an inch or two from the end of the board. For your next stroke, direct the middle of the cone to where the top edge of the cone was on your last spray, and do that stroke. Repeat until the board has been covered. Make sure your nozzle is about a foot from the board at all times, which means you may have to walk along the lengths of the longer boards rather than just pivoting at your shoulder.

Step 8: Construct Table Structure: Inner Aprons and Outer Aprons

Unlike a regular table, our four-piece table has two apron structures, which are connected by additional end aprons. Start off by constructing two rectangles. Ours are about 64 ½" by 10". The short endpieces should be screwed to the inside of the long apron pieces so that their endgrain will not be visible on your finished table. Then attach your two end aprons to your two long tabletop slats that will be on the end of the table. Decide how much of an overhang you want from the end apron to the outside of the two outer table slats. Even if your two tabletop end slats are different widths, all you have to do is make sure the distance from the apron to the outside edge is the same. We countersunk screws and then filled in the holes. If you have a Kreg jig, you can accurately countersink toenailed screws from the bottom so there are no holes on your tabletop.

We then clamped all four pieces together, making sure they were all lined up in the right place, and then drilled holes for our bolts. There are eight bolts in total, two on each end of each rectangle, about two inches in from either side. We first drilled a smaller pilot hole to ensure accuracy in our drilling location. The last picture is taken from underneath, and hopefully the captions will help you make sense of how the whole thing is put together.

Step 9: Add Leg Supports to Inner Aprons

We cut four pieces of scrap 2" × 4" the same length as our inner aprons to make the leg supports. The legs we purchased had machine screws coming out the top that attach to top plates. We screwed the top plates into each 2" × 4" leg support, then positioned the 2" × 4"s so that the legs would be in each corner of the table and screwed them into place.

Step 10: Attach Tabletop Slats to Inner Aprons

Now that the structure is assembled and bolted together, you can start attaching your tabletop! First, lay out your tabletop slats. The only two that are connected to the table thus far are the two longer end pieces. This is your last chance to rearrange them! Hopefully, your boards will be laid out between your two long end pieces with more than enough width of wood. This is good. After nailing all but one of your boards in place, you will rip (cut down the entire length of the board) your last two boards to the exact width it needs to be.

But before ripping those last two boards, you will be nailing the rest of your slats into place. We used a pneumatic nail gun and wood glue. First, mark where your nails will go in each of your slats. We decided to overhang our tabletop slats by ½" from each center structure piece, leaving about 4" between each matching board for the trough. To ensure even spacing, find something you can use as a spacer. We were lucky to find some long, ⅛" thick fiberboard in the scrap container. If you can't find anything long enough, you can simply use two of anything that is the same thickness: two quarters, for example.

To start nailing, we would put the spacer in place, put some glue on the skeleton where it would meet the tabletop slat, place the slat so it's spaced correctly, and then use the nail gun to nail it in place. We found it was faster to do one entire side and then the corresponding boards on the other side, rather than walking across the table after every slat.

When you get to your last two slats, measure the width they will need to be, making sure you are including the space you will need to leave for the spacers on either side of your slat. Rip them to the width they will need to be on the table saw, and then double check your measurement against your table with spacers on either side. When you are happy with your cut, do a quick sanding of the edges you have just cut, spray the end you have just cut with your spray finish (because it will be impossible to do so after it is nailed in place), and then glue and nail it into place. Your tabletop should now be complete!

Step 11: Final Spray Finish, Attaching Trough and Legs, Touch-up

If you feel you need to sand the ends of any boards to make them look more in-line with each other, do that now. If you feel the need to fill in your nail holes as we did (remember, it's just a picnic table), do that now. Spray on your last coats of finish, making sure all hardware (the machine screws in your legs, for example) are covered with tape. Cut the gutter to size. Attaching the gutter will be easier if the four tabletop parts are disassembled. Punch holes for screws in the gutter every foot or so. Use short screws to attach one side, and then carefully position the other tabletop half at an angle, bending the gutter's U-shape apart so you can get your screwdriver in place to screw in the gutter to the other tabletop half. Then reassemble your table.

We also put small scrap rectangles of metal on our outer aprons where it would touch the gutter so the wood would be a bit more protected from rot. If you are planting succulents, put some holes in the gutter (making sure the sharp side faces up so your legs don't scrape on the underside of the gutter) and fill it with some soil or volcanic rock that is lightweight and good for drainage. If you are planting beers, the holes are good too, and if you stick your feet all the way under on a hot day, the cold water will drip onto your toes. Screw on the legs and enjoy a leisurely outdoor lunch.

Paracord Laced Pallet, Hanging Chair

By Timothy Pratt (Twotim221)

http://www.instructables.com/id/Paracord-Laced-Pallet-Hanging-Chair/

Create a very comfortable, very easy-to-make chair from a pallet and some paracord. I know that there are a lot of different kinds of chair Instructables already, but I have never seen a chair like this before. It is so easy to make, and it is comfortable because it conforms to your body. I don't know how I came up with the idea, and as I was making it I wasn't even sure if it would work out. But it did and I am very happy with the results. This Instructable will show you everything I did to make the chair, but I am sure you will find ways you can customize yours to meet your needs.

Step 1: Tools and Materials

Tools:
- Drill
- Saw
- Lighter
- Sawzall (optional)

318

Materials:
- Paracord
- Pallet (I was able to get by with just one but it all depends on how much usable wood you can get off of each pallet)

I used pallet wood because it is hardwood and free, but, as with all treated wood, you need to use precaution when handling it. Make sure you are wearing a mask when cutting and gloves at all times. When you are finished with all the cuts and have drilled all your holes, it is important that you seal the wood.

I used paracord because it is small yet strong and does not stretch as much as other ropes. Paracord is also easier to work with because it doesn't unravel or fray like other types of rope, and because the ends can be melted to easily make lacing.

Step 2: Take Pallet Apart

There are many different ways to take apart pallets in order to use the wood for something else. I have found that prying them apart causes a lot of damage to the wood and is a lot more work than is necessary. So, my preferred method is to cut the pieces apart using a sawzall. All you have to do is cut through the nails that are holding it together and you are good to go (with minimal damage to the wood). If you want you can pop the remaining parts of the nails out of the wood. Just take the sawzall and cut right between the piece you would like to save (the top piece) and the thick frame. Try to cut just the nails and not too much of the wood. Once you get the hang of it, it will go really fast.

Step 3: Cutting the Wood to Size

Now here is where you need to decide how wide you would like your chair. I guess you should base the size on the hiney that will be sitting in it. With the pallet that I had I was able to cut the boards right down the middle (20"). But the size is up to you. The amount of board is also up to you. I ended up using 16 boards for my chair.

Warning: Make sure you look out for leftover bits of nails in the wood as you are cutting.

Step 5: Marking Wood for Lace Holes

Now what you want to do is take one of the boards and mark where you want to put the laces. I put my laces ½" in from the edge of the board and put them 2" apart. Depending on how you would like yours to look you can make the laces farther apart or closer together, as long as they are in far enough from the edge so that the board does not break once it has weight on it. Keep in mind also that if the laces are spaced farther apart, the boards will tend to pull away from each other more, making a gap where things might get pinched (fingers, "cheeks," etc.).

Step 6: Drill the Holes

Now that you have your holes marked you can start drilling. I used a drill press, but a regular drill will work just fine. I started by drilling all the holes in my first board, and then I used that board as a jig to do the rest. You will want a drill bit that is a little bigger than your paracord so that the cord fits easily through the holes.

Step 7: Start Lacing

Now comes the fun part. Start by placing two of your boards next to one another. Now lace the paracord through them just as you would a pair of shoes. Once you reach the end, cut the paracord, making sure you leave enough slack to tie a strong knot at the end. Now you can pull the paracord out and use it to measure the rest of the pieces you will need. When you cut the rest make sure you leave a little room for error. It's better to have too much than to have too little and have to start over.

Once you have cut your paracord to size, it is a good idea to melt the ends so that it is easy to get the cord through the holes. Now you can start lacing boards together.

Things to watch for as you're lacing:

- Make sure you are paying attention to what side of the board is up and what side is down so that you end up with all the good-looking sides facing up.
- It looks best to have all the knots on the bottom.
- Once you have finished a lace go back and pull each "X" to get the slack out.

Step 8: Hang and Enjoy

Now all you have to do is hang the chair from whatever structure you have available. I used some 2" × 4"s between the trees in my backyard (not the prettiest but it works). Just drill a couple of holes in each of the four corners you would like to hang the chair from and thread the paracord through them. I put the front cords back one board from the end so that it would be more comfortable on the back of my legs. For a somewhat laid-back chair attach the front and back cords farther apart from each other with the back cords low. For more of an upright chair, like mine, put them closer together with the back cords high. The whole thing is completely adjustable to your liking, so tweak it till it's comfortable for you.

Note: I used two strands of paracord per corner, which is strong enough to hold me, but you might want to braid more together for added strength. Getting into the chair can be a little tricky (kind of like getting into a hammock) but once you do, relax and enjoy.

Improvement: I think I would stain the boards next time, as this would look nicer and make the paracord stand out more.

Whiskey Barrel Bar Stools

By kminer49er

http://www.instructables.com/id/Whiskey-Barrel-Bar-Stools/

Sun and weather take a toll on outdoor furniture. I had four outdoor bar stools covered with plastic resin wicker that had cracked and split. I priced new outdoor bar stools, ($75 and up × 4.) I figured I could renovate my old stools for about the price a single new chair. The plastic wicker had to go, but the powder-coated steel frames still looked good. I repurposed an old whiskey/wine half-barrel to provide all the material for the seats, backs and bracing. If you are even a little bit handy, possess basic wood working skills, and have some ordinary tools, you can knock this out in a weekend. I wound up with great looking and very serviceable barstools from a single half-barrel and a hand-full of screws.

Step 1: Remove Resin Plastic Wicker

You can see how the plastic had cracked and split. I cut away the plastic wicker from the barstool frames using a utility knife; taking care not to scratch the powder coating.

Step 2: Materials List

- 1-Oak Half Barrel w/ Hoops
- Barstool frames (up to 4)
- Zink Coated Phillips Screws (per barstool)
  - 14 - #10 × 1-½" Oval Head
  - 8 - #10 × 1-¼" Pan Head
  - 9 - #12 × ⅝" Pan Head
- 1 qt. 'Spar' exterior polyurethane - oil based
- ½ pt. Wood Stain - oil based
- Sandpaper - Belts (80 grit)
- Sandpaper - Sheets (120 & 220 grit)

Optional:
- 1 pt. Rust Remover (for barrel hoops)
- 1 qt. Wood Bleach (oxalic acid)

Step 3: Tools & Personal Protective Equipment

- Circular Saw
- Belt Sander
- Electric or Cordless Drill
- Palm Sander
- #2 Phillips Bits and Holder
- Jig Saw
- 7/64" & 1/8" Steel Drill Bits
- Hand Saw
- Angle Grinder
- Hacksaw
- Utility Knife
- Sanding Block
- Wood Chisel
- Wood Rasp
- Rubber Hammer or Mallet
- Quick - Clamps
- Tape Measure
- Torpedo Level
- Steel Brush
- Long Handled Scrub Brush Use the correct PPE (safety equipment) to prevent injury
- Dust Mask
- Long Sleeve Chemical Resistant Gloves
- Face Shield
- Hearing Protection
- Safety Glasses
- Disposable Gloves for Staining

Step 4: Disassemble the Barrel & Barrelhead

The first thing I did was to pull out the barrel staves, taking care not to damage the hoops or barrel head. The barrel head was also made of oak sections that had been put together with dowels. Because the barrel was empty and allowed to dry out it, came apart easily. The dowels were pushed into the holes and cut flush. I sorted and stacked the staves by size. I did a mock-up to determine the count and placement of staves to get an idea of the positioning and proportion. I settled on using three of the larger staves for the back and five smaller ones on the base. I needed a total of 32 staves to do the four chairs and there were only 30 in the barrel. So I ripped the two largest staves in half with a circular saw.

Step 5: Sanding

A clamping worktable held the uneven staves securely so I could sand off the charring. The belt sander and 80-grit sandpaper made quick work of this part of the project. Be sure to use eye and hearing protection as well as a dust mask when doing any sanding. I did all my sanding outside to make cleanup easier. What sawdust the breeze didn't take away, I blew into the lawn with a leaf blower. Just how much charring you ultimately take off is up to you; but at least remove all the loose bits. I sanded off nearly all of the char.

Step 6: Prep the Hoops

I wanted to use sections of the barrel hoops to maintain a rustic look and provide additional bracing for the back and seat. The barrel hoops had powdery red rust covering both sides. I needed to remove or neutralize the loose rust so that the polyurethane would better adhere. I coated the hoops with a rust removing gel and worked it into the metal using a steel wire brush. Warning! This chemical is acid! Follow the instructions on the container! Use heavy rubber gloves; both eye protection and a face shield. I let the hoops sit and after about an hour (or however long it took me to sand the staves.) I used plain water and the steel brush to clean-off the gel. I dried the hoops thoroughly with an old rag.

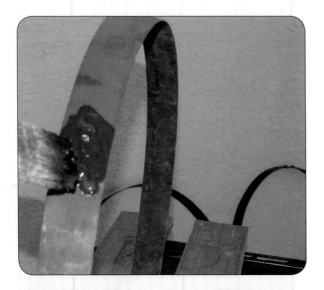

Step 7: Using Chemicals and More Sanding

I used a coarse plastic-bristled brush to work wood bleach into each stave. The main component is oxalic acid; commonly used to remove aging and stains from outdoor wooden decks. Warning! This chemical is also acid! Follow the instructions on the container! Use heavy rubber gloves, long-sleeves, eye protection as well as a face shield to prevent burns! After letting the bleach work about 30 minutes, I rinsed the surface with plain water and let dry. The bleach removed most of the weathered gray color, but it hardly touched the black stains left by the steel hoops. You can eliminate this step depending on how you want the finished surface to look. You could just sand everything down to the bare wood. Or if you want to keep the patina as is, lightly sand the surface and after removing the charring, apply an exterior (spar) polyurethane. Sanding down the the bare wood and protecting the surface with with a clear finish will give you a rich honey colored surface. I used a palm sander with 120 grit sandpaper to smooth out the back and prepare both sides for staining.

Step 8: Braces for Seat and Back

The staves were too short to span the full length of either the seat or the back. With a jig saw, I cut cross braces from the barrel head pieces. I positioned the back brace about ¾" of the distanced from the top and the seat brace roughly the same distance from the front. I sanded, prepped and stained all sides. When I did the mock-up, I saw that I needed to notch the stays for the seat-back to get a solid fit against the cross-brace and also sit flat against the curved back. I cut a tapering notch into the seat-back side pieces and took ⅜" out of the center stave (now repurposed as chair slats.) I used a handsaw, a wood rasp and a wood chisel to cutaway the wood a little at a time until I go a good fit.

Step 9: Stain and Finish

After a quick once-over with a tack cloth to remove any remaining sawdust, I brushed on a dark walnut oil-based stain; wiping off the excess with an old t-shirt. I let the stain dry overnight before applying a thin coat of oil based exterior spar polyurethane. I recommend using either the semi-gloss or satin finish. Stir, don't shake, the urethane often or the solids used to de-gloss the finish will stay on the bottom of the can. It took only a few hours for the first coat to dry. I roughed up the surface with a 220 grit on a hand sanding block and applied another light coat of polyurethane finish. The second coat also dried very quickly. You could shorten application and dry times by using a combination stain and varnish aerosol spray.

Step 10: Attaching the Barces

When the pieces were dry, I attached the seat and back braces using #10 × 1-½" oval head screws; one at end of the each brace. I used quick clamps to hold the braces in place. For the back-brace I angled the screws from the top of the brace into the steel frame. The seat brace was attached by angling the screws from the front into the steel frame. I held the braces in place with quick clamps while I drilled the ⁷⁄₆₄" pilot holes and attached them. Drilling pilot holes will prevent the screws from splitting the oak.

Step 12: Ready for the Patio Party

I now have four refurbished bar stools that are surprisingly comfortable and will hold up to the elements. The half barrel sells for about $30 at one of the big box home improvement centers. Adding in the screws, stain, polyurethane and other materials I spent less than $80.

Step 11: Attaching the Back and Seat Slats

The slats designated for the seat backs were attached to the frame with one 1-½" × #10 oval head screw at the top and one 1-¼" × #10 screw through the back brace. Again quick clamps were utilized to hold the slats in place while they were being fastened. The seat slats were attached from the bottom to hide the screws 1-¼" × #10 pan head screws. The outermost seat slats were attached to both the brace and the metal frame with the 1-¼" × #10 screws. I cut the hoops to fit with a hacksaw and used a metal file to remove any sharp edges. Each piece was attached with three ⅝" × #12 pan head screws; two sections for the back and one on the seat. Using an angle grinder, the screw heads were ground flat to look more like rivets. A piece of 18 gauge sheet metal with a hole drilled the diameter of the screw-head was used to protect the surrounding area while the grinder did its work.

How to Build an Awesome Sidewalk with Recycled Lumber

By Vyger

http://www.instructables.com/id/How-to-build-an-Awesome-Sidewalk-with-recycled-lum/

After reading that title you might wonder, why would anyone make a sidewalk out of wood? Well, there are a few very good reasons for doing it.

A Little History

More than 25 years ago my wood sidewalk started out as an experiment to see how practical it might be. We needed some kind of walkway for the country house we had just moved into. I thought of using the traditional concrete but in the climate that I live (Northeastern Montana) cement sidewalks have some problems. The ground here moves around a lot. It shrinks in the hot dry summers, sometimes making cracks that are 4" wide. In the winter it freezes 6' to 8' down, so the ground heaves up a lot. Between the shrinking in the summer and freezing in the winter concrete does a lot of cracking. Also cement stays cold and frozen all winter whereas wood warms up and the ice melts off of it anytime it gets above freezing. It was also the least expensive of my available choices. So I built a wood sidewalk. It lasted far longer than I ever thought it would, more than 25 years. But all things deteriorate and my sidewalk has been in need of replacing for a while now. Once again I found myself debating about what to use. I had been looking into making my own pavers but in the end I went back to wood, especially when I got used redwood for free.

My challenges for this project were:
- Come up with a design that could use all the different sizes of redwood I salvaged without producing a lot of waste.
- Resurface the older weathered wood so it matched with everything.
- Create a good-looking, practical sidewalk at a reasonable cost.

Step 1: The Wood

The wood I had acquired second-hand was not all nice, standard, same-size pieces. It was a mix of 2" × 4", 2" × 6", and 2" × 8" with varied lengths from 8' long to 12". In addition, the wood from the old deck was very weathered on the top side from years of exposure.

Step 2: The Tools

I have a 30-year-old Craftsman table saw that played a pretty major role in this project. Another key tool is a wood planer. I also used an 8 ½" miter saw, a cordless drill for driving screws, a circular saw for some of the difficult cuts of the longer boards, a square, a tape measure, hammer, dirt-moving tools, and lots of miscellaneous things. Lastly I used a Dremel.

Step 3: The Cost Breakdown

The final cost breakdown for this project is as follows.

- Six boxes of deck screws. The original price on each box was $7.50 per box, but I got them all when a local hardware store went out of business and auctioned everything off. I bought three large boxes of various packages of screws for $20.00. That would put the final price for the screws I used at about $5.00.
- ½ gallon of deck sealer, which I also bought at the auction. I bought four gallons for $20.00, so about $3.00 for the amount I used.
- A gallon of diesel fuel, which I mixed with used motor oil to treat the underside of the wood and support pieces as a preservative—about $3.00 (more on this later)
- Two trips in my pickup to get the free redwood, using roughly six gallons of gas, or about $18.00 for transportation.
- Finally, I ruined the blades on my planer after hitting a number of hidden screws in the wood, which is a hazard of working with used wood. The blades are double-sided, so I could use the other side, which means only half the blade was worn out. I bought a set of replacement blades for $28.00, figuring half of that for this project is $14.00.

The total was $43.00. Just to be safe I rounded it up to $50.00. That's pretty reasonable for the results that I got.

Step 4: A Close Shave

A wood planer shaves off the top layer of the wood to expose the good wood underneath. It is very important to check the lumber for any hidden screws or nails. The plane spins at very high-speed, and if it hits a metal object in the wood it takes a notch out of all the blades. From then on you will see a line down anything you plane where those blades are damaged. You can run the wood through again to take off the line but if you get to many dings in the blades you will have a real problem.

I start with the board just clearing the blades and work the depth down from there. It usually takes at least three passes to get it looking good. Remember that you are going to have to plane all the boards to the same size in order to avoid having some boards sticking up above others. Decide from the start which side is going to be the top. I usually run the bottom of the board through the plane at least once to take off any high spots, but you don't have to worry about cutting it down to fresh wood as it's not going to show. A plane makes big piles of chips and sawdust very quickly. Have a plan for dealing with it. I rototill all my sawdust into the garden so it's recycled.

Watch out for lead paint on old boards. If you suspect that they may have it dispose of them. If you plane them the lead will go everywhere in the fine dust from the planer.

Step 5: The Table Saw

Some of my boards were badly worn on the edges. A few had been steps, so they were very rounded from being walked on. You can use the table saw on these to cut 2" × 6"s down to 2" × 4"s. Also 2" × 8"s can become 2" × 6"s. Start by cutting off the worst edge; don't just try to cut it down completely in one pass.

Next run the board again and square up the other edge. You now should have a good, flat, square side that will work against the rip fence. Measure and set the fence for the final dimension (3 ½" for a 2" × 4") and again cut off the worst edge to make your 2" × 4". I was only able to salvage half of the one in the picture because of the big knot. In addition, be aware of any screw or nail holes in the board, if you can trim them out while cutting down the board, so much the better. Sometimes the holes actually line up with where you need them to be, and you can just reuse the hole.

Important: A Note about Safety

All new table saws come with guards on the blades. Mine did, but it broke many years ago, so that is why it's not on there in the photos. I do not recommend running the saw without the guard. These blades are so sharp and so fast that you will see you finger lying on the ground and wonder what it is before you even realize that yours is gone. I had a friend who sliced his finger right down the middle before he had a chance to pull his hand back. They sewed it back together but it never worked the same because of the damage to the joints. Treat this saw with absolute respect and you should have no problems. Never lose track of where that blade is when it is running. Also remember that table saws love to throw stuff—they can launch a hunk of wood with great speed. It's called kickback. Make sure you are not in the line of fire. Mine threw a chunk of wood through a window once. Always use sharp blades. A dull blade will tear up the wood and smoke and char the kerf. I always use carbide-tipped blades; they are definitely worth the money.

Step 6: The Layout and Design

I tried a number of different patterns but quickly decided on this one. It made best use of the sizes of wood that I had, and from the first layouts I did I thought it looked really interesting. It did make for some difficult cuts for the supporting boards, but that is just all part of the challenge.

I made this in sections; the length of each section was determined by the length of the longest 2" × 4" board that I had since they were the ones going lengthwise. The sections can come apart just by taking off the connecting 2" × 6"s where they come together. By doing this the sections are small enough that I can stand them up on edge if I need to get underneath them. The sidewalk sections are free floating. They are not attached to the ground. The support boards rest on bricks that can be adjusted to get it level.

For the supporting boards you can use the boards that are in the poorest condition. This is one of the reasons you should sort out your wood and decide what will be used for what. The support boards don't need to be planed. However, if they are going to be in contact with or close proximity to the ground they should be treated.

I have tried commercial wood preservatives and some of them just don't seem to work very well. Something that *does* work though is a mix of used motor oil and a half to a third part diesel fuel. This has been in use around this area for a very long time. I learned that they used to use it to treat wooden wagons. Some use it to treat flatbed trailers that are left out in the elements for years. I know from my own experience it works and is cheap. The oil penetrates into the wood and appears to seal it from moisture. It's that simple. Oil and water don't mix so if the wood is saturated with oil no water will get in. No water means no rot, and also the bugs really don't like to chew on it. The diesel fuel thins the oil and acts as a transport agent to move it deeper into the wood. I have seen fence posts that were treated with oil still in the ground after 30 years. Very little oil transfers to the ground, so it's not a pollution problem. One down side to it is that it smells for a while. It takes time for the diesel fuel to evaporate, but if you live where I do that's not a problem. It also is more flammable than just plain wood until it weathers for a while, but again that is not usually a problem for outside landscaping projects.

To apply it just paint it on with an old paint brush and let it soak into the wood. Pay special attention to the ends of the boards and any holes or cracks in the boards. Weathered wood with lots of cracks actually works very well for this because it gives the oil more places to soak in. If you have the time to wait you should let it stand for a few days until most of it soaks in. If you are in a hurry you can use it right away, but it might get a little messy.

327

Step 7: Complex Joints

I made the support boards so they were under each place where the ends of the top boards came together. Since I was using this pattern the support boards did not meet at a 45 degree angle. You can cut these types of angles and pieces by laying one board on top of the other and marking it for the cut. You don't need to try to draw the angles with a protractor; just align everything and mark them and make the cut. These joints were the only places that I used my circular saw.

Step 8: Section Two

For the next section I reversed the pattern I was using, which created an even more interesting look. Keep in mind that since there were no standard-sized lumber pieces I had to measure and cut each board to fit its specific place.

Step 9: Sealer

After completing the first two sections I put the sealer on it. I didn't want it to get wet before I had a chance to seal it. The wet sealer looks really impressive. Too bad it doesn't stay that way. It really shows off the redwood color.

Step 10: Section Three

Because this next section turns both right and left I had to change the pattern a little and send it in both directions.

Step 11: Section Three to the Left.
Again I used interesting angles.

Step 12: Section Three to the Right
Now the split is going to the right.

Step 13: Finished for the Season
I screwed the last boards down and declared my project finished, and it started snowing three days later. Perfect timing.

Laundry Room

Some people have a whole room devoted to cleaning their laundry while others just have a closet with their machines tucked away, while others yet have to trudge elsewhere to take care of business.

Regardless of the category you fall under, you can find something to help you out here. Learn how to completely fix your laundry room to make it more efficient and organized, or just find a way to keep your clothes from littering your floor before you get them cleaned, wherever that may be.

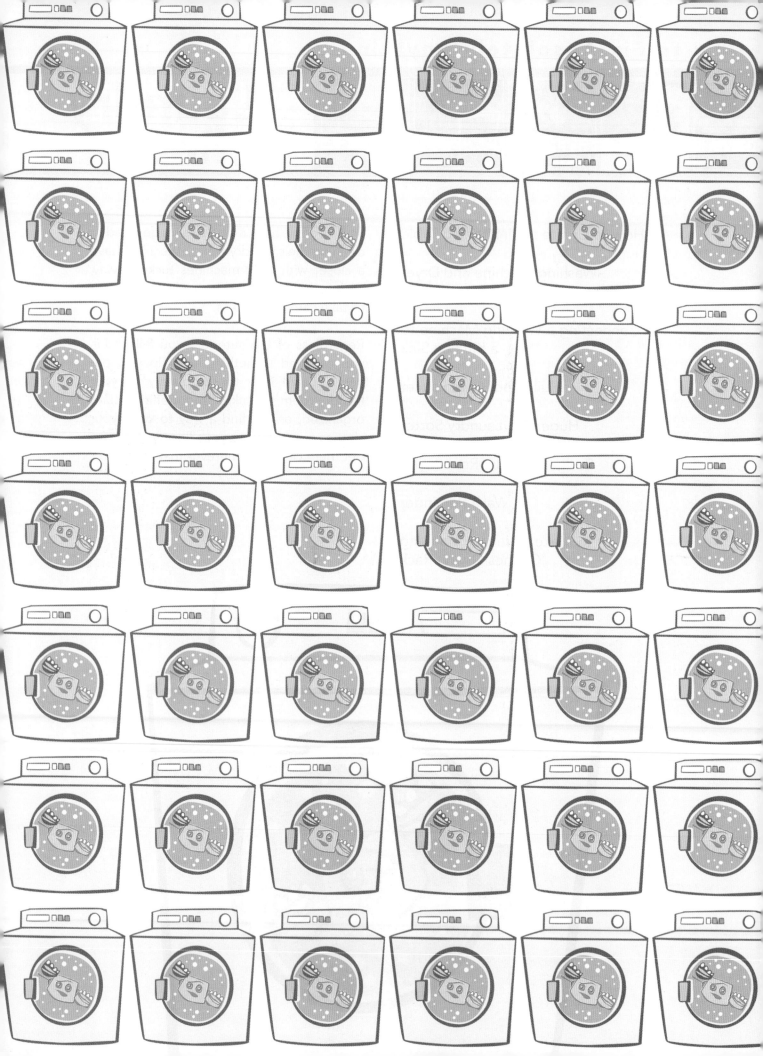

How to Create a Mini Ironing Table

By craftknowitall

http://www.instructables.com/id/How-to-Create-a-Mini-Ironing-Table/

If you do any amount of sewing, one thing you learn is that if you want your finished product to look great, you need to press as you go. If you have a small area for sewing, you will end up doing like I've done and set your ironing board and iron in the other room. That means sewing, getting up and moving to the other room to press, then returning to sew some more, again going to press, etc. I found myself skipping the ironing part whenever possible.

Here is how I rescued an old TV tray and turned it into a mini ironing table to go beside my sewing machine.

Step 1: Supplies

- A wood TV tray (rescue one from a yard sale or secondhand store, or $9 new)
- One yard Warm and Natural 100 percent cotton batting ($6 a yard)
- ½ yard 100 percent cotton fabric ($10 a yard, your choice of colors)
- Medium-size piece of cardboard
- Tape measure
- Yard stick
- Pencil
- Pinking shears ($20)
- Fabric shears (mine are Ginghers, $30)
- Box knife
- Staple gun with staples (your choice of style and cost)

Step 2: The Before

When I brought the TV tray home it looked like this:

Step 3: Cleaned Up

After cleaning, sanding, and staining, it looked like this:

Step 4: Measure It

Use the tape measure to measure the width and length of the top of the tray.

Step 5: Add Cardboard

Cut the cardboard so that it will fit the top of the tray without hanging over. I worried about messing up the stain on top of the tray by applying heat through the three layers of batting. I decided to add a layer of cardboard to protect the finished surface.

Step 6: The Batting

Cut three pieces of Warm and Natural batting to place on top of the cardboard.

Step 7: The Fabric

Cut the material so that it is 4" wider (my material shrunk so it was an inch short) and 4" longer than the top of the tray. Using the pinking shears, cut all the way around the material; this pinked edge will prevent any unraveling around the edges.

Step 8: Assembly, Part One

Lay the fabric right-side down on a flat surface. Center the three layers of batting on the material and then put the piece of cardboard on top of the batting.

Step 9: Assembly, Part Two

Now turn the TV tray upside-down and place its top on top of the cardboard/fabric stack.

Step 10: Stapling

Pull the edges of the material tightly to the underside of the tray and use the staple gun to staple it in place. Put one staple in the center of one side, then staple the center of the opposite side. Next, stretch the fabric and staple the centers of the two ends.

Step 11: More Stapling

Pull the fabric tight and put staples on each side of the first center staple. Repeat the process on the opposite side and then on the two ends. Keep repeating; add two staples each time, doing first one side and then its opposite side. This method will make the material on top of the tray smooth and taut.

Step 12: Corners

When you get to a corner, gather up the excess fabric and use two or three staples to keep it flat and neat.

Step 13: Finished

Done! You know what I like best about using a TV tray to make this mini ironing table?

Step 14: Storage

When it is not it use, it can be folded flat and put in a corner for storage. Yeah, I like that! Enjoy!

We all know washer and dryer pedestals are VERY expensive and are ridiculously priced. You can certainly buy another washer for the price of the two pedestals; or perhaps a new refrigerator! This instructible shows you how to make yourself a cheap pedestal or stand for your washer and washer is that you eliminate the need to bend over to pick up your laundry. Also you can place items under the pedestal such as soap, laundry detergents, etc. The pedestals are a practical accessory for front loading washing machines and dryers.

Step 1: Materials

Materials:

- Plywood (the thicker the better. mine is about an inch thick)
- 2" × 4" wood
- Drill or hammer
- Saw
- Screws or nails (3 inch screws/nails, 2 inch screws/nails)
- Glossy paint

All items can be bought at your local hardware stores. I got all these at home depot. The plywood cost $15 since it was very thick. The 3 pieces of 2" × 4" × 10" cost $2.35 each.

Since I already measured the base of both my washer and dryer, I went a head and had home depot cut the plywood for an extra 15 cents per cut thus eliminating back pains and muscle sore from cutting the plywood myself. I highly recommend doing this.

Step 2: Take Measurements

1. Make measurements around the base of your washer and dryer. My measurement was 27" around, a perfect square. Mark this measurement ion the plywood. This will serve as the top panel where the washer and dryer would sit. 27" × 27". (have Home Depot cut it)
2. Make measurements for the height of your pedestal. In this instructible, the height for my pedestal was 15". Most pedestals are around this height range.
3. Mark your measurement for height on the plywood and also your length. This will serve as the side panels. In this case two 15" × 27". (again, have Home Depot cut it)
4. Measure and mark the 2" × 4"s. Two 25" for the length and four 13" for the height. The four 13" would serve as the leg support . *note* 25" is the length because the plywood was about an inch thick. Depending on the thickness of your plywood, you just have to make the necessary adjustments. You don't want the side panels protruding on the side. We want to seamlessly connect the woods together. To do this, just subtract the thickness of the 2 side panels from the main length of the base of your washer or dryer. That will be the length of your 2×4's. Hope that made sense.

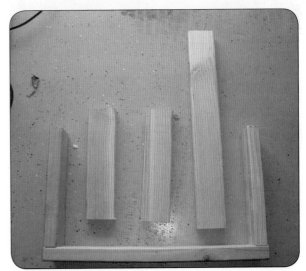

Step 3: Make the Cut

1. Cut the plywood—Top Panel and Side panels.
2. Cut the 2"×4"s.
3. Connect the one 25" with the two 13". You can use nails or screws which ever you feel comfortable.

I use screws this way I prevent the would from cracking. Also I drilled a hole before I screwed it in.

4. Do the same with the other 25" and two 13".
5. Connect the 2 × 4's into the side panels. Secure using screws or nails.
6. Place the top panel in place. Secure using screws and nails.
7. To cover the back, measure from each end of the side panels. That will be your size. Height will still be 15".

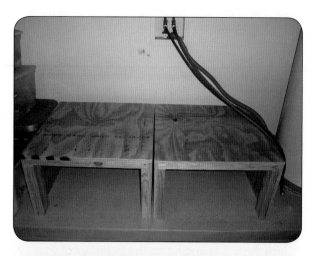

Step 4: Paint it!

Now paint that beautiful work of art to match your washer and dryer. You can brush or spray paint it! Which ever you choose, be creative.If you feel that you don't need to use the space underneath the washer and dryer, just measure and cut a piece of plywood and nail or screw it in place. That size would be 15" × 27" (in my case). After that, You are are done! You've basically have made a platform!If your washer and dryer are inside your house, instead of painting the wood, you might want to consider carpeting the top and side panels. This should help minimize the noise radiated from the washer onto the wood. You can also, instead of painting, cover it with some kind of vinyl, or tolex. Have fun and be creative.

Step 5: Relax and Enjoy!

And finally, enjoy your work of art. Say good bye to back pains and most of all to those ridiculously priced pedestals. Best of all, the total cost for this project? Less than $25. PRICELESS!!! Now if I could just find the time to make the drawers . . . to be continued!

I'm an apartment-dweller, and I managed to inherit a washing machine and dryer (no more collecting quarters and trips to the Laundromat—yay!). But there are no hookups in my apartment (boo!).

Here is my solution to this problem. Note that I never signed anything in my lease forbidding me to have a washing machine—you might want to check your own lease for details. Also, my downstairs neighbors are cool with their dishes rattling when I do laundry.

Step 2: Sink Connection

Another piece you need from Home Depot is a sink aerator thread to hose connection adapter (piece at left on photo; aerator at right). It's sold in the rack of small plumbing fittings (along with washers, sink replacement parts, etc.). I've found that hand-tightening the adaptor is about right—overtightening with a set of ChannelLocks makes the rubber washer squeeze out of its correct shape, causing a leak. The adaptor gets connected to the faucet. The hose gets connected to the adaptor. Knee bone connected to the shin bone.

Step 1: Extension Hoses

None of the hoses that came with the washer are long enough to reach the sink. The supply hose is female-hose fitting (both ends). I just cobbled one together out of plastic hose repair fittings and clear braided tubing (all available from Home Depot). I extended the drain hose with 1 ¼" ID braided tubing—it is a friction fit around the outside of the drain hose. I secured it with a hose clamp. This works fine with a corrugated drain hose; I'm not sure how well it would work with a smooth-surfaced hose.

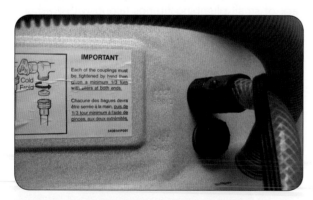

Step 5: Wrap-Up

When you disassemble the hoses, be sure you have a bucket around to drain them out.

Step 3: Connection to the Washing Machine

The supply hose needs to be connected to the cold hose connection. You are going to be controlling water temperature with the faucet controls (hot/cold/warm). Since the rinse cycle is usually cold, you need to hook up to this side to make it work. Note the hose cap on the unused hot side. This is actually important. The solenoid valves have enough slop in them that there is some leakage out of this connection, even when you're just running the machine on cold. I found this out the hard way.

Step 6: Wrap-Up, Part Two

The second use for the Velcro ties is to keep the hoses in place when the machine is not in use.

Step 4: Finishing Setup

You might notice the Velcro ties holding the hose together. I considered it good insurance, to keep the drain hose from flopping out of the sink mid-cycle. Make sure all the connections are tight; turn on the water to the temperature you want it. Fire it up and do your laundry! Note that if you wanted to do a cold rinse, you will have to change the faucet settings mid-cycle.

Build Your Own Faucet

By pribich

http://www.instructables.com/id/Build-Your-Own-Faucet/

When I discovered I needed a new faucet for my laundry room sink I didn't want to choose between a cheap faucet that will only last a few years and an expensive one. I decided to build my own.

The faucet is made from ½" copper pipe and solder fittings, two ball valves, and two ⅜ threaded fittings.

The specific pipe lengths, configuration, and installation will vary based on your needs and tastes so I leave that for each person to determine what will work best in their situation.

Step 1: Tools and Materials

Tools:

- Drill and drill bits
- Hand saw
- Tape measure
- Combination square
- Pipe cutter
- Mallet
- Wrench
- File
- Steel wool
- Pliers
- Safety glasses
- Heat resistant gloves (not pictured)

For Soldering:

- Wire pipe brush
- Sand paper
- Torch
- Solder flux
- Solder
- Brush (for applying flux)
- Lighter

Materials:

- Wooden blocks (One 8" in length, the other 3½")
- Bolts of greater length than the width of the block

- All pipe materials have ½" solder joints:
- Two ball valves
- Three 90 degree elbows (I bought extra in case of problems with soldering)
- One T-joint
- Two ⅜" threaded converters for attaching supply hoses
- One ⅜" pipe thread to ¾" hose thread adapter
- Copper pipe

Step 2: Building the Base

The spacing of the supply hookups on a normal faucet is 4". You want to ensure that the pipes go through the existing holes in your sink. Begin by using the combination square to draw two lines at 2" from each side of the 8" board. Then mark the halfway point of each line. Use these points to center the holes. Once these holes have been drilled, use a hand saw to cut from the end of the board into the ½" hole. Mark four spots on the edge of the board ⅜" from the edge and in the center. At each of these locations, drill a hole that is large enough for the shaft of the bolt. A larger hole will provide more leeway and will be helpful in ensuring that the two holes line up. A drill press would be very helpful in this step, but a hand drill and a steady hand will also work. Once the holes are drilled, push the bolts all the way through and attach the nuts, but do not tighten them yet. As the base will often be exposed to water, sealing and painting will help prevent decay and will increase the life span of your faucet.

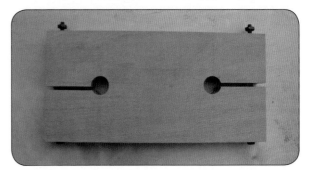

Step 3: Pipe Cutting and Fitting

The pipe cutter I used is much larger than necessary. A hack saw will also work fine. Measure all of the pieces carefully to ensure that the project fits together well. Compare lengths of pipe that are intended to be the same size to ensure symmetry.

To solder the joints:

1. Observe safety precautions. Read labels on the solder and flux and follow the listed safety procedures. Always wear safety glasses and gloves. Work in a well-ventilated area, as flux and solder can produce toxic fumes. Use lead-free solder to ensure no contamination of the water in the faucet or of you during assembly.
2. Wire-brush the fitting and sand the pipe.
3. Wipe both clean.
4. Apply soldering flux to both surfaces to be soldered, being careful not to over apply. Avoid skin contact by using a small brush.
5. Fit the pieces together.
6. Heat the pipe and fitting with the torch
7. Move the torch away and apply solder. There should be enough to go all the way around the pipe. Be careful not to over apply.
8. Observe caution, as the pipe will be very hot. The solder may remain soft until it has cooled completely.

Step 4: Assembling the Pipes and Fittings

The exact length of the pipes used will depend on your specific situation. Start by connecting the ⅜" threaded fittings to two equal lengths of pipe. Press the unsoldered end up through the holes in the base so that the threaded fittings are on the bottom. Make sure the length of pipe above the board is equal and tighten the bolts. Attach the valves, making sure that they both have room to turn freely. Once the valves are in place, connect both to the T-fitting using elbows. The center of the T-fitting should face forward, as this is where you will attach the pipe that caries water to the sink. Use a piece of pipe to ensure that it does not interfere with the valves. Fit an elbow onto the final piece to direct the flow of water downward. Adding a ⅜" threaded piece and the hose adapter will allow you to screw hoses onto your sink. It is wise to cut and fit all pieces before soldering to ensure they all fit together properly.

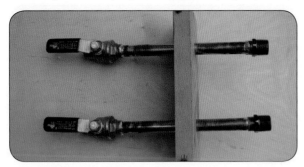

Step 5: Testing

The ⅜" pipe thread to ¾" hose thread will allow you to fit a garden hose to the bottom of the faucet. This will allow you to check one side at a time. Connect the hose (you may need a coupler, as both ends will be male) and check for leaks. Wiping the faucet dry first will ensure you spot any problems.

Step 6: Cleaning Up the Copper

A file will let you remove large pieces of solder that may have dripped during fitting. Steel wool will clean the copper without leaving harsh or obvious scratch marks.

Step 7: Installation

After you are satisfied that the joints are sound and the faucet looks attractive, you can install it in your sink. Shut off the water and open the old tap so the water can drain. Shut-off valves are notoriously problematic, so use penetrating or a lubricant (such as WD-40) and be careful not to turn it too hard. Forcing a frozen shut-off valve can lead to serious troubles. Fit the pipes through the holes in your sink and make sure the base sits flat. You can use the third hole, often used for the drain-stop lever, to screw or bolt the base of the faucet to the other small wooden block. In the case of my laundry room, the sink is plastic and I was able to drill through it. The best way to secure your faucet depends on your specific situation. Once the faucet is secure, attach the supply hoses. Plumbers putty or plumbers tape applied to the threads of the faucet will help ensure that the connection does not leak. Once you are satisfied with the connection, turn on the water supply. Check all connections. Wipe the faucet dry and look for leaks. Watch the area over the next few days to spot any slow leaks or drips.

This is a five-bin PVC laundry sorter that is built with PVC pipe, fittings, snap clamps, a piece of fabric, some laundry bags, and, of course, a few safety pins.

Step 1: Come Up with A Plan

What follows is my basic plan. I decided to put a lid on it (to keep my cat away). The lid certainly isn't required, but it is rather cool to use slip-on PVC tees to create things that you might not otherwise be able to do with PVC.

Step 2: Gather Your Materials

I'm assembling this laundry sorter out of PVC parts. Here's a rundown of what I used and where I got them. (Note: All PVC sizes are ½")

Structural PVC Fittings: (These fittings are made particularly for building things [they do not carry fluid], though you could use standard PVC fittings as well.)

- Eight PVC20 Three-Way Ls (these will be for the corners)
- Five PVC25 Tees (these will be for the middle supports and for the top of the lid)
- Eleven PVC10 Slip Tees (these hold the bag supports and also are used to hinge the lid)
- Two PVC15 Elbows (these are the corners of the lid)

Snap Clamps: (Snap clamps are PVC clips that are used to hold on both the lid fabric and the laundry bags.)

- Twelve for the bag supports
- Twelve for holding on lid fabrics

PVC Pipe Lengths:

I kept the lengths simple. I made the sorter three feet tall and six feet wide, so I only had two lengths to cut (with the section of the lid "edit" - more about that later). This is all ½" Schedule 40 PVC.

- Sixteen 3-foot cuts (four for bottom, four for top, six for uprights, two for lid)
- Eleven 18" cuts (two for bottom, six for top, three for lid). You will probably want to determine the size based upon the size bags that you are planning to use.

Other Stuff:

- Five laundry bags
- One piece of fabric to cover the top
- A bunch of safety pins to help attach the fabric

Step 3: Assemble PVC Frame

I started by assembling the base. I added the uprights and then built the the top frame. Notice how I slipped the PVC Tee fittings onto the pipe. I used three on one and four on the other; the extra on one side was a support for the middle of the lid. The only real tricky part was the length of the lid pipes. Because the hinges are offset, I had to trim one of the top pipes so that it fit with the offset. Once I got to that part in the project, I simply measured it in place and trimmed off the excess with a hack saw. I did not glue my PVC together. The fittings I was using had a tight enough fit to stay together.

Step 4: Attach Bags and Fabric Top

I attached my bags with some plastic clips called Snap Clamps. These clips are great because they allow you to easily clip fabric onto PVC pipe. The bags can be removed and washed when they get smelly or need to be changed. My wife found some discount fabric that we laid over the top, pulled tight, snapped on with snap clamps, and then fastened with a few safety pins (so that the excess fabric didn't flap around).

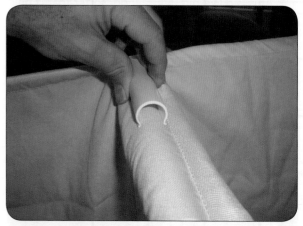

Step 5: Viola! Your Very Own Massive PVC Laundry Hamper

That's it—pretty basic and straightforward.

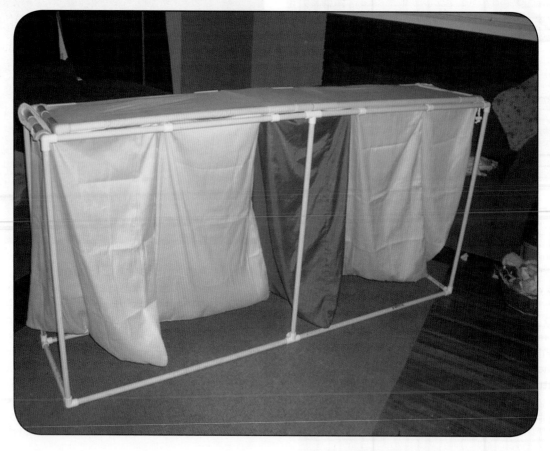

Our laundry room has been an embarrassment for the last ten years with its cluttered shelves, yawning gaps behind the washer and dryer, a cluttered sink, and dark, dingy cabinets. Well, I finally decided to do something about it. The problem with wanting to remodel the laundry room has always been money. I'm surprised, though, at how little this remodel job cost. My out-of-pocket for this project was around $50, but that's because I used materials and supplies that I already had on hand. I estimated what it would have cost if I were buying everything now and it came to less than $200. Still a very budget-friendly renovation!

Step 1: Materials

- Oil-based primer
- White satin paint
- Curtain track
- Drapery pins
- Tiles
- Tile grout
- Tile adhesive
- King-sized flat bed sheet
- Stainless steel paint
- Plywood for counter
- Storage containers
- Hooks
- Electrical tape
- Yellow spray paint
- Yellow latex paint
- Cabinet pulls
- Wood glue

Step 2: Hide Clutter

Because our laundry room is also where the water heater and central air are located, the biggest bang for my remodel job came from hiding this side of the room from view with a curtain. For this, I painted a king-sized sheet with a floral pattern and hung it from a drapery track with drapery hooks. (My younger sister came to town like a whirlwind of DIY kindness, and the ceiling track installation was one of the many helpful things she left in her wake. You can buy special tracks for ceiling installation, but my sister used a wall-mount version that cost about $20 and screwed it to the ceiling.)

For the sheet, I wanted a pretty pattern, but anything preprinted was too expensive. Instead, I bought a set for $16 and painted the flat sheet.

Not shown is the top hem sewn on the sheet. For this, I just folded the edge of the sheet over about four times and sewed the layers together into a hem, in which I inserted drapery hooks.

To hide the clutter around the sink, I added two cheap storage containers under the counter. One was screwed to the wall at the back of the cabinet and the other to the back of one of the doors. I also added hooks behind one of the cabinet doors. Now all the soaps, sponges, rags, and gloves are tucked out of sight.

Step 4: Tile the Sink Area

I have a great relationship with a local construction goods salvager, so tiles and PVC and such cost me pennies, if anything (sometimes I trade for cheese bread). This white-tiled countertop was free except for the tile adhesive and grout.

To tile around a sink:

1. Remove sink.
2. Roughen the surface with sandpaper.
3. Lay out tiles and make necessary cuts.
4. Set the sink back in its hole to test if it fits. Remove sink.
5. Butter tiles or counter top with adhesive and lay tiles.
6. Grout tiles. Wait 15 minutes and wipe with a sponge. Don't worry if there's still a light film of grout on the tiles. Let it dry another hour, then wipe with a dry cloth.
7. Set sink back in its hole.

Quick DIY tip: If you can't find edge tiles, paint the edge with porcelain paint. It'll make a budget job look expensive!

Step 3: Add Countertop Space

The last straw that finally made me do this laundry renovation was that I hate having to drag the washer or dryer out to look for fallen laundry. If there were a counter over the two appliances that braced against the wall, well, that task would be abolished.

I wanted a stainless steel or copper countertop, but didn't have the money. I did, however, have some stainless steel paint, so I made a faux stainless-steel countertop with a piece of plywood. A bit of wood glue added an interesting textured design.

Step 5: Tile the Backsplash

The color scheme for this remodel job was white, yellow, and gray. That's because I had some yellow and some gray tiles lying around. They weren't enough to tile a countertop, but were enough for a backsplash all around the sink and appliance walls. The combination made a big impact with a minimal budget.

First, I removed the old wood backsplash from around the sink area, then tiled rows behind the sink and washer and dryer. I made sure to leave the appropriate gap above the faux stainless steel counter support pieces so the board could slide in all the way to the wall and not hit tile. That "locked" the counter into place without having to screw the counter down anywhere (so I can remove it to work on the appliances when necessary).

If you don't have different color tiles, you can create a patterned look by painting the same tile with different craft finishes.

Step 6: Paint Walls and Trim

Always, the most bang you can get for your remodel buck is to paint. I had already started this renovation job when Ace Hardware sent me a coupon for a free quart of paint. I squealed with glee because that would give me just enough for the yellow that I needed for this small area. I had some high-gloss yellow trim and door paint, which I used to color-match the wall paint from Ace. The result? A sun-drenched look for our laundry room! Cost? Zero.

By the way, for small spaces like this laundry area, keeping a unified color instead of breaking it up into chunks of this or that will make the room look larger.

Step 7: Paint the Cabinets!

The floor-to-ceiling cabinets in our laundry area overpowered the space with their dark and dingy finish. White paint made the biggest impact toward lightening up the space and making it a happy area rather than a drag.

I had intended to add molding around all the cabinet doors, but after doing it on the two biggest doors, I gave up. Because the sides of the doors were

rounded, I had to fill the gaps with wood filler, and since the doors were heavy oak to start with, they turned out to be *really* heavy. I'd also intended to use glass on two of the doors (I had three 2 'x 3' pieces someone gave me—the perfect size!), but two of the glass pieces broke during handling, and the silicone adhesive I used for the one that didn't break looked hideous. I wouldn't recommend putting molding or glass on the doors yourself unless you have the right skills for the task.

Step 8: New Hardware

For about $4 I added new hardware to the cabinet doors. I had to hunt for a matching set at Habitat for Humanity, but found just enough to do the job.

Step 9: French-ify Your Doors and Windows

For $6 worth of electrical tape I turned the plain door into a French-pane version. How? Measure out the panes and apply electrical tape with the color of your choice to the glass. Cut. Done.

Wash Reminder

By Benjamin Bustard (Stryker)
http://www.instructables.com/id/Wash-reminder/

Never forget that you left wet clothes in the washer again! This Instructable shows how to make a clothes in the laundry reminder device.

Step 1: Why and How

The problem:

Our laundry room is next to the baby's room and you have to turn off the washer and dryer when he takes a nap. So my wife asked me to think of a way to remind her that she had clothes in the washer.

My solution:

Make a little device that can be turned on when the washer gets paused and will flash until turned back off reminding her to finish the laundry.

Material:

- 1 sheet of white ⅜ inch poster board (Michaels $5)
- 1 Red flashing LED (Free from halloween candy display package)
- 2 AA batteries w/ holder (Free from halloween candy display package)
- 1 on/off switch (Pulled from old toy)
- Small piece of red tissue paper
- Small piece of aluminum foil
- Washer with arrow image (made by my artist brother)

Tools:

- Exacto knife
- Metal ruler
- Glue gun
- Soldering iron
- Glue stick

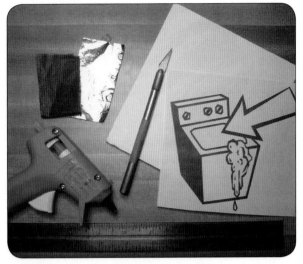

Step 2: Front Construction

1. Cut the poster board into 6 inch wide by 14 inch long piece
2. Measure 6 inches down and using your exacto knife and metal ruler remove a ³⁄₁₆ wide strip of foam leaving the poster board top untouched.
3. Measure 1 inch down and remove another strip of foam
4. Repeat steps 2 and 3 until a box is formed.
5. Now cut out the washer image and red part of the arrow.
6. Test fit the washer image and trace the inside of the arrow onto the posterboard.
7. Carefully cut out the arrow from the posterboard.
8. Double over and cut a piece of tissue paper a little bigger than the size of the arrow.
9. Glue the tissue paper and washer image to the poster board.
10. Trim any excess tissue paper.

Step 3: Inside Construction

1. Cut a hole through the washer where you want your switch to go. Make sure it's large enough for your switch to operate smoothly.
2. Solder up and test your battery holder, on/off switch and LED setup. I can't tell you exactly how to do this step because I don't know what you are using. Take a look at my insides picture to see how I did it.
3. Hot glue the battery holder, switch and LED to the posterboard.
4. Cut a piece of aluminum foil a little bit larger than the arrow and hot glue that down to help spread out the LED light.
5. Put some hot glue in 2 of the seams of the posterboard to make it a stronger box. Don't glue it all together because you will need to open it up to change the batteries.
6. Close it up with some pins or however you want and hang it up.

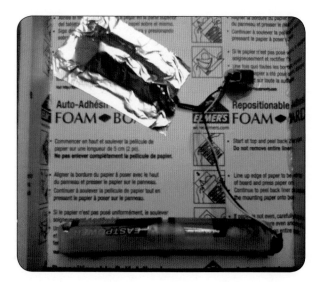

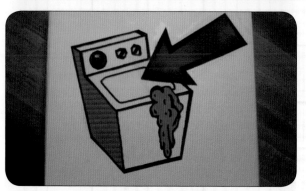

Step 4: Final note

This project only took a little bit of time and money so if forgotten laundry is a problem in your house, try making one of these. But don't blame me if your wife tells "you" to do the laundry if you don't like the way she does it . . . .

How to Make an Indoor Hanging Clothes-Drying Rack

By Jim Vanderlinde (coolbeansbaby68)
http://www.instructables.com/id/Inside-hanging-clothes-rack/

My wife came across an idea in which someone used a cut-down apple-picking ladder. I decided to make one for our laundry room.

Step 1: Rack Dimension Illustration

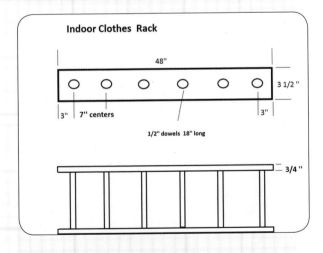

Step 2: Building the Rack

First, I bought a 1" × 8" × 8" pine board. I then cut it to be 4' long.

I then ripped two boards to be 3 ½" × 4" on the table saw.

Next, I put the two boards together and marked out 3" on center of the board for the first and sixth dowel on each end. Then I marked 7" on center for the remaining four dowels.

I then used a ½" drill bit and drilled all six holes. Next, I cut six ½" dowels 18" long and glued the ends before fitting them in the holes.

Step 3: Edges

First, I used a router and a 45 degree router bit to chamfer all the edges.

Then I sanded smooth the entire rack and put a coat of paint on it.

Step 4: Accessories

You will need:

- (4) screw eyes
- (4) pieces of #6 chain 5" long
- (4) ³⁄₁₆" × 2" toggle bolts

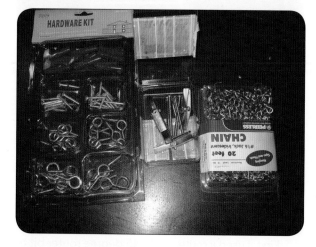

Step 5: Screw Eyes

I measured 2" in on all four sides. Then I screwed in the four screw eyes.

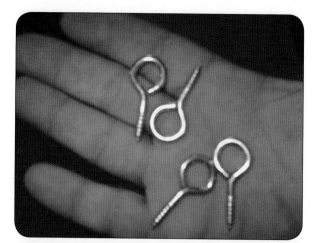

Step 6: Toggle Bolts

I first measured out from the wall 5" from each corner, then 18" out from there.

I drilled four ½" for the toggles bolts.

I then cut four 5" long pieces of chain and installed the toggles bolts in the holes and tightened them up.

Last, I hooked the chain to the screw eyes. It's finished and ready to hang clothes up to dry.

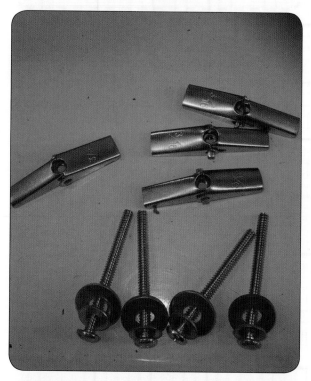

How to Fix Absolutely Anything

Dining Room

Dining rooms can be classy and elegant or you can just have a table tucked in the corner of your kitchen. Everyone's room is different and so are everyone's tastes. When you move into a new place it isn't going to be to your liking right away, but we can fix that! Take a look at this selection of dining tables and chairs and see how you can fix up your dining room and make it seem like it was designed just for you!

Fix Broken Wine Glass Foot

By misko13

http://www.instructables.com/id/Fix-broken-wine-glass-foot/

I just bought a batch of four wine glasses and one of them fell and broke its foot. It was a pity to throw it to the bin so I decided to fix it. For that I used Fimo modeling clay, which hardens after 30 minutes in the oven. It's actually become my favorite glass as it has more grip than the other glasses.

Step 1: Modeling

This clay is divided in six portions. To make the base I used three of them.

1. Make a ball with 2 ½ portions.
2. Flatten it until you get the dimension of the base wanted (do this on a tray covered with aluminum paper).
3. Place the glass in the middle and make sure it's straight.
4. Secure the glass to the base with the half portion left.

Step 2: Baking

Now make sure there are no fingerprints on the glass. You've probably had dirt on your hands while modeling the base, and if you leave any fingerprints on the glass it will also harden in the baking process.

Bake it for 30 minutes at 110 degrees Celsius (230 degrees Fahrenheit), let it go cold . . . and that's it!

Wash the glass before use.

It was your favorite chair until—SNAP!—a piece was broken. You might be getting ready to dump it or to put it in front of your house as a lost cause for someone else to adopt, but wait! It can likely be fixed, and you can have many years of satisfied sitting ahead of you.

All right, let's fix it!

Step 1: Clean the Wound

Remove the splinters at the ends of each piece. You want the two pieces to easily go back together and even have a slight gap between them for the epoxy to fill.

Step 2: Form a Tape Trough

To keep the epoxy from dripping all over the floor, use masking tape to form a trough on the underside of the rung. This will be an impromptu mold.

Step 3: Epoxy Time!

Time to glue it down! I'm using Loctite Epoxy here. The picture here is a little misleading. Do not just squeeze onto the rung! It's a two-part adhesive so you'll need to pour it onto another surface (cardboard is great), mix it up thoroughly, and then pour it onto the rung.

Feel free to tap the rung a bit to dislodge any air bubbles and make sure that the epoxy fills up the gap.

This is a five-minute epoxy, but that name refers to the time for the epoxy to set. It will take a full 24 hours for it to cure.

Step 4: Hello Again, Chair

When the epoxy has set you can remove the tape. After it has fully cured (again, 24 hours) then you can sand down any rough parts with sandpaper. You can also paint the epoxy to better match the rest of the chair.

And you're done! Next time go a little easier on the furniture, okay?

Fix a Torn Card Table

By rintheamazing

http://www.instructables.com/id/Fix-A-Torn-Card-Table/

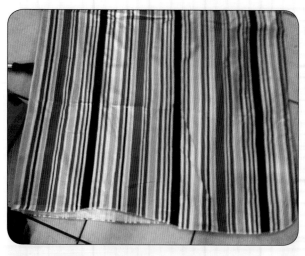

My vinyl-topped card table got all torn up on the top, allowing the wood to show through. I used a dollar-store tablecloth to recover the top and now it looks better than new.

Step 1: You Will Need...

- Your card table
- Flannel-backed vinyl tablecloth in a color or pattern you like
- A screwdriver (check the screws that hold the top of your table on to the leg assembly)
- Sharp scissors
- A stapler and staples (note: you will be tempted to use a staple gun. Unless the top of your table is a lot thicker than mine was, this will not work. My first attempt sent the points of the staple right through the wood and out the other side. You just want a regular stapler, but it needs to be one where you can open it out flat)
- Marker and ruler or other straightedge (optional)

Step 2: Remove Top Of Table From Leg Assembly

This picture shows the top already separated from the legs.

What you want to do here is turn the table over so the legs are sticking up in the air. Then look to see how the top is attached. In this case, there were screws going through those little metal tabs and into the table top. I just removed the screws, making sure to put them in a little dish so I wouldn't lose them.

Step 3: Cut Tablecloth

Spread your tablecloth out face-down on the floor.

Now is the time to decide which direction you want the pattern to go. This will be more important with stripes than it would be with a pattern such as polka dots or flowers. I opted to have the stripes run diagonally so I wouldn't have to worry about lining the stripes up perfectly with the edges of the table.

Place the table top face-down on the table cloth, aligning it with the pattern however you like. Then use your sharp scissors to cut the tablecloth parallel to the edge of the table, leaving a margin of around 4" to 5". This doesn't need to be super precise, but if you're more comfortable drawing a line with a ruler before you cut, then do that.

Cut the corners off your square of tablecloth so that the corners of the table are about 2" to 3" inches from the edge.

Step 4: Attach Tablecloth to Table Top

How neatly you want to do this is up to you. It is, after all, the underside of the table. I opted to fold each edge under before stapling the tablecloth down, but it's not really necessary.

The trick to getting the top nice and smooth is even tension. Fold the tablecloth over one corner of the table top, towards the center, and then staple it down. Then repeat with the opposite corner, pulling the tablecloth nice and tight around the table top.

As you start to staple down the sides of the cloth, you may want to mark where the screw holes are for attaching the leg assembly, as the cloth will be going over these holes. If you forget, as I did, then you'll just need to feel for them with your finger and use your screwdriver or the point of the scissors to poke a hole so the screws can go through.

Use as many staples as you need to get the tablecloth pulled nice and evenly around the table top. I spaced my staples about 6" apart. Be careful not to staple over any of the screw holes.

Don't worry if some of the staples go in crooked or look like they might not hold for long. The screws that attach the top to the leg assembly will help to hold everything in place.

Step 5: Reattach Leg Assembly

We're doing step 1 in reverse now. With the table top still face-down on the floor, align the leg assembly with the top.

If you haven't already done so, use something sharp to pierce the tablecloth where it covers the screw holes in the table top. Then use the original screws to reattach the leg assembly.

I find it best to put all the screws in and tighten them a little bit, then go back and tighten them all the way.

Step 6: Rejoice in Your Completed Repair

Turn the table back over so it's standing up on the legs.

Ta-da! Your previously torn up card table is now pristine and new-looking, and with a snazzy new color or pattern, to boot!

Gather some friends to play cards or eat snacks or whatever it is you use this table for, and congratulate yourself on a job well done.

This is an easy way to fix up old or used furniture. Why didn't we do this earlier?

Step 1: Before

Here's an old chair with a ratty seat cover. We got it from Craig's List about three years ago. The seats had been re-covered in a neat red silk that looked good but didn't wear well. After months of ignoring the shredded red silk, we finally yanked it off to discover the original black fabric, which also looked pretty bad. Since we were planning to have 40 people over for Thanksgiving the next day, it was the perfect time to start a new project. Right.

Step 2: Find Your Fabric

We headed off to the local fabric store to find some thick upholstery fabric. This will wear better than that thin silk, and hopefully stand up to years of daily abuse at our kitchen table. I chose some nice swirly blue stuff that should look good with the dark brown wood of the chairs. Thrift stores are also a great source for material—pick up an old jacket, skirt, tablecloth, or anything else with a thick fabric and neat design. Just make sure it can stand up to the level of use you'll be giving it. You don't need much fabric—just the size of the seat plus a couple of inches around each edge of the seat. Remember to measure your seats before running off to the fabric store, or else you'll have lots of extra fabric, or worse, not quite enough. (I'm planning to make cloth napkins from my leftovers. Eventually.)

Remove the chair seat and place it upside-down against the back of the fabric. (Remember the good stuff should be facing up when you're done.) Make sure it's properly aligned with your fabric's pattern, especially if there are stripes involved. Trim around the edge to leave enough fabric to fold over on all sides. Depending on the thickness of your cushion, this could be 2" to 5".

Staple the sides, again tugging firmly to make sure the fabric is tight over the top of the seat. Do the corners last. I found it best to take a fold on each side of the corner, then make a pleat along the diagonal—look at the pictures for inspiration, then do what works best for you. Again, yank staples and re-do anything you don't like.

Things to think about:

1. How many staples to use? My staples were kind of small, and I love stapling, so I used more than absolutely necessary. Scale as appropriate for your fabric, staple size, and entertainment, but make sure you use enough to share the strain across your fabric.

2. Where do the screws go? If you have to screw your seat back on, take care not to block the screw holes with lots of fabric or staples. You can go through one layer of fabric easily, but staples are a problem.

3. Is it tidy? Be sure to hammer down any staples that aren't flush, and trim any extraneous blobs of fabric.

Step 3: Staple!

This is the fun part—an excuse to use a staple gun. Ours is a sweet electric version that can punch through most anything. In any case, be careful—don't staple your fingers, your eyes, your leg, or anything else but the fabric and the seat back. Start with the flat front side and staple from the center out towards the edges. You want to make sure the fabric is smooth and tight, without bunches between your staples. This is much like wrapping a present—if you can do that, you can re-cover a chair.

Now spin the seat and tug the back of the fabric into position. Pull firmly against the front row of staples to be sure you've gotten rid of any wrinkles or bunches. Again, start stapling at the center and spread outwards. When the seat back starts to curve, make folds/tucks in your fabric. The goal is to have all the bunching under the seat, not on top. Try a few different things and see how it works. Remember, you can always pull the staples out and try again until you get it right.

Step 4: Stain Protect

We sprayed the new seat covers down with Scotch Guard. This little can held enough to do only six seats; luckily we only needed four. Set up some milk crates or other support structure and spray the seats according to package directions. Be sure to do this outside, as the vapors are pretty foul and probably carcinogenic. Let them dry overnight in a protected but well-ventilated area. If you can put them in a porch or garage this will protect you from the vapors while also protecting your shiny new seats from dangerously well-fed birds.

Step 5: Reassemble and Use

When the seats are dry, reassemble your chairs. These required a screwdriver. Use and enjoy your newly-refreshed seating, and wonder why you didn't do this earlier. Start checking out the rest of your furniture and wonder whether recovering a couch is really that much harder.

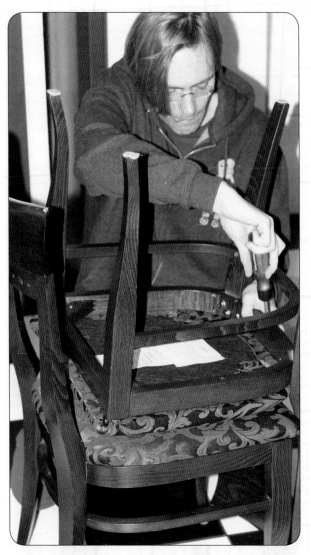

How to Make a Chandelier Using Mason Jars

By timpaslay

http://www.instructables.com/id/How-to-make-a-Chandelier-using-Mason-Jars/

We made this chandelier to be the centerpiece of our dining room.

Before I get started, I want to make a disclaimer: I am not an electrician and will not assume responsibility for any damage that occurs as a result of you attempting this project. If at any point you feel uncomfortable, hire an electrician! We have had this chandelier installed in our house for about two years without any problems.

There are a lot a steps involved but I will do my best to explain things in terms anyone can understand. So, here goes . . .

Step 1: Materials

You will need:

- Canning jars with lids (6 large, 9 widemouth, 6 small)
- Wire (18-2 lamp cord)
- #10 washers
- Hex nuts (that will fit your nipple, which is the threaded metal rod)
- Steel nipples
- Small hose clamp
- Four keyless Sockets
- 4" offset crossbar
- 4" PVC cap (found in plumbing section). We used this as the ceiling plate because it provides a lot of room to accommodate all the wires that are coming from the fixture.
- 3" machine screws (to attach the ceiling plate to the crossbar)
- Two acorn nuts
- Two wire nuts

Step 2: Prep the Jars

It may be hard to tell from the pictures, but only four of the jars contain lights. We have had some other people try to add more lights and some have experienced bulbs bursting. I think the ratio of lighted to non-lighted jars we have is close to ideal. You could try more if you like, just be prepared for what might happen.

Select the four jars you want to hold lights (make sure the socket and bulbs will fit) and then drill a hole large enough to accommodate the diameter of your steel nipple.

Next, drill four ventilation holes around the periphery of the lid. This will allow the heat created by the bulb to escape.

For the remaining 17 jars, you will need to drill a hole that is large enough to fit your wire.

For this first fixture I purchased 6" lengths of steel nipples and cut the 1" sections I needed with a circular saw and grinder with a fiber wheel. I recommend threading a nut on your nipple before you begin cutting so that when you are done you will be able to "rethread" your cut section by removing the nut. I purchased these materials from Home Depot.

Since then I have found a local hardware store that specializes in repairing chandeliers and lamps that carries individual nipples in ¼" increments. Now I buy as many as I need in whatever length I desire and don't have to worry about fouling up threads or sparks.

Step 3: Prepare Wiring

Now we will prepare our wire to string each jar. I am providing measurements and quantities to recreate a chandelier similar to the one in the pictures, but feel free to adjust anything you wish to create a fixture that fits your personal space.

Cut 21 lengths of wire at 2' each.

Then, use wire strippers and/or a razor blade to split the plastic coating on one end and reveal the metal wire underneath. You will want about ¾" of exposed wire.

For the 17 jars that will remain unlit, push the wire through the hole in your lid and string a washer onto one wire and then twist the two together to secure it.

Step 5: Assembling the Lids

Screw your hex nut onto your nipple. Next, push the nipple through the hole in your lid, and then screw on the keyless socket. Tighten everything together.

When you open your keyless socket, it will have a cardboard sleeve around it. Do not throw this away thinking it is packing material. For now you can remove it, but you will need to reinstall it later.

Step 4: The Lids

Now it's time to work on the lids that will hold the lights.

I documented the steps I took to create our first chandelier; since then I have refined the process a bit and will include tips I have learned from successive productions.

Step 6: Wire the Jars

Now we are ready to wire the lit jars. Take one of the four remaining 2' wire sections you have and feel the rubber insulation. One of the wires will have a ridge while the other will be smooth. The "ridged" wire will be connected to the silver screw of your socket, and the "smooth" will attach to the brass screw.

On the stripped end of your wire, pull the wires apart to about a ½" down (reference the picture above).

Insert this end of the wire into the steel nipple. Paying attention to which wire will go to which screw, separate the wires as they exit the nipple.

Loosen the screws and wrap the wire clockwise underneath them, then tighten them back down. Replace cardboard wrap.

Step 7: PVC Cap

Drill a hole through the middle of your PVC cap. We used a 1" spade bit (a hole saw will work as well) to accommodate all of our wires. Bundle all of your wires together and compare to your bit before you drill.

Our cap had raised writing on the center. You can sand this off with sand paper. It isn't a bad idea to give the entire cap a light sanding with a fine-grit sandpaper. It will help your paint stick. Paint it whatever color you desire.

If the cap is too deep for your liking, you can cut it down. We took off about an inch. I recommend carefully using a handsaw or coping saw. If you want to do it quickly with a miter saw, create a jig to hold it securely in place.

Next you will need to drill two smaller holes to connect your PVC housing to the mounting plate. Be sure figure out which holes you will use to connect your plate to the junction box and then decide which two holes you will use to connect the PVC housing. Make your holes large enough to accommodate 3" machine screws.

Step 8: Arrange the Jars

Screw all your jars to your lids. Gather the wires together, raising and lowering different ones to get the shape you want. This is definitely a two-person job. You need someone to hold all the jars in the air while someone else arranges them in an aesthetically pleasing grouping. You will also need to decide how far your chandelier is going to hang from the ceiling.

Once you have the shape you want and know the height at which it will hang, push all the wires through the PVC cap/ceiling plate and then through your hose clamp. Tighten your hose clamp as much as possible! It will be holding all the weight of the jars.

Although I didn't do it for the one hanging in our living room, I have decided it would be a great idea to wrap your wire bundle with a few layers of electrical tape before installing your hose clamp.

Step 9:

Cut all the wires back that are not connected to the keyless sockets. It is best to tag these wires from the very beginning so you don't cut something you shouldn't.

Strip the insulation of the "lit" wires, exposing about ¾" of wire. Group your four neutral wires and then separately group your four hot wires. Hot Wires=Smooth plastic coating; Neutral Wires= ridged plastic coating.

Create a "pig tail" from a small piece of wire. Using a 4" to 6" scrap of wire, strip the insulation from both ends. You can leave the two wires together in the center or you can pull them completely apart and have separate neutral and hot pigtails.

Attach the neutral pigtail to the group of neutral wires using an appropriately sized wire nut. Do the same for your hot wires.

I recommend installing the 3" screws (or whatever size you need based on your housing) to your mounting plate and fitting the housing over these. You will need to install the acorn nuts and then keep turning them until they hold the PVC housing tight against the ceiling. If you do it this way you need to make sure you insert the machine screws into the threaded holes in the mountain plate.

That's it. I love this unique light fixture and gotten lots of positive feedback. I hope you enjoy it as much as we do.

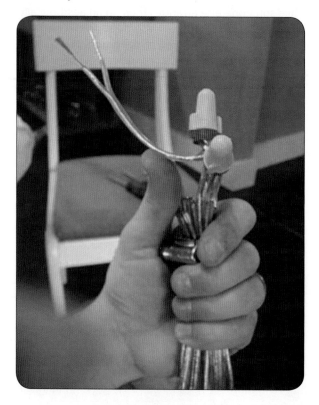

Step 10: Installation

All that is left is to install your new fixture. It is a good idea to have another set of hands during this step to help hold the weight while you make your connections.

Connect your "hot" pigtail to the black wire in the ceiling and the "neutral" pigtail to the white wire in the ceiling.

A couple of years ago we replaced our old, heavy, wooden garage door with a lightweight aluminum door. I hung on to the panels since they were made with high-quality pine wood and marine-grade plywood. I turned one of the panels into a workbench in my garage, and two others were reserved for a new dining room table.

I tossed around several ideas on how to fill the recessed pockets of the door sections. The first thought was to fill them with concrete and grind and polish the surface, much like a concrete countertop. However, if I did that, it would cover up most of the beautiful wood grain. So I decided on a clear epoxy. Because of this decision, I found out just how much epoxy is required to fill the recesses and cover an entire 48" × 83" table top, and also just how expensive it is! Sometimes, finding the right solution to upcycle materials will cost you more money than just buying new ones, but where is the fun in that? I don't think you could ever buy a table made from a garage door at the mega furniture stores.

Step 1: Getting Started and Planning
LET'S GET STARTED

Because this is such a specialized project, and I highly doubt many people have old wooden garage door sections lying around, please look at this more as an inspiration for other custom furniture. My approach to this project was to try to plan as much as possible, but the majority of the work was trial and error. I want to share lessons learned and ideas to make your own furniture as painlessly as possible.

CAD OVERKILL

I laid out the general idea of the table in CATIA—yes, I know, a little bit of overkill on the CAD software, but hey, it's what I do for a living so why not? I actually used the CAD model to calculate the exact amount of epoxy I would need. I had the option of just leaving both sections at their length (8') and using them side by side, or I could cut the sections in half and butt them up against one another. Leaving them long and side by side made for a really long, skinny table, whereas cutting them and stacking them end to end made for a semi-really-long and wide table. Stacking them also allowed for more symmetry due to how these garage doors were made. See pictures for an explanation.

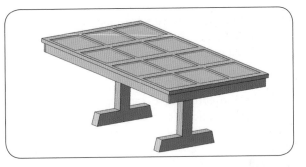

DISCLAIMER

I started by attempting to scrape the peeling paint off the doors. This proved to be very difficult as there was approximately 60 years' worth of paint stuck to the door. Since I wasn't using the painted side of the door for the top, I didn't spend a lot of time trying to remove paint. I basically wanted to make sure I didn't have loose paint chips coming off the bottom of the table.

Note: I want to point out that I have no idea if the paint on these doors was lead based. I made sure that any paint that could be peeled, picked, or knocked off was removed and sanded smooth. Any unsealed painted surface would not be exposed to food and would be out of reach of prying hands. Please keep this in mind when working with older painted materials.

Step 2: Sanding, Cutting, Scuffing, Beveling, and Brushing
KICKING UP SOME DUST

The doors had either been stained on the inside or had just absorbed many years' worth of dust and dirt, as they were definitely dark and dirty. I sanded the upper surfaces of the ribs with an orbital sander and finished them by hand. The surfaces of the pockets I also attempted to sand with the orbital sander, but it was pretty tricky, and I ended up eating up my sanding pads pretty quickly due to the disc bumping against the edges and tearing the pads. The thing I found that worked best was my metal grill brush. It would easily take the loose materials off and would do a sort of sanding action as well. I wasn't too worried about getting the surfaces of the pockets smooth since they were going to be filled with ½" of epoxy in the end. Please note that when sanding it is highly advisable to use a respirator or, at the very least, a dust mask.

ROUNDING THINGS OUT

After the cutting and sanding, I tried to round off the sharp edges created by the cuts. I wasn't very particular with this either since it was a worn, rustic, industrial look I was going for. Rounding over the edges also helped prevent splinters, which I was unfortunately blessed with many of from this project!

CLEAN UP THE ROT

The bottom section had some areas that were starting to rot, so I cut about an inch and a half off the bottom section. Then I cut each section in half. Once I cut the sections in half, I had to cut about an inch off what used to be each edge of the sections so the width of the edges would be the same. Again, please look at the pictures for clearer explanations.

Step 3: Nice Legs!
HEY TOOTS, NICE STEMS

Figuring out which style of legs to make was the next step. I thought about regular post legs, angled legs, pedestal legs, even tensegrity legs. Finally my wife showed me a wonderful how-to on making a farmhouse table. The legs were perfect (and very easy to make)! For the most part I copied what she had done, but I did make a few modifications to mine. The dimensions will vary based on the application, but I have included mine for reference.

TORCH IT!

Note: The following instructions are dangerous if proper caution is not exercised! I will not be held responsible for improper use of a blow torch!

The 2" × 4"s I bought were red pine so they would match the aged red pine of the garage door. I made all the cuts and glued and screwed them together. Once they were set, I torched them! A few years ago, I had come up with a way (I'm probably not the only one who has done this) to texture and age dimensional soft wood.

Very carefully sweep a torch over the wood, allowing the flame to scorch the wood. You don't want to burn the wood to ashes, just char the outer grains to a nice dark brown-black. I varied the amount of charring over the wood to give it some variety.

Once you have a level of blackening you are happy with, take a wire brush and scour off the charred wood. The more you burn it the more material you will remove. The flame burns the softer part of the grain and hardly touches the harder parts.

After you have removed most of the blackened grains, go over it with fine grit sandpaper to smooth out the top grains. You should end up with a very textured wood with beautiful darker color variations.

Another thing you can do is spray the wood with black spray paint and let it sit for a few seconds, then wipe it off with a rag and sand. This gives the grains even more texture, but it would have been too dark for my preference here.

I applied stain to the wood per the manufacturer's instructions, then applied three coats of polyurethane. This gave a wonderful look that complemented the table top. I wasn't going for an exact match, but a complementary look to make a pleasing flow of colors and textures.

Step 4: Substructure and Support
OVER-ENGINEERING AT ITS BEST

Since my background is in engineering and design with structural steel, it was only fitting that I over-engineer the bottom support of the table. I didn't want the slightest bit of sag, which is a problem with many tables over time. I built the frame of dimensional lumber first and then added it to the panels. I attached the frame to the panels on our flat and level living room floor.

I placed 2" × 4"s over each seam where the panels joined together.

I added notched 1" × 4"s perpendicular to those 2" × 4"s. These ran along the ribs of the door.

I then added a box of 1" × 4"s around the whole outside of the substructure.

In hindsight I would have used 1" × 3"s in place of the 1" × 4"s because they wouldn't have hung down so low and would have provided just as much support. I attached all the boards to the top with screws and glue. In the seams where the door panels met and where the 2" × 4"s laid on the panels, I applied Liquid Nails. I also bought a Kreg jig to create pocket holes to attach the 1" × 4"s to the door sections. This jig is one of the best investments I have made in tools! I suggest if you do any sort of woodworking that you get one!

Finally, after the frame was attached and adhesives dried, I took the whole thing outside for a final leveling sand. Where the panels met, it wasn't always smooth due to varying thicknesses of the panels and differing layers of paint. Since the door was outside I could see more areas that needed to be touched up than I could in the basement.

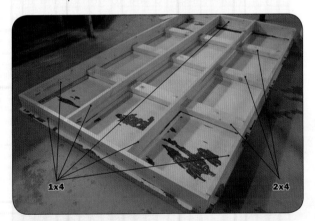

1x4   2x4

Step 5: Attach Those Nice Legs, Stain the Frame, and Seal the Top
DRILL, COUNTERBORE, AND SCREW

Plain and simple: pre-drill and counterbore the holes to get a nice tight connection and screw directly into the 2" × 4". Use lag bolts or other strong type of fastener with a wide head or shoulder. You could also add regular washers and lock washers to prevent any loosening of the screws.

I wanted the legs to be removable so the table can be disassembled for easier moving, therefore I did not use any adhesive.

SEAL THE DEAL

The next thing I did was to apply three layers of satin polyurethane to the ribs. I also applied—

what I thought was sufficient—one layer inside the pockets. The instructions on the epoxy explicitly tell you to apply a skim coat of the epoxy before pouring your flood coats. I assumed one layer of polyurethane was just as good. It almost was. I ended up with thousands of teeny tiny air bubbles on the base layer—just like the instructions said I would if I didn't listen. You can't actually see them unless you nearly put your face on the table and really look for them, but nevertheless they are there. (I am also my own worst critic so I am prone to look at all the mistakes I made.) More on the epoxy pouring in the next step.

Step 6: Now Comes the Hard Part!
POUR THE EPOXY ON ME . . . !

So my decision to pour epoxy into the pockets had my anxiety levels elevated! I had poured epoxy before, but it was in much smaller areas and it was usually tinted with sign paint, so air bubbles were not always a problem due to opaqueness. This, on the other hand, had to be nearly perfect, and I know from experience that I am nowhere near perfect in my projects. My goal was to only fill the pockets and leave the sealed wood exposed to create a nice contrast of finishes.

WHERE DO I BEGIN?

I won't go into explicit detail on pouring the epoxy as that could be a whole Instructable in itself. I will just pass on a few lessons I learned from such an undertaking.

In order to pour the epoxy to ½" thickness, I had to do four pours in each pocket. Each pocket pour required ¾ of a gallon each of the resin and hardener! Doing the math equals six gallons total of resin and hardener.

I researched online to find US Composites, and they were the least expensive that I found. (Note when buying epoxy - if you are buying a four-gallon kit, it means you get two gallons of resin and two gallons of hardener.)

Follow the directions; there's a reason they include them with their products, and they are found on several pages on their website.

Don't rush it.

Use a blow torch to remove air bubbles, and when you think you have them all removed, use your blow torch again. I wouldn't recommend a heat gun or hair dryer since those are using forced air and can stir up a lot of dust, which you do not want in your epoxy.

Did I mention following the directions?

NOW WHAT!?

Once all pockets had been completely filled, I noticed that when I had sanded the ribs, I had dipped the belt sander a little on some of the sides and the epoxy was flowing into those low edges, thus erasing any crisp clean edges from epoxy to rib. My solution? Pour more epoxy over the whole table top making it all one level. It worked, but it was a L-O-N-G day and I was bordering on insanity trying to ensure all bubbles were removed and all surfaces were level. I was also

chasing drips off the sides of the table since I didn't bother to hassle with barriers to contain the epoxy at the edges. Adding the top coat of epoxy required almost another gallon total, so I used seven gallons of epoxy when the whole project was finished! In the end, it was worth it since the finish made the wood grains pop more.

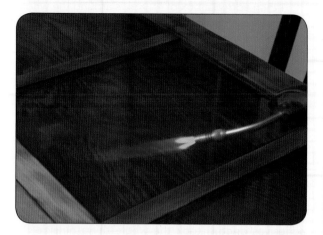

Step 7: Wrapping It Up
FINALLY

Overall it turned out beautifully in my opinion, even though it didn't have the look I was going for initially. I hope it inspired you to go out and use, reuse, and upcycle items to make beautiful furniture yourself! The less we throw away the better it is for everyone.

Installing T&G Flooring

By Brett Russell (bwrussell)
http://www.instructables.com/id/
Remodeling-Installing-TG-Flooring/

In this Instructable, the old linoleum and carpet floors in the kitchen and dining room are removed in favor of a wood-laminate tongue and groove (T&G) floor. Since the flooring comes with instructions and there are other well-done instructions all over the web, I will not go in-depth about the actual install, and instead will focus on some of the prep, not found in basic instructions, and tips I picked up along the way.

Step 1: Materials and Tools

Materials:

- Tongue & Groove flooring: I would suggest having at least half a box extra, more if the shape of your room necessitates a lot of cuts. Besides cutting boards, there will be warped or damaged boards as well.
- Underlayment pad: We used a pretty basic pad and so far have not had any problems. You will need slightly more than the area of your project.
- Underlayment board: This is sheets of particle board used to build up the sub-floor to match the carpet or to provide a smoother surface than the sub-floor. If your new floor won't come up to carpet and your sub-floor is nice then this is not necessary
- Wood Screws: For attaching the underlayment board, if necessary.
- Click-Seal, Cal-Flor, $16.99: This is a fairly new product for use with T&G floors that are going in places where water is likely to find its way onto the floor (entries, kitchens, and bathrooms). It is a wax/oil gel that goes onto the tongue as the floor is assembled. It doesn't actually glue the floor pieces together; it just reduces the water

absorption of the boards. It's a product that you won't know is working but it gives a little peace of mind when putting a non-sealed wood floor into the kitchen.
- Transitions: Again, you can reuse the old ones, if there were any, but like most everything in this project, this is a good time to change these to match the new style of the room.
- Tack strip: Only necessary if you cut a new edge to some carpet. If you are careful when removing the strips you can reuse them.

Tools:

- Hammer
- Tape measure
- T&G tools: This consists of a puller bar, a block, and edge spacers.
- Utility knife
- Screw driver and bits: only needed if you need to build up your subfloor
- Saw: We used a combination of a table saw, handheld circular saw, and standard wood saw.
- Pry bar: only needed if you are removing carpet
- Pliers: see above

Step 2: Remove Old Flooring

Linoleum:

Using a utility knife, cut out strips and pull them up. If the entire area is linoleum and it's in good condition then you can just leave it down for most T&G floors.

Carpet:

Use a piece of string and some nails to make a line, if the carpet needs to be cut. After the cut, or if it wasn't necessary, remove the trim around where the carpet will come up. If the carpet matches some in the rest of your house and it's in good condition then consider taking care while removing it so it can be used if you ever need a patch. If the carpeted area is large, cut it into manageable chunks. To remove the carpet, go around the edge, carefully removing the carpet from the tack strip. With the carpet now loose you can roll it up and store it or dump it.

The carpet pad is simple but a pain. It should be stapled down; you'll see the staples because the pad will be dimpled down wherever they are. Using needle-nose pliers, go through and pull as many of the staples as you can. Then roll or tear the pad up and dispose of it (or store it if it's in really good condition and you have space and a future use for it). Grab the pliers again and pull any staples you missed.

To get the tack strip up grab a small pry bar and a hammer. Knock the pry bar under the strip at each point it is nailed down and pop each nail out of the sub floor. Doing it this way you should be able to remove entire sections of the strip with splintering the wood or losing any tacks. This is particularly useful if you only cut out a section of carpet and now have an exposed, untacked edge, because the strips should be reusable.

Step 3: Prep Sub-Floor

Old Sub-Floor:

If your old sub-floor is all one thickness or doesn't have an underlayment step, follow the instructions provided by the flooring. Essentially the floor needs to be level, clean, and dry. Make sure there aren't any screw heads sticking up or staples leftover from any carpet pad that may have been down. Also if you pulled linoleum then you will probably need to scrape away some old glue.

New Underlayment:

If the old floor was a mix of carpet and pretty much anything else then there was probably an underlayment board under the anything-else section and now there is a step down where the carpet used to be. Start by measuring both the size of the bare sub-floor (the part that needs to be stepped up to match the old underlayment board) and the thickness of the old underlayment board. Your local hardware store should carry a variety of thicknesses that should match the old board. Plywood is a little cheaper than underlayment board but it is not as smooth, which is helpful for laying a T&G floor.

Cut the boards to fit in the room and screw them into the sub-floor below. As with using original sub-flooring, make sure it is clean and dry with no screws or nails protruding from its surface.

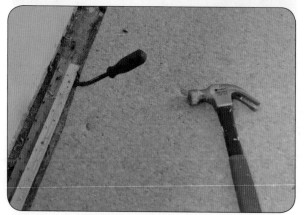

Step 4: Layout New Floor

The instructions in the T&G flooring should cover this pretty well, so here are just a couple of notes.

I read two different rules about board direction: perpendicular to the joists, and parallel to the predominant natural light source (perpendicular to the window it comes through). Personally, our room was much wider so we went with the boards in the wider direction, partially to match the flow of the room and partially to maximize the number of whole planks we could use. It happens to follow the joist rule and not the light one, but I haven't noticed any visual issues with the light. Also the joist rule is probably not a big deal unless the sub-floor flexes a lot (squeaking), and then it's probably important.

Consider the location of any protrusions in or out of the room's basic rectangular footprint (appliance slots or built-in desks spring to mind) when choosing a layout. Ease shouldn't be your first priority, but it makes a good tie-breaker if needed.

If you're really adventures go with a diagonal layout. It will involve a lot more cutting, precision, and thought, but the results are guaranteed to grab attention.

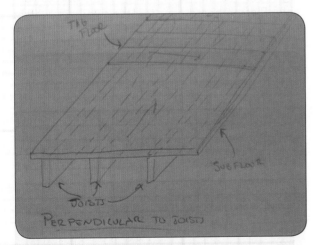

Step 5: Install New Floor

Again, the included instructions should cover the step-by-step stuff pretty well so I won't get into that.

This is when you use the click-seal. It goes on both tongues right before each board is installed. I didn't put it on every board, just the ones in the kitchen, under the dining table, and in front of the sliding door to the deck.

Be very careful when knocking the boards into place. If it is not seated properly or held firmly in place it can chip the laminate layer (that has the wood decal on it), forcing at least a partial scraping of the board.

NEVER use the "S"- or "2"-shaped puller bar on any board other than those at the end where it will be covered by trim. It chips the edge every time.

If a board just won't snap in place, set it aside and try it somewhere else. We had several boards that were literally impossible to attach in one place that fit right together in another. Some boards may be too warped to use anywhere, but even these might still work on an end or beginning where they get cut down.

When ending and starting rows think through the measurement several times. It's backwards and it will trip you up if you don't pay attention. The left side of the board is used on the right side of the room and visa versa.

Mix up the length of your starting boards so you don't get visible lines formed by close joints.

Step 6: Finishing Touches

Finish the floor off by installing, or reinstalling, the transition strips. There are so many different styles of transition strip I won't cover that here. If it's more complicated than cut to length and fix in place (nail or screw), it will come with instructions.

Remember to clean up any liquid spills as quickly as possible, and a damp mop with a mild detergent is the most you should be mopping with.

Chalkboard Table

By Randy Sarafan (randofo)

http://www.instructables.com/id/
Chalkboard-Table/

I can't tell you how many times I've been sitting at the dining room table and have been struck with a "brilliant" idea and haven't had anywhere to write it down. This table, in fact, was one such idea. I thought to myself, wouldn't it be great if the table were a chalkboard and I could sketch out my ideas right there as they came to me, rather than having to get up and find my notebook? And then I thought that I could also use it to label various food dishes on the table for the benefit of the vegetarian in the household. And why stop there? I could also easily resolve issues pertaining to seating arrangements with a few simple strokes. I could save money on place mats and table settings. I could draw funny pictures of cats being eaten by octopi. And in my mind, it was decided then and there that this table was going to—no, needed—to be made.

Step 1: Go Get Stuff

You will need:

- 3' × 5' × ¾" board
- Two 3' sections of 1" × 2"
- Wood or craft glue
- Some sort of large weight
- Chalkboard paint
- Two black IKEA trestles
- Brushes, rollers, trays, and drop clothes

- Two 6' aluminum extrusions (mcmaster.com PN#8427A67)
- Power drill and ¼" and ⁵⁄₃₂" drill bits
- Twelve wood screws and screw driver
- Chalkboard chalk
- Chalkboard eraser (optional)

Step 2: Glue

Glue your two 1" × 2" wood bars parallel and on edge such that they are running length-wise to your table. Place a board over top the two bars, weight them down, and let the glue dry.

Step 3: Paint

Paint the table surface with chalkboard paint. You can cover the top with your fine roller and the edges with your brush. Apply a thin and even coat and then let it dry as directed. Place a second coat and let dry again. It should look pretty good at this point. (Tip: to save the roller while the table dries, cover it in saran wrap to keep the paint on it from drying out.)

Step 4: Prepare Chalk Holders

Cut the aluminum extrusion to the size of the table using your hacksaw. The easiest way to measure this is to simply line it up with table and make a mark where it extends past the edge. Measure an inch in from each edge of the aluminum extrusion and make a mark. Next make marks at one foot intervals between each of these two holes. Drill ¼" holes a foot apart.

Step 5: Fasten Chalk Holders

Hold the aluminum extrusion up to the edge of the table. Make sure it is lined up where you want to install it and then drill ⁵⁄₃₂" pilot holes to correspond with the center of each hole in the aluminum extrusion. Once you have drilled all the pilot holes, attach the piece of aluminum with your screws.

Step 6: Chalk

Put some blackboard chalk in the chalk holder and you should be good to go.

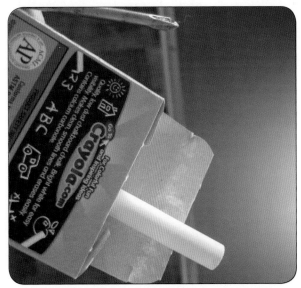

CONVERSION TABLES

One person's inch is another person's .39 centimeters. Instructables projects come from all over the world, so here's a handy reference guide that will help keep your project on track.

Measurement								
	1 Millimeter	1 Centimeter	1 Meter	1 Inch	1 Foot	1 Yard	1 Mile	1 Kilometer
Millimeter	1	10	1,000	25.4	304.8	—	—	—
Centimeter	0.1	1	100	2.54	30.48	91.44	—	—
Meter	0.001	0.01	1	0.025	0.305	0.91	—	1,000
Inch	0.04	0.39	39.37	1	12	36	—	—
Foot	0.003	0.03	3.28	0.083	1	3	—	—
Yard	—	0.0109	1.09	0.28	033	1	—	—
Mile	—	—	—	—	—	—	1	0.62
Kilometer	—	—	1,000	—	—	—	1.609	1

Volume										
	1 Milliliter	1 Liter	1 Cubic Meter	1 Tea-spoon	1 Tablespoon	1 Fluid Ounce	1 Cup	1 Pint	1 Quart	1 Gallon
Milliliter	1	1,000	—	4.9	14.8	29.6	—	—	—	—
Liter	0.001	1	1,000	0.005	0.015	0.03	0.24	0.47	0.95	3.79
Cubic Meter	—	0.001	1	—	—	—	—	—	—	0.004
Teaspoon	0.2	202.9	—	1	3	6	48	—	—	—
Tablespoon	0.068	67.6	—	0.33	1	2	16	32	—	—
Fluid Ounce	0.034	33.8	—	0.167	0.5	1	8	16	32	—
Cup	0.004	4.23	—	0.02	0.0625	0.125	1	2	4	16
Pint	0.002	2.11	—	0.01	0.03	0.06	05	1	2	8
Quart	0.001	1.06	—	0.005	0.016	0.03	0.25	.05	1	4
Gallon	—	0.26	264.17	0.001	0.004	0.008	0.0625	0.125	0.25	1

Mass and Weight						
	1 Gram	1 Kilogram	1 Metric Ton	1 Ounce	1 Pound	1 Short Ton
Gram	1	1,000	—	28.35	—	—
Kilogram	0.001	1	1,000	0.028	0.454	—
Metric Ton	—	0.001	1	—	—	0.907
Ounce	0.035	35.27	—	1	16	—
Pound	0.002	2.2	—	0.0625	1	2,000
Short Ton	—	0.001	1.1	—	—	1

Speed		
	1 Mile per hour	1 Kilometer per hour
Miles per hour	1	0.62
Kilometers per hour	1.61	1

Temperature		
	Fahrenheit (°F)	Celsius (°C)
Fahrenheit	—	(°C x 1.8) + 32
Celsius	(°F – 32) / 1.8	—

also available

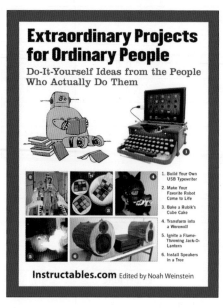

Extraordinary Projects for Ordinary People
Do-It-Yourself Ideas from the People Who Actually Do Them

by Instructables.com, edited by Noah Weinstein

Collected in this volume is a best-of selection from Instructables, reproduced for the first time outside of the web format, retaining all of the charm and ingenuity that make Instructables such a popular destination for Internet users looking for new and fun projects designed by real people in an easy-to-digest way.

Hundreds of Instructables are included, ranging from practical projects like making a butcher-block countertop or building solar panels to fun and unique ideas for realistic werewolf costumes or transportable camping hot tubs. The difficulty of the projects ranges from beginner on up, but all are guaranteed to raise a smile or a "Why didn't I think of that?"

US $16.95 paperback ISBN: 978-1-62087-057-0

also available

How to Do Absolutely Everything
Homegrown Projects from Real Do-It-Yourself Experts
by Instructables.com, edited by Sarah James

Continuing the Instructables series with Skyhorse Publishing, a mammoth collection of projects has been selected and curated for this special best-of volume of Instructables. The guides in this book cover the entire spectrum of possibilities that the popular website has to offer, showcasing how online communities can foster and nurture creativity.

From outdoor agricultural projects to finding new uses for traditional household objects, the beauty of Instructables lies in their ingenuity and their ability to find new ways of looking at the same thing. *How to Do Absolutely Everything* has that in spades; the possibilities are limitless, thanks to not only the selection of projects available here, but also the new ideas you'll build on after reading this book. Full-color photographs illustrate each project in intricate detail, providing images of both the individual steps of the process and the end product.

US $16.95 paperback ISBN: 978-1-62087-066-2

also available

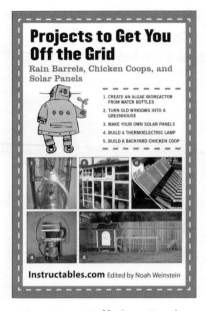

Projects to Get You Off the Grid
Rain Barrels, Chicken Coops, and Solar Panels
by Instructables.com, edited by Noah Weinstein

Instructables is back with this compact book focused on a series of projects designed to get you thinking creatively about thinking green. Twenty Instructables illustrate just how simple it can be to make your own backyard chicken coop or turn a wine barrel into a rainwater collector.

Illustrated with dozens of full-color photographs per project accompanying easy-to-follow instructions, this Instructables collection utilizes the best that the online community has to offer, turning a far-reaching group of people into a mammoth database churning out ideas to make life better, easier, and, in this case, greener, as this volume exemplifies.

US $14.95 paperback ISBN: 978-1-62087-164-5

also available

Practical Duct Tape Projects

by Instructables.com, edited by Noah Weinstein

Duct tape has gotten a reputation as the quick-fix tape for every situation. However, did you know that you can use duct tape to create practical items for everyday use? Did you also know that duct tape now comes in a variety of colors, so your creations can be fun and stylish? Originating from Instructables, a popular project-based community made up of all sorts of characters with wacky hobbies and a desire to pass on their wisdom to others, *Practical Duct Tape Projects* contains ideas from a number of authors who nurse a healthy urge to create anything possible from duct tape.

Practical Duct Tape Projects provides step-by-step instructions on a variety of useful and fun objects involving duct tape. Guided through each endeavor by detailed photographs, the reader will create articles of clothing, tools, and more.

US $12.95 paperback ISBN: 978-1-62087-709-8

also available

Backyard Rockets
Learn to Make and Launch Rockets, Missiles, Cannons, and Other Projectiles

by Instructables.com, edited by Mike Warren

Originating from Instructables, a popular project-based community made up of all sorts of characters with wacky hobbies and a desire to pass on their wisdom to others, *Backyard Rockets* is made up of projects from a medley of authors who have collected and shared a treasure trove of rocket-launching plans and the knowledge to make their projects soar!

Backyard Rockets gives step-by-step instructions, with pictures to guide the way, on how to launch your very own project into the sky. All of these authors have labored over their endeavors to pass their knowledge on and make it easier for others to attempt.

US $12.95 paperback ISBN: 978-1-62087-730-2

also available

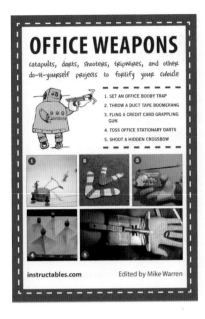

Office Weapons
Catapults, Darts, Shooters, Tripwires, and Other Do-It-Yourself Projects to Fortify Your Cubicle
by Instructables.com, edited by Mike Warren

Bored in your office? Did your coworker just prank you and you're wondering how to get him back? Is your boss constantly stealing your paperclips and you don't know how to keep his mitts away from your desk? *Office Weapons* gives you the complete step-by-step instructions for thirty different daring office pranks. Check out these simple but effective weapons fashioned from office materials and be prepared next time someone borrows your special stapler or leaves the copy machine jammed.

These projects are made by the best in the business; the office workers who actually need them! They say necessity is the mother of invention; leave it to the Instructables community to put that theory to the test!

US $14.95 paperback ISBN: 978-1-62087-708-1

also available

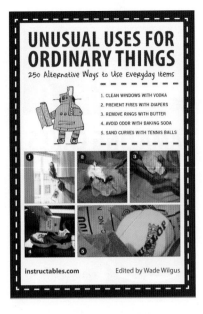

Unusual Uses for Ordinary Things
250 Alternative Ways to Use Everyday Items
by Instructables.com, edited by Wade Wilgus

Most people use nail polish remover to remove nail polish. They use coffee grounds to make coffee and hair dryers to dry their hair. The majority of people may also think that the use of eggs, lemons, mustard, butter, and mayonnaise should be restricted to making delicious food in the kitchen. The Instructables.com community would disagree with this logic—they have discovered hundreds of inventive and surprising ways to use these and other common household materials to improve day-to-day life.

Did you know that tennis balls can protect your floors, fluff your laundry, and keep you from backing too far into (and thus destroying) your garage? How much do you know about aspirin? Sure, it may alleviate pain, but it can also be used to remove sweat stains, treat bug bites and stings, and prolong the life of your sputtering car battery. These are just a few of the quirky ideas that appear in *Unusual Uses for Ordinary Things*.

US $12.95 paperback ISBN: 978-1-62087-725-8

also available

Amazing Cakes
Recipes for the world's most unusual, creative, and customizable cakes

by Instructables.com, edited and Introduced by Sarah James

With Instructables.com's *Amazing Cakes*, you'll be able to make cakes shaped like animals, mythical creatures, and vehicles. They may light up, breathe fire, or blow bubbles or smoke. They may be 3D or they may be animated, seeming to move of their own free will. Whether they're cute and cuddly (like a penguin) or sticky and gross (like a human brain!), these cakes have two things in common: They're (mostly) edible and they're amazing!

Instructables.com authors walk you through each step of the process as you cut plywood for cake bases, hardwire figurines for automation, and mix nontoxic chemicals for explosions and eruptions. The photos accompanying the step-by-step directions provide additional information about the processes.

US $12.95 paperback ISBN: 978-1-62087-690-9

also available

Meatless Eats
Savory Vegetarian Recipes from around the World
by Instructables.com, edited and Introduced by Sarah James

"Originating from Instructables, a popular project-based community made up of all sorts of characters with wacky hobbies and a desire to pass on their wisdom to others, *Meatless Eats* is made up of recipes from a cast of cooks who demonstrate their culinary savvy and flavor combinations.

Meatless Eats gives full step-by-step instructions for creating delicious vegetarian dishes that even die-hard carnivores will crave. Written by cooks who can't get enough of veggies, each recipe contains pictures for an easy follow-along guide, even for those who spend little to no time in the kitchen. Discover your inner vegetarian with these mouthwatering recipes."

US $12.95 paperback ISBN: 978-1-62087-697-8

also available

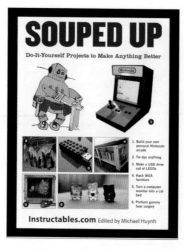

Souped Up
Do-It-Yourself Projects to Make Anything Better
by Instructables.com, Edited by Michael Huynh

Ever look around your house and get bored with the things you have? Too ordinary? Used it a million times? With this Instructables.com compilation, *Souped Up*, you can turn your ordinary into the extraordinary.

Learn how to:

- Make a USB drive out of LEGOs
- Build your own personal Nintendo arcade
- Perform gummy bear surgery
- Roast your own pig
- Hack IKEA furniture

Compiled from the best that the web has to offer, with more than one thousand full-color images and easy-to-understand how-to instructions, this collection is the perfect gift for anyone never satisfied with the status quo. Ever thought, "I could improve that"? These authors did too, and we've put together their best ideas for upgrades, hacks, and everything you need to get the most out of everything.

US $16.95 paperback ISBN: 978-1-62087-562-9